D1221686

Insects, Experts, and the Insecticide Crisis

THE QUEST FOR NEW PEST MANAGEMENT STRATEGIES

Insects, Experts, and the Insecticide Crisis

THE QUEST FOR NEW PEST MANAGEMENT STRATEGIES

John H. Perkins

The Evergreen State College
Olympia, Washington

PLENUM PRESS • NEW YORK AND LONDON

Library of Congress Cataloging in Publication Data

Perkins, John H.

Insects, experts, and the insecticide crisis.

Bibliography: p
Includes index.
1. Insect control—United States—History. 2. Insecticides—United States—History. 3. Insects, Injurious and beneficial—Research—United States—History. 4. Entomologists—United States—History. 5. Entomology—United States—History. I. Title.
SB934.P47 363.7'3 81-22658
ISBN 0-306-40770-1 AACR2

Warning: Mention of any insecticide or any other method of insect control in this book does not constitute a recommendation for use.

A Divison of Plenum Publishing Corporation
233 Spring Street, new York, N.Y. 10013

Printed in the United States of America

Preface

Science and technology are cultural phenomena. Expert knowledge is generated amid the conflicts of a society and in turn supplies fuel to fire yet further change and new clashes. This essay on economic entomology is a case study on how cultural events and forces affected the creation of scientific and technical knowledge. The time period emphasized is 1945 to 1980.

My initial premises for selecting relevant data for the story were ultimately not of much use. Virtually all debates about insect control since 1945 have been centered around the environmental and health hazards associated with insecticides. My first but inadequate conclusion was that the center of interest lay between those who defended the chemicals and those who advocated the use of nonchemical control methods. With this formulation of the problem, I was drawn to an analysis of how the chemical manufacturers had managed to dominate and even corrupt the work of entomological scientists, farmers, members of Congress, and regulators in the USDA and EPA. My own contributions to a policy study at the National Academy of Sciences were based on this premise.[1] More recently, Robert van den Bosch developed the "corruption theme" in considerable detail.[2]

After I left the National Academy of Sciences in 1974, I began to reformulate my thoughts about the economic entomologists to answer a question that had continually baffled me: Why did those entomologists most responsible for moving insect control toward less reliance on chemicals have such vastly different opinions about the research needs for their science? If the central problem were one of developing nonchemical control methods and removing the chemical industry from its preeminent role in shaping insect control practices, these disagreements had no easy explanation. I was completely unimpressed with one possible set of answers, namely that entomologists were stupid, without insight, or venal. My experiences with many entomologists completely convinced me that they were intelligent, creative (sometimes to the point of genius), and well motivated to serve some concept of the public welfare.

This book presents an answer to the question that so puzzled me. A major key to unraveling the intellectual tangle in the entomological literature was the realization that two possibly irreconcilable strategies had evolved in the years after 1945 to move insect control away from chemicals. It is my contention that the entomologists themselves have not recognized and explained the gulf which separates these two schools of thought. A second indispensible element of the answer was my realization that the socioeconomic organization of American farming led to certain imperatives that any purported insect control technology had to meet if it was to be voluntarily adopted by agriculturalists. Chemicals happen to meet those imperatives better than any alternative strategies. Heavy reliance on chemicals required no "corruption thesis," because it was largely a matter of social and technical practicality. The chemical industry has been guilty of excesses in marketing their products, but my analysis argues that the real problem lies in how the American people organized their food production system. Those who are working to reduce the environmental damages still being done by insecticides are urged to consider this argument carefully because of its important policy implications. Minimally, it suggests that merely increasing the regulations of insecticide use will at best treat the symptoms of the problem, not the root causes.

A word should be said about the methodology used in constructing this book. It was conceived as an exercise in the history of science and technology. I was particularly influenced by discussions on the sociology and philosophy of knowledge ignited in 1962 by Thomas Kuhn's *The Structure of Scientific Revolutions*. I was also guided by my own political interests in (1) reshaping the types of insect control practices employed in America and (2) reforming the injustices resulting from unequal distribution of wealth. I like to characterize the book as an "applied history of science," that is, an essay using some of the major ideas in the history of science in order to shed light directly on policy problems.

A number of sources were used for information. Oral interviews with some of the most eminent entomologists provided information that was invaluable. Many of the ideas stated in those interviews were available nowhere else. Most of those interviewed also agreed to share all or parts of their unpublished correspondence with me. These letters also provided insights of crucial importance to the analysis. Finally, considerable recourse was made to the published entomological literature and to unpublished correspondence available in the National Archives.

Who will find this work of interest? It was my intention to write for a number of different audiences, some so diverse that real problems emerged in finding language and approaches suitable for them. Entomologists are a primary audience, and I have included Chapter 6 and 7 largely for them as background on the philosophy of science. Policy makers are also a major audience. It is my belief that too many regulators and analysts attempt to find solutions without an adequate sense of the historical legacies muddling all policy debates. This book will hopefully illuminate the importance of history to the contemporary debate about insect control.

A variety of historians may find the book of interest. Historians of science and technology will find the conceptual approaches familiar, and the extensive details on entomology (Chapters 1–5) will outline the salient features of this little-studied discipline to them. Agricultural historians may find the book of interest, but they should be forewarned that this is not a typical work arranged in strict chronological order. Environmental historians, a new breed, may find the work of use as they attempt to unravel how culture and natural phenomena are related.

The final audience is simply members of the general public who read books. Insecticides are continually in the news, and I hope this essay provides useful background to all who care to delve behind the headlines to understand what is happening.

Authors always hope their books will be a "success," but how to measure that elusive quality is difficult. For my part I will be pleased if the argument developed here helps entomolgists clarify the goals, methods, and foundations of their own work. I would also hope that in some small way the book is a contribution to the ongoing struggle for a livable environment and a just political economy.

John H. Perkins

Olympia, Washington

REFERENCE NOTES

1. *Pest Control: An Assessment of Present and Alternative Technologies* (Washington: National Academy of Sciences, 1975–1976), 5 vols.
2. Robert van den Bosch, *The Pesticide Conspiracy* (Garden City, New York: Doubleday, 1978), 226 pp.

Acknowledgments

Most books cannot be written by an individual alone, and this one was no exception. Responsibility for all errors must remain mine, but many people deserve credit for their important contributions.

A number of people agreed to be interviewed, and their insights into the motivations for their work and that of others was of fundamental importance. Not all of them will agree with my interpretations, but each of them should know that I came to have a sincere appreciation for their creative efforts.

The entomologists who were interviewed were Perry L. Adkisson, James R. Brazzel, Harold Compere, Theodore B. Davich, Paul H. DeBach, Carl B. Huffaker, Edward F. Knipling, Charles G. Lincoln, L. Dale Newsom, and Reece I. Sailer. J. Ritchie Smith of the National Cotton Council of America provided important insights into how a trade association becomes involved with scientific work. Helen Bruner, Harriet Hanson, and Alice Smith graciously shared their memories of Lawrence Bruner and Harry Scott Smith.

Over a period of years, students made important contributions as research assistants for this study: Joseph Albrechta, Alex Echols, Keith Johnson, Jeffery Page, David Soloway, Martijn Steger, and Susan Tiefel. Beyond their work as research assistants, students in the Western College Program at Miami University provided a stimulating teaching environment that encouraged work on this book.

Staff, faculty, and administrative personnel at Miami University encouraged my work in ways too numerous to describe in detail. Of particular importance were Jane Goldflies, Diane Temple, Curtis Ellison, William Newell, Nancy Nicholson, Terry Perlin, Barbara Whitten, Mike

Lunine, and David Brown. Particular thanks go to Mike Lunine who made it possible for me to have sufficient leave time from teaching to finish the writing.

Most of the writing occurred while I was a visiting Research Associate of the Division of Biological Control at the University of California at Berkeley. Carl Huffaker served as my host while Robert van den Bosch and Leo Caltagirone provided overall administrative support. Many staff members at the "Gill Tract" provided essential service and a friendly, patient atmosphere in which to work. Especially important were Jane Clarkin, Johnnie Eaton, Joanne Fox, Grace Leach, Nettie Mackey, Ina Obee, and Helen Ward. Joanne Fox deserves a special thanks for typing most of the manuscript, and Nettie Mackey helped gather many of the illustrations from the files. Thanks also go to Bill Copper for preparing Fig. 1.

Judy Lindlauf, Audrey Streeter, Bettye Spicer, Laura Allen and Robin Erhart of The Evergreen State College provided valuable assistance to this project near its end. My special thanks go to Judy Lindlauf for overseeing the preparation of the final manuscript and organizing my life as a new Academic Dean so that I could finish it.

Librarians and archivists perform indispensible services for all historical research. I am particularly indebted to Douglas Helms, Helen Ulleberry, and Harold Pinkett of the National Archives in Washington, D.C. Thanks also go to the staff of the Gianni Foundation Libary at the University of California at Berkely: Martha Chan, Phyllis Donald, Grace Dote, Virginia Fox, Jeannie Imazumi, and Sophit Lee.

Mary Sebrechts and Don Nielson of the U.S. Department of Agriculture generously supplied photographs for some of the illustrations.

Alice Patience prepared Fig. 14.

Over a period of years, it has been my pleasure to discuss various aspects of entomological history with a number of people. Particularly important insights came from talks with Jim Bradley, Leo Caltagirone, Donald Dahlsten, Richard Daum, Thomas Dunlap, William Friedland, Richard Garcia, Andrew Gutierrez, Ken Hagen, Douglas Helms, Peter Kenmore, Carolyn Merchant, Brian O'Farrell, David Pimentel, Carroll Pursell, Margaret Rossiter, Kathey Sheehan, James Shideler, Pritam Singh, Ray Smith, Robert van den Bosch, Knox Walker, and David Williams.

Several people read part or all of this manuscript, and I wish to give special thanks for their criticisms, even those I did not accept. They included Charles Cooper, Carl Huffaker, Carolyn Merchant, Richard Norgaard, Barbara Perkins, Ray Smith, and two anonymous reviewers. Thanks also go to Kirk Jensen of Plenum Publishing Corporation for his patience and support in the completion of this manuscript.

Finally, financial assistance is what makes the world go around, and at various times vital help was extended to this project. A fellowship from the Josiah Macey, Jr., Foundation, awarded with the help of Everett Mendelsohn, launched me into this study. Miami University's Extramural Support Incentive Program administered by James Pyle provided a needed boost somewhat later. The majority of the necessary funds to complete this project came from the National Science Foundation (SOC 76-11288). My sincere thanks go to Ronald Overmann, other NSF staff members, and the innumerable reviewers and panel members who make the NSF a major positive contributor to American scholarship.

It goes without saying, of course, that the persons and institutions who have supported this work in various ways must not be held responsible for my results, judgments, and opinions.

Contents

PART II • A SEARCH FOR ALTERNATIVES

CHAPTER 3

Strategies I: Integrated Pest Management

CHAPTER 4

Strategies II: Total Population Management

CHAPTER 5

Traumas

PART III • ENTOMOLOGY IN ITS CULTURAL CONTEXT

CHAPTER 6

A Conceptual Framework

CHAPTER 7

The Philosophical Foundations

CHAPTER 8

Revolutionary Farmers

CHAPTER 9

Entomologists and the Revolution

CHAPTER 10

Entomology and Agricultural Production

List of Figures and Tables

Insects, Experts, and the Insecticide Crisis

PART I

The Insecticide Crisis

Leaders from entomology, the farming industries, government, and the chemical industry generally agree that agricultural insect control practices after 1945 were heavily dominated by the use of insecticides. Research in the entomological profession was similarly heavily preoccupied with insecticides, although its orientation toward experiments with insecticides declined after about 1955. The immediate source of the heavy interest in insecticides came from dramatic successes of DDT and other new insecticides invented during and following World War II.

It is difficult to understand the enthusiasm with which the new chemicals were greeted without looking at the cultural complexity surrounding insect control practices. A number of facets must be traced independently. In Chapter 1, we examine first the introduction of insecticides; second, the invention of DDT; and third, the general impacts of DDT and other new insecticides on insect control practices, the science of entomology, the insecticide industry, and the farming industries. Chapter 1 concludes with a case study of insecticides and the apple industry. Euphoria with insecticides was short lived. Chapter 2 outlines the development of the insecticide crisis.

CHAPTER 1

A New Technology

THE INTRODUCTION OF INSECTICIDES

Insecticides are the foundations of most insect control strategies in agriculture, particularly in the industrialized countries. Their present status as an integral part of agricultural technology reflects many successes in the invention and development of particular compounds for use by the farming industries. Moreover, reliance on insecticides presupposes a stable chemical industry to manufacture, formulate, and market the toxic materials. This chapter outlines the major events in the invention of insecticides and the development of the insecticide industry.

The use of insecticides had a diffuse initiation in the ancient past, but little effort was made to exploit them systematically until the nineteenth century. An unknown inventor's discovery in about 1868 that the dye Paris green could kill insects launched a new era in the deliberate use of toxic substances for commercial purposes.[1] Oil, sulfur, nicotine, rotenone, pyrethrum and other materials were known and used before the advent of Paris green, but pyrethrum may have been the only such compound produced and traded on a significant scale before Paris green.[2] In addition, Paris green was the first compound used other than sulfur of which the chemical identity was known. The toxic principle in Paris green was arsenic, the element subsequently used in London purple and lead arsenate. By 1910, Paris green and lead arsenate were the most widely used insecticides sold on a commercial basis.[3] The total annual sales of the industry were estimated to be about $20 million.[4]

The commercialization of the insecticide industry was accompanied by substantial fraud including adulterating legitimate products and making extravagant claims for absolutely worthless junk. Indeed, some of the insecticides sold in the latter part of the nineteenth century were decidedly destructive to the plants upon which they were used.[5] Outraged denunciations of such shenanigans came from the pen of entomologist Benjamin Dann Walsh, and the developing community of professional entomologists was a powerful force advocating federal and state regulations of the industry.[6] The leadership exercised by entomologist E. Dwight Sanderson from New Hampshire and by Harvey W. Wiley, champion of pure foods and drugs in the USDA, led to the passage of the Insecticide Act of 1910.[7] Under the Act, manufacturers were required to portray accurately on the label the efficacy of the insecticide; if inert ingredients were contained, the label had to so state. Standards of purity and strength were established for the two most widely used materials, lead arsenate and Paris green.[8]

Economic and political conditions during World War I forced technolgocial and structural changes in the American chemical industry that had far-reaching consequences for insecticides and insect control practices. Severe shortages of Paris green occurred in 1917 and 1918, owing to a diminished supply of one of its necessary ingredients, acetic acid. The USDA recommended the substitution of lead arsenate for Paris green.[9] The industry's capacity to manufacture arsenical insecticides jumped with the increased wartime demand for arsenic in making lead shot, signal flares, the poison gas diphenylcholoroarsine, and plate glass.[10]

In 1917, Bert R. Coad, a USDA entomologist, made a discovery that further increased the sales opportunities of arsenical insecticides. Coad found that calcium arsenate, known but little used since the early part of the century due to its tendency to burn foliage, was effective in killing the cotton boll weevil.[11] Production of calcium arsenate rose from almost nothing in 1917 to over 13 million pounds in 1923. Boll weevils had entered the U.S. in southern Texas in 1892 and created great havoc over the entire cotton belt before it reached Virginia in 1922.[12] The market for calcium arsenate was accordingly large, and it, along with lead arsenate, was the leading insecticide from 1917 till after World War II.[13]

World War I also had a stimulating effect on the development of an entirely different class of insecticides based on synthetic organic molecules. At the outbreak of hostilities in Europe in 1914, the U.S. had almost no capacity to produce the lifeblood of a synthetic chemicals industry, coal-tar intermediates. The country relied almost entirely on German imports for such chemicals to support its small dye industry; most dyes were also imported from the Germans. The termination of trade in intermediates and dyes from Germany in 1915 stimulated American chemical manufacturers to begin their own manufacture of coal-tar intermediates, which in turn could support the manufacturing of dyes, medicinal chemicals, and explosives. Seventeen companies entered the field in 1915. Despite explosions, fires, and deaths from working with the unfamiliar, volatile, and highly flammable materials, a domestic industry was created within a few years.[14] The entry of the U.S. into World War I created a further demand for explosives that could now be met, whereas it could not have been earlier.

The manufacture of explosives had a direct spinoff effect on the development of synthetic insecticides that presaged the later successes of DDT. Paradichlorobenzene (PDB) was a by-product of the chlorination of monochlorobenzene for picric acid production for explosives. Before World War I it was seldom isolated or weighed. In 1918, the U.S. Tariff Commission's *Dye Census* did not even mention its value. In 1919, however, 131,000 lb. of PDB were reported with an average value of $0.07/lb. By 1921, manufacturers reported 402,000 lb. produced with a value of $0.16/lb.[15]

PDB's jump from obscurity stemmed from the work of USDA entomologist E. B. Blakeslee, who found it to be highly effective against the peach tree borer. This insect was formerly controlled with difficulty by hand removal from beneath the bark of peach trees, but PDB allowed a more effective and considerably less labor-intensive method for control.[16] By the early 1940s, 1.5 million lb. of PDB were used for peach tree borer control and 12.5 million lb. for clothes moth control.[17] The tear gas chloropicrin was also found to be insecticidal in 1916 and thus changed from a wartime product to one of peace.[18]

Development of the synthetic insecticide industry was continued during the 1920s and 1930s. Ethylene oxide, thiocyanates such as Lethane, phenothiazine (to substitute for lead arsenate in codling moth control), and xanthone (with the unappealing tradename "Genicide") were introduced and achieved some commercial successes.[19] In addition, sales of pyrethrum and rotenone-containing insecticides increased.[20] By 1940, the insecticide industry was firmly established; it had achieved its successes both by increasing sales of older materials and by bringing out entirely new materials based on the wizardry of chemical research. Yet more profound changes in insecticide technology were still to come. The creation of DDT opened the door to a host of new discoveries based upon the nearly infinite possibilities of synthesizing new molecules.

THE DISCOVERY OF DDT

DDT's discovery was the culmination of a research effort motivated purely by commercial concerns, but the compound's adoption was inextricably enmeshed in the politics of war. The saga began in Switzerland in 1932 when the firm J. R. Geigy SA of Basel began a search for moth poisons with a high affinity for wool. In 1935, the company broadened the potential commercial range of its research goals to include materials useful as seed disinfectants.[21] The following year Paul Herman Mueller, one of the Geigy staff chemists, defined the biological objective of the research as a synthetic contact insecticide.[22] Within a few years, Mueller had discovered that diphenyltrichloroethane showed substantial insecticidal activity against flies. Mueller proceeded to synthesize and test many derivatives of the compound, and he found in September, 1939, that the substance p,p′-dichlorodiphenyltrichloroethane (DDT) had extraordinary contact-killing power, as well as long duration outdoors, where the compound was exposed to weathering.

World War II's outbreak in 1939 isolated the Swiss and made them dependent upon their abilities to raise their own food. Swiss farmers, in efforts to increase their yields, began to use DDT (in Geigy's trademarked product Gesarol) against the Colorado potato beetle in 1941. At the same time that food supplies became critical, refugees from the war zone came into Switzerland infested with lice. The potential for typhus epidemics was thus high, and the Geigy company began work in 1941 to test the possible effectiveness of DDT against human lice.[23] By September 1942, they had placed a ton of Neocid (a trademarked product containing DDT and intended for control of human lice) at the disposal of the Swiss army commander for the control of lice on refugees.[24] Thus, within three years of its initial discovery by Mueller, DDT was recognized in Switzerland as an effective synthetic organic insecticide for use in both agriculture and public health. Furthermore, Geigy was producing the material in Switzerland in substantial amounts.

The Geigy company began to inform its foreign subsidiaries and associates, as well as foreign governments, about DDT within two years of its initial discovery. In September of 1941, the company informed its U.S. subsidiary of a "new insecticide" that in the form of a one-percent dust was effective against the Colorado potato beetle. The initial reaction of the U.S. company to this nonspecific information was unenthusiastic because lead arsenate was successfully employed in controlling the potato pest in the U.S.[25] In 1942, the Geigy company informed diplomatic representatives of the belligerent powers in Bern about DDT and sent samples of the material to Geigy representatives outside Switzerland with instructions to approach the governments of the countries in which they were located.[26] In the fall of 1942, U.S. Geigy officials presented samples of DDT to Ruric Creegan Roark of the USDA.[27] Roark and his staff accepted the material, tested it, and became enthusiastic over its potential. The grounds for their enthusiasm were partially technical, but political considerations resulting from the war were of equal or more importance.

In 1940, USDA research became oriented toward military goals when Secretary of Agriculture Henry Wallace directed all personnel "to consider their possible contributions to national needs as the defense program approaches the stage of 'maximum effort.' "[28] The initiation of open hostilities in December 1941 caused the USDA to complete the transformation from a peacetime organization to one totally committed to war. On December 11, Secretary of Agriculture Claude Wickard ordered a complete review of all work: "Every activity now must be measured by the contribution it can make to a victorious conclusion of the war."[29]

Military personnel requested that the USDA give special attention to the development of repellents and insecticides for lice and mosquitoes. The USDA's Division of Insects Affecting Man and Animals (DIAMA) had a laboratory at Orlando, Florida, that was chosen in 1941 as the major research site for defense-related projects. By May 1, 1942, a nucleus of researchers was located at Orlando under the direction of Walter E. Dove and his assistant, Edward Fred Knipling.[30]

By the end of the summer of 1942, the Orlando group had achieved some small successes. In August, MYL* powder was recommended to the armed forces for body louse control, but it was effective for only one week, too short a period when men are under the pressure of war.[31] The development of mosquito repellents and mosquito larvicides was not as far along as the antilouse powder. Researchers of DIAMA had recommended indalone to the army as an interim mosquito repellent and felt that esters and alcohols offered more promise of good repellent activity than other types of compounds. Although R-612 (2-ethyl-1,3-hexanediol) was then known to be a good repellent, there were problems in making the compound commercially available. The DIAMA personnel also discussed the possibility of developing nonwettable or floating preparations of Paris green for use against surface-feeding mosquito larvae.[32] Beyond these achievements, however, the Orlando staff had been able to accomplish little aside from the establishment of colonies of mosquitoes and lice for experimental purposes.

The development of the DIAMA laboratory in Orlando was paralleled by the emergence of a severe shortage of agricultural insecticides. Federal and state entomologists recognized that the shortage could adversely affect wartime goals for food production. Supplies of pyrethrum

* U.S. Army louse powder, based on pyrethrins and other materials.

and rotenone were of special concern because they were imported and thus subject to disruption by war. Japan was, at the time, the major source of pyrethrum for the U.S.[33] By the summer of 1942, supplies of rotenone were quite short, and there were allegations that some South American companies were hoarding their supplies in order to force a higher price for the material in the U.S.[34]

Roark, head of the USDA's Division of Insecticide Investigations (DII), directed his staff to meet the needs of the military by searching for new materials with insecticidal activities. He also began collecting statistics on the needs for all types of pesticides by farmers in different regions of the country.[35] Roark's staff spent much effort in attempts to find synergists for pyrethrum to stretch the effectiveness of this scarce commodity. By October 1942, DII had conducted 350 tests on houseflies and found six synergistic materials for pyrethrum. The division had also screened 800 new chemicals for activity against phytophagous* insects, flies, and roaches.[36]

The stage was thus set for Roark's receipt of DDT from the Geigy company on October 16, 1942. The laboratories of both DII and DIAMA were operating and many compounds were being screened routinely and, if promising, put through a series of tests to determine whether they had any possibility of practical use. The USDA was under pressure to provide insect control materials for both military and agricultural uses. Roark later recorded the excitement generated by DDT's arrival:

> Evaluation of the preparations . . . reached us within a week or two. . . . We immediately undertook an investigation of the active insecticide principle . . . by a series of reactions together with synthesis the structure of DDT was determined.
>
> On February 26, 1943, Dr. Haller visited the Geigy Company in New York, informed them of our interest in their preparation and inquired as to the possibility of its manufacture in this country. At that time, it was not known by any of us that the Geigy Company had a manufacturing outlet in this country; in fact there was some pessimism that the product (DDT) was impractical because it would be necessary to import it from abroad. Dr. Haller informed the Geigy people of the chemical composition of DDT, then known as GNB Conc., and how it might be made commercially. They stated that while they had not been informed about its chemistry, that should the product be of value it could be made in this country. Within a few days they confirmed our findings as to the chemical identity of DDT.
>
> The Division of Insecticide Investigations began to make inquiry into the availability of the necessary raw materials, chloral, chlorobenzene, and sulfuric acid. In May, 1943, Wm. Lee, Research and Development Division,

* *Phytophagous* insects are those that feed upon plants. *Entomophagous* insects feed upon other insects.

> Quartermaster Corps, and Dr. Haller visited the Cincinnati Chemical Works, Norwood, Ohio, and encouraged them to proceed as rapidly as possible with the production of DDT. . . .[37]

Knipling, director of the Orlando laboratory from 1942 to 1946, summed up his recollections about how DIAMA had worked with the new chemical from Switzerland in the months immediately after its introduction. His laboratory received a sample of Gesarol Dust Insecticide in November 1942 from DII and quickly found that DDT was a good louse powder. "Our chief worry was: Can the chemical be used safely on man? The Food and Drug Administration was attempting to determine the answer to this question. After several months of intensive study they concluded that in dust form DDT was entirely safe to use. By May 1943, DDT was recommended to the armed services as a safe and effective louse powder."[38]

The effectiveness of DDT as a mosquito larvicide was also quickly established. Christian C. Deonier of the USDA began work in October 1942 on the development of a larvicide but had not made much progress by February 1943, when DDT was tried for the first time. DDT was recommended as a larvicide dust in May. Other uses of the chemical were also established by May: DDT residual oil spray for control of flies, mosquitoes, and bedbugs, and a combination of benzyl benzoate and DDT spray for treatment of scabies. By July 1943, the uses of DDT had been expanded to include a larvicide spray for mosquitoes, treatment of clothing for louse control, and tests of 5% DDT aerosols. In the latter part of 1943 and in 1944, three other major developments with DDT insecticides qualified for recommendation to the armed forces: DDT residual spray emulsion (Triton Z100), control of dog flies by spraying their breeding places, and the use of DDT aerosols in industrial plants for the control of mosquitoes.[39]

Initial production of DDT in the U.S. was channeled almost exclusively to the armed forces, a policy that, in spite of the shortage of agricultural insecticides, delayed the adoption of DDT for agricultural purposes. In late summer of 1943, shortly after the Orlando laboratory had recommended DDT for certain uses by the armed forces, the USDA sent limited supplies of DDT to the state agricultural experiment stations.[40] Entomologists published their initial results in the February 1944 issue of the *Journal of Economic Entomology*. The range of insects against which DDT was tested in 1943 included the oriental fruit moth, the California red scale, various cotton insects, the codling moth, the European corn borer, and others. More extensive tests with DDT came with the growing season of 1944, but many problems remained unresolved by the fall of that year. DDT still could not be recommended for commercial agricultural use.[41] Some of the field studies of 1944 had not repeated the results obtained in 1943, and there were still uncertainties about what percentage of DDT to use and how much residue of DDT could safely be left on the finished commodity.[42]

Despite the initial problems of adapting DDT to use in agriculture, a Special Committee on DDT chaired by USDA's Sievert A. Rohwer reported in December 1944 that the future of DDT looked very promising for an extraordinarily large range of peacetime tasks:

> We feel that never in the history of entomology had a chemical been discovered that offers such promise to mankind for relief from his insect problems as DDT. There are limitations and qualifications, however.
>
> Subject to these, this promise covers three chief fields: public health, household comfort and agriculture. As public health we include control of the insects which carry diseases that have scourged humanity, such as malaria, typhus and yellow fever. Household comfort is taken to cover such things as flies, fleas, bedbugs and mosquitoes. Agriculture includes not only farms, gardens and orchards, but forests, livestock and poultry.[43]

The optimism of Rohwer and his colleagues about DDT was largely confirmed in the five-year period after DDT was released for civilian use in 1945. DDT's usefulness in public health purposes led in 1948 to the award of the Nobel Prize for Physiology and Medicine to Mueller. For the first time in history, entomologists envisioned the possibility of controlling or eradicating malaria, typhus, yellow fever, filariasis, dengue, and other diseases transmitted by insects. At the very time the prize was awarded, the Health Division of the Rockefeller Foundation, the Italian High Commission for Public Health, and the United Nations were in the midst of a joint campaign to rid the entire island of Sardinia of its ancient association with malaria, a project that was largely successful by the end of the decade.[44] Similar successes in agricultural insect control also took place and are discussed in more detail shortly.

The successes of DDT stemmed from its technical superiority to competing insecticides available at the time and to the sociopolitical pressures stemming from World War II. More importantly for the long run, DDT's successes stimulated a search for more synthetic organic pesticides. The USDA estimated that 25 new pesticides were introduced between 1945 and 1953. The more important of them were BHC (benzene hexachloride), chlordane, toxaphene, aldrin, dieldrin, endrin, heptachlor, parathion, methyl parathion, and tetraethylpyrophosphate.[45] Invention, development, and adoption of these insecticides profoundly altered (1) insect control practices and the science of entomology, (2) the insecticide industry, and (3) farm production practices.

IMPACT OF THE NEW INSECTICIDES

The major, direct effect of the new synthetic, organic insecticides was a shift in the constellation of insect control techniques relied upon by farmers. The techniques affected were chemicals, sanitation and other farming practices, mechanical control, biological control, and quarantines.

Chemical control techniques were the type most immediately altered. In general, the use of older compounds decreased as use of the new materials increased. For example, DDT and BHC were influential in reducing the uses of lead and calcium arsenates in the U.S. The total amount of insecticides used per year increased.[46] Not only were older chemicals replaced by newer ones, but the new inventions were sufficiently cheap and effective to warrant adoption for control of insects not previously considered to be subject to chemical control. For example, the cheapness of DDT caused insect control strategies in forestry to shift from cultural practices to chemical methods.[47] Similarly, the widespread use of DDT to control malaria after 1945 resulted from the compound's cheapness and persistence, traits lacking in the older insecticides. In short, DDT's low acute mammalian toxicity, persistence, cheapness, and broad-spectrum activity made it more useful than any other single insecticide developed before it.

The fortunes of biological control techniques, especially those dependent upon entomophagous insects, can only be said to have declined as a result of the introduction of DDT and the other synthetic organic insecticides. The percentage of research papers in the *Journal of Economic Entomology* on the general biology of insect pests and on their biological control dropped from 33% in 1937 to 17% in 1947, while the amount devoted to the testing of insecticides rose from 58% to 76%.[48] By 1950, Paul H. DeBach of the Division of Biological Control, University of California, Riverside, noted that the use of DDT had resulted in increases in the cottony-cushion scale, a pest of citrus formerly under complete biological control. DeBach and his colleagues attributed such insecticide-induced outbreaks to the destruction of entomophagous insects in the citrus groves (Chapter 2).

Control measures based on habitat sanitation and farming practices (cultural control) were altered by the advent of the new insecticides but in a different way. Chemicals did not interfere with cultural control, but they offered an alternative. For example, the western corn rootworm *(Diabrotica vergifera)* could be controlled by crop rotation before DDT.[49] Both BHC and DDT were suggested in 1948 as alternatives to crop rotation for control of this insect by entomologists of the Nebraska Agricultural Experiment Station.[50] Aldrin came to replace DDT and BHC as the insecticide of choice in the 1960s.[51] Corn, especially in the Corn Belt, tends to be a more valuable crop than the alternative crops with which it can be rotated, such as wheat, oats, barley, and soybeans. Farmers began to prefer chemical control to crop rotation for economic reasons.[52]

The fate of mechanical control (destruction of individuals by physical means such as pressure or temperature) after the introduction of DDT and the other new insecticides was much the same as that of cultural control. Chemicals were cheaper and more effective, so they replaced mechanical control. No statistics on the extent of mechanical control practices exist for the postwar period, but they probably survived only in small areas, such as households, or as a by-product of some procedure performed for other reasons, such as plowing for weed control.

Legal control, the exclusion of insects by quarantines, was the technology most unchanged by the introduction of DDT and other new chemicals. Widespread adoption of air travel made the maintenance of quarantine systems more important than ever in order to exclude alien pests from the U.S.[53] Administration of quarantines changed only in that DDT and the other new insecticides were sometimes adopted by quarantine inspectors to destroy infestations discovered in items of commerce.

DDT and the other new chemicals elicited proposals for a concept of control seldom considered in prewar times: permanent control by eradication of a pest species. Gordon Harrison eloquently described the transformation of operations against malaria from control to eradication, and some agricultural entomologists soon followed suit.[54] The power of the new chemicals to evoke quests for final solutions became an important part of entomology that lives with it to the present day (Chapter 4).

The more immediate impact of the new insecticides was that they stimulated the development of a new paradigm for agricultural entomology: the major tool for controlling insects would be the application of toxic chemicals to them. Other methods were not forgotten, dismissed from research, or left totally unused; but they were for the most part relegated to secondary importance. This chemical control paradigm attracted many entomologists away from competing lines of research and provided numerous problems for them. Particularly important were the questions of which chemical, applied how, at what time, and in what amounts. Entomologists continued to maintain that insects could be controlled by many different means, but when drawing up their own research plans, they tended to select a chemical as the foundation of the experimental design.

All across the nation, farmers and entomologists alike scrambled to exploit the technological power of the new insecticides. Neither group had much choice in the matter. Farmers who refused or neglected to adopt profitable techniques risked being forced out of business by their technically more progressive neighbors. Scientists who preferred other lines of research risked professional stagnation by not investigating what were on the surface the most marked advances in insect control every demonstrated.

DDT's successes during and after World War II also had immense impacts on the chemical insecticide industry. Scientists in the chemical industry and professional entomologists developed new uses for DDT as the chemical industry expanded its ability to make the compound. The Cincinnati Chemical Works at Norwood, Ohio, a subsidiary of the Geigy company began production of the material in 1943.[55] By 1945, 14 companies manufactured the material, and 16 formulated DDT into insecticides for sale.[56] Total production of DDT by U.S. firms rose from about 10 million lb. in 1944 to over 100 million lb. in 1951.[57] U.S. production peaked in 1962–1963 at 188 million lb.[58] By then, DDT was used in agriculture, public health, and a wide variety of consumer specialty items.

The pesticide industry in general underwent a tremendous growth in the years 1939–1954. Establishments producing primarily insecticides and fungicides increased from 83 to 275. Value added to the materials by the manufacturers increased from $3.8 million to $62.1 million, and the total value of the shipments from these manufacturers increased from $9.2 million to $174.6 million.[59] One corporation, Merck and Co., Inc., saw its total sales jump from $20 million in 1939 to $61.6 million in 1946. "Practically all the increase came from the new products [synthetic vitamins, sulfa drugs, DDT, and the fermentation antibiotics (penicillin and streptomycin)], which were also responsible for most of the company's comfortable $6 million profit last year," announced one business magazine.[60]

Journalists covering the chemical industry in the years following 1945 traced a $3.8 billion expansion in plant capacity between 1947 and 1949[61] and believed that the new materials such as synthetic insecticides would be the source of the highest profit margins in the years ahead.[62] Chemicals were seen as the "premier industry of the U.S."[63] A ranking of the big five companies (DuPont, Union Carbide, Dow, Allied, and Monsanto) by relative investments in research correlated almost exactly with their ranking in sales growth during the war years.[64] Most of the expansion of plant capacity was financed by borrowing instead of internal profits. This practice increased fixed costs of production and thus made net profits more sensitive to variations in sales than would have been the case had expansion been financed internally.[65]

Public announcements by two companies, Monsanto and DuPont, corroborated the general statements made in the business press. DuPont increased its annual expenditures for new plant facilities from $34.7 million in 1945 to $116.7 million in 1948. Monsanto began manufacturing DDT in 1944 and offered preferred stocks for sale as a means of financing that and other capital expenditures in 1946. Both companies discussed their activities concerning the new insecticides (plus many other new compounds) with considerable pride.[66]

A comprehensive history of the insecticide industry has not been written, and it is beyond the scope of this study to attempt it. Nevertheless, evidence from the news media and public announcements of involved companies is consistent with the hypothesis that the industry had been transformed in important ways by the early 1950s. Research to find new synthetic insecticides was the pathway to growth and profits; production of the old standard materials like lead arsenate was at best a pedestrian way to make money. Agressiveness in sales was necessary because of external debts to be repaid and because the marketing of a stream of new products required the constant education of potential customers about their benefits.

In these two respects, novelty and agressive sales, the insecticide industry was apparently consistent with other segments of the American chemical industry. Alfred D. Chandler, Jr., argued in 1977 that diversification through innovation became a conscious strategy of growth in the 1920s for many industries, especially those dealing with chemicals. George Eastman of Kodak fame was one of the first major pioneers in the strategy when he decided that constant innovation was a better way to compete than reliance on patents. By 1910, many companies had established research departments.[67] Further study is needed to determine if the insecticide industry followed the same pattern, but the available evidence indicates that it did.

Synthetic, organic insecticides thus had major impacts in three areas: insect control practices in agriculture were altered; research patterns in entomological science were reoriented; and the insecticide industry was transformed. Farming was the *raison d'être* of both professional entomology and the insecticide industries, but the complexities of insect control varied between commodities, regions, and individual farms. In order to explore how the new chemicals actually fit into farming practices, we turn to a case study of the apple industry. Apple producers were one of the biggest consumers of insecticides; only cotton producers exceeded their purchases in the years before 1945.[68] Their handling of the new insecticides was exemplary of the career of the new materials.

INSECT CONTROL AND THE APPLE INDUSTRY

Apple trees probably originated in southwestern Asia between the Caspian and Black Seas south of the Caucasus. They were cultivated in Europe at least 2000 years before their introduction to the U.S. They grew readily here, and exports began in the eighteenth century. Apples were widely cultivated throughout North America during the nineteenth century, but they were primarily a minor crop on diversified farms until the last one to two decades. Little was done to fertilize the trees or spray them for insect and disease control. Apples that appeared in urban markets usually came from nearby rural areas and were usually damaged in minor ways from insect or disease attack.[69]

Transformation of the apple industry from a small sideline business to a specialized, commercial industry occurred between approximately 1850 and 1930. In North America, western New York on the south shore of Lake Ontario was recognized as a superior region for apple production by 1860; by 1900, it was one of the foremost apple growing areas of the entire U.S.[70] Other areas of the northeast and midwest were also heavy centers of apple production in 1900. In addition, Washington, Oregon, and California were sites of rapid growth in the new industry. Oregon became the first large western producer in the 1870s and was connected by ship to its markets in California.[71] Washington State surpassed New York and became the largest producer of commercial apples in the Nation by the 1930s.[72] Its growth was almost entirely dependent upon the expansion of the railroads into the Pacific Northwest. The Northern Pacific Railroad came to the Yakima Valley and the Great Northern Railroad to the Wenatchee–Okanogan Valley in 1886 and 1892, respectively.[73] Other areas in North America such as Nova Scotia in Canada also entered commercial apple production in the last part of the nineteenth century and became major production centers. Nova Scotia's apple market was in Britain.[74]

Emergence of the commercial apple industry was accompanied by increased specialization of apple producers in their one main crop. Commercialization was also accompanied by a reduction in the number of varieties of apples produced. Delicious became a favored variety in Washington, for example, and other varieties declined.[75]

A complex of factors affecting all of agriculture after the Civil War affected the growth of the commercial apple industry. Increases in population, urbanization, incomes, education, and transportation all combined to create an increased demand for apples, especially high quality fruits.[76] The apple industry boomed in response to the heavy demand, and production soared until 1930. In Washington, for example, production rose from an annual average of 7.5 million bushels in 1911–1915 to 38 million bushels in 1930.[77] The heady prosperity enjoyed by successful growers was reflected in the value of their land. Irrigated orchards in Washington brought a phenomenal $2500 per acre in 1910.[78]

The bubble burst after 1910 and became worse with the onset of the agricultural depression in the 1920s and 1930s. Between 1910 and 1930, growers were afflicted with poor marketing practices. Apple producers in the Pacific Northwest attempted to meet these problems by cooperative marketing arrangements, most of which failed.[79] After 1930, the general economic drop affected nonagricultural industries as well. Land values in Washington orchards dropped to a little over $300 per acre.[80] The number of bearing trees in the U.S. dropped 35% from 1930 to 1940, and the number of nonbearing (young) trees dropped 51%.[81] In short, apple producers were pulling out established trees and not planting new ones. The bust came in 1929 for the large Nova Scotian apple industry, and a Royal Commission was appointed by the province to see what was the matter. They concluded that increased competition on the British and European markets from surplus U.S. apples was a major handicap.[82]

It is difficult to trace personal tragedies in any financial reversal involving so many people in different countries, but economists provided somewhat impersonal statistics. G. P. Scoville of Cornell University assumed that an apple grower should receive an income of 5% from his investment plus an hourly wage equal to that achievable in nearby industrial establishments. Therefore if his net receipts did not exceed 5% of his capital investment, the man received no income from his labor. Scoville calculated that between 1913 and 1940, the average New York apple grower received labor income less than that of the hired man in 23 of the 28 years. Only in 1913 and 1936 was the average grower able to receive as much as $200 per year for his labor efforts. In 10 of the 36 years between 1913 and 1948, growers received a labor income of less than zero.[83] A similar dismal picture was painted for the Washington State industry.[84]

World War II created an economic bonanza for apple growers in the United States. Domestic demand for apples recovered with rising incomes. In 1943, 72% of the New York producers had labor incomes higher than hired men's wages, and the mean was $5948. An average grower in Niagra County, New York, received a total income of $9514 in 1943 or a 30.4% return on his invested capital.[85] The question facing the apple industry at the end of the war in 1945 was whether or how long the new good times would last.

Growers in Washington faced particularly difficult problems, because a number of changes in the national apple industry had taken place in the period since 1930. Washington growers had traditionally relied on their ability to raise a high-quality (nonwormy) fresh apple that stored well. Their fruit was transported to large eastern markets where it either brought a premium price in comparison to inferior eastern apples or was sold out of storage after the eastern apples had been marketed. Eastern growers, however, had responded to the competitive threat posed by the westerners with improved production practices. Increased spraying for insect and disease control plus thinning excess blossoms allowed them to produce large, blemish-free apples just about as efficiently as the westerners. Proximity to large markets such as Chicago and New York gave the eastern growers a decided advantage in transportation costs compared to the western producers.[86]

Furthermore, all apple growers were faced with a competitive threat from the citrus industry. Per capita consumption of citrus increased from 18.7 lb. in 1909–1913 to 50.3 lb. in 1935–1939; simultaneously per capita consumption of fresh apples dropped from 63.8 lb. in 1909 to 40.8 lb. in 1939. Consumption of dried, canned, and juiced fruits increased while fresh fruits declined.[87] The great American habit of orange juice for breakfast thus edged apples out of their top position in the fruit market, and the food processing industry paid less for apples than individual consumers seeking fresh fruit.

Another factor affecting the apple industry was the increase in labor costs engendered by the war. The cost of harvesting apples for fresh market in New York State, for example, rose from $0.14 per bushel in 1937–1940 to $0.31 in 1946–1950; haresting as a percent of the total cost of production rose from 17% to 24% in the same period.[88] The Washington State Apple Commission noted in November, 1946, that labor costs in Washington were up 277% in the period 1939–1945. In 1939 labor costs in Washington were estimated to be $0.26 per box and in 1945 the figure was $0.98 per box (a box in Washington is approximately equal to a bushel).[89] Rising labor costs during the war years were acceptable to growers because the demand for apples was so strong. With the return of peace and uncertainty of demand, high labor costs became a threat to continued prosperity for orchard owners. Economists urged continued research to lower labor costs as well as the cost of other inputs in apple production. Cooperative marketing for Washington apples was also recommended.[90]

The stage into which the new insecticides were introduced can thus be summarized as follows: Apple growers had gone through very tight years since 1910, and wartime conditions brought the first prosperity they had seen in about 30 years. Continuation of good times was tenuous, however. Competition from the citrus industry, shifting consumer preferences in favor of processed compared to fresh fruit, and skyrocketing costs for labor all loomed as factors threatening orchard owners with a return to the "bad old days." In addition, the nation's largest apple growing region, Washington State, was faced with additional competitive threats from improved orchards of the east.

High competition in the apple industry plus the specter of renewed poverty defined the arena into which the new insecticides were introduced. Whether they would be adopted or not was to be answered in the context of uncertainty and fear. Such conditions breed high premiums for short-term factors compared to long-term considerations. If the new insecticides offered the least bit of advantage in lowering the production costs of blemish-free, fresh fruits, then the grower who failed to adopt them truly risked his continued existence in the commercial apple production industry.

Apples were plagued with insect and disease pests before their commercial production began. The economic importance of the various pest species before commercialization, however, was minimal. Apples consumed on the farmstead simply had the damaged portion removed; those sold in nearby markets formed only a small portion of the income of the producer, and the consumers were of necessity tolerant of damaged fruit. Commercial production by specialized producers brought with it a change in the economics of pest control. Producers dependent upon apples for a large portion or all of their income had more incentives to maximize the quality of their produce so as to maximize their receipts.

Lead arsenate was introduced as an insecticide for gypsy moth control beginning in 1892–1893 and quickly found use in apple orchards.[91] During the first half of the twentieth century, lead arsenate was the primary insecticide used in commercial apple production, and apples provided the major market for lead arsenate.[92] The major target was the codling moth, an insect introduced into the U.S. from Asia. This creature was known throughout the U.S. as the most persistent, destructive, and difficult insect pest in apple orchards. Without treatment it regularly damaged between 20% and 95% of the apples in every orchard. Plum curculios were considered the second most serious insect pest.[93]

Costs of controlling insect pests of apples varied from year to year and between different regions. Nevertheless, commercial orchardists considered annual expenses for insect control to be highly significant. In Washington, expenditures for spray materials and labor to apply them ranged from 16% to 18% of all production costs between 1942 and 1944.[94] Some of the costs were for disease control, so not all of them can be attributed to insect pests. Not only were costs of spraying significant in Washington, they had increased since 1925 whereas costs of spraying in the eastern orchards had not. In 1943, the cost of spraying Washington apples was about $0.25 per box and that of New York apples was $0.21 per bushel.[95] Resistance of the codling moth to lead arsenate was suspected in some areas as early as 1928.[96]

Codling moth was important enough to force apple production out of certain areas. In 1930, for example, apples were grown in all parts of the Yakima Valley in Washington. By 1945, however, production in the lower parts of the Valley had virtually disappeared in favor of other types of fruits. The upper Yakima Valley had cooler temperatures that promoted better coloring in the apple, and the higher temperatures in the lower part of the Valley aggrevated the codling moth situation. Growers usually had to apply poisons three times each summer to control the moth in the upper Valley, but in the lower Valley seven applications were necessary.[97]

USDA entomologist Howard Baker exaggerated the situation in 1952, but he captured the mood of at least some growers with the statement, "As recently as 1944, apple growers throughout the United States feared that the codling moth would put them out of business."[98]

Baker's major error was his failure to account for the diversity among apple growers. Some indeed probably were put out of business, such as those in the lower Yakima Valley. Others, however, continued to produce, and indeed made handsome returns during the war years, as noted above.

Systematic surveys of insecticide-use patterns do not exist for the U.S. before 1964. Nevertheless, knowledgeable students of the apple industry agreed that DDT became the material of choice for codling moth control by the early 1950s. Use of lead arsenate declined but did not disappear. The reason for DDT's rapid adoption was first and foremost its effectiveness against codling moth. With lead arsenate, the best farmers could hope for was about 15% wormy apples. With DDT, the rate of wormy apples was frequently about 1–2% or less.[99] Tests in Colorado indicated that 36.9% of the apples were wormy when lead arsenate was used compared to 6.4% when DDT was the insecticide.[100] Such experimental results do more than show that a smart farmer could increase his short-term profits by adopting DDT. They suggest he would have to be somewhat derelict not to!

New insecticides, particularly DDT, were important changes for the apple industry, but they constituted only one part of the total change in insect control practices. New machines and new formulations of the chemicals were also introduced in the late 1940s and both gave considerable evidence of their abilities to further reduce the costs of insecticide application. The costs of spray materials and labor to apply them in Washington, for example, had risen from $12.98 per acre in 1910 to $60.92 in 1940; the percentage of the total insect control costs occupied by labor in the same period rose from 31% to 45%.[101] Clearly the price of labor had risen faster than the costs of chemicals.

Airblast application machines changed the situation considerably.[102] Prices of pesticides continued to rise, but the new machines were so much more efficient in terms of labor that the total costs of pest control dropped to $53.61 per acre in 1950; labor's portion of this cost was now only 10%.[103]

One of the major reasons the new machines made better use of labor was they they could apply a concentrated insecticide rather than one highly diluted with water. An experiment on the use of concentrated DDT to control codling moths on pears in California in 1947 indicated that dilute formulations of DDT applied with high-pressure sprayers cost $16.83 per acre. Use of the concentrated formulation in an airblast sprayer cost only $2.03 per acre.[104] In Washington, the average number of hours per acre spent on spraying apples dropped from 29.7 in 1926–1928 to 6 in 1950.[105] The combined factors of reduced codling moth damage plus the reduction in labor costs to apply sprays signalled the end of lead arsenate's domination in the apple orchard.

DDT's effectiveness in controlling codling moth and the ever-rising price of labor also provided the foundation for the demise of sanitation practices and other cultural techniques aimed at keeping moth populations low. In 1942, the Extension Service of Washington State College advised apple growers to clean up dropped and cull fruits so as to destroy overwintering codling moth larvae. Producers were also advised to scrape the old bark off their trees in order to remove the larvae and to apply bands soaked in beta-naphthol to kill larvae seeking shelter under them.[106] By 1950 the Extension Service had dropped their recommendations for sanitation and cultural controls and recommended DDT as the most efficient and economical material for codling moth control.[107] DDT triumphed over the older materials and the labor-intensive methods of sanitation and cultural control. Knowledgeable entomologists working in Washington lamented years later that the Extension Service's recommendations were effective.[108]

DDT's adoption in apple production was not an unmixed blessing despite its ability to lower production costs. Orchard owners benefitted from less damage from codling moth and lower labor bills, but those who worked in the orchards may have preferred that their jobs not be curtailed. Biologically, DDT induced outbreaks of mites, particularly of the European red mite and the Pacific mite.[109]

Entomologists E. J. Newcomer and F. P. Dean from Washington State College noted this problem the first time they used DDT in 1944.[110] They sought a solution to the mite problem with a strategy that unfortunately became all too common in the post-DDT era. They combined DDT with other materials in order to find a concoction that would kill the mites as well as the codling moth; parathion and other materials gave adequate control of mites.[111] In 1950, the Extension Service in Washington summarized all of the new tests for mite killers and recommended either parathion or TEPP (tetraethylpyrophosphate). In addition, outbreaks of wooly apple aphids induced by DDT were to be controlled by BHC.[112]

Washington apple growers were now "safe." They could use DDT to kill codling moth and induce outbreaks of mites and wooly apple aphids, which could in turn be killed with parathion, TEPP, and BHC. In 1952, entomologist Howard Baker of the USDA noted that experimentation on control of apple insects had once been directed toward the discovery of a substitute for lead arsenate. "Now, it is directed toward working out a complete spray program that will take care of all pests that may be present."[113] Michigan entomologist Brian Croft estimated in 1975 that apples were sprayed between 12 and 20 times per year for a variety of insect and disease problems.[114] Some of the chemicals changed after 1952, but it is important to note that the techniques developed were responses to a complex of needs of apple producers. The attractiveness of new chemicals that killed more codling moths with less labor precisely reflected the competitive situation faced by apple producers. Similarly, the development of complex mixtures of insecticides to kill pests induced by DDT was compatible with the economic situation. For their part, growers accepted the new chemicals and went about their business of trying to stay in business.

Was the codling moth the cause of the problems faced by apple growers? An apple grower might perceive the moth as his major problem. An economic planner would have been just as reasonable to say that the economic and social system was at fault because it was conducive to producers raising more apples than consumers could purchase. Alternatively, a cynic might argue that greedy orchard workers demanding too much for their labor was really the cause of distress in apple production. Other scapegoats could be found, but all would suffer from the parochialism of narrow interest evident in the three above. The important point is that DDT was adopted by apple producers because it was a technical fix to a portion of their problems. Apple growers were ecstatic about its successes, but DDT did nothing to address the fundamental social and economic questions facing producers.

It is also important to note that the change in techniques of insect control in apple production led to a demand for further changes. A new type of chemical industry was essential to the new practices. Less labor was required, so employment patterns were altered. In New York, some orchardists didn't survive, and only 25% as many were in business in 1959 compared to 20–30 years earlier. Those remaining were more specialized and operated more acres.[115] The new machines reduced labor but required more acreage to support their higher costs. Farmers with fewer than 60–80 acres and 15,000 to 20,000 bushels per year found it uneconomical to use them in New York.[116] Changes in insect control practices were certainly not the only factors involved in the transformations, but they were important. Apples were typical of many agricultural enterprises that underwent a shift toward more use of insecticides, higher capital inputs, and a concomitant reduction in labor (Chapter 8).

CONCLUDING REMARKS

The world into which DDT and other new insecticides entered in 1945 was largely shaped by a variety of factors that had operated since 1900 and before. DDT's success in meeting wartime emergencies endowed it with a popularity that accelerated its adoption and enhanced its reputation as a "friend" useful against "enemies." DDT and the other new insecticides offered the promise of profitable sales to the chemical manufacturers and reduced production costs to farmers.

An interesting synergism thus developed that "chemicalized" insect control practices. The sale and use of insecticides met the interests of both chemical manufacturers and farmers. Insecticide sales and the number of new products on the market increased as toxic substances became part of agricultural production technology. Government regulation protected farmers against fraudulent insecticides and established chemical manufacturers against "disreputable" manufacturers. Entomologists served as justices of the peace in bringing the farming and chemical industries together. Their professional status increased as they successfully showed farmers which chemicals were best to use.

The happy marriage was unproblematic on the surface. But two questions were to raise their heads in a short time. What if the use of the chemicals posed unacceptable risks to society as a whole? What if the chemicals failed to do the job they were supposed to do? We turn to these disturbing realities in the next chapter.

REFERENCE NOTES

1. L. O. Howard, *A History of Applied Entomology* (Washington, D.C.: Smithsonian Inst., 1930), p. 64 (hereafter cited as Howard, *History*).
2. Walter S. Hough and A. Freeman Mason, *Spraying, Dusting and Fumigating of Plants* (New York: The Macmillan Co., 1951), pp. 3–9 (hereafter cited as Hough and Mason, *Spraying*).
3. Harold H. Shepard, *The Chemistry and Action of Insecticides* (New York: McGraw-Hill Book Co., 1951), pp. 15, 21 (hereafter cited as Shepard, *Chemistry*).
4. Adelynne Hiller Whitaker, *A History of Federal Pesticide Regulation in the United States to 1947*, Ph.D. Thesis, Emory Univ., 1974, p. 101.
5. *Ibid.*, pp. 1–7.
6. *Ibid.*, pp. 7–10.
7. *Ibid.*, pp. 81–102.
8. 36 Stat. 331, Sect. 7.
9. Williams Haynes, *American Chemical Industry* (New York: D. Van Nostrand Co., Inc., 1945), Vol. 3, p. 112 (hereafter cited as Haynes, *Chemical*).
10. *Ibid.*, p. 115.
11. B. R. Coad, Recent Experimental Work on Poisoning Cotton-Boll Weevils, USDA Bull. No. 731, July 19, 1918, 15 pp.
12. J. Douglas Helms, *The Cotton Boll Weevil in Texas and Louisiana, 1892–1907*, M. A. Thesis, Fla. State Univ., 1970, 127 pp; Howard, *History*, pp. 124–132.
13. Shepard, *Chemistry*, pp. 25–26.
14. Haynes, *Chemical*, Vol. 3, pp. 209–215.
15. *Ibid.*, p. 110.
16. Hough and Mason, *Spraying*, pp. 11–12. E. B. Blakeslee, Use of Toxic Gases as a Possible Means of Control of the Peach-Tree Borer, USDA Bull. No. 796, Oct. 21, 1919, 23 pp.
17. Shepard, *Chemistry*, p. 272.
18. Hough and Mason, *Spraying*, p. 12.
19. Haynes, *Chemical*, Vol. 4, p. 332; Vol. 5, pp. 315–316.
20. Haynes, *Chemical*, Vol. 5, pp. 316–317.
21. Andreas Buxtorf and M. Spindler, *Fifteen Years of Geigy Pest Control* (Basel: Buchdruckerei Karl Werner AG, 1954) (hereafter cited as Buxtorf and Spindler, *Fifteen*

Years). This book was originally published several years earlier under the title *10 Jahre Geigy Schadlingsbekampfung*. Although it is a company-sponsored, enthusiastic history, it contains a thorough review of the Geigy company's efforts to discover, test, manufacture, and market DDT insecticides.

22. Insecticides are frequently classified as stomach or contact materials. The former must be ingested by the insect before poisoning occurs. The latter can kill merely by contacting the outside of the animal. An obvious advantage of contact poisons is that killing may be affected before the insect dines on the protected woolen textiles, while a stomach poison could begin to protect only after damage is done to the cloth. Some materials such as DDT possess both stomach- and contact-killing properties.
23. Paul Herman Mueller, *Histoire du DDT* (Alençon: Maison Poulet-Malassis, 1948). I thank Christine Newman for translating the article.
24. H. Mooser, *Schweiz. Med. Wochenschr.* 74 (1944): 947; quoted in T. F. West and G. A. Campbell, *DDT* (London: Chapman and Hall, 1950), pp. 3–4 (hereafter cited as West and Campbell, *DDT*).
25. Victor Froelicher, The story of DDT, *Soap and Chemical Specialties* 20 (1944): 115, 117, 119, 145 (hereafter cited as Froelicher, DDT); quoted in West and Campbell, *DDT*, p. 6.
26. Buxtorf and Spindler, *Fifteen Years*. There is some ambiguity about what type of information was given to the Germans. Mueller implies that the information was delivered only to the U.S. and the United Kingdom, but Buxtorf and Spindler imply that the information was also given to the Germans. The latter authors display a picture of a patent from the Deutsches Reich along with patents from France, the U.S., Switzerland, and the United Kingdom.
27. Froelicher, DDT.
28. Henry A. Wallace to Chiefs of Bureaus and Officers, Aug. 23, 1940, Record Group 7 (Records of the Bureau of Entomology and Plant Quarantine), National Archives (hereafter records from this group are cited as RG7NA).
29. Claude R. Wickard to Chiefs of Bureaus and Heads of Offices, Dec. 14, 1941, RG7NA.
30. Walter E. Dove, "Historical References to Man and Animal's Contribution to War Effort," n.d., RG7NA. Knipling assumed the directorship of the laboratory in June 1942 and guided it for the duration of the war years. He later wrote that the real moving influence in getting the laboratory started came from Col. William S. Stone and Gen. J. S. Simmons (U.S. Army), who sat on committees of the National Research Council. According to Knipling's estimation, the Office of Scientific Research and Development gave the Orlando facility $815,000 between March 1942 and October 1945. In addition, the laboratory received from other agencies equipment, aircraft, personnel, and administrative supervision. The total cost of operating the research station was estimated to be approximately $1 million [Edward F. Knipling, "Insect Control Investigations of the Orlando, Florida, Laboratory during World War II," in *Annual Report of the Smithsonian Institution, 1948* (Washington, D.C., 1948), pp. 331–348] (hereafter cited as Knipling, Insect Control).
31. Knipling, Insect Control.
32. Ruric C. Roark to Percy N. Annand, Aug. 27, 1942, RG7NA.
33. W. H. White to Percy N. Annand, Jan. 28, 1942, RG7NA.
34. F. C. Highbee to R. E. Moore, July 29, 1942, RG7NA. Data collected by the Department of Commerce on imports of pyrethrum and rotenone amply demonstrate the fall in supplies during 1942 and 1943 compared with earlier years:

Pounds of Pyrethrum and Rotenone Imported (Millions)[a]

Year	Pyrethrum	Rotenone
1939	13.6	5.9
1940	12.6	6.6
1941	11.0	8.0
1942	9.5	3.8
1943	6.8	4.1

[a]Source: Harold H. Shepard, *The Chemistry and Action of Insecticides* (New York: McGraw-Hill, 1951), pp. 147, 159.

35. Ruric C. Roark to Percy N. Annand, Jan. 2, 1942, RG7NA.
36. Avery S. Hoyt to Morse Salisbury, July 2, 1942, RG7NA.
37. Ruric C. Roark to Percy N. Annand, Jan. 6, 1945, RG7NA.
38. Knipling, Insect Control.
39. Walter E. Dove, "Contributions to War Effort: Summary of More Important Developments to January 24, 1945," n.d., RG7NA.
40. Fred C. Bishopp to D. L. Van Dine, Sept. 2, 1943, RG7NA.
41. Annonymous, DDT not recommended for agricultural use, *Oil Paint Drug Rep.* 146 (Nov. 6, 1944): 4.
42. Agricultural Association discusses DDT, *ibid.*, Vol. 146 (Oct. 30, 1944): 3.
43. Report of Special Committee on DDT (S.A. Rohwer, Chairman) *J. Econ. Entomol.* 38 (1945): 144.
44. S. W. Simmons, "The Use of DDT Insecticide in Human Medicine," in *DDT*, Paul H. Mueller, ed. (Basel: Birkhäuser Verlag, 1959), pp. 264–265. Gordon Harrison discussed the frustration of the Sardinian Campaign because it failed to eradicate the malarial vector. *Anopheles labranchiae*, even though transmission of malaria was halted, in *Mosquitoes, Malaria and Man* (New York: E. P. Dutton, 1978), Chap. 24.
45. Production and Marketing Administration, *The Pesticide Situation for 1952–53* (Washington, D.C.: USDA, 1953), p. 4 (hereafter cited as Production and Marketing Administration, *Pesticide Situation*).
46. *Ibid.*, pp. 4–5, 16.
47. Samuel A. Graham, *Forest Entomology*, 3rd ed. (New York: McGraw-Hill Book Co., 1952), p. 10.
48. D. Price Jones, "Agricultural entomology," in *History of Entomology*, Ray F. Smith, Thomas E. Mittler, and Carroll N. Smith, eds. (Palo Alto, California: Annual Reviews, Inc., 1973), pp. 326–327.
49. E. Dwight Sanderson and Leonard Marion Peairs, *Insect Pests of Farm, Garden and Orchard*, 2nd ed. (New York: John Wiley and Sons, 1921), p. 144.
50. Roscoe E. Hill, Ephraim Hixson, and Martin H. Muma, Corn rootworm control test with benzene hexachloride, DDT, nitrogen fertilizers and crop rotation, *J. Econ. Entomol.* 41 (1948): 392–401.
51. Velmar W. Davis, Austin S. Fox, Robert P. Jenkins, and Paul A. Andrilenas, Economic Consequences of Restricting the Use of Organochlorine Insecticides on Cotton, Corn, Peanuts, and Tobacco, *Agricultural Economic Report No. 178* (Washington, D.C.: USDA, 1970), p. 14.

52. John H. Berry, "Effect of restricting the use of pesticides on corn–soybean farms," in *Economic Research on Pesticides for Policy Decision Making*, proceedings of a symposium, Apr. 27–29, 1970 (Washington, D.C.: USDA, 1971), p. 139.
53. C. L. Metcalf, W. P. Flint, and R. L. Metcalf, *Destructive and Useful Insects* (New York: McGraw-Hill Book Co., Inc., 1951), p. 354.
54. Gordon Harrison, *Mosquitoes, Malaria and Man* (New York: E. P. Dutton, 1978), Chap. 25.
55. Buxtorf and Spindler, *Fifteen Years.*
56. Agricultural Research Administration, USDA, "Producers of DDT and DDT Insecticides," mimeo, 1945.
57. Production and Marketing Administration, *The Pesticide Situation*, p. 7.
58. Economic Research Service, DDT Used in Farm Production, *Agricultural Economic Report No. 188* (Washington, D.C.: USDA, 1969).
59. Bureau of the Census, U.S. Department of Commerce, *Census of Manufacturers: 1954*, Vol. 2, Pt. 1 (Washington, D.C.: Government Printing Office, 1957). The figures quoted are for firms classified in Standard Industrial Code 2897.
60. Anonymous, Merck means over 1200 fine chemicals, *Fortune*, June, 1947, pp. 104–111+.
61. Anonymous, The chemical surge, *Business Week*, Mar. 18, 1950, pp. 117–118 (hereafter cited as Chemical surge, *Business Week*).
62. S. B. Self, Chemists goal, *Barron's* Jan. 7, 1946, pp. 9+.
63. Anonymous, The chemical century, *Fortune*, Mar. 1950, pp. 68–76+.
64. J. V. Sherman, New Products assure growth in chemical industry, *Barron's*, Feb. 19, 1945, pp. 9–10.
65. Chemical surge, *Business Week.*
66. For DuPont, see *Annual Report 1946* and *Annual Report 1948* (Wilmington, Del.: E. I. DuPont de Nemours and Co., 1947, 1949). For Monsanto, see *Report of 44th Annual Meeting of Stockholders*, Mar. 27, 1945; *Report of 45th Annual Meeting of Monsanto Stockholders*, Mar. 26, 1946; and *Prospectus*, Apr. 8, 1946; all published by Monsanto Co., St. Louis, Mo. The entry of DuPont into DDT production was noted in *Oil, Paint, and Drug Reporter*, Jan. 24, 1944, p. 37. Monsanto's activities with DDT were reported in *ibid.*, Aug. 21, 1944, p. 40.
67. Alfred D. Chandler, Jr., *The Visible Hand* (Cambridge: Harvard Univ. Press, 1977), pp. 374–375, 473–476.
68. Harold H. Shepard, *The Chemistry and Action of Insecticides* (New York: McGraw-Hill Book Co., 1951), p. 18. Shepard notes that in 1941, 56% of the lead arsenate produced was used on apples.
69. R. M. Smock and A. M. Neubert, *Apples and Apple Products* (New York: Interscience Pub., Inc., 1950), pp. 1–3 (hereafter cited as Smock and Neubert, *Apples*).
70. J. C. Folger and S. M. Thomson, *The Commercial Apple Industry of North America* (New York: The Macmillan Co., 1921), p. 3 (hereafter cited as Folger and Thomson, *Apple Industry*).
71. Joseph W. Ellison, The beginnings of the apple industry in Oregon, *Agric. Hist.* 11 (1937): 322–343.
72. Chester C. Hampson, "Trends in the apple industry," *Wash. Agric. Exp. Stn. Bull. No. 277*, Feb. 1933, p. 9 (hereafter cited as Hampson, Trends).
73. Hoyt Lemmons and Rayburn D. Tousley, The Washington apple industry. I. Its geographic basis, *Econ. Geog.* 21 (1945): 161–182 (hereafter cited as Lemmons and Tousley, Apple industry, I).

74. Willard V. Longley, Some economic aspects of the apple industry in Nova Scotia, *Nova Scotia Dept. of Agric. Bull. No. 113*, Nov. 1932, pp. 1, 7.
75. Hampson, Trends, p. 8.
76. Folger and Thomson, *Apple Industry*, pp. 10–15.
77. Rayburn D. Tousley and Hoyt Lemmons, The Washington apple indsutry. II. Economic considerations, *Econ. Geog.* 21 (1945): 252–268 (hereafter cited as Tousley and Lemon, Apple indsutry, II).
78. C. H. Zuroske, Washington Apple Production Costs and Labor Requirements, *Wash. Agric. Exp. Stn. Bull. No. 644*, Oct., 1962, 16 pp. (hereafter cited as Zuroske, Washington apples).
79. Joseph Waldo Ellison, Cooperative movement in Oregon apple industry, 1910–1929, *Agric. Hist.* 13 (1939): 77–96; Joseph W. Ellison, Marketing problems of northwestern apples, 1929–1940, *Agric. Hist.* 16 (1942): 103–115; C. Brewster Coulter, The big Y country: Marketing problems and organization, 1900–1920, *Agric. Hist.* 46 (1972): 471–488.
80. Zuroske, Washington apples.
81. Tousley and Lemmons, Apple industry, II.
82. "Royal Commission Investigating the Apple Industry of the Province of Nova Scotia," *Report* (Halifax: Minister of Public Works and Mines, King's Printer, 1930), pp. 10–11.
83. G. P. Scoville, Fruit Farms Analysed: 36 Years of Farm Business Records in Niagra County, *Cornell Univ. Agric. Econ. 769*, Feb. 27, 1951, 38 pp.
84. Tousley and Lemmons, Apple industry, II; Lemmons and Tousley, Apple industry, I.
85. The average figure of $5948 comes from Scoville, Fruit Farms. Data on Niagra County growers come from G. P. Scoville, Apple Costs, 1943, *Cornell Univ. Agric. Econ. 509*, Feb., 1945, 20 pp.
86. Tousley and Lemmons, Apple industry, II.
87. *Ibid.*
88. Van Travis and B. F. Stanton, Costs and Use of Labor in Harvesting Apples for Fresh Market, Hudson Valley, New York, 1959 and 1960, *Cornell Univ. Agric. Econ. Res. 63*, Apr. 1961, 13 pp.
89. Washington State Apple Commission, *Apple Research Digest*, No. 4, Nov., 1946, p. 3.
90. *Ibid.*, Nos. 1–84 (Nov., 1946–Dec., 1953), constantly advocated ways to reduce packing costs and bruising. Tousley and Lemmons strongly recommended a renewed effort to establish cooperative marketing for Washington apples, in Apple industry, II.
91. Edward H. Forbush and Charles H. Fernald, *The Gypsy Moth* (Boston: Wright and Potter Printing Co., State Printers, 1896), pp. 142–143, 473.
92. C. L. Metcalf and W. P. Flint, *Destructive and Useful Insects*, 2nd ed. (New York: McGraw-Hill Book Co., Inc., 1939), pp. 244–245 (hereafter cited as Metcalf and Flint, *Destructive*). In 1941, 55.6% of the lead arsenate used in the U.S. was on apples (Shepard, *Chemistry*, p. 18).
93. Metcalf and Flint, *Destructive*, pp. 599, 594.
94. Calculated from figures in W. M. Bristol, Washington Apple Production Costs for the 1944–45 Season, *Wash. Agric. Exp. Sta. Bull. 474*, June, 1946, 24 pages; M. T. Buchanan, Washington Apple Production Costs During the 1943–44 Season, *Wash. Agric. Exp. Stn. Bull. 446*, July, 1944, 14 pages; and M. T. Buchanan, A. W. Peterson, and G. A. Lee, "Washington Apple Production Costs, 1939–43," *Wash. Agric. Exp. Stn. Bull. 429*, May, 1943, 11 pp.

95. Tousley and Lemmons (Apple industry, II) analyze comparative cost changes between Washington and New York. See M. T. Buchanan, Washington, for Washington State figures; Scoville, Apple costs, for New York data.
96. Walter S. Hough first studied Colorado codling moth larvae resistant to lead arsenate in 1928 [Relative resistance to arsenical poisoning of two codling moth strains, *J. Econ. Entomol.* 21 (1928): 325–329].
97. Lemmons and Tousley, Apple industry, I.
98. Howard Baker, "Spider mites, insects, and DDT," in *Insects: The Yearbook of Agriculture, 1952*, p. 562 (hereafter cited as Baker, Spider mites).
99. *Ibid.*
100. J. H. Newton and George M. List, Codling moth and mite control in 1948, *J. Econ. Entomol.* 42 (1949): 346–348.
101. Calculated from Zuroske, Washington apples.
102. For an early review of the airblast machines, see O. C. French, Spraying equipment for pest control, *Calif. Agric. Exp. Stn. Bull. 666*, May, 1942, pp. 34–38; see also James G. Horsfall, *Fungicides and their Action* (Waltham, Mass.: Chronica Botanica Co. 1945), p. 78.
103. Calculated from Zuroske, Washington apples.
104. Arthur D. Borden, Control of codling moth on pears with a DDT spray, *J. Econ. Entomol.* 41 (1948): 118–119.
105. Zuroske, Washington apples.
106. Recommendations for Codling Moth, Orchard Mite, and Scale Control in Washington for 1942, *State Coll. of Wash. Ext. Bull. 279*, Feb., 1942, 12 pp.
107. Spray Programs for Insects and Diseases of Tree Fruits in Eastern Washington, *State Coll. of Wash. Ext. Bull. 419*, Feb., 1950, 29 pp (herefater referred to as Spray programs, *Ext. Bull.*, 1950).
108. S. C. Hoyt and J. D. Gilpatrick, "Pest management on deciduous fruits: Multidisciplinary aspects," in *Integrated Pest Management*, J. Lawrence Apple and Ray F. Smith, eds. (New York: Plenum Pub. Co., 1976), pp. 133–147.
109. Baker, Spider mites; E. J. Newcomer and F. P. Dean, Studies of orchard acaricides, *J. Econ. Entomol.* 41 (1948): 691–694.
110. E. J. Newcomer and F. P. Dean, Effects of xanthone, DDT, and other insecticides on the Pacific mite, *J. Econ. Entomol.* 39 (1946): 783–786.
111. Newcomer and Dean, Studies.
112. Spray programs, *Ext. Bull.*, 1950.
113. Baker, Spider mites.
114. B. A. Croft, "Tree fruit pest management," in *Introduction to Insect Pest Management*, Robert L. Metcalf and William H. Luckmann, eds. (New York: John Wiley and Sons, 1975), p. 481.
115. B. F. Stanton, B. A. Dominick, Jr., and S. C. Fan, Variability in Apple Production Costs and Returns, *Cornell Univ. Agric. Econ. Res. 17*, May, 1959, 35 pp.
116. C. G. Garman, How to Increase Efficiency in Spraying Apples: Some results of a study made by K. L. Robinson of 56 fruit tree farms in New York State in 1946, *Cornell Univ., Agric. Econ. 654*, Jan. 1948, 11 pp.

CHAPTER 2

Crisis

Widespread adoption of the new insecticides in American agriculture was essentially complete by the early 1950s, but it was not uncontested. Safety to humans and other species constituted a recognized problem from the beginning, but the exact nature and magnitude of the threats continues to be a subject for bitter debate. A second sort of problem emerged almost simultaneously with the introduction of the new insecticides. Are they a stable technological tool? Resistance of insects to the poisons and the destruction of natural enemies of insect pests threatened to unleash the tremendous reproductive power of pest species in a way that would render the insecticides useless or worse in the eyes of their users.

Problems of safety were primarily *external*, in that people other than users of insecticides were usually adversely affected. Resistance and the destruction of natural enemies, on the other hand, were *internal* problems, because they affected first and foremost the very people who were using the chemicals. Adverse publicity about insecticides has tended to focus more on the external problems, but a careful examination reveals that the internal factors provided the major impetus to innovate in entomology. In this chapter we explore how both sets of problems developed.

HAZARDS TO HUMANS AND OTHER SPECIES

It is interesting to note that one of the first doubts about DDT's safety was published even before the compound was released for general civilian use. During the middle and late 1940s, entomologists, public health officials, conservationists, and others were much concerned about hazards of the new chemicals to humans, livestock, and wildlife.[1] Despite the early worries about harm from the new insecticides, no easy consensus was reached about the magnitude or permanence of the damage.

Most of the entomological profession, plus the chemical and farming industries, became staunch defenders of the new materials. Polarized against them were elements of the medical profession, some wildlife specialists, and a few spokesmen from the food processing industries. Two federal actions initiated in 1949 provided the focal point for these adversary opinions.

First, the Food and Drug Administration (FDA) announced a long-planned series of hearings to establish legal limits on the amounts of pesticide residues that could remain on fruits and vegetables.[2] Such hearings had been provided for by the Food, Drug, and Cosmetic Act of 1938 (FDCA). Residues of poisons, particularly arsenic, lead, and fluorine, had been the source of many battles between the FDA and the apple industry in the days before World War II.[3] The hearings would have been held before 1949 but for the interference of World War II and then the drastic change in insect control practices engendered by the advent of the new chemicals.[4] Second, the Congress established a Select Committee to Investigate the Use of Chemicals in Foods and Cosmetics in 1950.[5] James J. Delaney (D., N.Y.) became chairman, and the "Delaney Commmittee" held extensive hearings from 1950 to 1952 on a wide variety of problems associated with chemicals coming in contact with consumers from different routes. Insecticides constituted a major portion of the testimony heard by the Committee.

Federal and state entomologists viewed both exercises as a threat to food production because of the possibility that new regulations would constrict the use of the new insecticides.[6] By implication, they viewed the "interference" of the FDA and the Congress as a threat to the legitimacy of expertise held by the entomological profession.[7]

Neither federal investigation diminished the social legitimacy of chemical control techniques. Congressman A. L. Miller (R., Nebr.), a physician and member of the Delaney Committee, introduced legislation that required a chemical manufacturer to present evidence on the safety of its product to the FDA and receive a "tolerance" or legal limit to the amount of residue that could appear on harvested food and feed; the tolerance had to be determined before the product could be marketed. Miller's amendment to the FDCA passed in 1954 and thus legitimized the use of insecticides by establishing legal doses that were considered insignificant.[8] The FDA's extensive hearings were mooted by the legislation, because the Miller Amendment established a new method for obtaining a tolerance. Entomological expertise was thus saved by the collective judgement of the Congress that certain levels of the poisons could be tolerated as a daily part of our existence. The Congress put entomologists and the chemical and farming industries on notice that the poisons were considered serious enough to merit specific and detailed regulation, but the threat was not judged sufficient to eliminate chemicals altogether or even to call for a decrease in their use.

Hearings by the FDA and the Delaney Committee obscured for a period the concern over hazards to wildlife by the new insecticides. Sporadic reports were made in the late 1940s and through the 1950s about isolated cases of damage caused by use of the chemicals. Rachel Carson, a person whose story has been told elsewhere,[9] ended the complacency over hazards to the environment, however, with her best-selling *Silent Spring* (1962).[10] Her thesis was that the use of insecticides (and other pesticides) was indiscriminate and that even when used as directed the materials frequently resulted in harm to people and wildlife. She also recognized the serious internal problems of resistance and destruction of natural enemies. Carson by no means rejected the use of chemicals in principle, but she argued that research leading to nonchemical means of control should be pursued. She later testified before the Senate that an individual citizen should have the freedom not to be poisoned by another person's pesticides.[11]

Entomologists on the whole probably did not agree with most of Carson's ideas, but their public responses were muted. E. F. Knipling, head of the USDA's Entomological Research Division (ERD), prepared for internal use within ERD a vigorous defense of insecticides.[12] Knipling disagreed with Carson's contention that pesticides were a substantial threat to man and animals; he also felt Carson had presented a one-sided story with insufficient attention to the benefits of chemicals. He agreed, however, that nonchemical control techniques should be developed and argued that ERD was already pursuing such paths. The USDA's public response was somewhat milder than Knipling's paper and took no issue with Carson's general argument. Instead, the Department emphasized that they already understood the problems and had taken steps to alleviate them.[13] As will be developed later, USDA's assertion of change to correct the problems was justified, and it was primarily Knipling's influence that had led to the move away from chemicals.

R. K. Chapman, an extension entomologist from the University of Wisconsin, prepared a bitter and defensive critique of Carson's book after public discussion of *Silent Spring* in Madison. The document was signed by his entire Department for circulation within only a limited segment of the University community.[14] P. J. Chapman (no relation), an entomologist from Cornell University, gave his opinion to a slightly larger audience of fruit growers in New York; his mixed review of Carson appeared in the *Proceedings* of the New York State Horticultural Society,[15] a publication outlet that wasn't exactly private but certainly did not reach a wide audience beyond the farming community and agricultural scientists in New York.

The most strenuous criticisms against *Silent Spring* published in widely circulated journals came not from entomologists but an M.D. (William J. Darby) in *Chemical and Engineering News*[16] and a bacteriologist (I. L. Baldwin) in *Science*.[17] Darby had had long experience with certain toxicological hazards of pesticides and had testified before the Delaney Committee. Nevertheless, his review was highly emotional. He appeared to be more upset with the fact that an "outsider" with little experience in the study of pesticides had raised disturbing questions than with the minor errors he justifiably noted.

Darby's review is perhaps best interpreted as the epitome of professionalism dedicated to the analysis of narrowly conceived problems; he had neither the imagination nor the skill to see beyond the end of his nose, which was apparently attached to the question, were people dropping dead in the street from pesticide poisoning? The answer to that question was clearly no, and Carson never argued otherwise. Her problem was the subtle and long-term hazards that the chemicals posed to humans and entire ecosystems plus the instability produced by resistance and destruction of natural enemies.

Baldwin's review was more reasoned and he granted the correctness of some of Carson's points. Baldwin agreed that chemicals had been used "without adequate testing, or . . . under improper conditions. Sometimes lives have been lost or health had been destroyed."[18] He complained vigorously, though, that Carson had presented a biased case against the accused, because she did not describe the benefits of pesticides. Baldwin took particular exception to Carson's argument [19] that entomologists might be biased by the research support they received from the chemical industry. Baldwin went on to recommend that those who read *Silent Spring* should also read a series of reports [20] issued by the National Academy of Sciences in which the benefits and costs of pesticides were more judiciously balanced. He was chairman of the committee whose reports he recommended, and his language clearly reflected his attitude that a competent group of scientists were already working on the problems caused by pesticides. Like Darby, Baldwin was irritated to find an "outsider" wading into the pesticide situation with such a comprehensive critique.

Carson's supporters among reviewers of her book clearly outnumbered her detractors. Thirteen of the twenty reviews located gave her a clearly positive bill of health; only Darby was able to find nothing of use in her work, and the others gave her a mixed reception.[21] Several professional entomologists later recalled that her book was needed and welcome, but at the time they did not publish their views.[22] Reece I. Sailer, then of the USDA, helped Carson gather information on biological control, but only on a *sub rosa* basis. He felt constrained by the cavalier attitudes of his peers at USDA and elsewhere toward the potential problems of insecticides in the environment.[23]

Carson's outcry had little in the way of immediate impact. President John F. Kennedy asked his President's Science Advisory Committee (PSAC) to prepare an appropriate policy response to Carson's argument; their report in 1963 largely vindicated *Silent Spring* by urging increased research on nonchemical means of control and efforts to get farmers to adopt them.[24] Senator Abraham Ribicoff (D., Conn.) subsequently led the Senate through an extensive series of hearings on the federal capability of responding to Carson and PSAC. Ribicoff's committee produced only minor legislation that (1) ended the ability of a chemical manufacturer to register a product "under protest," i.e., against the wishes of the government, and (2) allowed the registration number of the pesticide to be printed on the label.[25]

In the long run, it is perhaps difficult to overestimate the impact of Carson's work. She articulated a philosophy of how civilized people ought to relate to nature and its care.[26] Carson's technical critique of insecticides launched from a philosophical foundation ultimately found a home in a new movement, environmentalism, in the late 1960s and 1970s. She must be regarded as one intellectual founder of the movement, even though she perhaps did not intend to do so nor did she live to see the real fruition of her work.

If we examine the situation in the early 1960s however, the impact of the concerns about hazards from insecticides must be judged small in inducing entomologists to innovate. By 1962 definite efforts to redirect research had already been made. Debates over safety played no more than a secondary role in entomological thinking. The situation was reversed by the end of tbe 1960s, but by then genetic resistance to pesticides and the destruction of natural enemies demanded that entomologists seek tools other than chemicals to accomplish their goals. It was the internal threat of technological failure that was most important in creating the climate for innovation, not the external threat of social unacceptability arising from health and environmental hazards.

RESISTANCE

The contemporary entomologist believes as a matter of principle that insect populations can develop genetic resistance to insecticides.[27] A recent policy study in the U.S. judged that resistance was a fundamental justification for increased efforts to find nonchemical control measures for insects.[28] The seeming ease with which resistance to insecticides is now accepted as a real and recurring problem obscures the fact that recognition and explanation of the phenomenon came only from tedious empirical work combined with the neo-Darwinian synthesis in which evolutionary theory and genetics were merged.

Axel Leonard Melander, an entomologist then serving as professor and head of entomology at Washington State College, is generally credited as being the first person to document resistance.[29] He noted in 1908 that lime–sulfur washes failed to kill the San Jose scale on apples in the area of Clarkston, Washington, whereas the treatment had previously been highly effective and the law required its use throughout the State. Melander titled his paper with a question, "Can Insects Become Resistant to Sprays?" His argument was couched to refute the notion that the problem lay in the use of adulterated preparations of lime–sulfur, which was widely believed in the areas where resistance first appeared. Melander suggested the resistant insects were endowed with genetic material conferring an ability to withstand the poison.

Resistance of insects to insecticides remained a relatively small problem before World War II in terms of the failure of control in the field. Henry Joseph Quayle working at the Citrus Experiment Station in Riverside, California, documented resistance to hydrocyanic acid fumigation in three citrus insects, the red scale [*Aonidiella aurantii* (Mask.)], the black scale [*Saissetia oleae* (Bern.)], and the citricola scale [*Coccus psuedomagnoliarum* (Kuw.)].[30] Quayle's colleagues, Alfred Mullikin Boyce and others, identified resistance of citrus thrips [*Scirtothrips citri* (Moult.)] to tartar emetic–sucrose in the San Fernando Valley of California.[31] Walter Seneff Hough of the Virginia Agricultural Experiment Station demonstrated that the codling moth [*Laspeyresia pomonella* (L.)] had become resistant to lead arsenate in Colorado and Washington.[32] The fact that field failures of control due to resistance first appeared in citrus and apples was undoubtedly due to their intensive treatment with insecticides.

Hough in his work with codling moths was convinced by 1943 that he was working with a genetic phenomenon.[33] but his published works give little evidence that he was particularly interested in the theoretical population genetics underlying the resistance phenomenon. Quayle, on the other hand, was interested in the theory as well as the practical dimensions of resistance. He concluded in 1938 that resistance to hydrocyanic acid fumigation in three of the most important scale insects on citrus was due to a natural selection process as articulated by Theodosius Dobzhansky in his 1937 classic, *Genetics and the Origin of Species*.[34] Dobzhansky at the time was professor of genetics at the California Institute of Technology in Pasadena, not far from Quayle's post at the Citrus Experiment Station in Riverside. The two men were undoubtedly in touch with each other in 1937, as Dobzhansky cited Quayle's as yet unpublished review,[35] and Quayle in turn relied on Dobzhansky's interpretation of his data on resistance in order to provide a theoretical perspective.

The interchange between theoretician Dobzhansky on the one hand and applied entomologists Quayle and Harry Scott Smith (also at the Citrus Experiment Station) continued after Dobzhansky left Cal Tech for Columbia in 1940. His second edition of *Genetics and the Origin of Species* (1941) cited Quayle's 1938 work in great detail as a major example demonstrating the genuine effectiveness of natural selection operating within historical times and subject to study in both field and laboratory.[36] The additional evidence from Riverside that resistance to hydrocyanic acid in red scale was a sex-linked recessive trait[37] and that the reproductive potential of the resistant race was lower than that of the nonresistant[38] was particularly useful for Dobzhansky's theories. Dobzhansky agreed with Smith's conclusion that the frequency of the resistant gene in the population was a function of the intensity of fumigation with hydrocyanic acid.[39]

Smith's presidential address to the American Association for Economic Entomology (December, 1940)[40] was a brief yet remarkably clear explanation of the implications of natural selection of genetic variants within insect populations for applied entomologists. He concluded that no method of insect control was likely to be permanent. It is difficult to tell how influential Quayle and Smith's synthesis of theory and practice was on other applied entomologists. Quayle in 1943 felt a vigorous argument was needed to convince his peers about the generality of resistance.[41] His argumentation was apparently needed because others working on resistance of red scale to hydrocyanic acid persisted in referring to the uncontrolled varieties as "so-called resistant strains" until 1942.[42] The enduring value of Quayle and Smith's interactions with Dobzhansky, however, may be inferred from the fact that their conceptualization of resistance as a prime example of natural selection and a fundamental problem for entomology was never seriously challenged.[43]

DDT and the other new organosynthetic insecticides changed the phenomenon of resistance from a limited curiousity to a major feature of entomology. A major factor in the shift was the development of resistance in insect populations directly threatening human health and comfort. Of particular importance was the recognition in several countries between 1946 and 1948 that the common house fly (*Musca domestica* L.) was no longer controlled by DDT. The situation developed first in Europe, but the U.S. was not far behind.[44] By 1948, resistant flies were considered serious by entomologists working on fly control around dairy farms in California, New York, New Jersey, and elsewhere. Economic losses from resistant flies were not serious, but they were considered a genuine menace to human comfort and health.

Resistance in mosquitoes was more threatening, because some species of mosquito were known vectors of diseases in humans. Yellow fever, dengue, and malaria especially had been endemic in the U.S. into the twentieth century, and all of them were transmitted by mosquitoes. The discovery of resistant strains of Culicine mosquitoes in Italy in 1947[45] and in Florida in 1948–1949[46] were disturbing, although in the U.S. the immediate problem was more one of nuisance biting from salt marsh mosquitoes than actual threats of disease outbreaks. The major worry on a worldwide scale was resistance in Anopheline mosquitoes, which transmitted malaria. By 1951, only one report of Anopheline resistance, from Greece,[47] had been noted, but the threat was so clear that medical entomologists began to show concern.

In 1951, human head lice, vectors of typhus, were found in Korea to be resistant to DDT.[48] Outbreak of the Korean War in 1950 made this development of genuine concern, because typhus for years had been known as a severe scourge under wartime conditions. In fact, DDT's meteoric rise to fame during World War II had been based in large part on its role in controlling an outbreak of typhus in Naples during the winter of 1944–1945.[49] DDT-resistant lice found in Korea therefore were seen with alarm by U.S. military officials.

In late 1951, entomological and medical authorities gathered at a conference on Insecticide Resistance and Insect Physiology, held by the National Research Council at the request of the Army. Discussions indicated that students of the resistance phenomenon had no serious questions with the basic theory articulated earlier by Quayle, Smith, and Dobzhansky: resistance was a phenomenon of genetics and natural selection.

Despite the ease with which conference participants accepted a theory of resistance, they were divided on which research lines would be most likely to yield a solution. Moreover they had no unified opinion on the long-term future of insecticides as the foundation for their control technologies. As a result, the Conference recommended a series of eight action for the Army, seven of which presupposed that chemicals in one way or another would continue to be a mainstay of control techniques for insects of medical importance. The last recommendation listed (and therefore possibly the last in order of priority) was for increased research on nonchemical methods of control.[50] Entomologists testifying before the Delaney Committee expressed a similar, conservative judgment that chemicals would remain the foundation for insect control.[51]

Known cases of agricultural insects resistant to insecticides mounted in the late 1940 and early 1950s. Especially important were two-spotted spider mites (1949) and spider mites (1952) to organophosphorus insecticides; and codling moth, cabbage looper, imported cabbage worm, and tomato hornworm, among others, to DDT.[52] These cases, like those in medical entomology, created inconvenience and worry, but did not raise the specter of disaster sufficient to elicit widespread political support for research on alternative control methods. Only when the boll weevil developed resistance to chlorinated hydrocarbon insecticides in 1954–1955 were concerted efforts made to invent new control methods.

The train of events began when John S. Roussel and Dan Clower of Louisiana State University analyzed complaints of cotton growers that the insecticides they relied upon for boll weevil control (toxaphene, BHC, and others) were not effective in some areas. They concluded that the boll weevil was resistant to the insecticides.[53] Within a short period, a mixture of Toxaphene, DDT, and methyl parathion was discovered to be effective against the resistant boll weevils,[54] and it eventually received widespread use.[55] Cotton production continued in the deep South despite the presence of resistant boll weevils, but its damages plus the threat of new types of strains resistant to organophosphorus compounds hung a dark cloud over the region. In 1958, Robert C. Coker, representing the National Cotton Council, sought aid for the distressed industry from Congress in the form of more research on boll weevils.[56] The research stemming from Coker's plea had far-ranging effects on entomological science (Chapter 4).

Anthony W. A. Brown, a Canadian, announced in 1960 that the "golden age" of chemical control had passed.[57] Since Brown's prophesy, chemicals have by no means been discarded, but the cognitive structure of the science has changed drastically, and resistance was a foremost factor in the change.

THE DESTRUCTION OF NATURAL ENEMIES

The assumption underlying the use of insecticides was that if you squirt toxic chemicals on a pest insect, the insect will die. Observations that the application of insecticides could cause an increase in pest populations were thus on the surface counterintuitive. How could a poison cause an insect population to grow faster? Three possible explanations were suggested in 1956 by W. E. Ripper, an English entomologist[58]:

1. The insecticide eliminated the natural enemies (parasitic and predatory insects) of the pest, and the pest individuals not killed by the chemical quickly regained their numbers to again become pests. Alternately, an insect infrequently found before using an insecticide suddenly became common, and thus a pest, because the natural enemies keeping it scarce had been killed by the insecticide.*
2. The insecticide stimulated reproduction in the pest species, either directly or indirectly by altering the chemical composition of the plant upon which the pest was feeding.
3. The insecticide killed other plant-eating species and thus freed the pest insect from unfavorable competition; the pest situation thus became worse than it had before.

His conclusion was that the first hypothesis was almost invariably correct and that the second was occasionally important. Ripper believed the last hypothesis was not likely in any case.

Ripper's original synthesis of the problem has not been altered in any major way since 1956. Its ease in acceptance undoubtedly stems from the fact that examples of resurgence and secondary pest outbreaks had been known for decades before 1956.[59] Their increased incidence in the years after 1945 demanded the attention of entomologists.[60] Systematic theory to explain the phenomenon came from a small, close-knit group of researchers who specialized in biological control and insect ecology. H. S. Smith, whose thoughts on resistance were noted above, was the central figure.

Smith received his Master's degree from the University of Nebraska in 1908 and shortly thereafter began research on the gypsy moth at the USDA's parasite introduction laboratory in Melrose Highlands, Massachusetts. He was subsequently hired by A. J. Cook in 1913 to be the Superintendent of the State Insectary of the California State Commission on Horticulture.[61] When the state legislature transferred the biological

* The first case is called *resurgence,* while the second is called a *secondary pest outbreak.*

control work to the University of California in 1923, Smith became an associate professor at the Citrus Experiment Station, now the Riverside campus of the University. In that location, he served as a guiding light and inspiration for furtherance of work in insect ecology and biological control.[62]

Smith's own work was not directly concerned with the induction of pest outbreaks by insecticides, but his influence on a number of key entomologists was strong, and together they served as leaders in the subject. Two of Smith's proteges were particularly important in demonstrating the reality of insecticide-induced pest outbreaks. Curtis Paul Clausen was hired by Smith as Assistant Superintendent of the State Insectary in 1916; later he led the USDA's foreign parasite introduction work between 1920 and 1951. During the latter period, in 1936, he prepared a brief review of biological control in which he discussed how insecticides could create pest problems.[63] Clausen's article did not attract wide attention at the time, and Ripper in 1956 did not even discuss Clausen's contributions to the theory of insecticide-induced outbreaks. The infrequency with which such outbreaks occurred before 1945 was undoubtedly a major cause of the neglect Clausen's paper suffered.

Paul Hevener DeBach was a second man to receive Smith's inspiration for work on natural enemies of insect pests. He carried his interest in insect ecology directly into experiments that supported the hypothesis that insecticides could cause pest outbreaks by destroying natural enemies.

DeBach was an undergraduate majoring in entomology at UCLA when Harry Smith was invited to give a guest lecture on biological control. From then on, DeBach knew that biological control was the subject in which he intended to specialize. Smith served as his major professor for the Ph.D. degree and, after DeBach's short stint with the U.S. Public Health Service and the USDA, hired him as an assistant entomologist at the Citrus Experiment Station in 1945.[64]

DeBach's work was primarily on citrus, the crop that had at that time enjoyed more success in terms of biological control than any other.[65] Smith and DeBach were intensely interested in measuring the effectiveness of natural enemies years before DDT was introduced.[66] DeBach and his colleagues were among the first to begin experiments with DDT and other new insecticides in citrus, but he recognized in 1946 that the chemicals could potentially cause more problems than they would cure. He even went so far as to turn what was on the surface an entomological disaster into a useful scientific tool: the "insecticidal check method" for measuring the effectiveness of natural enemies.[67] Smith had suggested in 1929 that insecticides could be used to kill beneficial species, which would allow the researcher to follow the population of the pest supposedly kept under control by the beneficial. If the pest increased in numbers more when the beneficial was absent than when present, then a case was made that the natural enemy was an important element keeping the pest under control.

In 1946, DeBach collected evidence that DDT and other materials could kill natural enemies and thus release pest populations of long-tailed mealybugs [*Pseudococcus longispinus* (Tar.)],[68] cottony-cushion scale [*Icerya purchasi* (Mask.)],[69] and citrus red mite [*Paratetranychus citri* (McG.)].[70] By 1950, DeBach and other workers in California had extended the studies of detrimental effects of insecticides and shown that the California red scale [*Aonidiella aurantii* (Mask.)] and the yellow scale [*Aonidiella citrina* (Coq.)] had effective natural enemies whereas previously they were supposed not to have had such control factors.[71]

DeBach argued at a symposium on biological control in 1950 that a strong ecological approach was needed to avoid the pitfalls of using chemical poisons.[72] Only ecological understanding could protect a farmer from discovering that the use of insecticides might be worse than the original disease for which they were applied. DeBach's insecticidal check method was particularly important in establishing beyond all reasonable doubt that the counterintuitive induction of pest outbreaks by insecticides has a reasonable and simple explanation.

COTTON: THE CRISIS IN MICROCOSM

Environmental hazards, resistance, and the destruction of natural enemies generated vigorous debate within the entomological research community, but such arguments were pale in comparison to the pressure generated when the phenomena erupted in the field and threatened commercial agricultural production. Only occasionally have the three become serious enough to raise the specter of totally eliminating the production of a particular commodity. A few such incidents, however, have had a powerful influence on the thinking of entomologists and their research policies.

The production of cotton has utilized more insecticide than any other single crop in the U.S. since about 1950. It is not surprising, therefore, that some of the worst "horror stories" about insecticides have come from that crop. As Robert van den Bosch once phrased it, ol' king cotton has had a melancholy addiction to chemicals.[73]

Here we examine how health hazards, resistance, and the destruction of natural enemies acted in consort in the lower Rio Grande Valley

(LRGV) of Texas to encourage new patterns of entomological thinking. The worst of the disaster came *after* significant efforts to innovate had already begun, so it cannot be said that the situation described here directly caused the innovations.

Boll weevils were the major, recurring insect pest of cotton in the LRGV after 1892. DDT was not particularly toxic to boll weevils, but compounds that followed it, such as benzene hexachloride, toxaphene, endrin, aldrin, and others, were highly effective. Development of resistance to the chlorinated hydrocarbons, described earlier in this chapter, sent shivers down the backs of cotton growers and entomologists, but it did not occur in the LRGV until the early 1960s. No major disasters were immediately forthcoming, however, because calcium arsenate, organophosphate, and carbamate insecticides were readily available. Entomologists and farmers simply shifted to the use of alternative materials, and methyl parathion or other organophosphate insecticides became the standard treatment for boll weevils; for effective treatment, the organophosphates were frequently mixed with chlorinated hydrocarbon insecticides.[74]

Unfortunately, boll weevils were not the only insects attacking cotton in the LRGV. By the time boll weevils became resistant to chlorinated hydrocarbons, entomologists from other areas had already noted that insects formerly considered of minor or no importance had been appearing in more significant numbers due to the new insecticides.[75] Of particular importance were two moths, the bollworm [*Heliothis zea* (Boddie)] and the tobacco budworm [*Heliothis virescens* (Fabricius)]. These two insects lay their eggs on cotton leaves, and the larvae (worms) devour the flower buds ("squares") and fruit ("bolls") of the plant. The larvae are almost indistinguishable, and they were probably confused in some studies before 1953. The two species are frequently called "*Heliiothis* spp."

Texas A & M University recommended treating for "bollworm" (no distinction between the two species) in the early 1950s with various mixtures of DDT, BHC, sulfur, and parathion.[76] Although it may not have been well understood at the time, the DDT and parathion were to control the outbreak of *Heliothis* spp. induced by the poison for boll weevils. The complete switch in tbe late 1960s to organophosphates for controlling boll weevils resistant to chlorinated hydrocarbons made the situation with *Heliothis* spp. even worse.[77] Widespread use of insecticides by the agricultural community in the LRGV caused a near disaster to the regional economy. Damage to the public health of the area and a near collapse of the control technologies created a real question of whether cotton would continue to be grown in the LRGV.

George L. Gallaher was a physician practicing in Harlingen, Texas, one of the small cities of the LRGV. He noted as early as 1959 a large number of pesticide poisonings among "crop-dusting" pilots,* the loaders of the aircraft, and general farmworkers. Gallaher proceeded to organize the Harlingen Poison Control Center at Valley Baptist Hospital in the spring of 1960.[78] The medical treatments and epidemiological studies performed over the next ten years by Gallaher and several colleagues painted a grim picture of an epidemic of pesticide poisonings that was slowly brought under control. Citrus and other crops are grown in addition to cotton in the LRGV, so not all of Gallaher's results should be ascribed to cotton cultivation. The heavy use of aerially applied insecticides on cotton, however, make that crop the probably source of most of the injuries.

The Harlingen Poison Control Center treated about 20 poisoning cases per year from 1960 through 1963. A sudden and dramatic increase occurred 1n 1964 wben nearly 70 cases were recorded. Gallaher correlated the sudden increase with a 400% increase of the amount of pesticide used in 1964 and a switch from the relatively nontoxic chlorinated hydrocarbons to the more dangerous organophosphates.[79] A majority of them involved teenaged boys exposed while they worked as loaders, mixers, or flagmen for aerial applicators.[80] Fewer than 10 cases were reported in 1967, but 1968 yielded a crisis. A total of 118 cases were treated in Harlingen and other valley hospitals; 23 poisonings occurred in a single incident affecting workers in one field. Men and boys working in aerial application again suffered the most, with over 60% of the poisonings attributed to this group. The situation in 1969 improved again, with less than 20 cases reported. Improvement was due to improved safety practices among workers, a decrease in the use of insecticides, and a switch from parathion to the somewhat less toxic methyl parathion.[81]

As serious as the health problems were, internal failings of insecticides were ultimately of more importance in forcing change. The *Heliothis* spp., unleashed by the insecticides directed against boll weevils, developed resistance to chlorinated hydrocarbons and carbamates in the early 1960s.[82] Temporary relief was obtained from the use of higher amounts of organophosphate insecticides added to the mixture containing DDT and toxaphene. Breakdown of the control system came in 1967 and 1968 when growers learned that the tobacco budworm was becoming resistant to the organophosphate insecticides as well as the chlorinated hydrocarbons and carbamates. Farmers sprayed their fields in

* Most insecticides were applied as sprays by the 1960s, not as dusts.

excess of 20 times per year and still were not able to control the tobacco budworms. Texas A & M entomologist Perry L. Adkisson believed the pressure he and his department were under to do something amounted to a genuine crisis. Either a new solution had to be found or cotton might cease to be produced in the Valley.[83]

The anguish of the Texas entomologists was heightened by what they saw across the river in the areas of Matamoros and Altamira, Mexico. Peak production in the Matamoros area was in the 1950s when 500 thousand bales were produced in response to the high cotton prices prevalent during the Korean War. By 1971, only 500 bales were expected.[84] Production in Altamira began in the 1960s but had almost ceased by the early 1970s.[85]

The major factor leading to the demise of cotton cultivation and all of its associated industries on the Mexican side of the border was thought by the entomologists to be the problem of controlling the tobacco budworm once it became resistant to organophosphates.[86] Resistance was undoubtedly important, but it was not the only consideration. The Mexican government, in contrast to the American, did not subsidize cotton production. Further, irrigation water was inadequate in the area around Matamoros,[87] and the Altamira area was hit by severe hurricanes in 1966 and 1967.[88] Since subsidies were given to food and feed crops, farmers in the Matamoros area found it more profitable to switch from cotton production.[89] These factors, combined with resistance, made cotton production in eastern Mexico uncompetitive on the world markets. Regardless of the complex causes, however, the demise of an industry due even in part to insect control problems spelled failure to the entomological profession, a condition that threatened their prestige and credibility.

The Americans continued to produce, but they had to alter their practices. Entomologists at Texas A & M University advised them to use early maturing varieties, control boll weevils entering diapause, and destroy stalks on an areawide basis. Furthermore, acceptable damage levels from cotton fleahoppers and *Heliothis* were increased, and insecticides recommended for their control were reduced. These strategies were designed to keep populations of the boll weevil low and protect the natural enemies of the tobacco budworm.[90] The tobacco budworm thus came again under control by natural enemies, and the crisis of king cotton's melancholy addiction was "solved."

Adkisson and his colleagues based their new practices on the philosophy of integrated pest management (IPM). Details of IPM's development are covered in the following chapter. For the moment it is sufficient to note that IPM's success in the LRGV was a significant milestone in the rise of IPM to a prominent position in the policy area surrounding the insecticide crisis.

THE INSECTICIDE CRISIS IN THE POLICY ARENA

Insecticides are now the foundation of most insect control techniques. Their use has aroused heated, emotional debate, and dozens of policy statements have been issued over the past 30 years. Almost every conceivable position has at one time or another been defended. The range has been from Wagnerian trumpetings about the essentiality of insecticides to prevent imminent famine and pestilence to virtual denials that they really are needed at all.

As noted above, the instability of insecticidal technologies plus the fear of environmental contamination were the *primary* problems debated from the 1950s through the 1970s. Without doubt, these primary issues will continue to attract attention directly to the insecticides during the 1980s and beyond. A number of indirect, *secondary* issues, however, made the arguments more complex after the mid-1960s. A growing human population, dwindling supplies of fossil fuels and land, the conditions needed to create new agricultural production technologies, and the adverse impact of industrialized economies on less developed countries all combined to make resolution of the primary problems more difficult. Collectively, the secondary issues defined the political arena in which the primary issues were to be debated. Their importance to the battles over insecticides necessitates a brief exposition of the issues at stake.

Currently, somewhat over 4.4 billion people live on the earth.[91] Medium variant projections of the United Nations estimate that by 2000 this number will rise to 6.4 billion. By 2075, a total of 12.2 billion people are projected to be living on the earth.[92] Efforts have been made to estimate the largest possible number of individuals that can be supported by the global ecosystem, but all such studies suffer from the imprecision of the assumptions upon which they are based. Regardless of the ultimate potential of the earth to support human life, it is clear that presently a substantial portion of the population is poorly nourished. Over 400 million persons (about 10% of the earth's population) are chronically malnourished, and more are subject to poor-quality diets or sporadic bouts of severe malnutrition.[93]

Insects are estimated to reduce food production before harvest by 14% on a global basis.[94] and additional amounts of food are lost after harvest in food storage facilities. Reducing losses to insects would in no way *guarantee* help to those most in need of additional nourishment, because hunger is more a consequence of sociopolitical patterns of wealth distribution than a lack of physical supplies of food.[95] Nevertheless, substantial food losses to insects in the presence of famine raises the argument that better pest control is needed to feed millions of starving people.

Nobel Laureate Norman Borlaug directly connected the use of insecticides such as DDT with the prevention of famine.[96] Former Secretary of Agriculture Earl Butz argued that without pesticides, farmers "could not produce enough food for 206 million Americans."[97]

In a simplistic sense, Borlaug, Butz, and others who raised the apocalyptic specter of famine in defense of insecticides were correct. Under current systems of agricultural organization, farmers in the industrialized world could not produce in their accustomed manner without insecticides and other types of pesticides (Chapters 8 and 10). Agricultural production practices, dietary habits, and food distribution mechanisms, however, are all subject to social manipulations, some of which could lead to better diets for all people at current or reduced levels of production. Predictions of imminent famine, especially in the industrialized nations, are unlikely to be true, and the prophets of doom are presenting a misleading and distorted viewpoint. The political importance of the insecticides-or-famine allegation, however, cannot be denied. Any attempt to resolve the primary problems associated with insecticides must simultaneously handle the secondary issue of population–food balance as well.

A far more serious and difficult question surrounds the continually decreasing per capita supplies of fossil fuel and arable land in the world. If their incomes permit it, most people in the world would prefer to consume a diet high in animal protein and dairy products rather than starchy energy-rich foods such as cereals, potatoes, and cassava.[98] Consumption of animal products, however, requires heavier inputs of land, energy, and other natural resources compared to a diet based on vegetable food.[99] More grain and forage must be grown to support a livestock industry than would be required if people subsisted on grain directly.

Approximately 0.62 hectares of arable land per person are available in the U.S., but in the world as a whole only 0.38 hectares are available.[100] In the absence of significant technological breakthroughs in land productivity, it is unlikely that the total world population will ever have the option of subsisting on a diet of grain-fed animals. Land resources simply aren't sufficient, and land resources are dwindling as population increases.

Projected declines in fossil fuel supplies, particularly natural gas and petroleum, plus loss of arable land to urbanization, transportation, and soil erosion will decrease the land-per-person ratios from their current levels. The fact that insect control can increase the productivity of land and energy inputs makes insect control technology an important component in efforts to improve agricultural production efficiency. Resolution of the insecticide crisis will therefore occur in the context of important and needed efforts to improve land and energy productivities in agriculture.

The final secondary issue is the growing restiveness of the third world countries with the policies of the industrialized nations, particularly those of North America and Western Europe.[101] Revolts against European colonialism and American neocolonialism were the hallmark of relationships between the industrialized north and nonindustrialized south after World War II. Third world countries will continue to struggle to control their futures instead of leaving it in the hands of multinational corporations headquartered in the U.S. or Europe. Price differences between agricultural raw materials and manufactured goods will be the subject of debate as nonindustrialized countries seek a larger share of the world's economic production. Control of land use in the third world will be a constant source of friction. Agricultural production will continue to be a crucial component of all economies and especially in countries of the third world. Insecticides in turn are important components of certain types of agricultural production practices. Resolution of the insecticide crisis will therefore be connected with the larger struggle between the have and have-not nations.

Secondary issues will make resolution of the insecticide crisis more difficult, but they should not obscure the fundamental fact that many alternative techniques for controlling insects have been known to professional entomologists for many decades. Biological control, alteration of farming practices, mechanical devices, use of resistant crop plants, and other techniques have and will continue to play important roles in crop production. The real question is to what extent and how can the alternatives replace the use of toxic chemicals. A plethora of answers, frequently conflicting, to this paramount policy question have come forth during the last two decades:

- The insecticide crisis is overblown; it's really not that bad, so no worry is necessary.
- Insecticides may have problems, but in most cases they're more cost-effective than the alternatives.
- The alternatives really don't work very well.

- Entomologists are ignorant, stupid, or corrupted by the insecticide industry; thus they can't or won't provide good advice to farmers.
- Farmers are ignorant, stupid, or greedy; thus they can't or won't change to the alternative.
- Everybody wants to change, but incentives for change are lacking. Fine-tuning of the farm economy will elicit the needed changes.
- It's all a matter of research and education. Give the university and USDA scientists enough resources, and insect control technologies will change in the proper directions.

Contradictory judgments on insecticides notwithstanding, important policy changes have occurred in the years since *Silent Spring* was published. New research monies were poured into USDA and state university laboratories. New laws were passed that put increasingly stringent environmental safety requirements upon the development and use of insecticides. Every president since Dwight David Eisenhower issued a major policy declaration on insecticides and other pesticides

TABLE I
Production and Sales of Synthetic Organic Insecticides, Fumigants, and Rodenticides in the United States, 1963–1978[a]

Year	Production (million lb.)	Sales (million lb.)	Sales (million $)
1963	478	435	207
1964	447	445	218
1965	490	475	240
1966	552	482	273
1967	496	489	301
1968	573	511	304
1969	571	493	294
1970	490	444	307
1971	558	497	343
1972	564	539	381
1973	639	605	471
1974	650	692	645
1975	660	546	765
1976	566	502	808
1977	570	545	1000
1978	605	509	1038

[a]All figures are taken from U.S. Department of Agriculture, *The Pesticide Review* for the years 1966, 1968, 1970, 1971, 1973, 1975, 1976, 1977, and 1978. Data for years before 1969 were corrected by subtracting production and sales figures for calcium and lead arsenates.

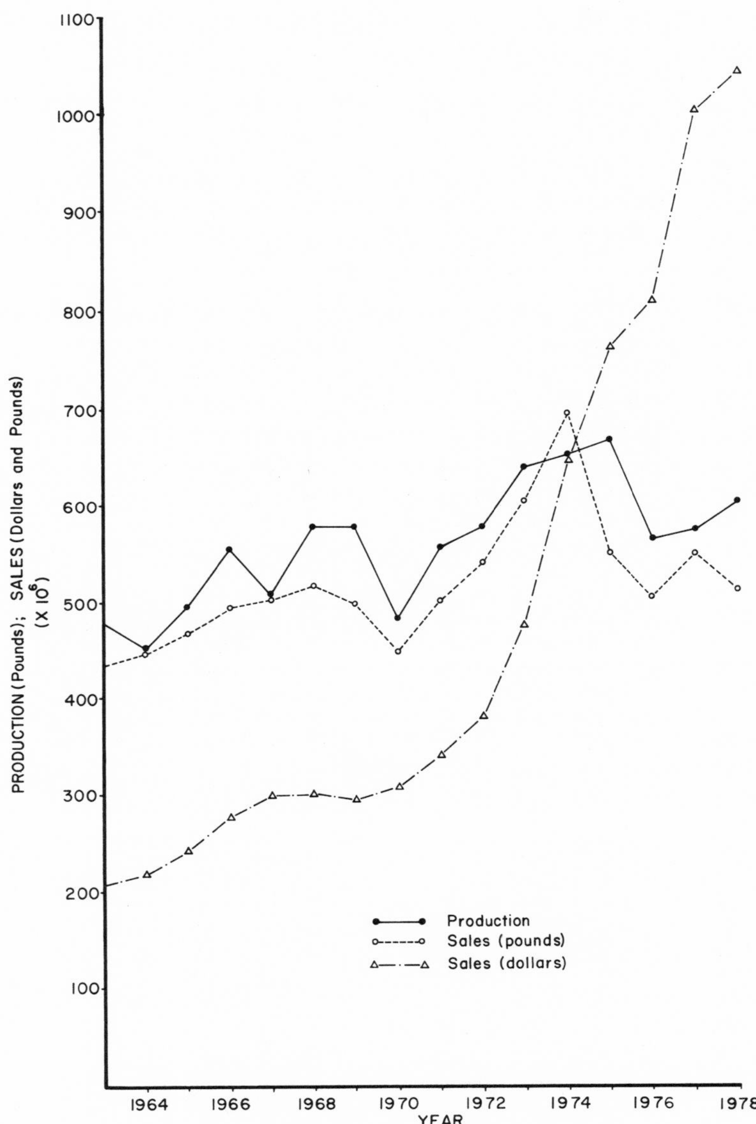

FIGURE 1. Production and sales of synthetic organic insecticides, fumigants, and rodenticides in the United States, 1963–1978. Despite large annual fluctuations, both production and sales (in lb.) are still rising. (See Table I for exact figures and sources.)

and the need to encourage alternatives. Despite these efforts, production and sales of insecticides and other pesticides in the U.S. are still growing (Table I, Fig. 1). Global sales also continue to increase, and the insecticide industry foresees increments in sales of over 13% during the next five years.[102]

Despite virtually universal agreement by all analysts that further research on insect control was needed in order to foster changes in farming practices, the continued dominance of insecticides remains a stumbling block of considerable proportions. Given the importance of innovation in efforts to resolve the insecticide crisis, surprisingly little attention has been given to the processes by which entomologists attempt to design control techniques less dependent upon insecticides. Policy makers have tended to assume that entomologists, if given sufficient funding and laboratory support, will respond by finding the new insect control techniques everyone seems to want. Examining the validity of this assumption is a key element of this essay.

REFERENCE NOTES

1. Roger Conant, No joy in an insect-free world, *Entomol. News* 55 (Dec. 1944):258–259. Discovery of DDT residues in milk was viewed with particular alarm by both medical personnel and entomologists because of milk's importance as a food for infants. Entomologists learned by 1947 that direct treatment of cows with DDT for fly control caused residues to appear in milk; further investigation indicated that mere treatment of barn walls led to the residue problem. The USDA recommended against use of DDT around dairy animals, and newspaper publicity brought the problem to the public. [See testimony of F. C. Bishopp before the Delaney Committee (U.S. Congress, House Select Committee to Investigate the Use of Chemicals in Food Products, *Chemicals in Food Products,* Hearings on H. Res. 323, 81st Congress, 2nd sess., 1951, pp. 387, 409, 521–522, 527–528); New York Times, U. S. seeks to keep milk free of DDT, April 23, 1949, p. 19; New York Times, Hazard to health from DDT denied, July 11, 1949, p. 25.]

   The series "Correspondence Relating to Bureau Programs and Plans, 1930–1951," General Administrative Records, Record Group 7, National Archives (RG7NA), contains reports of conferences and meetings between the Bureau of Entomology and Plant Quarantine (BEPQ), USDA, Public Health Service, Food and Drug Administration, and the chemical industry on the problems posed by toxic residues; BEPQ's Fred C. Bishopp was clearly concerned about the problem. Edward F. Knipling of the BEPQ argued for more tests on the chronic toxicity of insecticides to livestock in 1948 (E.F. Knipling to P.N. Annand, Aug. 3, 1948, RG7NA). Bishopp (Asst. Chief of BEPQ) agreed (F.C. Bishopp, office memo., Aug. 3, 1948, RG7NA).

   Thomas R. Dunlap provides a critical review of the knowledge on toxicological hazards in the period 1945–1950 [*DDT: Scientists, Citizens and Public Policy,* Ph.D. Thesis, Univ. of Wisc., 1975, pp. 72–75 (hereafter cited as Dunlap, *DDT*)].

   Results of studies on insecticides during the late 1940s reflected the ambivalent attitude in the scientific community towards DDT. The compound at 5 lb. per acre caused definite wildlife losses while losses from 1 lb. per acre were much smaller or undetectable. The seriousness of losses at either dose remained controversial. Those who expressed concern were for the most part employees at the Fish and Wildlife Service. [See Clarence Cottam, DDT and its effects on fish and wildlife, *J. Econ. Entomol.* 39 (1946): 44–52; John L. George and Robert T. Mitchell, The effects of feeding DDT-treated insects to nestling birds, *J. Econ. Entomol.* 40 (1947): 782–789; Lowell Adams, Mitchell G. Hanavan, Neil W. Hosley, and David W. Johnston, The effects on fish, birds, and mammals of DDT used in the control of forest insects in Idaho and Wyoming, *J. Wild. Manage.* 13 (1949): 245–254; Earl S. Hearld, Effects of DDT–oil solutions upon amphibians and reptiles, *Herpetologica* 5 (1949): 117–120; and John L. George and William H. Stickel, Wildlife effects of DDT dust used for tick control on a Texas prairie, *The Am. Midl. Nat.* 42 (1949): 228–237.]

Others expressed less concern, especially about "light" damage from low doses of DDT. [See S. Charles Kendeigh, *"Bird Populations Studies in the Coniferous Forest Biome during a Spruce Budworm Outbreak," Biol. Bull. No. 1,* Dept. of Lands and Forests, Ontario, 1947, 100 pages; Charles T. Brues, Changes in the insect fauna of a New England woodland following the application of DDT, *Harvard Forest Papers No. 1,* 1947, 18 pp.; C. H. Hoffman and E. P. Merkel, Fluctuations in insect populations associated with aerial applications of DDT to forests, *J. Econ. Entomol.* 41 (1948): 464–473; and C. H. Hoffman and J. P. Linduska, Some considerations of the biological effects of DDT, *Sci. Mon.* 69 (1949): 104–114. See also Dunlap, *DDT,* pp. 90–118.

2. Federal Register, Sept. 17, 1949, p. 5724.
3. James Whorton provides a thorough discussion of the problems, *Before Silent Spring* (Princeton: Princeton Univ. Press, 1974), 288 pp. (hereafter cited as Whorton, *Before Silent Spring*). See also Dunlap, *DDT,* pp. 34–63.
4. Whorton, *Before Silent Spring,* pp. 246–249.
5. U.S. Congress, House Resolution 323 (81:1), June 20, 1950.
6. F. C. Bishopp to Bailey D. Pepper, Mar. 30, 1951, RG7NA; S. A. Rohwer to Stanley B. Freeborn, Nov. 23, 1949, RG7NA.
7. It is interesting to note that the USDA did not have a uniform opinion on the need for new regulations. Bishopp testified that no new laws were needed, but E. L. Griffen (assistant chief, Insecticide Division, Production and Marketing Administration) believed that the manufacturer should have to prove his product safe and effective before registration (*Chemicals,* pp. 558–559).
8. 68 Stat. 511–517.
9. Paul Brooks, *The House of Life: Rachel Carson at Work* (Greenwich, Conn.: Fawcett Pub., Inc., 1972), 303 pages; Frank Graham, Jr., *Since Silent Spring* (Greenwich, Conn.: Fawcett Pub., Inc., 1970), 288 pp.
10. Rachel Carson, *Silent Spring* (Boston: Houghton Mifflin Co., 1962), 368 pp. (hereafter cited as Carson, *Silent Spring*).
11. U.S. Congress, Senate, Committee on Government Operations, *Intragency Coordination in Environmental Hazards (Pesticides)* Hearings, Part 1, 88th Congress, 1st Sess., 1964, p. 216.
12. E. F. Knipling, Comments on Rachel Carson's articles entitled "Silent Spring," July 18, 1962, mimeo, 8 pages; copy supplied by E. F. Knipling, personal communication, Aug. 18, 1977.
13. United States Department of Agriculture, Comments on Rachel Carson's articles in the New Yorker, mimeo, 2 pp. Knipling believes that this public release was prepared by staff writers and that he probably reviewed it before release.

14. Dunlap, *DDT*, pp. 150–155.
15. P. J. Chapman, The use of chemicals to control pests, *N.Y. State Hortic. Soc. Proc.* 108 (1963): 168–175. I thank David Pimental for bringing this article to my attention.
16. W. J. Darby, Silence, Miss Carson, *Chem. Eng. News* 40 (Oct. 5, 1962): 60, 62–63.
17. I. L. Baldwin, Chemicals and pests, *Science* 137 (1962): 1042–1043.
18. *Ibid.*, p. 1042.
19. Carson, *Silent Spring*, pp. 258–259.
20. Committee on Pest Control and Wildlife Relationship, *Part I: Evaluation of Pesticide–Wildlife Problems; Part II: Policy and Procedures for Pest Control; Part III: Research Needs* (Washington, D.C.: National Academy of Sciences, 1962, 1963), Publications 920-A, 920-B, and 920-C.
21. *Book Review Digest*, 1962–1964, lists 18 reviews. The articles by P. J. Chapman and I. L. Baldwin were not indexed.
22. Personal interviews with Carl B. Huffaker (Mar. 17–18, 1977), Paul DeBach (Mar. 22–23, 1977), and L. D. Newsom (June 1–2, 1978). Robert L. Metcalf recalled he had been shocked by Carson's criticisms but reluctantly came to believe she had served a useful purpose (recorded in *The Insect Alternative*, NOVA series, WGBH, Boston, 1978, pp. 4–5).
23. Reece I. Sailer, personal interview, May 15–16, 1978. Paul DeBach also helped Carson gather information, but he mentioned no inhibitions about his activities (personal interview, Mar. 22–23, 1977).
24. President's Science Advisory Committee, *Use of Pesticides* (Washington, D.C.: Government Printing Office, 1963), 25 pp.
25. 78 Stat. 190.
26. Carson, *Silent Spring;* see especially p. 297.
27. F. J. Oppenoorth, Development of resistance to insecticides, in *The Future for Insecticides*, Robert L. Metcalf and John J. McKelvey, Jr., eds. (New York: John Wiley & Sons, 1976), p. 41.
28. *Contemporary Pest Control Practices and Prospects*, (Washington, D.C.: National Academy of Sciences, 1975), Vol. 1, p. 2.
29. A. L. Melander, Can insects become resistant to sprays? *J. Econ. Entomol.* 7 (1914): 167–172; A. L. Melander, Tolerance of San Jose scale to sprays, *Wash. Agric. Exp. Stn. Bull. No. 174*, Feb., 1923, 52 pp. Years later (1951), F. H. Babers and J. J. Pratt, Jr., argued that priority for noting resistance really belonged to J. B. Smith, The influence of environment on the life history of insects, *Gard. and For.* 10 (1897): 334. The recognition of resistance as an important phenomenon, however, occurred in ignorance of Smith's work. Melander deserves the credit for stimulating interest in the subject among professional entomologists. See F. H. Babers and J. J. Pratt, Jr., Development of Insect Resistance to Insecticides—II, *Bur. of Entomol. and Pl. Quar. E-818*, May, 1951.
30. For a review, see H. J. Quayle, The increase in resistance in insects to insecticides, *J. Econ. Entomol.* 36 (1943): 493–500 (hereafter cited as Quayle, Increase).
31. A. M. Boyce, C. O. Persing, and C. S. Barnhart, The resistance of citrus thrips to tartar emetic–sucrose treatment, *J. Econ. Entomol.* 35 (1942): 790–791.
32. For a review, see Walter S. Hough, Development and characteristics of vigorous or resistant strains of codling moth, *Va. Agric. Exp. Stn. Tech. Bull. 91*, Nov., 1943, 32 pp.
33. *Ibid.*
34. H. J. Quayle, The development of resistance to hydrocyanic acid in certain scale insects, *Hilgardia* 11 (No. 5, 1938): 183–210. Theodosius Dobzhansky, *Genetics and the*

Origin of Species, 1st ed. (New York: Columbia Univ. Press, 1937), 364 pp. (hereafter cited as Dobzhansky, *Genetics*).

35. Dobzhansky, *Genetics*, 1st ed., p. 345.
36. Theodosius Dobzhansky, *Genetics and the Origin of Species*, 2nd ed. (New York: Columbia Univ. Press, 1941), pp. 190–192.
37. R. C. Dickson, Inheritance of resistance to hydrocyanic acid fumigation in the California red scale, *Hilgardia* 13 (1941): 515–522.
38. Dobzhansky, *Genetics*, 2nd ed., p. 192.
39. *Ibid.*
40. Harry S. Smith, Racial segregation in insect populations and its significance in applied entomology, *J. Econ. Entomol.* 34 (1941): 1–13.
41. Quayle, Increase.
42. H. R. Yust and R. L. Busbey, A comparison of the susceptibility of the so-called resistant and nonresistant strains of California red scale to methyl bromide, *J. Econ. Entomol.* 35 (1942): 343–345.
43. Dobzhansky's effort to forge a new synthesis between genetics and evolution also benefitted from Quayle and Smith's thoughts. Garland E. Allen notes that Dobzhansky's work was an important component in the triumph of the neo-Darwinian theory of evolution by natural selection in the 1940s. The episode can be seen as an extraordinarily fruitful cross-fertilization between practical and theoretical scientists. See Garland E. Allen, *Life Sciences in the Twentieth Century* (Cambridge: Cambridge Univ. Press, 1978), pp. 134–141.

    Even in the 1960s, Ernst Mayr of Harvard University argued that "typological thinking," a metaphysical presupposition, had for centuries been a barrier to understanding evolution. A typologist believes there exists an ideal "type" for every species, and variation is an illusion or imperfection in nature. The opposite metaphysical view is that of the populationist, "who believes only variation is real and abstract statistics describe an illusory 'average' representing the species." The difficulty some entomologists had in accepting the reality of resistance and its origins in a population may have reflected the argument between typologists and populationists. See Ernst Mayr, *Animal Species and Evolution* (Cambridge: The Belknap Press of Harvard Univ. Press, 1963), pp. 5–6.
44. For reviews, see: W. V. King and J. B. Gahan, Failure of DDT to control house flies, *J. Econ. Entomol.* 42 (1949): 405–409; F. H. Babers, Development of Insect Resistance to Insecticides, *Bur. of Entomol. and Pl. Quar. E-776*, May 1949, 31 pp. The European cases of resistance were most intensively investigated in Italy: for a review see A. Missiroli, Riduzione o eradicazione delgi Anofeli? *Riv. Parassitol.* 8 (1947): 141–169.
45. Ezio Mosna, Su una caratteristica biologica del *Culex pipiens autogenicus* di latina, *Riv. Parassitol.* 8 (1947): 125–126; and *Culex pipiens autogenicus* DDT-resistenti e loro controllo con octa–klor e esaclorocicloesano, *Riv. Parassitol.* 9 (1948): 19–25.
46. E. F. Knipling, Present status of mosquito resistance to insecticides, *Am. J. Trop. Med. Hyg.* 1 (1952): 389–394.
47. A. W. A. Brown, The challenge of insecticide resistance, *Bull. Entomol. Soc. Am.* 7 (1961): 6–19 (hereafter cited as Brown, The challenge).
48. *Ibid.*
49. Anonymous, Typhus in Naples, *Life* 16 (Feb. 28, 1944): 36–37; Frederick C. Painton, The second battle of Naples—against lice, *Reader's Digest* 44 (June, 1944): 21–22; Allen Raymond, Now we can lick typhus, *Sat. Ev. Post* 216 (Apr. 22, 1944): 14–15+.
50. National Research Council, Division of Medical Sciences, *Conference on Insecticide Resistance and Insect Physiology* (Washington, D.C.: National Academy of Sciences, 1952). NAS–NRC Publ. No. 219, 99 pp., see especially p. 88.

51. U.S. Congress, House, Select Committee to Investigate the Use of Chemicals in Food Products, *Chemicals in Food Products,* Hearings on H. Res. 323, 81st Congress, 2nd sess., 1951, pp. 166–168, 189, 382, 640, 661, 774, 791, 891–892.
52. Brown, The challenge.
53. John S. Roussel and Dan Clower, Resistance to the chlorinated hydrocarbon insecticides in the boll weevil (*Anthonomus grandis* Boh.), *La. Exp. Stn. Circular No. 41,* La. State Univ. and Agric. and Mech. College, Sept. 1955, 5 pp. plus tables.
54. J. K. Walker, Jr. and R. L. Hanna, Control of boll weevils resistant to chlorinated hydrocarbons, *J. Econ. Entomol.* 53 (1960): 228–231.
55. Perry L. Adkisson, personal interview, May 30–31, 1978; *Pest Control: An Assessment of Present and Alternative Technologies, Vol. 3, Cotton Pest Control* (Washington, D.C.: National Academy of Sciences, 1975), pp. 58–60 (hereafter cited as NAS, *Cotton Pest Control*).
56. U.S. Congress, House, Committee on Appropriations, *Department of Agriculture Appropriations for 1959,* Hearings, Part 2, 85th Congress, 2nd sess., 1958, pp. 449–466.
57. Brown, The challenge.
58. W. E. Ripper, Effect of pesticides on balance of arthropod populations, *Annu. Rev. Entomol.* 1 (1956): 403-438.
59. J. W. Folsom's study in 1925–1926 of induced outbreaks of cotton aphids by calcium arsenate is one of the first examples [Calcium arsenate as a cause of aphid infestation, J. Econ. Entomol. 20 (1927): 840–843]. Studies in the 1930s on citrus and apples indicated that those crops, too, could suffer from induced pest outbreaks [see, for example, W. L. Thompson, Cultural practices and their influence on citrus pests, *J. Econ. Entomol.* 32 (1939): 782–789; A. M. Boyce, The citrus red mite *Paratetranychus citri* McG. in California and its control, *J. Econ. Entomol.* 29 (1936): 125–130; and H. M. Steiner, Effects of cultural practices on natural enemies of the white apple leafhopper, *J. Econ. Entomol.* 31 (1938): 232–240].
60. One sign of the relative lack of interest in the subject before the 1930s can be inferred from L. O. Howard's failure to cover it in his paper in 1926, The parasite element of natural control of injurious insects and its control by man, *J. Econ. Entomol.* 19 (1926): 271–282.
61. C. P. Clausen and S. E. Flanders, Harry Scott Smith, 1883–1957, *J. Econ. Entomol.* 51 (1958): 266–267.
62. Paul DeBach, personal interview, Mar. 22–23, 1977; Carl B. Huffaker, personal interview, Mar. 17–18, 1977.
63. C. P. Clausen, Insect parasitism and biological control, *Ann. Entomol. Soc. Am.* 29 (1936): 201–223. Harvey L. Sweetman of Massachusetts State College prepared a similar but briefer statement for his work, *The Biological Control of Insects* (Ithaca: Comstock Pub. Co., 1936), 278–280.
64. Paul DeBach, personal interview, Mar. 22–23, 1977.
65. Richard L. Doutt, "The historical development of biological control," in *Biological Control of Insect Pests and Weeds,* Paul DeBach, ed., (New York: Reinhold Pub. Corp., 1964), pp. 31–38.
66. Harry S. Smith and Paul DeBach, The measurement of the effect of entomophagous insects on population densities of their hosts, *J. Econ. Entomol.* 35 (1942): 845–847.
67. Paul DeBach, An insecticidal check method for measuring the efficacy of entomophagous insects, *J. Econ. Entomol.* 39 (1946): 695–697.
68. *Ibid.*
69. *Ibid.*
70. Paul DeBach, Predators, DDT, and citrus red mite populations, *J. Econ. Entomol.* 40 (1947): 598.

71. Paul DeBach, The necessity for an ecological approach to pest control on citrus in California, *J. Econ. Entomol.* 44 (1951): 443–447.
72. *Ibid.*
73. Robert van den Bosch, The malencholy addition of ol' king cotton, *Nat. Hist.* 80 (No. 10, 1971): 86–91.
74. NAS, *Cotton Pest Control*, pp. 57–62; J. R. Brazzel and D. E. Shipp, The status of boll weevil resistance to chlorinated hydrocarbon insecticides in Texas, *J. Econ. Entomol.* 55 (1962): 941–944.
75. James R. Brazzel, L. D. Newsom, John S. Roussel, Charles Lincoln, F. J. Williams, and Gordon Barnes, Bollworm and tobacco budworm as cotton pests in Louisiana and Arkansas, *La. Tech. Bull. No. 482*, Dec. 1953, 47 pp.
76. Texas A & M Univ. Ext. Ser. and USDA, *1952 Cotton Insect Control Guide: Lower Rio Grande Valley of Texas* (College Station: Texas A & M Univ., 1952), pamphlet.
77. 1967 was the first year Texas A & M dropped all recommendations for chlorinated hydrocarbons for control of boll weevils. See Texas A & M Agric. Ext. Ser., *South Texas guide for controlling cotton insects* (College Station: Texas A & M University), leaflet L-561, issues for 1964, 1966, 1967 (hereafter cited as Texas A & M, *South Texas guide*).
78. George L. Gallaher, Agricultural poisons, *Tex. State J. Med.* 61 (1965): 336–339.
79. G. L. Gallaher, Recent experiences with parathion poisoning, Paper presented at Texas Medical Assn. annual meeting, Dallas, May, 1967, 8 pp., xerox copy in possession of author.
80. G. A. Reich, G. L. Gallaher, J. S. Wiseman, Characteristics of pesticide poisoning in south Texas, *Tex. Med.* 64 (No. 9, 1968): 56–58.
81. Donald A. Smith and J. S. Wiseman, Pesticide poisoning, *Tex. Med.* 67 (No. 2, 1971): 56–59.
82. Perry L. Adkisson, personal interview, May 30–31, 1978; J. R. Brazzel, Resistance to DDT in *Heliothis virescens*, *J. Econ. Entomol.* 56 (1963): 571–574; J. R. Brazzel, DDT resistance in *Heliothis zea*, *J. Econ. Entomol.* 57 (1964): 455–457.
83. NAS, *Cotton Insect Control*, p. 60; Perry L. Adkisson, personal interview, May 30–31, 1978; Texas A & M, *South Texas guide*, Leaflet No. L-561, issues for 1967 through 1971.
84. Billy C. Duck, Food crops attract Mexican farmers away from cotton, *Cotton Int.* 38 (1971): 88–89 (hereafter cited as Duck, Food Crops).
85. H. Reiter Webb, Cotton acreage in Latin America jumps by 5%, *Cotton Int.* 40 (1973): 201–202, 210 (hereafter cited as Webb, Cotton acreage).
86. Perry L. Adkisson, personal interview, May 30–31, 1978.
87. Webb, Cotton acreage.
88. Hasso von Eickstedt, Mexico ups production techniques, *Cotton Int.* 36 (1969): 108, 110–111.
89. Duck, Food crops.
90. Dale G. Bottrell and Perry L. Adkisson, Cotton insect pest management, *Annu. Rev. Entomol.* 22 (1977): 451–481.
91. *World Population Estimates* (Washington, D.C.: The Environmental Fund, 1979), pamphlet.
92. Paul R. Ehrlich, Anne H. Ehrlich, and John P. Holdren, *Ecoscience* (San Francisco: W. H. Freeman, 1977), pp. 222–227.
93. *Ibid.*, pp. 290–291.
94. H. H. Cramer, *Plant Protection and World Crop Production* (Leverkusen, Federal Republic of Germany: Farbenfabriken Bayer AG, 1967), p. 483. See also Ray F. Smith and Donald J. Calvert, "Insect pest losses and the dimensions of the world food

problem," in *World Food, Pest Losses, and the Environment,* David Pimentel, ed. (Boulder, Colorado: Westview Press, 1978), pp. 17–38.

95. The most complete study on the relationship between nutrition and economics is Alan Berg's *The Nutrition Factor* (Washington, D.C.: The Brookings Inst., 1973), 290 pp. See especially pp. 40–49.
96. Norman E. Borlaug, "Mankind and civilization at another crossroad," Food and Agriculture Organization of the United Nations, Rome, Nov. 8, 1971, c 71/LIM/4, 73 pp.
97. Quoted in David Pimentel, J. Krummel, D. Gallahan, J. Hough, A. Merrill, I. Schriner, P. Vittum, F. Koziol, E. Back, D. Yen, and S. Fiance, Benefits and costs of pesticide use in U.S. food production, *BioScience* 28 (1978): 772, 778–784.
98. Berg, *The Nutrition Factor,* pp. 40–42.
99. David Pimental, P. A. Oltenacu, M. C. Nesheim, J. Krummel, M. S. Allen, and S. Chick, The potential for grass-fed livestock: resource constraints, *Science* 207 (Feb. 22, 1980): 843–848.
100. John H. Perkins and David Pimental, "Society and pest control," in *Pest Control: Cultural and Environmental Aspects,* David Pimentel and John H, Perkins, eds. (Boulder, Colorado: Westview Press, 1980), p. 10.
101. See Richard J. Barnet and Ronald F. Mueller, *Global Reach* (New York: Simon and Schuster, 1974), 508 pp.; and Frances Moore Lappé and Joseph Collins, *Food First* (Boston: Houghton Mifflin Co., 1977), 466 pp.
102. Anonymous, A look at world pesticide markets, *Farm Chemicals,* Sept., 1979, p. 61.

PART II

A Search for Alternatives

Chemical control of insects was the supreme technology among farmers by 1955. Entomologists for the most part adhered to the chemical control paradigm in the decade following World War II, i.e., their searches for solutions to insect problems were dominated by quests for adequate chemical spray programs. Only a few entomologists designed their research efforts around other goals and concepts.

Yet by 1955, signs of technological failure were clearly evident. Resistance, resurgence, and the outbreak of secondary pests created problems for the farming industries. In addition concerns about the safety of residues raised the possibility that social pressures might preclude the use of some of the new insecticides. These crises enhanced the stature of entomologists who never adopted the chemical control paradigm. By 1960, they had a substantial list of accomplishments that were seen in a new light given the ever growing problems with insecticides (see page 59 for a partial list).

The emergence of new avenues of research was stimulating, but the very plethora of possibilities created its own problems. Which paths of research were most likely to be successful? Should entomologists pursue all with equal vigor, or should priorities be made? If choices were to be made, as they inevitably would be given limitations in funds, then by whom, how, and for what purpose?

Moreover, overreliance on insecticides had by 1960 made many entomologists leary of ever again placing their hopes on just one technique of control. The genetic plasticity of insect populations suggested that they could evolve resistance to any single technique that entomologists might devise. Therefore entomologists began to grapple with a more difficult question: How can we combine two or more control techniques into programs in which each individual method could synergize the effectiveness of others and thus create a level of suppression greater than that provided by a single technique? Also, entomologists hoped that the use of two or more control practices would forestall or preclude the emergence of resistance in the target pest population. Alternative efforts to articulate strategies for combining control techniques became the prime focus for debate in the 1960s and 1970s.

Entomologists based largely in the land grant universities of California and the mid-South created one strategy, Integrated Pest Management (IPM). Other workers based largely in the USDA developed another, Total Population Management (TPM). In this essay, both IPM and TPM are referred to as *paradigms,* a term made popular by Thomas Kuhn's *The Structure of Scientific Revolutions* (1962). Further discussion of Kuhn's theories and their limitations is deferred until Chapter 6, but as a first approximation his notion of *paradigm shift* as the unit of scientific change helps explain the major events of economic entomology since 1945. The chemical control paradigm failed, and rival schools of entomologists articulated two new paradigms, IPM and TPM, as conceptual guides to research.

In this section, we examine how each new paradigm came into existence. Chapters 3 and 4 cover IPM and TPM, respectively, while Chapter 5 outlines the traumatic experiences each had in its development.

EXEMPLARY TECHNICAL ADVANCES IN ENTOMOI

• **1932–1943** Reginald H. Painter (Kansas State University), a
in Kansas, Nebraska, and the USDA and elsewhere develop
Pawnee wheat, resistant to the hessian fly; by 1946 this variety of wheat
leading one grown in central and eastern Nebraska. Painter codified the principles of using host plant resistance in his major book, *Insect Resistance in Crop Plants* (1951). Breeding for plant resistance became a major research line.

• **1939–1950** Ralph T. White and Samson R. Dutky (USDA) developed and disseminated the milky disease for biological control of the Japanese beetle on 93,000 acres in the eastern U.S. The usefulness of insect pathogens was thereby established.

• **1945–1950** James K. Holloway (USDA) and Carl B. Huffaker (University of California) achieved biological control of the Klamath weed in California with insect enemies of the plant. It was the first major success in the biological control of a weed in the U.S. and demonstrated that opportunities for biological control research continued even after the advent of the new pesticides.

• **1937–1959** Edward F. Knipling, Raymond C. Bushland, and other USDA colleagues developed the sterile male technique and eradicated the screwworm fly from Curaçao and Florida. Use of sterile males (an autocidal technique) was an entirely new and previously unforeseen avenue of research that became viable after 1955.

• **1917–1956** Carroll M. Williams (Harvard University) and many others established that a sequence of hormones regulates growth and metamorphosis of insects. Williams reported the first extract of juvenile hormone in 1956. Hormonal control of insect growth, an old field of biological research, thus entered the field of insect control as a new avenue for study.

• **1956–1960** Leo Dale Newsom and James Roland Brazzel (Louisiana State University) identified diapause in the boll weevil. Brazzel, then at Texas A & M university, Theodore B. Davich of the USDA, and others translated this observation into a new way to use insecticides—the diapause control method—by 1960. Neither the physiology nor the insecticides used were markedly new, but their successful combination revitalized the notion that basic biology still had much to contribute to insect control.

• **1959** Peter Karlson and Adolf Butenandt (Max-Planck-Institut für Biochemie) coined the term "pheromone" and thus crystallized the long-developing field of insect attractants into a new subfield of entomology.

CHAPTER 3

Strategies I

Integrated Pest Management

HUFFAKER AND THE HUFFAKER PROJECT

Entomology departments and Washington bureaucracies alike were alive with the hum of "integrated pest management" (IPM) during the 1970s. Both scientists and government officials saw ways out of the pesticide crisis through this strategy in which chemicals and nonchemical methods of control were used to keep pests below damaging numbers. IPM was not a control technique for insects *per se,* rather a concept of *how* insect control should be researched and conducted. Numerous studies were guided by an IPM-like philosophy during the period 1900–1970, but usually they were conducted in isolation from one another. They never constituted a major public policy issue, nor was their underlying conceptual base made explicit. The contemporary IPM concept became a political and intellectual entity through a major research program during the 1970's, "The Huffaker Project," named after its director, Carl Barton Huffaker.

Huffaker was born in the small town of Monticello, Kentucky, in 1914. He received his undergraduate and master's training at the University of Tennessee and his Ph.D. at Ohio State University. He began his professional life in the early 1940s as a specialist in mosquito ecology and control. In 1944 Huffaker became one of the first researchers to use DDT as a residual house spray against malaria-bearing mosquitoes, but his major interest was the role of physical factors (e.g., temperature, humidity, and plant habitat conditions) in the natural control of animal and plant populations. This interest in physical plant ecology was important in Harry Scott Smith's decision to hire him as an assistant entomologist in the University of California's Division of Biological Control in 1946.[1]

Huffaker's first assignment was to work on the biological control of Klamath weed with James K. Holloway, a USDA man also stationed at the Albany, California, research station. Harry Smith had developed an interest in this project some years earlier through correspondence with A. J. Nicholson in Australia where workers were finding some success in controlling the weed with insects imported from Europe. Klamath weed (*Hypericum perforatum* Linnaeus, also known as St. John's Wort) was a native of Europe and Asia that thrived readily on the range lands of northern California, southern Oregon, and other places in the western U.S. It arrived in the U.S. in 1900 without any effective natural enemies and developed large populations. By 1946, an estimated two million acres of rangeland in California were so infested with the unpalatable and toxic Klamath weed that they were unusable for commercial cattle ranching. One beetle, *Chrysolina hyperici,* had already been imported from Australia when Huffaker arrived in 1946, but he was involved with the importation, release, and evaluation of *Chrysolina quadrigemina* (then called *C. gemellata*). The latter insect eventually became the major factor controlling the weed.[2]

Chrysolina quadrigemina's effect on Klamath weed was so fantastic that the plant became an infrequent roadside and range weed over most of its former habitat within ten years. Figures 2 and 3 were taken from the same place in Humboldt County, California. They show how dramatically the range land was cleared of Klamath weed. Success in this venture was a tremendous boost for biological control, particularly for use against weeds in the U.S. *Chrysolina's* success encouraged Huffaker's enthusiasm for biological control as his research specialty, and it furnished a meeting ground for his two major interests, entomology and ecology.

In the 1950s, Huffaker had two further successes with biological control that reinforced his notion that natural enemies could, if properly exploited, provide enormous relief to farmers. The first was a series of studies he conducted with his colleague Charles E. Kennett on the cyclamen mite (*Steneotarsonemus pallidus* Banks), a severe pest of strawberries. Huffaker and Kennett discovered that to get good control of cyclamen mite, a grower needed a healthy population of *Typhlodromus cucumeris* Oudemans, a predatory mite that fed on the cyclamen mite. Unfortunately for the growers, the predatory mite was not always present when cyclamen mite populations developed. Therefore Huffaker

FIGURE 2. Rangeland infested with Klamath Weed, partially cleared by *Chrysolina* spp., Humboldt County, California, 1948. [Original photograph by J. K. Holloway (USDA). Originally published in C. B. Huffaker and C. E. Kennett, Some aspects of assessing efficiency of natural enemies, *Can. Entomol.* 101 (1969): 405–447.]

FIGURE 3. Same as Fig. 2, totally cleared, 1966. [Original photo by Junji Hamai. Source: as in Fig. 2.]

and Kennett suggested that it might be possible to control the cyclamen mite by introducing it and its predator when they planted their fields. The predator would insure that cyclamen mite would not grow to damaging numbers.[3]

Huffaker and Kennett's scheme was never adopted, possibly because of the counterintuitive nature of their solution. Only trained ecologists had enough faith to introduce a pest in order to destroy it! Growers instead resorted to such practices as applying a spoonful of parathion into the crown area of the plant to kill any cyclamen mites that might get into their fields. Even costs of up to $150 per acre for parathion compared to $2–3 per acre for distribution of the two mites did not dissuade them. Seizures of strawberries for excess residues of the insecticide were somewhat more persuasive, and some growers also began switching to a one or two year plant–harvest–replant cycle for strawberries in place of the more traditional two- to four-year cycle. Cyclamen mites were less troublesome under such conditions.[4] William Allen's development of endosulfan, an insecticide that preferentially killed cyclamen mites rather than its predator,[5] presented a more attractive scheme to growers than Huffaker and Kennett's biological control. Nevertheless the whole episode strongly reinforced Huffaker's belief that natural enemies were both powerful and underutilized.

Moving toward his second success, Huffaker picked up on a study of biological control of the olive scale [*Parlatoria oleae* (Colvée)], a severe pest of olives and other deciduous fruits. A tiny wasp [*Aphytis maculicornis* (Masi)] imported from Iran provided much relief, but it could not function efficiently in the hot, dry summer months in California's central valley. At this time, Paul DeBach was exploring in Afghanistan for parasites of other scale insects and found *Coccophagoides utilis* Doutt, another small wasp that parasitizes olive scale. Huffaker, Kennett, and G. L. Finney colonized it on the olive scale in 1957, and it provided sufficient parasitism during the period when *Aphytis* was inactive to give complete biological control of the scale insect, not only on olive but on some 200 other plant species attacked by this scale (Figs. 4 and 5).[6]

Effective control was in itself a significant accomplishment, but the example of two parasites working in harmony provided an important instance relevant to a dispute then current in the biological control field: should a complex of parasites be introduced to let the best one(s) establish their own superiority or should only the single best parasitic species be introduced so as not to have other less efficient species interfere with the work of the best one?[7] In the case of olive scale, the answer was clearly in favor of multiple introductions, because neither *Aphytis* nor *Coccophagoides* alone provided the control they did together.

FIGURE 4. Olive scale outbreak on olives, induced by the use of DDT to destroy natural enemies. [Originally published in C. B. Huffaker, C. E. Kennett, and G. L. Finney, Biological control of olive scale, *Parlatoria oleae* (Colvee) in California by imported *Aphytis maculicornis* (Masi) (Hymenoptera: Aphelinidae), *Hilgardia* 32 (No. 13, 1962): 541–636.]

By 1960, Huffaker was clearly established as an insect ecologist and biological control specialist. His successful ventures persuaded him of the untapped utility of biological control, even in the face of stiff competition from insecticides, and undoubtedly were an important factor leading his peers to select him in 1966 as an organizer of a biological control program for U.S. participation in the International Biological Program. Huffaker's subsequent efforts with the IBP eventually blossomed in 1972 into the "Huffaker Project," but the pathway was complex, and the research effort actually undertaken was considerably altered from that originally envisioned. Changes flowed as much or more from political considerations as from scientific factors, because the Huffaker Project was far more than a mere exercise in research. It was, at minimum, also the following:

- The largest scientifically coordinated research project ever launched for insect control; 18 universities, elements of the USDA, and private industry supplied over 300 researchers who worked

FIGURE 5. Olives without olive scales due to effective biological control. [Same source as Figure 4.]

over seven years and spent about $13 million producing over 250 scientific papers.[8]

- An effort to organize research so as to transcend disciplinary, organizational, political, geographic, and crop-specialty barriers that usually inhibited cooperation among entomologists and other agricultural and engineering scientists.
- A "revival" movement to show the entomological community by example that there was a new, viable way of conceptualizing insect problems and searching for solutions.
- A political salvation for the Nixon administration, whose EPA was under severe pressure from environmentalists and the courts to ban DDT.
- A demonstration that the power to shape agricultural research was no longer confined to a constituency of agriculturalists and agricultural scientists, even though those two groups still retained a preponderance of influence.

Launching the Huffaker Project (1972–1978) was complex both in the coalescence of the participating scientists and in the gathering of political support from federal agencies. Different intellectual traditions of entomological and ecological work and widely scattered university departments merged their efforts. As with most fruitful marriages, much happiness was accompanied by some grief; without doubt it changed the nature of the entomological landscape for the duration of the 1970s and probably much longer.

THE INTELLECTUAL TRADITIONS

Classical Biological Control

Harry Scott Smith and Curtis Paul Clausen of the University of California and the USDA, respectively, each headed sizable research units in biological control in the days before World War II. Their origins and contributions to the theory of induced pest outbreaks were discussed in Chapter 2, but that work was somewhat incidental to their interests in classical biological control*: the careful importation and release of insect predators and parasites to control pest insects and weeds. Each was a major contributor to the establishment of biological control as a modern science, which in turn was the major background for Huffaker. Clausen's *Entomophagous Insects* (1940),[9] for example, was one of the first systematic compilations of information on the biology of natural enemies.

Smith became quite interested in the precise mechanism by which parasites and predators could regulate their hosts and published a paper in 1935 arguing that natural enemies regulated their prey in a "density-dependent" fashion. That is, when the prey population was high, natural enemies had a higher rate of parasitization or predation on them compared to when the host population was low. Furthermore, Smith argued that insect populations oscillated about an equilibrium because of the action of density-dependent biotic factors.[10] Belief in density-dependent regulation was the foundation for confidence in the ability of biological control to function reliably in crop production systems.

Research in classical biological control was inherently international because it involved the search for natural enemies abroad, their importation, and their release in the U.S. (or other countries). The outbreak of World War II interfered with such research, and USDA researchers closed their stations in Europe by November 1939, and in Japan in November 1941.[11] Some of the staff took up new duty stations in South America, but many went into the armed forces. Clausen's cadre of work-

* *Classical* biological control will be distinguished from *augmentative* biological control in a later discussion.

ers was thus dissipated, and the budgets and personnel for the USDA's biological control research dropped. Funds for biological control did not recover to their prewar levels during 1945–1950 even though other research lines did.[12]

Clausen retired from 31 years' service in the USDA in 1951 at the age of 58. Whether he retired early simply for a change of pace or because of his disenchantment with the USDA's support of biological control in the postwar years is not known. In any case, he succeeded Smith as chairman of the University of California's Division of Biological Control. At the time it was a statewide division headquartered in Riverside with an outpost in Albany attached to the Berkeley campus. The USDA's efforts in biological control were first merged with the Division of Bee Culture and then with the Division of Insect Identification, where they remained until the Agricultural Research Service was reorganized in 1972.[13] Clausen served at the University of California until his second retirement in 1959; thus during the 1950s he was chairman of the only research organization in the U.S. devoted exclusively to work in biological control.

Despite its auspicious beginnings near the turn of the century, it is fair to say that biological control in the U.S. nearly died as a recognizable field of research from the 1940s through the 1960s. Attacks against it even included the ridiculous and ignorant assertion that funds expended on biological control posed a threat to the nation's food supply![14] The enormous infatuation with insecticides was clearly the major cause precipitating its near demise.[15]

Even within the University of California system, biological control did not always fare well. Many California entomologists were as intrigued with the seemingly unbeatable powers of the new chemicals as were researchers elsewhere. Furthermore, when Clausen retired in 1959, the Department of Biological Control went through a series of personnel disputes and reorganizations that undoubtedly left a certain amount of demoralization within the staff. Charles A. Fleschner was Clausen's successor at Riverside, but within two years he so antagonized his colleagues that a substantial majority of them requested he resign. Robert van den Bosch was particularly active in the campaign against Fleschner, but the Dean of the Riverside campus supported his incumbent chairman.[16] Van den Bosch later transferred to the Berkeley campus. The issue over Fleschner's leadership was rendered moot in 1963 when the statewide Department of Biological Control was broken apart and its respective elements became parts of the departments of entomological science at the Riverside and Berkeley campuses.

Biological control thus suffered from academic and political doldrums in the decade after 1945, but it was by no means wiped out. Smith's students and proteges continued their work; DeBach, Huffaker, and Richard L. Doutt were especially important, and other major contributors in California included van den Bosch, Kenneth S. Hagen, and Powers S. Messenger. Their field may not have been the most prestigous in entomology but the *espirit de corps* of the California group was sufficient to produce in 1964 a landmark tribute to Harry Scott Smith and the field he helped develop: *The Biological Control of Insect Pests and Weeds.*[17] Smith died in 1957, so he never saw the mammoth volume he inspired. Paul Oman, Ted Gardner, and Reece I. Sailer were still active in the much-reduced USDA effort in biological control. Together and with foreign colleagues, these researchers kept the spirit of biological control alive, and slowly they breathed a revival into it.

Renewal was most evident first at the USDA in 1955 when E. F. Knipling requested that Oman prepare plans for expanded work in biological control, to begin in 1957.[18] Three years later, Knipling directed that Oman and Sailer draw up plans for the establishment of a new laboratory dedicated to biological control research.[19] In 1963 it began operations in Columbia, Missouri, under the direction of Frank R. Lawson.

Sailer had hoped to become Director of the Columbia laboratory, but once he understood its research directions, he was just as happy that Knipling had appointed Lawson. Sailer's approach to biological control was classical, but the USDA lab placed more emphasis on the mass rearing and release of predators and parasites rather than classical biological control.[20] Such an approach can be called *augmentative biological control,* whereby natural enemies are reared and applied in somewhat the same manner as an insecticide. The parasites or predators become a "package" to be pulled off the shelf and released at the farmer's initiative. *Classical biological control* relies more on the natural propagation of the natural enemy to keep a pest under control. We will return later to further discussion of the social and philosophical implications of the differences between the two approaches. For the moment, suffice it to say the laboratory's establishment was a significant achievement and a decided boost by the USDA for research on nonchemical methods of control. It should be noted as well that initiative for the laboratory began well before *Silent Spring* was written.

A second source of revitalization in biological control came via a complex pathway from Europe. William Robin Thompson, a Canadian, became the Director of the Commonwealth Institute for Biological Control (CIBC) in 1949.[21] CIBC, based on former British colonies, was an attractive organizational model because it was international and served a large population base. At the time, only the USDA, the University of California, and the Dominion Parasite Laboratory in Canada (which was incorporated into CIBC) rivaled it in size or breadth of territory. The USDA and CIBC were inspirational to a group of French and other continental entomologists who began in 1948 to organize a European counterpart, ultimately known as the Commission Internationale de Lutte Biologique contre les Enemis des Cultures (CILB). A. S. Balachowsky of the Pasteur Institute served as one of the guiding spirits for launching CILB in 1955 and its journal, *Entomophaga* ("insect eating"), in 1956.[22] CILB met the needs of Europe in that the member countries formed a larger area than any one country, but it was not as far flung as CIBC. Furthermore, the United States declined to join, even though an invitation was extended from Balchowsky in 1956.[23] As a result, CILB was confined largely to western Europe, the Mediterranean basin, and a few former colonies of France and Belgium.

Pest insects, of course, paid no attention to political boundaries, so a truly global organization for biological control was still needed. Bryan P. Beirne, then director of Canada's Entomology Research Institute, chaired a committee to plan a global organization in 1964, and the International Advisory Committee on Biological Control (IACBC) was born. IACBC membership was confined to individuals, as opposed to governments or organizations. Nevertheless its secretary (F. J. Simmonds) and chairman (Beirne) had close ties to the CIBC.[24] Researchers associated with CILB were at first suspicious that IACBC was simply CIBC out to supplant them in their special relationships as adisers to the United Nations.[25] Difficulties between IACBC and OILB (CILB became OILB, O for Organization, in 1965) were finally resolved in 1968, and a new organization based on the OILB structure was ratified by the International Union of Biological Sciences in 1969. The new International Organization for Biological Control (IOBC) replaced OILB in 1971 with DeBach of California's Riverside campus as its first president.[26] Both individual and institutional memberships were allowed, and regional suborganizations permitted more specialized attention to local problems.[27]

The maze of negotiations necessary to create an international organization for biological control tended to obscure the ultimate scientific significance of the diplomacy involved. Only with effective cooperation between nations, however, could the search for natural enemies of insect pests proceed. IOBC in some ways has remained a paper organization, but clearly its formation, argued at length during the 1960s, reflected some organizational progress in support of biological control.

A third boost for the morale of biological control researchers came from the organization of the International Biological Program (IBP). Huffaker was asked in 1966 by the U.S. National Committee for the IBP to organize a project on the biological control of spider mites as one element of the IBP.[28] At about the same time, he and Paul DeBach organized the International Center for Biological Control run jointly on the Berkeley and Riverside campuses of the University of California.[29] Training in biological control was one major objective of the Center and provided a needed complement to the research carried on under the auspices of the IBP. Cooperation between Berkeley and Riverside through the Center was also a way of regaining some of the benefits biological control workers had previously enjoyed in the old state-wide department. Little in the way of extra funding was attached with the original work on the IBP projects; rather, Huffaker's role as coordinator of the spider mite project was to achieve enhanced research productivity through cooperation and faster communication.

Congress appropriated $4 million to the National Science Foundation (NSF) for use in IBP projects during fiscal year 1970.[30] Huffaker, in collaboration with other biological control specialists, submitted a proposal in October 1969, for managing and coordinating research on the biological control of aphids, mites, scale insects, rice pests and cereal leaf beetle, and on the effects of pesticides on natural enemies.[31] Most of the planned research was classical biological control.

Charles F. Cooper, Program Director for Ecosystems Analysis at NSF, was responsible for managing the proposal's review. Ultimately, he and his reviewers were instrumental in rather drastically altering Huffaker's proposed research directions. Cooper believed that Huffaker's project in biological control had the potential for achieving fast practical results that would appeal to the Congress. He argued that NSF could not support research aimed merely at improved crop protection practices, but that development of general theories in biological control was an area the Foundation could sponsor. Cooper favored the research, but he believed it necessary for Huffaker to emphasize explicitly the important theoretical components of the proposed research.[32]

In early 1970, Cooper went further and proposed two major reorientations: (1) organize the work around two or three major world crops that could be studied with systems analysis and mathematical modeling; (2) use the broadest possible connotation of "biological control" for selection of control techniques in experimental designs.[33] The first request asked Huffaker and his colleagues to bring a growing element of basic ecology into the work. Systems analysis and mathematical modeling of ecosystems had been developed in the 1950s by a number of workers including Howard T. Odum, Kenneth Watt, and J. S. Olson.[34]

Before 1969, few applied entomologists used such techniques in their work.[35] Research in classical biological control used mathematical models only to the extent of simple differential equations describing pest population growth and the effects of predation and parasitism from natural enemies. Systems analysis sought to bring the concepts of energy flow and materials cycling in ecosystems into a mathematical formation. In addition, improved mathematical models of population dynamics could provide increased understanding of how crop plants, pests, and natural enemies interacted. Further coupling of *economic* data with *biological* factors offered the hope of identifying optimum management techniques that farmers could apply in the field.[36]

Enlarging the scope of "biological control" brought Huffaker and his colleagues into the midst of a semantic dispute that had begun in the 1950s and continues to this day. Huffaker's original IBP project was largely in classical biological control: the exploration, introduction, and establishment of parasites from abroad to control pest populations in this country. High skills in natural history, field observations, and taxonomy were essential for such research.

Development of the sterile male technique, the use of hormones and pheromones for control of pests, the artificial release of natural enemies, and the deliberate breeding of crop plants for resistance came to be referred to by some entomologists (generally *not* those in the IBP effort) as "biological" methods of controlling insects. Skills essential for developing these methods were in the areas of physiology, biochemistry, and genetics. Moreover, with the possible exception of breeding resistant host plants, the new types of "biological control" usually did not offer permanence as did the establishment of effective, self-sufficient natural enemies. Human intervention was required on a periodic basis to use such practices.[37] Thus a suggestion to broaden the concept of "biological control" implicitly demanded that researchers acquire skills and background they didn't necessarily have and that they acquire a philosophy of control (continual intervention) that they did not ordinarily apply to their work. Huffaker and his associates agreed to Cooper's suggestions for change because (1) classical biological control could still be heavily involved, and (2) the NSF would not make any award without this general reorientation.[38] The award was made in June, 1970.[39]

Reorientation of the proposed work created some difficulties, nonetheless. Huffaker was now the principal investigator for a project to manage and coordinate what was becoming known as *integrated control, integrated pest management*, or *pest management*. Yet even as late as March, 1970, Huffaker did not consider his own specialty to be integrated pest management.[40] He was well acquainted with the field and had no hesitations with its ecological philosophy; but it was not the ground on which he felt most comfortable, particularly regarding the use of insecticides. Integrated pest management gave considerable attention to the use of insecticides in ways that minimized their damage to natural enemies of insect pests. Researchers in that area often included various poison treatments in their experimental design. Huffaker, on the other hand, had done almost no direct experimental work with insecticides for nearly 25 years; he had concentrated on environmental effects and the interactions of pests and their natural enemies. The conduct of work to be coordinated under NSF and IBP auspices demanded marriage to a friendly but different group of researchers with an intellectual heritage different from those dedicated more specifically to classical biological control. We turn now to the origins and development of that group and then to how the merger occurred to create the Huffaker Project.

Ecologists Armed with Chemicals

It is easy to look over the record of specialists in biological control and conclude that they were ecologists as much as entomologists. That is, people like Smith, DeBach, and Huffaker determined the qualitative natural history and the quantitative biotic and physical factors governing the distribution and abundance of organisms. Such investigators seldom paid much attention to designing insecticide treatments for crops, and when they did so it was always with an eye toward preservation of natural enemies of the pest species.

What is not so readily recognized, especially since *Silent Spring* so roundly condemned the unthinking use of insecticides, is that a small group of entomologists was seriously dedicated to investigations with insecticides from an ecological perspective. Detailed comparative studies of different types of chemical treatments therefore did not always preclude equally serious study of the biotic and physical factors that governed the numbers and locations of pests. Serious ecologists armed with potent insecticides were not the norm of those who spent their time studying chemical treatments, but they had a powerful impact on the development of the contemporary science. It is this group that joined the biological control specialists to create the Huffaker Project.

The development of ecologically based studies on insecticides had a diffuse origin in the U.S., but the University of California was clearly the major site. The University of Arkansas was also an important location, but entomological inventions in the two places were largely independent until the late 1960s. A. D. Pickett and his colleagues in eastern Canada developed a remarkably similar approach for "harmonizing" the use of biological and chemical control techniques in apple orchards during the decade 1945–1955.[41] Their work, too, was largely independent of the efforts in California.

California research leading to integrated control began in the late nineteenth century with the arrival of Charles William Woodworth to the Berkeley campus. Woodworth was born in Champaign, Illinois, in 1865. He took his bachelor's training at the University of Illinois with Stephen A. Forbes, the first American entomologist to adopt the newly coined word *ecology* as descriptive of the types of studies he performed. Woodworth's first position was as entomologist and botanist in the Arkansas Experiment Station, but he left in 1891 to accept a position at the University of California. Woodworth was the first scientifically trained entomologist to be hired in a permanent position within the University. He was dubbed as a "kerosene entomologist" by George Compere, an early advocate and practitioner of biological control in California. (Kerosene emulsions were at the time one of the few insecticides available and the phrase seems to indicate that Compere believed Woodworth was too devoted to the use of chemicals.) Compere's complaints were somewhat unjust, however, because Woodworth was sufficiently interested in biological control to write one of the first papers, in 1908, that distinguished density-dependent and density-independent mortality factors.[42]

Woodworth was in no way shy about testing and advocating the use of insecticides when he thought them warranted. In fact, he began work with arsenical sprays for codling moth during his first year in California.[43] He was nonetheless a severe critic of the use of chemicals when he believed they were used improperly. Half of the costs of treating crops were wasted, he argued, owing to inappropriate application of materials. Woodworth argued that expert entomologists should help in making decisions in the field, and he was an early proponent of legislation to regulate insecticides.[44]

Woodworth's complaints about the ineffective or useless application of insecticides were not prompted so much by the occurrence of resistance, outbreaks of secondary pests, or health and environmental hazards. That potpourri of problems resulting from insecticides was not yet recognized. Instead, he was probably more concerned with costs of treatment and use of ineffective insecticides. California farmers in the late nineteenth century relied heavily on an "export" market to the eastern U.S.; frequently they had to compete with goods that were raised in the East as well. Hence any expenditures made by farmers had to be economical if California growers were to remain competitive with their eastern counterparts.

Regardless of the reason for Woodworth's stand against indiscriminate spraying and dusting, he exercised a tremendous influence in the shaping of professional entomology within the state of California for many subsequent decades. He headed entomology at Berkeley for 28 years, from 1892 to 1920. Among those he hired onto the University staff were Edward Oliver Essig and William B. Herms; the latter succeeded Woodworth as chairman in 1920, and Essig became chairman in 1943. Each of these entomologists retained the critical yet accepting stance toward insecticides that had originated with Woodworth. Abraham Ezra Michelbacher was hired by Herms in 1931, and Essig produced a young Ph.D. student, Ray Fred Smith, in 1946.[45] Michelbacher and Smith, plus a number of their colleagues, moved the critical stance toward insecticides from a mere attitude to a paradigm for guiding research and later to a foundation for public policy.

Michelbacher was trained at the University of California by Essig and began his career before the days of DDT and the other new insecticides. In 1938 he observed alfalfa fields in the northern part of the San Joaquin Valley that were severely infested with caterpillars of the alfalfa butterfly (*Colias eurytheme* Boisduval). He observed that the levels were sufficiently high to heavily damage the field, but on close inspection of the larvae he discovered that many of them were parasitized by the tiny wasp *Apanteles flavicombe* Riley (now known as *Apanteles medicaginis* Muesebeck) (Fig. 6). During a subsequent visit to the field, Michelbacher noted that the parasitization had protected the alfalfa from any significant damage.

From 1939 to 1942 Michelbacher, joined by Smith, made a series of observations on the alfalfa in the area. They concluded in 1943 that the wasps were capable of keeping the alfalfa butterfly under control so long as a high proportion of the caterpillar were parasitized in the early growth stages. They strongly recommended that insecticides not be applied to the alfalfa unless it was certain that the number of parasites present was incapable of keeping the pest under control. They especially cautioned against the use of any contact insecticide unless it were known for certain that it would kill the larvae of the butterfly; otherwise, they feared, the wasp would be killed and the larvae not—the key to creating an outbreak of the caterpillars.[46]

Michelbacher and Smith's 1943 study on the alfalfa butterfly must be seen as a landmark venture for them even though the alfalfa butterfly was not known as one of the most severe insect pests. For both entomologists, the experience of discovering that a potentially destructive pest was frequently kept in control by a common, native parasite created a strong appreciation for the power of natural biological control. More-

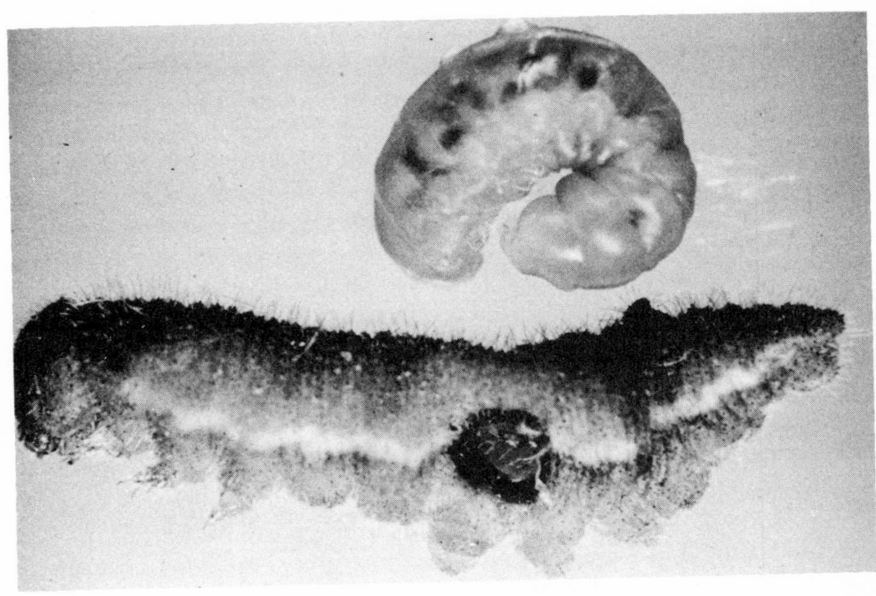

FIGURE 6. Larva of alfalfa butterfly (bottom) that was parasitized by *Apanteles medicaginis* (top).

over, they realized that chemical control practices against the butterfly should protect the parasite. The importance of conserving natural enemies while using insecticides became an important theme in their subsequent work.

Michelbacher's later work in the 1940s and 1950s centered mainly on pests of walnuts, and many of his experiments were oriented toward developing insecticide treatments that would not destroy the benefits of natural enemies. He argued in 1945 that ecology was fundamental to the conduct of insect control. He was especially critical of "insurance" treatments in which growers sprayed an insecticide just in case a pest infestation might develop; such activity was in Michelbacher's view a sign of "failure" of expert knowledge. He believed, as did other entomologists of a similar persuasion, that recommendations of insecticides should be based upon basic research on the biology of the pest species.[47] Michelbacher in 1952 may have been the first to use the term *integrated control* to refer to the notion of protecting natural enemies when using insecticides.[48] It was largely Ray Smith, however, who became the tireless organizer of his colleagues and growers into groups that could take the rhetoric of "integrated control" out of the scientific journals into the field.

Michelbacher began the process of transferring the practice of integrated control to the field even before the term was invented. In 1945 he and the Merced County extension agent toured alfalfa fields subject to severe defoliation from alfalfa butterfly. The agent, W. H. Akison, and Floyd Redfern, a large grower, organized a meeting of alfalfa growers with Ray Smith in May, 1946, to hear the case for hiring a trained entomologist to survey their field for alfalfa butterfly and the wasp parasite; only when the evidence indicated that the wasp would not control the caterpillar would the entomologist recommend that chemical treatments be used. Growers owning a total of 10,285 acres agreed to form the Westside Alfalfa Pest Control Association, with Redfern as president. Smith placed a student in his class at Berkeley, Kenneth S. Hagen, as the supervising entomologist.[49]

Results from the first year's work with the Westside Alfalfa Pest Control Association clearly encouraged both Smith and Hagen to pursue the supervised approach to insect control as a way to insure that insecticide treatments would be applied only when evidence existed that natural enemies could not take care of the job. Smith continued to staff the Westside Association with students during 1947 and 1948; he also organized the Westley Pest Control Association and the Tracy Pest Control Group to serve growers in other parts of the San Joaquin Valley.[50]

Smith's energetic efforts to promote supervised control efforts in the late 1940s came at precisely the time that DDT and other new insecticides were coming into use. During 1945 and 1946 DDT was used experimentally for *Lygus* bug on alfalfa grown for seed. By 1948, over 98% of the treated acres were sprayed or dusted with DDT. Sulfur and calcium arsenate passed into disuse on alfalfa insects as they did on other crop pests.[51] The pest control districts disappeared, but larger growers continued to utilize their own field checkers and, later, pest management advisors. Smith passed the report of Hagen's first summer's work along to Percy Nichol Annand, then chief of USDA's Bureau of Entomology and Plant Quarantine.[52] Annand was interested in maintaining nonchemical control options in the age of new insecticides.[53] He found Smith's work interesting,[54] but the USDA was no more able to stem the rush to heavy reliance on chemical control than was Smith.

For Hagen, the experience with the Westside Alfalfa Pest Control Association in 1945 was somewhat different. It was his first venture into professional entomology. He was so struck by the effectiveness of the parasitic wasp that he switched his major interests from taxonomy to biological control,[55] for which he earned his Ph.D. in 1952 under Doutt. His successors in the Westside Association job, Vernon Mark Stern and Robert van den Bosch, pursued their degrees under Ray Smith's direction. The early 1950s were inauspicious times for biological control and Doutt and Smith later recalled that enthusiasts were ridiculed as a "lunatic fringe" of the entomological profession.[56] Persistence and the spotted alfalfa aphid, however, brought Smith, Hagen, Stern, and van den Bosch together again in the last half of the 1950s. By this time, all were on the staff of the University of California, and the aphid served as the catalyst for a major theoretical and practical development in entomology.

The spotted alfalfa aphid [*Therioaphis maculata* (Buckton)] first appeared in southern California in 1954. It spread rapidly over a majority of California's alfalfa acreage in 1955 and caused an estimated loss of nearly $13 million that year.[57] Growers used three organophosphate insecticides (parathion, malathion, and TEPP) to control the insect, but trouble in the form of insecticide resistance came in the late summer of 1956 near Hinkley on the Mojave Desert. Repeated treatments with insecticides, furthermore, had decimated the natural enemies of the pest, and severe resurgences followed with high damage.[58] Repeated and heavy reliance on insecticides had thus created the standard pattern for crisis and disaster so common in the post-1945 era.

Van den Bosch, then at the Riverside campus, and several co-workers imported parasites of the aphid from Europe and the Middle East. *Praon exsoletum* (Nees) and *Trioxys complanatus* Quilis became established by 1957, but their potential effectiveness was threatened by the heavy use of insecticides.[59] Smith and Hagen found that native predators, especially several species of lady beetles, could provide considerable assistance in controlling the aphid during the early part of the summer as long as they were not destroyed by toxic chemicals.[60] Given the potential for native predators and imported parasites to control the insect under most circumstances, Stern and van den Bosch launched a search for an insecticide that could provide economical control of the aphid and leave sufficient natural enemies that further treatments might be avoided. They found their compound in demeton (Systox®) during extensive field studies in 1956 and 1957. As little as 0.7–0.9 oz. of the compound per acre could provide a relatively selective kill of aphids compared to their predators and parasites.[61]

The practical implications alone of the work of Stern, van den Bosch, Smith, and Hagen were sufficient to mark it as substantial and noteworthy. They had developed a system whereby an alfalfa grower, working perhaps with the aid of an experienced entomologist, could enjoy the benefits of both chemical and biological control methods to keep the aphid from destroying his crop. Net costs of the integrated program were considerably lower than exclusive reliance on chemicals and its effectiveness was more reliable than dependence on biological control alone.

They went beyond the case of the spotted alfalfa aphid, however, and created a general theory of integrated control that was presented as an eloquent companion paper to specific studies on the aphid.[62] "The Integrated Control Concept" (1959) is now frequently cited as the beginning of the integrated pest management movement, but it should be clear from the previous discussion that integrated control, albeit without the name, had emerged through an evolutionary process over a period of many decades. Woodworth certainly helped to create a tradition within the University of California in which chemicals were studied critically for both their positive and negative impacts. Harry Scott Smith and his close associates created a center of expertise on biological control and kept alive the belief after 1945 that the importation and release of natural enemies was by no means obsolete in the new age of chemicals. Michelbacher clearly appreciated both threads of entomological thought, and his impact on Ray Smith's approach to insect control was large. Smith in turn provided the organizational and intellectual leadership to create a body of scientific workers dedicated to integrated control.

In 1959, integrated control theory contained a number of essential components:

1. *Recognition of the ecosystem.* Crop plants, pest organisms (insects, weeds, plant pathogens, and others), and man, together with the physical environment, make up the unified ecosystem. Pest control had to be recognized as an activity that could alter the entire ecosystem with both beneficial and deleterious results. The control of one pest species could not be considered unrelated to the activities of other organisms. Furthermore, human economic activities and interests were integrally tied to the manipulation of the ecosystem. Insect control had to consider especially the fluctuations of the pest species and those of its parasites and predators.
2. *Economic injury levels and economic thresholds.* Mere presence of a pest organism in a farmer's field did not create cause for alarm. Only a population of the pest sufficiently high to cause crop injury equal to or greater than the cost of controlling the pest was deleterious; such a level was the *economic injury level.* Control measures in integrated control were to be taken at the *economic threshold,* a population density somewhat less than the economic

injury level; thus action was indicated somewhat before the level at which actual damage was anticipated.

3. *Augmentation of natural enemies.* Classical biological control, in which a new parasite or predator was imported from another area, was the primary means of augmentation envisioned in the 1959 paper. Also important were (a) periodic release of natural enemies, (b) artificial release of the pest species when it was normally low to provide food for natural enemies, (c) selective breeding and release of natural enemies so that they could withstand adverse climates or insecticides, and (d) modification of the environment (such as dust control) to make it more suitable for the activities of natural enemies.
4. *Selective insecticides.* Chemicals were important but had to be used with care in order to preserve natural enemies. Selective killing of the pest could be accomplished with (a) materials of selective toxicity, (b) treatment of selected areas to leave reservoirs of natural enemies, (c) proper timing of application to spare natural enemies, and (d) use of short-lived compounds that break down in the environment before killing too many natural enemies. Disease organisms of pest insects, such as *Bacillus thuringiensis* Berliner, were only then starting to receive much use, but such biotic insecticides could provide considerable selective killing power for use in integrated control schemes.
5. *Supervised control.* Integrated control presupposed substantial knowledge of the population dynamics of an insect pest and its natural enemies. Many growers would have neither the time nor the skill to check their fields properly to make integrated control work. Therefore, the University of California scientists recommended that professional entomologists evaluate a grower's insect problems and recommend the proper course of action. Smith and Hagen pioneered the use of supervised control in California in the 1940s, but the concept was not an original innovation with them. As will be developed shortly, Dwight Isely in Arkansas had instituted similar schemes for cotton many years earlier.

Smith and Hal T. Reynolds of the Riverside campus in 1965 refined the integrated control concept to include all methods of control: chemical, biological, cultural, genetic, attractants, and repellents.[63] This enlargement began to change it from merely a philosophy and strategy of insect control into a scheme for production management on the farm. *Cultural control* was the key to this shift because it included selection of crop plant variety, fertilization, irrigation, weed control, planting dates, harvesting dates, and any other farm practice that had an impact on the size of a pest population. Significantly, as will be developed in the next chapter, Smith and Reynolds excluded eradication of a pest:

> The philosophy of pest control based on eradication of the pest species is the antithesis of integrated pest control. Nevertheless, eradication may be a legitimate goal under special circumstances. However, these circumstances do not prevail for most agricultural and forest pests. In most situations our goal should be to manage pest populations so as to eliminate them as pests but not to eradicate them.[64]

In 1975, Smith became involved in cooperative efforts with plant pathologists, weed scientists, and nematologists so as to include their pest control activities along with the insect control in integrated pest management.[65] Smith and his colleagues perhaps had not sought to become "master agriculturalists" concerned with the total management of land areas, but their quest for ecological holism led them ever closer to this all-encompassing role. Along the way, they transformed the idea of integrated control from a concept of combining biological control with chemical control into a paradigm that provided a general set of guidelines and assumptions to guide those researchers who adhered to it.

LAUNCHING THE HUFFAKER PROJECT

Joining classical biological control to ecologically based research on chemicals was by no means unpleasant, unwelcome, or unprecedented. In fact, in a small way it had already occurred in the 1959 paper by Stern, Smith, van den Bosch, and Hagen. Stern and Smith both had their appointments in the entomology departments at the Riverside and Berkeley campuses, respectively; van den Bosch and Hagen both had their appointments in the Department of Biological Control, with van den Bosch at Riverside and Hagen in Berkeley. Thus within the University of California system, researchers transcended potential departmental and campus barriers to cooperate. Of course, the four had already had a long association for over ten years that considerably eased the problems that sometimes are associated with scientific work across bureaucratic boundaries.

Cooperation within California was certainly important for the intellectual growth of the integrated pest management paradigm. NSF funding of a large research effort on crop systems, however, was only partly a scientific question; it was also political. Clearly it was to Huffaker's advantage to have a broad base of research representing many states and crops and oriented toward widely recognized problems. A series of events transpired during the late 1960s that brought the California entomologists into a working relationship with a small group of entomologists in Texas, Arkansas, Louisiana, and Mississippi (TEXARLAM). Enhanced collaboration developed among these states that was important to the final launching of the Huffaker Project. In order to understand how that cooperation developed, we turn to some of the earlier events in entomology in the TEXARLAM region.

Agricultural production in the South diversified after 1900, but cotton remained an important foundation along with a few others such as sugar cane, citrus, cattle ranching, and timber. Boll weevils generally predominated over all other insects in demanding the continued attention of southern entomologists. The crisis created by boll weevils resistant to the chlorinated hydrocarbon insecticides in the Lower Rio Grande Valley (LRGV) of Texas in the late 1960s was discussed earlier (Chapter 2). Events flowing from Perry Lee Adkisson's efforts to stem that disaster had far-reaching impact on the Huffaker project.

Adkisson became chairman of the Texas A & M University Department of Entomology in 1967, just as the situation in the LRGV became critical. He was approached by John McKelvey of the Rockefeller Foundation and asked to organize an interuniversity research project to find cotton varieties resistant to insects. Adkisson pulled together workers from his own university, Mississippi State University, the USDA, and the University of California at Davis. He also invited Smith and Reynolds from the University of California (Berkeley and Riverside, respectively) to advise his department on how they might cope with the problem created by overreliance on insecticides. Smith and Reynolds were already committed to integrated control, and their collaboration with Adkisson and his Department provided an important foundation for enlarging cooperative projects between their universities.

More importantly, Adkisson began to draw upon the philosophy of Isely, his teacher at the University of Arkansas. Even though Isely had had an immensely important personal role in directing Adkisson into entomology in the first place, Adkisson had not had much occasion up to that point to draw specifically on Isely's thoughts. Adkisson had come to Texas in 1958 to work on the pink bollworm [*Pectinophora gossypiella* (Saunders)], a pest that was virtually under control by the time Adkisson arrived due to legally mandated stalk shredding and fall plowing. Because the insect was no longer such a significant pest, Adkisson had occupied himself with research on the basic physiology of the insect.[66] The recalcitrance of the boll weevil and the outbreaks of bollworms and tobacco budworms brought him for the first time to the need to delve into Isely's previous work. His cooperative work under the Rockefeller Foundation grant brought him into closer contact with other entomologists who had also been powerfully affected by Isely's teachings.

Isely was a Kansan by birth and education who began his professional life with the USDA's Bureau of Entomology in 1912. In 1921 he accepted a position with the University of Arkansas, where he spent the remainder of his professional career until his retirement in 1956.[67] He was never especially enthusiastic about biological control, but he had a keen interest in the effect of the physical environment on insect populations.[68] It is possible that his appreciation for climatic factors on insect population growth was conditioned by his location in Arkansas: boll weevils were a perennial pest in at least parts of Arkansas after 1906, but the State is far enough north that cold severely limits the insects' ability to overwinter. The boll weevil was therefore more sporadic in its damage in Arkansas than it was further south in Mississippi and Louisiana.[69] Isely's major contribution to cotton insect control was the design and implementation of *spot dusting,* a supervised control program in which trained scouts examined fields to see if they really needed treatment. His first scouting program began on a small scale in 1924–1925 when calcium arsenate was the best insecticide available[70]; it continued on a larger scale in the postwar years after the new synthetic organic materials replaced the old insecticides.[71]

Isely thus played a role analogous to that played by Smith in California. He was an ecologist as much as an applied entomologist, and he believed in the necessity and possibility of supervised control. He preceded Smith in time, but during his active years he had little influence outside of Arkansas and the mid-South region. Like Smith, Isely also trained a number of students, and it was they rather than Isely himself who were ultimately to carry his attitudes into a larger sphere of influence: Charles Gatewood Lincoln received his bachelor's degree under Isely, went to Cornell and was a colleague of Charles Edmund Palm, an earlier student of Isely's. While at Cornell, Lincoln taught Leo Dale Newsom from Louisiana, and they began a friendship that stretched over many decades. Lincoln returned to Arkansas after completion of his Ph.D. and eventually succeeded Isely as chairman of entomology; Newsom returned to LSU and also became chairman of entomology[72]; Adkisson trained under Isely and Lincoln at Arkansas from 1946 to 1950. While there, he was the roommate of Jake R. Phillips. Adkisson went on to Texas in 1958, and Phillips became a professor of entomology at Arkansas under Lincoln's chairmanship.[73] Thus, Isely's influence travelled throughout the TEXARLAM region. When resistance, resurgence, and secondary pest outbreaks became the order of the day in the 1950s, his philosophy on the need for ecological insights still resided in a reservoir of people he had trained or influenced indirectly. The shared attitudes of Adkisson–Newsom–Lincoln–Phillips became an important ingredient in the Huffaker Project.

The award to Huffaker from NSF in 1970 was to sponsor a working conference to draw up a proposal for research on a series of important crops. NSF indicated to Huffaker that the proper proposal could receive funding in the range of millions of dollars. Megabucks waiting to be plucked from NSF coffers, of course, opened up a serious problem: who's in and who's not? Huffaker gathered many of his Berkeley colleagues to discuss particular crops and people on May 25, and the consensus was that the integrated control philosophy was to be the guiding principle.[74] Unfortunately, the IPM paradigm was not a strict algorithm indicating the exact way to proceed; it was a loose set of research guidelines buttressed by a series of experiences during the previous 25 years. Especially important were their efforts against alfalfa caterpillar and spotted alfalfa aphid. Substantial judgments thus remained to be made.

The contacts developed among Smith, Reynolds, and Adkisson made it obvious that Adkisson was compatible with the IPM philosophy as acquired through Isely. Inclusion through Adkisson of cotton's problems in the boll weevil belt was highly attractive politically. Newsom had close ties through Lincoln to the TEXARLAM group. In addition, he had previously worked with Smith on a White House policy study on cotton insects, and it was obvious that he shared the basic tenets of the IPM philosophy.[75]

An unofficial coordinating committee coalesced to implement the conference: Huffaker, Smith, Reynolds, Newsom, and Adkisson.[76] The group they selected gathered at Berkeley in October 1970, and planned the largest, most expensive, coordinated research project ever attempted in entomology outside the USDA structure.

Huffaker and his conferees faced two important topics: (1) What techniques for nonchemical control should be emphasized, and how should priorities be set? Prominent candidates included cultural methods, importation and establishment of natural enemies, plant resistance, hormones, sterile male methods, and development of selectivity in chemicals. How to set economic threshold levels was also considered an important topic. (2) What crops and institutions were to be included? In May, Huffaker and other University of California people had tentatively selected cotton, alfalfa, stone and pome fruits,* and pine trees as crop systems.[77] Entomological research philosophy was clearly at stake

* For example, peaches (stone) and apples (pome).

in the first question, but the second touched the sensitive nerve of precisely who and what universities might get support. Moreover, any crop excluded from the proposal would subject the researchers to the political pressures of commodity trade associations and their legislators who felt that their insect problems were every bit as worthy as those included.

Huffaker believed that only three or four crop systems could be included, but the conference discussed seven: cotton, alfalfa, citrus, soybeans, stone and pome fruits, pine trees, and broad leafed trees. Only the last was omitted from the final proposal. Undoubtedly, one of the factors leading to the inclusion of more crops than originally thought possible was the internal competition set up within the conference. Newsom, for example, remembers that his major goal in attending was to "lobby" for the inclusion of soybeans, a crop just beginning to be grown in rotation with cotton in the South. Newsom pointed out that soybeans grown in the more northerly areas of the Midwest in rotation with corn were almost free of insect pests. In the South, however, a number of insects could potentially develop into serious problems, prompting heavy use of insecticides as had already occurred on cotton. Newsom successfully argued that it would be a sign of keen foresight to develop integrated control techniques for southern soybeans *before* rather than *after* a pesticide disaster had occurred.[78]

The Berkeley conferees added no new crops that had not already enjoyed the "patronage" of someone invited to the conference to discuss them. Pressures developed later to have corn and grain sorghum included,[79] but Huffaker and his colleagues held firm on the six crops agreed to at the conference. Each crop subgroup met in January 1971, to complete the detailed planning for the research on their crop,[80] and preliminary drafts were sent to NSF in August; the final proposal was sent about two months later.[81]

The massive amount of work proposed is suggested by the fact that each copy of the proposal weighed in excess of six pounds! Aside from the heavy emphasis on systems analysis and modeling, the proposed work was not radically different from work already underway by the researchers involved. Frank R. Lawson and his associates at the USDA lab in Columbia, Missouri, provided a concise articulation of the guidelines for the proposed research, which Huffaker used in the proposal[82]:

1. Identify "real" pests compared to those induced by insecticide use.
2. Establish economic injury levels for real pests with due regard for unintended damage done by insecticides.

3. Identify the key factors controlling populations of the real pests, e.g., a natural enemy or a resistant crop variety.
4. Identify factors controlling pests induced by insecticides.
5. Identify alternative possibilities for controlling real and induced pests.
6. Use systems analysis and modeling to guide planning, execution, and refinement of research program; include biological, economic, and social considerations in the model.

Huffaker and his colleagues were aware of the need to cooperate with the USDA and they had included appropriate USDA researchers in the first proposals to NSF under the IBP project on classical biological control. Furthermore, Edward F. Knipling, director of the Entomological Research Service, ARS, William E. Waters, director of Forest Insect Research, FS, and Frank R. Lawson had participated in the October conference in Berkeley. Knipling, Waters, and Lawson were also included in the overall steering committee of the proposal.[83] Mere participation of USDA personnel in the research guidance, however, was not enough to eliminate differences of viewpoints between the USDA and the university entomologists. Waters and Lawson were intellectually closer to the Huffaker group, but Knipling had a different set of priorities for research. Given unlimited research funds, he was a supporter of the efforts envisioned for the Huffaker Project: but research funds were limited, as usual, and Knipling soon became at best an uncertain supporter and perhaps even a political adversary of the Huffaker Project.[84] His different priorities for research reflected a different paradigmatic vision for research, which will be the subject of the next chapter.

The NSF by tradition supported only basic research instead of applied studies, so this part of the IBP program with its applied orientation took NSF onto somewhat unfamiliar ground. Research proposed in the Huffaker proposal further compounded the Foundation's sense of unease: not only was it applied, it was *agricultural* research and hence led NSF into a bureaucratic intrusion on the turf of the USDA. That agency already had an established system of laboratories plus its extramural funding to the land grant universities through the Cooperative State Research Service. NSF and USDA had agreed in March that NSF could expand research on insect control,[85] but Huffaker's proposal was a major test of that agreement's viability.

Environmental as well as bureaucratic politics also impinged upon the NSF's handling of the proposal and ultimately were an important key to its funding. DDT and other pesticides had been under fire by the Environmental Defense Fund's (EDF) suits since 1966, and by 1971 its future use was seriously in doubt. EDF's suit against the EPA forced the latter to commence cancellation procedures against DDT in January.[86] Montrose Chemical Corporation, DDT's major manufacturer, and Crop King Company (Yakima, Washington) requested an expert advisory committee selected by the National Academy of Sciences to examine the EPA's cancellation. Recommendations from the committee to reduce use of the chemical rapidly came in September,[87] shortly before the final proposal was submitted by Huffaker.

Thirty other companies plus the USDA demanded that EPA hold a public hearing which began in August. Cross-examination of witnesses testifying for and against DDT turned the hearings into a grueling public display of sharply divided scientific opinion on the costs and benefits of the chemical. EPA and EDF were pitted against USDA, the chemical industry, and some farming companies.[88] EPA chose not to act on the recommendations of the expert advisory committee while the public hearings were underway. Hence when the Huffaker proposal arrived in Washington, the atmosphere in Washington was one in which a cloud of uncertainty hung over the future of chemical control. Any proposal for research on reducing reliance on chemicals would surely have looked welcome and needed.

Concurrent with the administrative maneuvering on DDT, the Congress began making serious legislative moves designed to prevent environmental damage from pesticides. In February, Congressman W. R. Poage (D., Tex.) introduced a complete revision of the Federal Insecticide, Fungicide and Rodenticide Act (FIFRA). This bill had been prepared by an interagency task force convened by the Council on Environmental Quality and bore the support of the Nixon Administration. It provided explicit directions for the EPA to consider short and long term effects "on man and the rest of the environment" from pesticides before registering a pesticide for use.[89]

Senator Gaylord Nelson (D., Wis.) introduced the same revision of FIFRA into the Senate and also, in May, a bill providing both the USDA and the NSF $2 million each for expanding their research on "integrated biological–cultural" methods of pest control. His remarks at the bill's introduction made it clear that he had drawn heavily on the opinions and expertise of some of the leading members of the Huffaker proposal,[90] such as R. Smith, Newsom, Adkisson, and others. Nelson clearly intended his bill to provide the NSF with the wherewithall to fund the Huffaker proposal.

Leaders of the Huffaker proposal took little part in the debate on the new pesticide law and the cancellation hearings on DDT, but Huffaker sent copies of the Nelson bill to the directors of each of the subprojects and asked them to contact senators and congressmen from the states affected so as to gather needed political support for the bill.[91] In the late summer, van den Bosch organized entomological witnesses from the Huffaker proposal to testify in favor of the Nelson Bill.[92] Budgetary policy forced the USDA and the NSF both to deny the need for Nelson's bill, but they favored its intent. Favorable testimony from 17 entomologists, 9 farming and timber organizations, and 3 environmental groups (including the EDF) clearly sent word to the Nixon Administration that the Huffaker proposal had attracted powerful support from scientific, farming, and environmental interest groups.[93]

The USDA had also begun moving toward IPM ideas in 1970 following the parathion poisonings of workers in the tobacco fields of North Carolina. Ned Bayley, Director of Science and Education, asked James Roland Brazzel, a former student of Newsom's at LSU, to develop programs of supervised control with scouts paid from the federal treasury. Brazzel's committee launched two pilot programs in 1971 and began in May, 1971, to plan for a large increase in 1972.[94] Brazzel was also at the time a leading figure in the Pilot Boll Weevil Eradication Experiment which had just begun in the late summer of 1971. USDA argued that boll weevil eradication was "integrated control," but leaders from the Huffaker project disagreed, a subject to which we return in Chapter 5.

Bayley invited Huffaker to present his proposal to the Agricultural Research Policy Advisory Committee (ARPAC), a joint federal–state group that advised the USDA on priorities for research. Huffaker met with ARPAC in October, where he was received with considerable enthusiasm by both the committee and Bayley. Bayley apparently wanted to incorporate the Huffaker proposal administratively with other activities such as Brazzel's pilot pest management projects as one cornerstone for future USDA directions in pest control[95]; eradication experiments exemplified by the boll weevil effort provided another. Speculations were raised by both state entomologists and personnel elsewhere in Washington that Bayley was simply out to grab politically popular sciences and bring them all into his domain in the USDA.[96] At the same time, some state entomologists feared too-close links with the USDA because of Knipling's dedication to eradication projects.[97]

Regardless of what may have motivated Bayley, he was the key figure in moving the USDA into a cooperative agreement with the NSF and EPA to support the Huffaker proposal.[98] Also important was the interest of Warren Muir, a staff member at the Council on Environmental Quality, who kept up steady but quiet pressure from near the White House for a major federal effort on such pest management research.[99] Budgetary questions from the Office of Management and Budget (OMB) were cleared rapidly in December once the Nixon Administration decided to use the Huffaker proposal as a cornerstone of its environmental program in 1972. OMB personnel directed the NSF, USDA, and EPA to fund the Huffaker proposal at a level of $3.5 million for 1972 using redirected funds from other programs. OMB specifically referred to the "very real possibility" that DDT would be banned as justification for the urgency of funding the Huffaker research. The agencies were ordered to make the necessary arrangements in time for Richard Nixon to announce it in his environmental message to the Congress in early February.[100] NSF's peer review had already approved the project's scientific merit, but high-level political support guaranteed adequate funding at least for the first year.[101] Once the full support of the White House came behind it, the Huffaker Project had arrived!

THE SIGNIFICANCE OF THE HUFFAKER PROJECT

A committee convened by the Council on Environmental Quality in mid-1977 concluded that the achievements of the research were "excellent" and the knowledge base created made it possible to decrease insecticide usage in the U.S. by "50% or more."[102] Such a reduction did not occur (Fig. 1). Barriers between knowledge generation and knowledge use are complex in the field of insect control.

Sociopolitical changes in the conduct and administration of insect control research were also effected by the Huffaker Project. At the level of the research scientists, disciplinary, university, state, and to a certain extent crop specialty barriers were softened if not broken by the interactions created through the Huffaker Project. Most of the workers were entomologists, but a few agronomists, plant pathologists, weed scientists, agricultural economists, and systems analysts found their way into the complex. Modeling of insect–plant interactions was the most significant novelty in terms of entomology's previous history. Cooperation across disciplines and bureaucratic-political boundaries, however, was not unique to the Huffaker Project as we will see in the next chapter.

Of more fundamental significance was the entrance of new interest groups into the politics of funding entomological research. Traditionally, only the scientists and the farming and chemical industries paid much attention to appropriations for entomologists. Support from the environmental "movement" for the Nelson bill marked unique novelty in the politics of entomology. It came from both the entrance of governmental organizations such as CEQ, EPA, and NSF into the turf traditionally held by the USDA and from the support of the Sierra Club, the

Environmental Defense Fund, and others. Here IPM differed markedly from its rival, TPM. Huffaker himself was not a direct participant in the environmental slug-fest over DDT that emerged in the aftermath of Rachel Carson. Yet the work he was so prominently involved in found an important ally in the political movement inspired by *Silent Spring*. It's quite possible that the NSF would have funded at least a small version of the Huffaker Project even without the ruckus raised over DDT. However, the involvement of the White House in the funding decision and the size of the Huffaker Project surely flowed from the tide launched by Carson. A new movement in entomology thus basked in the heat created by the profession's earlier addiction to the "miracle" chemicals.

REFERENCE NOTES

1. Carl B. Huffaker, personal interview, Mar. 17–18, 1977.
2. James K. Holloway, "Projects in Biological Control of Weeds," in *Biological Control of Insect Pests and Weeds*, Paul DeBach, ed. (New York: Reinhold Pub. Corp., 1964), pp. 656–658.
3. C. B. Huffaker and C. E. Kennett, Experimental studies on predation, *Hilgardia* 26 (1956): 191–222.
4. Huffaker, personal interview.
5. Ray F. Smith, "Development of Integrated Control in California," 18 pp. plus 7 pp. references, mimeo, 1972; William W. Allen, H. Nakakihara and G. A. Schaefers, The effectiveness of various pesticides against the cyclamen mite on strawberries, *J. Econ. Entomol.* 50 (1957): 648–652.
6. C. B. Huffaker, C. E. Kennett, and G. L. Finney, Biological control of the olive scale, *Parlatoria oleae* (Colvée), in California by imported *Aphytis maculicornis* (Masi) (Hymenoptera: Aphelinidae), *Hilgardia* 32 (1962): 541–636; C. B. Huffaker and C. E. Kennett, Biological control of *Parlatoria oleae* (Colvée) through the compensatory action of two introduced parasites, *Hilgardia* 37 (1966): 283–335.
7. A. L. Turnbull and Donald A. Chant argued for introducing only the single best parasite in The practice and theory of biological control of insects in Canada, *Can. J. Zool.* 39 (1961): 697–753.
8. Council on Environmental Quality, Scientific review of the Huffaker project for integrated pest management—the principles, strategies, and tactics of pest population regulation in major crop ecosystems, unpublished report, Sept. 15, 1977 (hereafter cited as CEQ, Scientific review).
9. Curtis P. Clausen, *Entomophagous Insects* (New York: McGraw-Hill Book Co., Inc., 1940), 688 pp.
10. Harry S. Smith, The role of biotic factors in the determination of population densities, *J. Econ. Entomol.* 28 (1935): 873–898.
11. C. P. Clausen to K. A. Bartlett, Nov. 22, 1939; C. P. Clausen to P. N. Annand, Nov. 22, 1941; both in Record Group 7, National Archives (RG7NA).
12. C. F. W. Muesebeck to F. C. Bishopp, July 7, 1952, RG7NA; *U. S. Budget*, 1939 through 1951 (Washington, D. C.: Government Printing Office); Reece I. Sailer, personal interview, May, 1978.

13. *Ibid.*; R. I. Sailer, ARS agencies involved in Biological Control Research, rough draft, May 24, 1971, copy supplied by R. I. Sailer; K. S. Hagen and J. M. Franz, "A history of biological control," in *History of Entomology*, Ray F. Smith, Thomas E. Mittler, and Carroll N. Smith, eds. (Palo Alto: Annual Reviews, Inc., 1973), pp. 433–476 (hereafter cited as Hagen and Franz, *History*).
14. Donald Lerch, Search for biological controls poses threat to Nation's food supply, *Agric. Chem.* (Nov., 1964): 21–22, 103–104.
15. The brief recapitulation of the history of biological control given here in no way does justice to the field as a whole. For more complete studies, see Hagen and Franz, *History*; Richard L. Doutt, "The historical development of biological control," in *Biological Control of Insect Pests and Weeds*, Paul DeBach, ed. (New York: Reinhold Pub. Corp., 1964), pp. 21–42; and F. J. Simmonds, J. M. Franz, and R. I. Sailer, "History of biological control," in *Theory and Practice of Biological Control*, C. B. Huffaker, ed. (New York: Academic Press, 1976), pp. 17–39.
16. Paul H. DeBach, personal interview, Mar., 1977.
17. Paul DeBach, ed., *Biological Control of Insect Pests and Weeds* (New York: Reinhold Pub. Corp., 1964), 844 pp.
18. E. F. Knipling to P. W. Oman, Oct. 31, 1955, files of R. I. Sailer.
19. Sailer, personal interview. Knipling received support for such a laboratory from the California State Board of Agriculture in 1958 (see Romain Young to Ezra Taft Benson, Mar. 18, 1958 and E. F. Knipling to M. R. Clarkson, Apr. 8, 1958, files of R. I. Sailer).
20. Sailer, personal interview; R. I. Sailer to B. P. Beirne, Jan. 14, 1964, files of R. I. Sailer. See also the Quarterly Reports, Biological Control of Insects Research Laboratory, USDA, 1965–1972, copies held at USDA Biological Control of Weeds, Albany, Calif.
21. Hagen and Franz, *History*.
22. A. S. Balachowsky, La Commission Internationale de Lutte Biologique contre les Enemis des Cultures (CILB), *Entomophaga* 1 (1956): 5–18.
23. E. F. Knipling to A. S. Balachowsky, Feb. 20, 1957, files of R. I. Sailer. Knipling promised full cooperation with CILB even though USDA did not join.
24. International Advisory Committee for Biological Control, *Biological Control Information Bulletin No. 1*, Oct. 1965.
25. R. I. Sailer to W. H. Anderson, Sept. 9, 1965, files of R. I. Sailer.
26. P. DeBach to Members of IUBS Ad Hoc Committee for IOBC, Oct. 15, 1970, files of R. I. Sailer; F. Wilson, Conference Report, International Organization for Biological Control, *PANS* 16 (1970): 393–395.
27. By-Laws of the Council of IOBC passed at its meeting, Rome, Apr. 2, 1971, 3 pp., mimeo, files of R. I. Sailer.
28. Huffaker, personal interview. The U. S. National Committee for the International Biological Program began operations at the National Academy of Sciences in 1965 (U. S. Congress, Senate, Committee on Labor and Public Welfare, *International Biological Program*, Hearings, 91st Congress, 2nd sess., 1970, p. 16).
29. Paul DeBach and Carl Huffaker, A proposal to establish an International Center of Biological Control at the University of California, unpublished paper, Berkeley and Riverside, California, May, 1967.
30. U. S. Congress, Senate, Committee on Labor and Public Welfare, *International Biological Program*, Hearings, 91st Congress, 2nd sess., 1970, p. 17.
31. August G. Manza to Program Director, Ecosystem Director, Oct. 29, 1979, files of C. B. Huffaker. The full title of the proposal was "Management of an Integrated, Inter-Institutional Program in Biological Control, as part of the U.S./International Biological Program (IBP)."

32. Charles F. Cooper to Carl B. Huffaker, Dec. 1, 1969, files of C. B. Huffaker.
33. Huffaker, personal interview; Carl B. Huffaker to Charles Cooper, Mar. 20, 1970; Carl B. Huffaker to Frank Blair, Apr. 23, 1970. Letters from the files of C. B. Huffaker.
34. Richard G. Wiegert, "Simulation model of ecosystems," in *Annu. Rev. Ecol. Syst.*, Richard F. Johnston, Peter W. Frank, and Charles D. Michener, eds., 6 (1975): 311–338; Orie L. Loucks, Emergence of research on agroecosystems, in *ibid.*, 8 (1977): 173–192 (hereafter cited as Loucks, Emergence).
35. A pioneering effort was R. W. Stark and Ray F. Smith, "Systems analysis and pest management," in *Biological Control*, C. B. Huffaker, ed. (New York: Plenum Press, 1971), pp. 331–345.
36. Loucks, Emergence.
37. Major developers of classical biological control, such as Harry Scott Smith, were not opposed to some of the practices of "biological control" in the broad sense of the term. Indeed, Smith and some of his colleagues, especially Stanley E. Flanders, were developers and proponents of mass releases of parasites during the early 1930s. They cautioned, however, that such mass releases had to be based on a sound knowledge of the biology of the host and parasite. Effectiveness was the exception, not the norm, for most release programs. See H. S. Smith and S. E. Flanders, Is *Trichogramma* becoming a fad?, *J. Econ. Entomol.* 24 (1931): 666–672; Paul DeBach and K. S. Hagen, "Manipulations of entomophagous species," in *Biological Control of Insect Pests and Weeds*, Paul DeBach, ed. (New York: Reinhold Pub. Corp., 1964), pp. 429–458.
38. Huffaker, personal interview; C. B. Huffaker, Status of U.S./IBP project in biological control, unpublished report, July, 1970.
39. Wilbur W. Bolton, Jr. to Loy L. Sammet, June 3, 1970, NSF grant GB-19519, from the files of C. B. Huffaker.
40. Huffaker, personal interview; C. B. Huffaker, "Summary of a pest-management conference—a critique," in *Concepts of Pest Management*, R. L. Rabb and F. E. Guthrie, eds. (Raleigh: North Carolina State Univ. Press, 1970), pp. 227–242.
41. A. D. Pickett, W. L. Putnam, and E. J. LeRoux, "Progress in harmonizing biological and chemical control of orchard pests in eastern Canada," in *Proceedings Tenth International Congress of Entomology*, 1956, Vol. 3, (Ottawa? 1958), pp. 169–174.
42. Ray F. Smith, The origins of integrated control in California: An account of the contributions of Charles W. Woodworth, *Pan-Pac. Entomol.* 50 (1974): 426–440 (hereafter cited as Smith, Origins); C. W. Woodworth, The theory of the parasitic control of insect pests, *Science* 28 (1908): 227–230.
43. C. W. Woodworth, Spray and band treatment for the codling moth, *Cal. Agric. Exp. Stn. Rep.*, 1891, pp. 308–312.
44. Smith, Origins.
45. Department of Entomological Sciences, *Documentation for Departmental Review*, unpublished report, Univ. of Calif., Berkeley, Oct., 1975, p. 5; biographical data on Michelbacher from *American Men of Science* (New York: Jacques Cattell Press).
46. A. E. Michelbacher and Ray F. Smith, Some natural factors limiting the abundance of the alfalfa butterfly, *Hilgardia* 15 (1943): 369–397.
47. A. E. Michelbacher, The importance of ecology in insect control, *J. Econ. Entomol.* 38 (1945): 129–130.
48. A. E. Michelbacher and O. G. Bacon, Walnut insect and spider-mite control in northern California, *J. Econ. Entomol.* 45 (1952): 1020–1027. I thank K. S. Hagen for bringing this article to my attention.

49. [K. S. Hagen and R. F. Smith], First annual report of the entomologist for the Westside Alfalfa Pest Control Association, mimeo, Jan., 1947; K. S. Hagen, personal communication, June, 1979.
50. D. E. Bryan and R. F. Smith, First report of the entomologist for the Westley Pest Control Association, mimeo, 1948; R. E. Beer, Ray F. Smith, V. M. Stern, and R. van den Bosch, Second annual report of the entomologists for the Westside Alfalfa Pest Control Association, mimeo, 1948; E. Goldsworthy and Ray F. Smith, First annual report of the entomologist for the Tracy Pest Control Group, mimeo, 1948; V. M. Stern and Ray F. Smith, What has supervised control done for the Westside Alfalfa Pest Control Association? mimeo, 1948; L. A. Bascom and Ray F. Smith, Second annual report of the entomologist for the Westley Pest Control Association, mimeo, 1949.
51. Ray F. Smith and William W. Allen, Chemical control of the alfalfa caterpillar in California, *J. Econ. Entomol.* 42 (1949): 487–495.
52. Ray F. Smith to P. N. Annand, Nov. 25, 1947, RG7NA.
53. P. N. Annand, Preventive entomology, *J. Econ. Entomol.* 40 (1947): 461–468.
54. P. N. Annand to Ray F. Smith, Dec. 5, 1947, RG7NA.
55. K. S. Hagen, personal communication, June, 1979.
56. R. L. Doutt and Ray F. Smith, "The pesticide syndrome–diagnosis and suggested prophylaxis," in *Biological Control*, C. B. Huffaker, ed. (New York: Plenum Press, 1971), pp. 3–15.
57. Ray F. Smith, John E. Swift, and Jack Dibble, Rapid spread of alfalfa pest, *Calif. Agric.* 10 (Feb. 1956): 5, 15.
58. Vernon M. Stern and Robert van den Bosch, Field experiments on the effects of insecticides, *Hilgardia* 29 (1959): 103–130 (hereafter cited as Stern and van den Bosch, Field experiments).
59. *Ibid.;* R. van den Bosch, E. I. Schlinger, E. J. Dietrick, and I. M. Hall, The role of imported parasites in the biological control of the spotted alfalfa aphid in southern California, *J. Econ. Entomol.* 52 (1959): 142–154; R. van den Bosch, E. I. Schlinger, E. J. Dietrick, K. S. Hagen, and J. K. Holloway, The colonization and establishment of imported parasites of the spotted alfalfa aphid in California, *J. Econ. Entomol.* 52 (1959): 136–141; K. S. Hagen, G. A. Viktorov, Keizo Yasumatsu, and Michael F. Schuster, "Biological control of pests of range, forage, and grain crops," in *Theory and Practice of Biological Control*, C. B. Huffaker, ed. (New York: Academic Press, 1976), pp. 397–442.
60. Ray F. Smith and Kenneth S. Hagen, Impact of commercial insecticide treatments, *Hilgardia* 29 (1959): 131–154.
61. Stern and van den Bosch, Field experiments.
62. Vernon M. Stern, Ray F. Smith, Robert van den Bosch, and Kenneth S. Hagen, The integrated control concept, *Hilgardia* 29 (1959): 81–101. The companion papers are those noted in 58 and 60.
63. R. F. Smith and H. T. Reynolds, " Principles, definitions, and scope of integrated pest control," in *Proceedings of the FAO Symposium on Integrated Control* (Rome: Food and Agriculture Organization, 1966), pp. 11–17.
64. *Ibid.*, p. 15.
65. Ray F. Smith, Proposed intersociety consortium for plant protection, *Bull. Entomol. Soc. Am.* 22 (1976): 37.
66. Perry Lee Adkisson, personal interview, May 30–31, 1978. A review of pink bollworm problems in Texas can be found in Perry L. Adkisson and J. C. Gaines, Pink bollworm

control as related to the total cotton insect control program of central Texas, *Tex. Agric. Exp. Stn.* MP-444, July 1960, 8 pp.
67. Floyd Miner, Dwight Isely, 1887–1974, *J. Econ. Entomol.* 69 (1976): 298–299.
68. Charles Gatewood Lincoln, personal interview, June 6–7, 1978.
69. Dwight Isely and W. J. Baerg, The boll weevil problem in Arkansas, *Ark. Agric. Exp. Stn. Bull. 190*, Jan. 1924, 29 pp.
70. Dwight Isely, Control of the boll weevil and the cotton aphid in Arkansas, *Ark. Agric. Exp. Stn. Bull. 496*, June, 1950.
71. Charles Lincoln, W. P. Boyer, and Floyd D. Miner, The evolution of insect pest management in cotton and soybeans: Past experience, present status, and future outlook in Arkansas, *Environ. Entomol.* 4 (1975): 1–7.
72. Leo Dale Newsom, personal interview, June 1–2, 1978; Lincoln, personal interview.
73. Lincoln, personal interview.
74. C. B. Huffaker to R. L. Doutt, R. F. Smith, C. S. Koehler, W. W. Allen, K. S. Hagen, P. S. Messenger, R. van den Bosch, Y. Tanada, D. Jensen, L. A. Falcon, W. C. Batiste, L. E. Caltagirone, D. Price, D. Wood, R. W. Stark, and D. L. Dahlsten, May 27, 1970, files of C. B. Huffaker (hereafter cited as C. B. Huffaker to Doutt *et al.*).
75. President's Science Advisory Committee, *Cotton Insects* (Washington D.C.: Government Printing Office, 1965), 19 pp.
76. Adkisson, personal interview.
77. C. B. Huffaker to Doutt *et al.*
78. Newsom, personal interview; idem, An assessment of the potential for control of soybean insect pests with minimum use of conventional insecticides, unpublished paper delivered to the Organizing Work Conference for Proposal on The Principles of Pest Population Regulation and Control for Major Crop Ecosystems, Berkeley, Calif., Oct. 19–20, 1970, files of C. B. Huffaker.
79. P. L. Adkisson to Carl B. Huffaker, Oct. 20, 1971, files of C. B. Huffaker.
80. Carl B. Huffaker to Charles Cooper, Dec. 16, 1970, files of C. B. Huffaker.
81. August G. Manza to National Science Foundation, Nov. 1, 1971, files of C. B. Huffaker.
82. C. B. Huffaker and R. F. Smith, Application to National Science Foundation, The Principles, Strategies and Tactics of Pest Population Regulation and Control in Major Crop Ecosystems, Umbrella to the Proposal, unpublished grant proposal [Aug. 1971], pp. 33, 45–47, files of C. B. Huffaker. See also C. B. Huffaker and Ray F. Smith, "The IBP program on the strategies and tactics of pest management," in *Proceedings, Tall Timbers Conference on Ecological Animal Control by Habitat Management*, No. 4, Feb. 24–25, 1972, pp. 219–236; C. B. Huffaker, personal communication, May, 1980.
83. C. B. Huffaker and R. F. Smith, Management, coordination and special servicing of application, 9 pp.
84. Perry Adkisson delivered a complete copy of the proposal to Knipling on Sept. 23 in Lubbock, Texas. He reported Knipling to be unenthusiastic about funding for NSF before funding to USDA for pilot tests (P. L. Adkisson to Carl Huffaker, Oct. 5, 1971, files of C. B. Huffaker). Adkisson was probably referring to Knipling's interest in the Pilot Boll Weevil Eradication Experiment, which had begun in August and was underfunded. Knipling's work is covered in detail in Chapter 6.
85. U. S. Congress, Senate, Committee on Agriculture and Forestry, *Pest Control Research*, Hearings, 92nd Congress, 1st sess., 1971, pp. 13–14 (hereafter cited as U.S. Congress, Senate, *Pest Control Research*). It is likely the agreement was forged in anticipation of Huffaker's proposal.

86. Environmental Protection Agency, Cancellation of registration under the Federal Insecticide, Fungicide, and Rodenticide Act of products containing DDT, PR71-1, Jan. 15, 1971; copy attached to Edmund M. Sweeney, Consolidated DDT Hearing (Washington, D.C.: EPA, 1972), mimeo, 439 F 2d 584 (1971) (hereafter cited as Sweeney, Consolidated DDT hearing). Cancellations were also made of products containing TDE (*Ibid.*, PR71-3 and PR71-5).
87. DDT Advisory Committee, *Report* (Washington, D.C.: EPA, Sept. 9, 1971), 58 pp. The *Report* argued that "rapid and continuous decrease in the use of DDT" would accomplish the same purpose as "immediate suspension" (p. 43). The latter was the EPA's legal tool for immediately prohibiting sales of DDT in the market place. Even though the committee was clearly in favor of reducing all significant additions of DDT to the environment, they shied from explicitly recommending "immediate suspension." Their reasons for avoiding the legal term are not clear, but their reluctance to use it may have contributed to the EPA's decision not to suspend DDT in the fall of 1971.
88. Sweeney, Consolidated DDT hearing.
89. U. S. Congress, House, Committee on Agriculture, *Federal Pesticide Control Act of 1971*, Hearings, 92nd Congress, 1st sess., 1971 pp. 3–8, statement of John Quarles, Environmental Protection Agency.
90. Carl B. Huffaker to Drs. Adkisson, Armbrust, Caltagirone, DeBach, Newsom, Stark, Smith, May 17, 1971, with attachment [Gaylord Nelson], S. 1794, To provide a viable alternative to the Nation's rigid reliance on pesticides, 8 pp., files of C. B. Huffaker.
91. *Ibid.*
92. Lincoln, personal interview.
93. U. S. Congress, Senate, *Pest Control Research*, pp. 1–174.
94. James R. Brazzel, personal interview, May 26–27, 1978; J. R. Brazzel to D. R. Shepherd, July 21, 1970; and Ned D. Bayley, Parathion Safety Program, Pesticide Use Management, and Related Matters, unpublished paper, Nov. 30, 1970, files of J. R. Brazzel.
95. Carl B. Huffaker to Ned Bayley, Sept. 14, 1971; C. B. Huffaker to Steering Committee, IBP/NSF Proposals, Oct. 14, 1971; files of C. B. Huffaker; Huffaker, personal interview.
96. H. T. Reynolds to Carl B. Huffaker, Oct. 22, 1971; P. L. Adkisson to Carl B. Huffaker, Oct. 20, 1971; files of C. B. Huffaker.
97. H. T. Reynolds to C. B. Huffaker, Oct. 22, 1971; Robert L. Rabb to C. B. Huffaker, Oct. 21, 1971; and T. W. Fisher to C. B. Huffaker, Nov. 9, 1971; files of C. B. Huffaker.
98. C. B. Huffaker to Steering Committee, IBP/NSF Proposals, Oct. 14, 1971, files of C. B. Huffaker.
99. Huffaker, personal interview.
100. Donald B. Rice to William D. McElroy, Dec. 30, 1971 and Donald B. Rice to Earl L. Butz, Dec. 30, 1971, both in files of J. T. Callahan, NSF. Quote is from latter letter.
101. Huffaker, personal communication, July, 1979.
102. CEQ, Scientific review, p. 48.

CHAPTER 4

Strategies II

Total Population Management

AN ALTERNATIVE RESEARCH STRATEGY

The Huffaker Project was only one center of vibrant activity as entomologists attempted to escape from the dilemmas posed by chemicals. A second strategy, total population management (TPM),* developed alongside integrated pest management (IPM). Just as IPM was manifestated in a large-scale research project, so too did TPM become a visible political entity in a multimillion dollar, interstate experiment: the Pilot Boll Weevil Eradication Experiment (PBWEE), 1971–1973. Unfortunately for the layman and policy maker, proponents of both strategies frequently used the term *intergrated* in referring to their respective efforts. Thus, confusion developed in the 1970s as the genuine distinctions between the two paradigms were lost in a flood of rhetoric about "integrated control." Ultimate goals provide the key to unraveling the differences: TPM aggressively entertained the notion of the eradication of some, but not all, major pest species from large geographic areas, while IPM expressly rejected such ideas and argued eradication should be entertained only in special cases when the target insect was distributed over limited areas of land.

TPM, like IPM, was not a control technique *per se* but a concept of how to organize research and practice involving different control tech-

* My use of the phrase *total population management* is derived from language used by E. F. Knipling. Designation of TPM as a formal construct parallel to IPM, however, is my responsibility.

niques. Two major, formerly independent research lines provided the basis for the articulation of TPM: insecticidal control and the sterile male technique. Eradication as the proper goal toward which entomologists should work in some cases flowed from the fact that the first two successful demonstrations of the sterile male technique against screwworm flies totally eliminated its target from an island in the Caribbean and then from the state of Florida. Later versions of the paradigm sought to encompass all conceivable techniques into a unified package for research and practice. Especially important were host plant resistance, traps baited with pheromones and other attractants, and augmentative biological control. As in IPM, TPM sought to "integrate" the different techniques so as to obtain the most efficient use of each.

Many people, entomologists and otherwise, were involved in transforming TPM from ideas on paper into action programs involving laboratories, bench scientists, field workers, and farmers. One, however, stands out as preeminent in the creation of TPM—Edward Fred Knipling, who worked with the USDA from 1931 until and beyond his retirement in 1973. Knipling was both the chief theoretician of TPM and the administrative head of efforts to transform it from theory to practice. He was director of entomological research in the USDA from 1953 until 1970; during this time he was the key figure in the creation of PBWEE. It would be impossible to understand the origins, growth, and strength of either TPM or PBWEE without the conscious realization that both scientific and administrative leadership were combined in one person. We turn first to a brief description of Knipling's career and then to the development of TPM and PBWEE.

EDWARD FRED KNIPLING[1]

Knipling was born in Port Lavaca, Texas, in 1909. His father had immigrated to the U.S. from Germany in the late 1800s, and his mother was born in the U.S. of German parents. He was the ninth of ten children who grew up on their parents' cotton and livestock farm along the Texas gulf coast. He received as a youngster his first introduction to two insects that were to occupy major portions of his thoughts in later years: the screwworm fly [*Cochliomyia hominovorax* (Coquerel)] and the boll weevil (*Anthonomus grandis* Boheman). Screwworm flies attacked livestock, and boll weevils were the bane of cotton farmers from the Southeast to Texas. Both were constant companions on the Knipling farm, and young Knipling, like many other farm children, put in many an hour doctoring wormy animals and picking up fallen cotton "squares" (buds).

Knipling was not a collector of insects as a boy, but he liked to watch their behavior during his youth in rural Texas. His initial schooling was difficult, partly because he had to become Americanized from his German-speaking homelife, and partly because competition was keen for rural children when they entered the town school in Port Lavaca. He persevered, however, and ultimately completed his bachelor's degree in entomology at Texas A & M University in 1930. He was the only boy in his family to pursue a higher education, and he continued it through his master's (1932) and doctoral degrees (1947) at Iowa State University. As with most students, his future profession was in no way foreordained. He knew he didn't want to pursue farming as a career; hence, he went to college. He enjoyed genetics as an undergraduate, but he chose entomology because of more potential for employment. Pragmatic considerations in Knipling's case produced a happy match between personal interests and opportunities for work.

Knipling had only one employer during his entire career: the USDA. He first worked in 1930 as a temporary field assistant for the Bureau of Entomology, but after receiving his master's degree he entered the full-time civil service as a junior entomologist. From that point on, his career can best be described as "straight up" in the hierarchy of the Bureau of Entomology and Plant Quarantine. He worked first in Texas on a population survey of screwworms in an effort to see if their population could be decreased by trapping adult flies.

Ironically, this first assignment contained an element of significant historical accident. While at Iowa State working on his master's degree, Knipling became acquainted with Ernest William Laake, a USDA entomologist on leave to pursue his Ph.D. Knipling's first permanent assignment was to have been on stored-products insects in California; but unknown to him at the time, Laake asked his superior, Fred Corry Bishopp, to assign Knipling to Laake's staff in Texas for work on screwworms. Knipling was unaware of the maneuvering behind the scenes, but he was pleased to return to Texas and work on livestock pests. If Laake had not intervened, Knipling's career might have taken a decidedly different course. Screwworm flies were well-suited to suppression with sterile males, as will be mentioned shortly. Had Knipling gone to work on stored-products insects, he might never have pursued one of his major scientific triumphs.

Knipling held a number of different posts over the next eleven years. His primary work at all of them was with flies and mosquitoes affecting man and animals. Knipling also began to advance within the Bureau. Bishopp offered him the job of laboratory leader in Portland, Oregon, for work on mosquitoes; in 1942 Bishopp and Emory C. Cushing asked

Knipling to transfer to the Orlando, Florida, laboratory for work on the control of insects of military importance. In Chapter 1, we touched upon the work of this station, where, under Knipling's direction, DDT was adapted for use by the American and allied armed forces. Knipling recalls the exhilaration felt by him and his many colleagues at DDT's success as one of the highest points of his career. His enthusiasms resulted from both the scientific and political dimensions of DDT's contributions to winning the war. We will return to this experience shortly.

Knipling continued his advancement within the USDA in the postwar years. He took a short leave of absence to complete work for his Ph.D. at Iowa State and then, at Bishopp's request, went to Washington in 1946 to head the Division of Insects Affecting Man and Animals (DIAMA). Knipling's work after the war continued to be strongly oriented toward the development of new uses of synthetic insecticides, and he also established a program within DIAMA on their toxicology to livestock. When resistance began to emerge as a serious problem, Knipling was keenly interested in following its development and understanding its implications for future control practices (see Chapter 2). His extensive experience with both the promise and problems of insecticides was possibly a factor leading Avery S. Hoyt, chief of the Bureau, to offer Knipling the position of assistant chief in charge of research when Bishopp retired in 1953.[2] Knipling by that time had also achieved great professional prestige, a fact demonstrated by his election to the presidency of the American Association of Economic Entomologists for 1952.

Research in the USDA was substantially reorganized shortly after Knipling became assistant chief. The Bureau was disbanded and partly replaced by the Entomology Research Branch (ERB) within the newly created Agricultural Research Service (ARS). Knipling became chief of the ERB, and his job continued much as it had been. He lost research on forest and stored-products insects, but more important was the separation of regulatory entomology (quarantine administration, large-scale control programs) from research. He was now freed from immediate competition for funds with regulatory personnel.

One of Knipling's first decisions after reorganization was to upgrade and expand the research facilities of his new ERB. He was successful in adding a host of new laboratories over the next 15 years. In 1957, the ERB was elevated in status to become the Entomology Research Division within ARS. Knipling continued as its director until 1970 when he asked to be relieved of administrative duties so as to devote more time to writing. He formally retired in 1973, but continued as a collaborator on special projects.

Knipling's administrative contributions to entomology were clearly demonstrated by his important leadership positions between 1942 and 1970, a span of 28 years during which his profession was transformed. Had he been simply an administrator, his impact might not have been so great. Knipling, however, was also intimately involved scientifically in two major episodes of the transformation.

USHERING IN THE NEW INSECTICIDES

Chapter 1 recounted how the USDA's Orlando, Florida, facility was the major center for war-related entomological research and served as the focal point for work on DDT. Clearly this work was the beginning of the meteoric rise to fame of DDT and other new insecticides. Knipling participated heavily in these events as he authored or coauthored 27 scientific papers from 1944 to 1946. All of them were based primarily on the work done at Orlando and clearly signaled a new emphasis in Knipling's personal research. He had published 29 papers between 1934 and 1943, many of which dealt with taxonomic questions, reports of new distributions of recognized pests, and behavioral–ecological observations; only 8 of the 29 papers dealt with chemical control.[3] His work during the war thus nearly doubled his research bibliography and 100% of it was devoted to chemical control methods.

Exigencies of war were unquestionably the primary reason for Knipling's switch to a heavy emphasis on chemical control. Only chemicals, especially after DDT, offered the rapidity of action in control procedures needed for military operations. Dramatic success from the use of DDT was clearly influential in maintaining Knipling's interest in the new chemicals in the postwar years. He continued to write prolifically, and the majority of the 36 articles he published between 1947 and 1953 were focused on the use of insecticides. We noted in Chapter 3 that early, dramatic successes influenced the subsequent interests of Carl Huffaker and Ray Smith. Knipling, too, had the same sort of experience. He and his colleagues were dramatically successful in devising control methods for lice, mosquitoes, bedbugs, chiggers, and other vermin that for centuries had vexed humans. For the first time, they could be easily controlled with inexpensive and simple chemicals.

Patterns in which early successes shape subsequent interests can be found in many fields of endeavor, scientific and otherwise. What is most important to note in Knipling's case are the specifics of his research situation compared to those of Huffaker and Smith for example. Contrasts between the three scientists shed considerable light on their subsequent attitudes toward the chemicals. Knipling became familiar with the new insecticides as they provided for the first time in history a power to control insects attacking the human person; controlling diseases like malaria and typhus with cheap chemicals had a powerful appeal then and even today despite our increased knowledge about resistance and possible hazards to wildlife and humans. Huffaker shared some of this excitement through his work with DDT in malarial control, but his memorable first successes lay more in biological control: insecticides were irrelevant to biological control in Klamath weed; after the introduction of two effective parasites, olive scale was a pest only when chemicals were used thoughtlessly; and cyclamen mite could be controlled biologically, but chemicals had more appeal to farmers. Smith became familiar with the chemicals in a context similar to Huffaker's: alfalfa caterpillar was frequently controlled by a native parasite and the problem was to avoid killing the natural enemies with insecticides; spotted alfalfa aphid could not be reliably controlled with insecticides alone but only with integrated biological and chemical control.

Knipling, given his experience during the war years, saw chemicals as essentially useful and, in his particular case, the *only* tools available. He quickly recognized the problems of resistance, resurgence, and hazards, but he continued his basic enthusiasm for chemicals. Huffaker and Smith were not opposed to the use of chemicals, but their perceptions of risks and benefits led them to consider the materials as tools of the last resort, to be used only if all else fails. In all three cases, the attitude toward the new chemicals reflected the experience each reseacher had early in his own career.

Despite his thoughtful enthusiasm for the synthetic insecticides, Knipling continued to believe in the late 1940s that in some cases the chemicals were at best mere palliatives. They had to be used again and again, thus constraining human behavior to the whims of pest population dynamics. In addition, some pests such as screwworm flies were not amenable to attack with insecticides. He returned, therefore, in the late 1940s to a research idea that he had originated in conversations with Raymond C. Bushland in the screwworm laboratory in Texas before the war.

Knipling's notion was that if screwworm flies could be raised in large numbers in the lab, sterilized, and released, they would mate with native females and leave them incapable of producing fertile eggs. Screwworm populations would therefore drop and the insect would no longer be a pest. War interrupted Knipling's work on the idea, but he and Bushland discussed it from time to time in Orlando. Once in Washington, he began again to think about it more concertedly. That he brought such an outlandishly novel idea to successful development was sufficient to mark him as one of the primary contributors to entomology in the postwar years. We turn first to the development of the sterile male technique and then to its impact on his subsequent articulation of TPM and PBWEE.

STERILE MALES: A FRUITFUL INNOVATION

It is essential to understand the biology and early "control" measures for the screwworm fly in order to appreciate the novelty and complexity of the sterile male technique. Screwworm flies are native to the tropical Western Hemisphere. It is uncertain how long the species has been in the U.S., but reports dating from 1825 suggest that it was present since at least the early nineteenth century. The insect may have been in the region now encompassed by the state of Texas since the seventeenth century.[4] From the earliest reports in the nineteenth century up to 1933, screwworms were a pest primarily in the southwestern U.S., particularly Texas. During the late nineteenth century and early twentieth, the insect was known as a pest in the gulf coast states, but its appearance there was not chronic. The insect was introduced into Georgia and Florida as a permanent resident during 1933–1934.[5]

Damage from this insect is aesthetically distasteful (Fig. 7). An adult female lays 200–400 eggs near a wound of a warm-blooded animal. The eggs hatch within 12 hours, and the maggots begin to feed upon the damaged tissues. Larvae complete their feeding in about five days and drop from the animal to the soil where they burrow into the ground, pupate, and emerge as adult flies in about two weeks. The life cycle (Fig. 8) of the insect thus requires as little as 20 days, but under adverse conditions it may take as long as two and one-half months.[6]

Before the advent of the sterile male technique, the fly overwintered only in the southernmost parts of Texas and Florida. During the period from April to November each year, flies from Florida would invade Georgia and Alabama and sometimes would reach as far north as the Carolinas. Flies from Texas would travel into Oklahoma, Kansas, Missouri, and sometimes further north. Shipments of infested cattle to northern feedlots also caused the fly to appear during summer months as far north as Iowa, the Dakotas, and even Canada.[7] Cold weather each fall, however, eliminated the fly in all but the southernmost areas of the U.S.

Infested animals that did not receive treatment frequently died. An attack by one female fly was not always lethal, but an infested wound

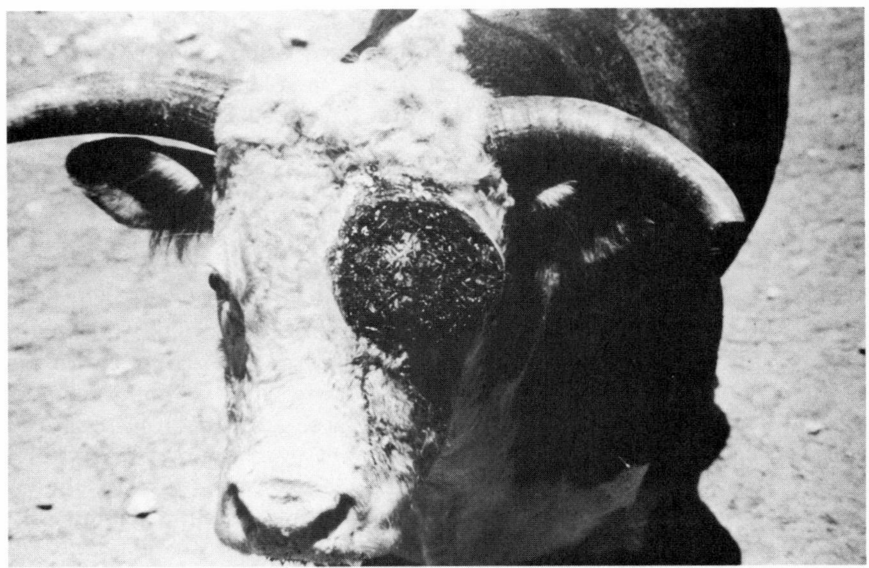

FIGURE 7. Hereford with infestation of screwworm fly larvae. [Source: USDA/APHIS.]

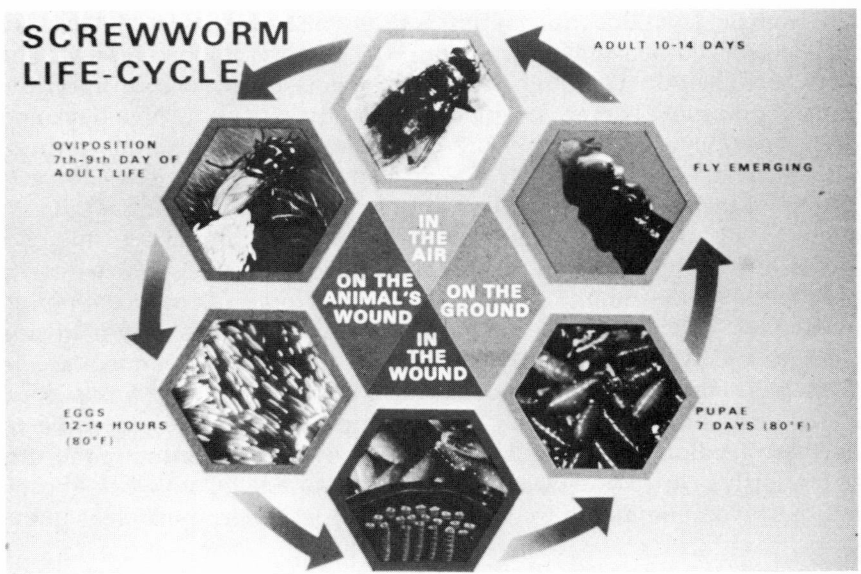

FIGURE 8. Life cycle of screwworm fly. [Source: USDA/APHIS.]

was more attractive to other females than was a noninfested wound.[8] Thus once an animal became infested with maggots it was likely to receive additional, fatal attacks. Treated infestations, on the other hand, were generally not lethal. Affected animals usually could be identified and treated while the wound was healing.

Good management practices that protected livestock from wounds lowered the predisposition to attack by screwworms and thus served to control the insect. Such management practices were expensive in skilled manpower and materials. A rancher therefore encountered economic losses from the screwworm: either he suffered the loss of untreated animals or he incurred the expense and trouble of preventing and curing infestations. In the Texas cattle country and in the Southeast after 1933, screwworms were regarded as the primary insect pest of livestock. Estimates of losses varied but they ranged in the tens of millions of dollars per year.[9]

The Bureau of Entomology began its first concerted effort against the screwworm in 1912 from headquarters at Dallas, Texas. A second laboratory was established in Uvalde, Texas, in 1916.[10] In 1917 Bishopp published the first USDA recommendations for control of the insect.[11] Bishopp mistakenly believed that screwworms bred primarily in the carcasses of dead animals and only occasionally in living flesh. Therefore he recommended that all dead animals be burned within a few days of their death. Bishopp also recommended that ranchers avoid calving, branding, castrating, and dehorning during the warm months where screwworm flies were active. If infestations developed despite precautions, they could be treated with chloroform, carbolic acid, pine tar, or tannic acid.[12] During the 1920s, USDA entomologists and chemists identified benzol and pine tar oil as the most efficient chemicals to use. Bishopp revised his recommendations accordingly in 1926.[13]

Livestock growers of the Southeast were unprepared for the screwworm fly when it was introduced in 1933, and one of the most destructive outbreaks ever recorded came in 1934. Bureau entomologists launched an educational program on screwworm control at the request of livestock growers, and Congress appropriated $1.1 million during fiscal years 1936–1938 to control the invading insect. The educational program was successful and estimated total dollar losses dropped from $3 million in 1934 to about $23,000 in 1935.[14] Congress also established in 1934 a new research laboratory at Valdosta, Georgia, with five entomologists and a budget of about $100,000 per year, a large operation at the time. Knipling was assistant director of the facility.[15]

The idea of controlling screwworm flies with the sterile male technique originated with Knipling sometime in 1937 after he returned to

Texas. The two major factors he determined to be of importance were (1) that the insect is comparatively rare in nature, and (2) that it is possible to raise large numbers of them in the laboratory.[16] By a "creative leap of the imagination,"[17] Knipling reasoned that it might be possible to find something that would be harmless to laboratory-related flies yet lethal to the insects once released in nature. For example, something might sterilize the flies. Once that something was found, it would be possible to rear large numbers of affected flies in the laboratory and then release them into nature where they would in turn mate with and render sterile the comparatively few wild flies.

Implementation of the sterile male technique, however, required more than simply the germ of an idea in Knipling's head. A number of specific scientific puzzles had to be solved before the idea could be translated into a usable technology. A primary piece of knowledge that was absolutely essential was the precise identification of the insect. Bureau entomologist Emory C. Cushing, during graduate work in 1933 at the School of Tropical Medicine of the University of Liverpool, distinguished between two closely related species now known as *Cochliomyia hominovorax* and *Cochliomyia macellaria*.[18] Before Cushing's work, it was assumed that all maggots infesting wounds were the relatively abundant *C. macellaria*. Once the distinction between the two species was made, it was necessary to reinvestigate each to determine its biology. *C. hominovorax* was identified as a parasite capable of living only on live animals and thus was the true screwworm; *C. macellaria* prefers to feed on carcasses only and was thus not a major threat to livestock.[19] The sterile male technique could never have been perfected had not the confusion of the two species been removed.

A second major advance was made in the mid-1930s when Roy Melvin and Raymond C. Bushland developed a method of obtaining screwworms in the laboratory.[20] Previous to 1936, the only method of obtaining screwworms was collection from nature or raising them on deliberately wounded animals, usually goats. The latter process was both expensive and offensive to research workers. An artificial medium allowed the mass rearing of insects, an absolute necessity to the sterile male technique.

Arthur W. Linquist, a Bureau entomologist, made a third major advance when he estimated from screwworm population surveys that the insect was rare in nature.[21] Its rarity meant that raising enough flies artificially to "attack" the wild population was feasible.

Knipling incorporated the knowledge of artificial rearing and relative scarcity as he began to think quantitatively about the sizes and yearly changes of screwworm populations in nature. Based on screwworm surveys taken in the southeast during the mid-1930s, he estimated that the flies overwintering in Florida produced no more than 500,000 flies per week. Knipling also began to develop mathematical models of the screwworm population and then to estimate the fate of the population if it could be stopped from reproducing.[22] Later experiments for testing the sterile male technique were based on Knipling's theoretical calculations, and the mathematical models were probably persuasive to skeptics of the technique's potential.

The final technical element crucial to the creation of the sterile male technique was not added until the 1950s: a practical way to sterilize the flies. Because no effective chemical sterilants were found, Knipling began thinking about ways of damaging the genetic material of the screwworm fly. Lindquist provided the decisive clue when he sent him a reference to Herman J. Mueller's work in the January, 1950, issue of *American Scientist* on the sterilizing effect of X-rays on *Drosophila,* the common fruitfly. Knipling immediately wrote Mueller, outlined the biology of the screwworm fly, and inquired whether Mueller thought there was any hope of controlling the insect through the release of flies sterilized by radiation. Mueller replied that there was reason to be optimistic about such an idea provided that the sterilized males were able to compete for females adequately with the wild males.[23]

With this encouragement, Knipling in 1950 persuaded Bishopp and Sievert A. Rohwer, both assistant chiefs of the Bureau, that research on the sterilizing potential of radiation was justified.[24] Bishopp and Knipling's funding requests to the Atomic Energy Commission were rejected, but Knipling maintained his enthusiasm for the idea. He talked to his colleague Raymond Bushland about a possible set of experiments on sterilizing flies with X-rays, and Bushland was "raring to go."[25] The latter, working at the Bureau's laboratory in Kerrville, Texas, arranged to irradiate the flies at the Brooke Medical Center, Fort Sam Houston, in San Antonio. He soon had success: the screwworm male could be irradiated, sterilized, mated competitively with normal females, and the resulting egg masses were not fertile.[26] Subsequent work, conducted in spite of budgeting problems, demonstrated that gamma rays from cobalt-60 sources were adequate and cheaper for sterilizing.[27]

Laboratory experiments were encouraging but it was still necessary to test the procedure in the field. In late 1951 and early 1952, Bushland released sterilized flies on Sanibel, an island off the coast of Florida, and demonstrated that natural populations of the screwworm could be reduced by the release of sterilized flies. Sanibel was within flight range of flies from mainland Florida, however, so that it was not possible to eradicate the insect on the island.[28]

Shortly after the experiment on Sanibel, Knipling received a routine letter from B. A. Bitter, veterinarian on the island of Curaçao of the Netherlands Antilles, who wanted information on the screwworm, a particularly damaging pest in that area of the Caribbean. Knipling had to look up the location of Curaçao in an atlas, but when he saw that it was a small island, about 170 square miles, isolated from other locations infested with screwworms, he realized that Curaçao might be the place to plan a definitive experiment on whether the sterile male technique could control screwworms in an area.[29]

Knipling responded cautiously to Bitter and informed him of the encouraging results they had just had with a new method of screwworm control. He asked if Bitter might be interested in attempting a similar experiment on Curaçao, and Bitter said he was interested. Knipling and Bishopp visited the agricultural attaché of the Netherlands Embassy in Washington to make arrangements for a more detailed investigation of the suitability of Curaçao as a testing ground for the sterile male technique.[30]

A. H. Baumhover was sent by Knipling to Curaçao in June 1953 to plan for the experiment. On the basis of Baumhover's report, final plans for the operation were developed by Knipling, Lindquist, and Bushland.[31] Bushland, Baumhover, and Weston D. New arrived in Curaçao in early March 1954, and sterile flies were first released on March 26.[32] Releases continued twice weekly until January 6, 1955, except for one four-week period. The planned release rate was 100 flies per square mile until July and August when it was increased to 400 per square mile. The last fertile eggs were found in November.[33] Releases on sterile males had eradicated screwworms from Curaçao!

In retrospect, perhaps the most astonishing fact about the sterile male technique is that it worked at all. It was expensive and complex as a research operation. Mass rearing of sterile flies required a skilled, dedicated crew, thousands of pounds of hamburger (Fig. 9), and large buildings; sterilization necessitated precision radiation equipment used exactly at the right time in the fly's life cycle; and release in the proper area at the correct time required aircraft, pilots, and other staff (Figs. 10 and 11). All were essential ingredients without which the technique would fail. Results speak for themselves, however, and entomology was permanently changed. Subsequent successes of the sterile male technique against screwworm flies included eradication of the insect from Florida and the southeast in 1958–1959 and suppression of it over the vast grazing lands of Texas starting in 1962. Currently, the USDA and the government of Mexico are engaged in an attempt to eradicate the insect in all of Mexico north of the Isthmus of Tehuantepec[34] (Fig. 12).

FIGURE 9. Preparation of growth medium for rearing sterile screwworm flies. [Source: USDA/APHIS.]

FIGURE 10. Sterile screwworm flies ready for aerial release. [Source: USDA/APHIS.]

FIGURE 11. Aerial release of sterilized screwworm flies. Note box at rear of aircraft that was just jettisoned. [Source: USDA/APHIS.]

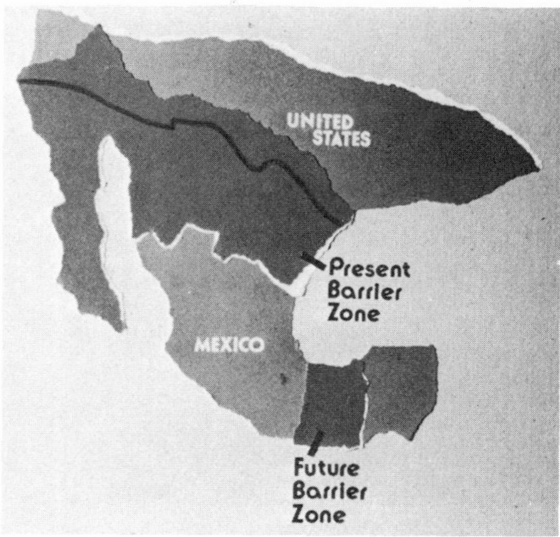

FIGURE 12. Geographic area in joint U.S.–Mexico program to eradicate the screwworm fly. [Source: USDA/APHIS.]

CHANGING RESEARCH DIRECTIONS

A number of items acted in consort to force shifts in USDA research directions between 1953 and 1958. First, Knipling became chief of research in 1953. He brought enthusiasm for the new insecticides qualified by his recognition that they were weak, especially in terms of resistance. After 1955, he saw tremendous possibilities for changing insect control programs through the use of sterile males, if the technique could be adapted for use with other species. Second, Congress passed the Miller Amendment to the Federal Food, Drug, and Cosmetic Act in 1954, which allowed the establishment of limits on the amount of insecticide residues on farm produce whenever possible. Third, boll weevils became resistant to the chlorinated hydrocarbon insecticides in the mid-South in 1954–1955. For the first time, a major agricultural industry was under severe pressure from the "Achilles Heel" of insecticidal techniques.

Knipling saw both the need and the possibility for redirecting the science of entomology. As head of the largest entomological research establishment in the world, he was in a position to exercise both scientific and administrative leadership. Precisely where to lead the troops of research entomologists was the major question.

Knipling met with his research team leaders in August 1954 to consider what new or expanded lines of investigations they should develop. Without setting priorities, the ERB as a whole concluded that classical biological control, systemic insecticides, insect vectors of plant disease, and crop resistance to insects were four lines of research that should be expanded.[35] At this time, it will be recalled, resistance of boll weevils to insecticides had not been confirmed and the sterile male experiments in Curaçao were still in progress. Thus these August 1954 judgments provide some insight into the thinking within ERB immediately before two crucial developments had occurred. Conspicuously absent from the list compared to later recommendations were research on insecticide resistance and the sterile male technique. Research on both was underway, but neither appeared as a priority item for expansion at the time. General advisory committees composed of growers and scientists agreed the following spring with the internal thinking of ERB.[36]

The boll weevil (Fig. 13) had been a persistent, serious pest for over 50 years, and insecticide-resistant varieties led within two years to a substantial shift in ERB's outlook. This shift became evident when the ERB advisory committees shifted investigations on "physiology, toxicology, and resistance" from level three to level one in priority.[37] Ironically, shifting cotton insect research into new avenues to avoid resistance problems was plagued with difficulties, the source of which illustrates some of the complexities of setting research priorities.

FIGURE 13. Boll weevil feeding on cotton. [Source: USDA/APHIS.]

Ky Pepper Ewing was head of research on cotton insects under Knipling. In contrast to Knipling, he resisted the notion that boll weevils had become resistant to chlorinated hydrocarbon insecticides. He tried to persuade Dale Newsom not to release LSU's data gathered in 1954–1955 until more information was available. Ewing was aware that resistance had been shown in other insects, but he feared that release of Clower and Rousell's data would damage both the insecticide and cotton-growing industries. Newsom recalls that Ewing was reluctant to accept the idea of genetic heterogeneity within boll weevil populations and may not have accepted the theory of organic evolution.[38] Ewing was an evangelical Methodist,[39] and perhaps he held fundamentalist beliefs contrary to evolution. Regardless of the cause, Ewing did not easily accept the conclusion that boll weevils had evolved resistance.

Another influential voice in agreement with Ewing was Knipling's former boss and mentor, Bishopp, who after retirement took on a special assignment to examine the boll weevil situation; he argued that evidence was not sufficient to rule out poor application and bad weather as the cause of failure in insecticidal control. He was adamant " . . . that we must not lose faith in our proven insecticides and other insect control practices." Bishopp's thesis, moreover, was plausible because 1955 had a mild winter followed by an extremely wet summer in Louisiana and Mississippi.[40] Such conditions were conducive to high boll weevil populations and poor prospects for chemical control even if resistance had not developed. Thus Ewing's and Bishopp's skepticism about resistance was based on reasonable suppositions and could not be lightly dismissed.

Knipling was therefore faced with a difficult position in reorienting research in the very area where the resistance problem threatened to reach crisis proportions. In correspondence within the USDA, he was convinced by August 1955 that boll weevil resistance was real: "To me, the data show rather conclusively that resistance had developed."[41] Yet to the Commissioner of Agriculture and Immigration of Louisiana, he hedged less than one month later. He acknowledged the reports of difficulties in controlling boll weevils, but he was reluctant to accept resistance as the sole cause for failure without further evidence.[42] Given Knipling's earlier concerns about resistance, it appears that for a short time he modified his own views to accommodate those of Ewing and Bishopp, perhaps to maintain peace within his own research division.

Disagreements among the professional entomologists notwithstanding, grower advisory committees to the USDA began to demonstrate their own concern with boll weevil resistance in 1956 when they moved research on the problem from 16th out of 22 priority topics established in 1955 to 5th out of 28.[43] In subsequent years, further research removed all doubts about the reality of resistant boll weevils[44]; and in 1957 and 1958, research on them remained a high order of priority within ERB and among growers.[45] Moreover, Ewing retired in 1957, and Bishopp's special assignment ended. Entomologists more convinced of the seriousness of resistance moved into decision-making positions within USDA.

Resistance as a general phenomenon plus the never-ending need to apply insecticides had led Knipling some years earlier to seek more fundamental means of attacking pests. Success of the sterile male technique against screwworm flies on Curaçao in early 1955 opened a new line of research in entomology, and Knipling quickly began thinking about other applications. He suggested to Ewing that the Cotton Insects Division consider starting studies on its applicability for eradication of the pink bollworm [*Pectinophora gossypiella* (Saund.)], and he also began theoretical work on whether the technique might be applicable to the codling moth [*Laspeyresia pomonella* (L.)].[46] A timely intervention from hard-pressed cotton growers was the trigger for action in which Knipling's new ideas for revamping entomological research moved from theory to research and field experimentation.

Robert R. Coker, president of Coker's Pedigreed Seed Co. of Hartville, South Carolina, and J. F. McLaurin, another cotton producer from South Carolina, introduced a resolution at the 1958 annual convention of the National Cotton Council (NCC) declaring the boll weevil to be the number one enemy of cotton production. Its passage solidified the entire cotton industry, from growers to textile manufacturers, behind a movement to alleviate damage from this insect.[47] Coker then testified in March, before Jaime L. Whitten's (D., Mass.) House Subcommittee on Agricultural Appropriations, that compared with the damage done by boll weevils, little federal research was directed toward reducing the problem. Coker had no specific suggestions for research projects, and Whitten's comments suggested that he (Whitten) may have first regarded Coker's request as simply an attempted raid on the treasury. Nevertheless, the House provided the USDA $25,000 for a study on needed research for the boll weevil.[48]

Knipling as director of the ERD chaired the effort, entitled the Working Group on Boll Weevil Research Programs. They concluded in their report of December 30, 1958, that the future of conventional chemical control for boll weevils was seriously threatened with possibly disasterous results to the cotton industry. In keeping with Knipling's continuing priority to raise the research capability of ERD, the Working Group recommended the establishment of a new, interdisciplinary laboratory near Mississippi State University.[49] Congress appropriated $1.1 million for its construction, and the Boll Weevil Research Laboratory (BWRL) was dedicated in 1962.[50] A brand new, sophisticated laboratory plus Knipling's selection of an eager young entomologist, Theodore B. Davich, as its director signaled a new era in the USDA's research on boll weevils.

Davich, born in 1923, grew up in a coal-mining town of West Virginia. Upon his release from the armed forces after World War II, he enrolled at Ohio State University with the notion of learning enough horticulture to go into greenhouse agriculture. Davich's plans changed rather suddenly as Dwight Moore DeLong, a long-time Ohio State professor, captured his imagination with the lore of entomology. From then on, he was dedicated to the study of insects. Davich obtained his graduate training at Wisconsin and immediately accepted a position at Virginia Polytechnic Institute's experiment station in Holland, Virginia, in 1953. At the time, he considered research in the federal entomological laboratories to be moribund, but he quickly changed his mind a few years later. Davich attended the annual meeting of the Entomological Society of America in Houston in December 1954.[51] What usually would have been a perfunctory ritual for a professional entomologist turned instead into a transformation of his research interests, career development pattern, and ultimately of his employer.

Bushland gave the first oral presentation of the Curaçao experiment at the Houston meetings. The standing-room-only crowd was nearly tumultuous in its electric excitement on hearing of the dramatic success of the sterile male technique. Bushland's successor on the program even offered to relinquish his own time so that questions could continue. Davich, too, was transfixed by the experience, and he occupied his time driving back to Virginia thinking how he might join the federal research team that had just demonstrated such foresight, creativity, and genius. He duly filed his civil service applications, and in 1956 joined the USDA's Cotton Insects Research Laboratory at College Station, Texas.[52] The fact that Davich clearly shared Knipling's vision for the future directions of entomological research was undoubtedly fundamental in Knipling's recommendation in 1960 that Davich become director of the BWRL. It was here that Davich and his staff worked closely with Knipling to produce basic scientific knowledge on boll weevil biology and important components of the PBWEE.

Knipling made clear at the Laboratory's dedication that eradication, if feasible, was the goal:

> Congress expects more than minor improvements. . . . Therefore, the objective of the research should be to find ways of reducing losses to a minimum

> or to eliminate the problem entirely. For my part, I feel that we should gear our thinking and direct our research efforts to the development of practical ways of eradicating the insect.[53]

SCIENTIFIC PRELUDE TO THE PILOT BOLL WEEVIL ERADICATION EXPERIMENT

Scientific developments in three areas provided the basis for attempting an eradication experiment: development of the reproduction–diapause (r-d) control method, adaptation of the sterile male technique for boll weevils, and a refined theory for designing attacks on total populations leading to eradication.

Control by r-d was an unusual and highly effective method for applying ordinary insecticides. For most crops, including cotton, the usual timing of insecticide applications was during the growing season when the insect was damaging the developing plant. Control by r-d, in contrast, timed the insecticide application so that it killed those weevils that gave rise to the individuals destined to overwinter and infest the following year's crop. Applications began in late summer at about the time a grower normally ceased use of insecticides because his cotton crop was no longer susceptible to boll weevil damage; applications continued until the cotton plants were destroyed by frost or chemical applied by the grower.

Newsom and Brazzel provided a basis for r-d control when they demonstrated in 1956–1957 a fundamental fact of boll weevil biology that had remained obscure to that time: weevils that survived the winter were those that achieved a state of diapause in the fall. Diapause is a physiological state characterized by high fat storage and low physical activity. In order to attain diapause, a weevil must feed heavily on cotton in the weeks before the onset of frost.[54]

Brazzel moved to Texas A & M University in late 1957 and translated diapause from an observation in basic biology into a new control method: kill boll weevils in the fall with insecticides and there will be no diapausing population; infestations in the following year will then be much lower than would otherwise occur. Brazzel teamed up with Davich and demonstrated the soundness of the idea in 1959 at Presidio, Texas. Their method was known as *diapause control*.[55]

Knipling added a refinement to diapause control in 1963 by arguing from theoretical population models that controlling the generation of boll weevils producing the individuals going into diapause would cause even greater reductions in the overwintering population. Elimination of the last reproductive generation led to the name *reproduction–diapause control.* P. L. Adkisson of Texas A & M and a number of his colleagues, plus Davich, E. P. Lloyd, and others in Mississippi, confirmed Knipling's predictions.[56] Adkisson's group ran a large-scale test of r-d control on the Texas High Plains in 1965 and obtained a 98% reduction in over-wintering boll weevils.[57] This result, perhaps more than any other, ignited interest in the eradication experiment, because it suggested that only 2% of the weevil population remained to be killed in order to achieve 100% annihilation.

Release of sterile males was the complement of r-d control in an eradication experiment as long as they could be reared and sterilized in large numbers. Boll weevils, in contrast to screwworm flies and a few other insects, had no known artificial diet until the late 1950s. Erma S. Vanderzant, joined by Davich, led the development of the first in 1957. She and Davich continued to refine the diet in the early 1960s. Mechanical arrangements essential for handling thousands of gallons of diet material plus millions of boll weevils were developed after Vanderzant's work by Robert T. Gast at the BWRL.[58] A tragic explosion and fire at the BWRL later killed Gast, and he was memorialized by having the first mass-rearing facility built for boll weevil production named for him.

Once artificial diets were developed, Davich and other co-workers began searching for a means to sterilize the insect. Initial tests with gamma radiation in the early 1960s produced the discouraging result that, while the insects could be sterilized, they were almost dead after the treatment.[59] Boll weevils thus presented a biological problem not found in the screwworm fly, and it plagued the subsequent eradication experiments. Davich and other USDA workers then turned to a search for chemicals that could be added to the artificial diet so as to sterilize the growing insects. Thousands of compounds were screened, and ultimately busulfan, sometimes combined with hempa or other materials, was identified in 1969.[60]

Artificial diets and sterilization techniques were sufficiently advanced to allow Davich and others at the BWRL to try five small-scale eradication trials in 1962, 1964, and 1967. They judged that only two of the experiments demonstrated the suppressive powers of sterile males, and an introduced population of gravid females was eradicated in one area. Continual problems of raising and sterilizing boll weevils, plus the migration of new weevils into the test areas, frequently confounded these experiments, however.[61]

Progress in theory development was the final building block for an eradication effort. Knipling as an administrator in Washington was somewhat removed from the research action in Texas and Mississippi during the period 1960–1966, but he followed the developments on boll weevils extremely closely. He also wrote prolifically on the theory of a wide variety of nonchemical means of insect control, particularly the sterile male technique and how it could function in conjunction with other suppressive practices. One of 38 papers he wrote in this period, "Some Basic Principles in Insect Population Suppression" (1966), was particularly important to the field of entomology. It outlined his theory for attacking total populations of pest populations and, in some cases, for eradicating them from wide geographic areas. He expanded these basic ideas into a large, comprehensive document published in 1979, but the core ideas were clearly present much before then.[62]

Knipling argued from simple mathematical models that use of insecticides alone produced a highly efficient kill rate when the target population was large, but inefficient control when it was small. Conversely, sterile male releases were efficient when the target population was small, but inefficient when it was large. Efficiency was maximized when the two techniques were combined so that insecticides first killed large numbers of insects and sterile male releases subsequently blocked reproduction of the pest. He then illustrated his theory with a hypothetical argument about how insecticides combined with sterile male releases could be "integrated" into a program to eradicate the boll weevil.

Knipling believed the most significant implication of his theoretical results was that the two complementary techniques allowed a pest controller to overcome the law of diminishing returns. According to this law, with increasing inputs of insecticides, each additional unit of chemical applied killed a smaller proportion of target insects. Thus, in theory, killing 90% of the pests might require one unit, 99% two units, 99.9% three units, and so forth. A 100% kill rate, essential for eradication, might therefore never be achieved. Sterile male releases, however, killed more efficiently as the target population diminished. Thus a combination of insecticides followed by sterile male releases might overcome the law of diminishing returns affecting insecticides alone and achieve eradication.

Knipling's paper was not important as a harbinger of research to come, because as already described such research on boll weevils was underway when he presented it in 1965. Rather, its importance lay in the fact that he delivered it upon receiving the most prestigious award given by his profession, the Founder's Memorial Award of the Entomological Society of America. His work of many years was thus honored, and he used the occasion formally to codify his thoughts. The paper in retrospect was a landmark signaling the maturation of the TPM paradigm by a highly prestigious individual. The fact that Knipling was further honored in 1966 with the Rockefeller Public Service award, the National Medal of Science, and election to the National Academy of Sciences gave even greater prominence to his work.[63]

Paradigms inspire and guide research, and appropriately Knipling ended his paper with an exhortation to the entomological profession:

> The development of procedures for achieving and maintaining complete control of specific insect populations will not be easy. . . . Research costs will be high just to develop the basic information needed. . . . The high cost of control, the high losses in spite of control efforts, and the undesirable side effects of current methods of control obligate us to take an entirely new look at some of the most costly and most troublesome of our insect problems. . . . These are the reasons for my interest, my confidence, and my enthusiasm for research on methods that eventually can be employed to meet many of our most important insect problems by applying the basic principles of insect population suppression discussed with you on this occasion.[64]

THE PILOT BOLL WEEVIL ERADICATION EXPERIMENT

Knipling concluded in early 1968 that r-d control and adaptation of the sterile male technique were sufficiently advanced to justify a full-scale eradication experiment.[65] One year later, the National Cotton Council (NCC) established the Special Study Committee on Boll Weevil Eradication chaired by Robert Coker.[66] Coker's committee consisted of cotton growers from across the south plus entomologists Knipling, Brazzel, Davich, Adkisson, and David Young of Mississippi State University. Knipling chaired a subcommittee to select a site for the experiment, and his group held a whirlwind of visits across the South in June. Their report, finished by August, recommended a location centered in Jefferson Davis and Covington Counties, Mississippi (Fig. 14). They emphasized the need for urgency in moving forward because of the danger that the boll weevil might become resistant to the organophosphate insecticides and because public pressure was increasing against the use of insecticides in general.[67]

Knipling's subcommittee also outlined a carefully coordinated set of techniques to be used over a period of three years in order to achieve eradication. They included, in chronological order, (1) insecticides during the growing season of the first year, (2) r-d control the first fall, (3) defoliation, dessication, and stalk destruction the first fall, (4) pheromone traps in the spring of the second year, (5) early season insecticide treatment the second year before boll weevil populations were actually damaging, (6) release of sterile males the second year, and (7) insecticides

FIGURE 14. Area of Pilot Boll Weevil Eradication Experiment, with eradication and buffer zones encompassing portions of Mississippi, Louisiana, and Alabama.

during the second growing season when necessary. Steps 2–7 would be repeated during the second and third years.[68]

Coker's full committee accepted the subcommittee's report in September, and in October active politicing began. Coker met with Undersecretary of Agriculture Philip Campbell and George W. Irving, administrator of the Agricultural Research Service (also Knipling's immediate superior in the USDA). Preliminaries finished, Coker formally requested Secretary Clifford Hardin's approval of the project on October 20. Hardin agreed to an experiment beginning in 1970, but Knipling and Brazzel then put the brakes on because a facility to raise sufficient sterile males would not be ready to go on time.[69]

Bottlenecks on the construction of the rearing facility were soon removed, and in March 1971 Coker announced that the PBWEE would begin that year. The USDA, the cotton industry, and Mississippi were joined in an experiment that ultimately cost $5.25 million. Coker simultaneously directed the Special Study Committee to immediately begin to think in terms of commencing a systematic eradication effort all across the cotton belt.[70] Initiation of PBWEE thus coincided with efforts on the part of NCC to launch a nationwide program. This precommittment to eradication in advance of a determination of its scientific feasibility became a haunting point in later years.

The PBWEE was not an unqualified success, as we develop in the next chapter. It is important to understand, however, that its launching was a major event in entomology. It was scientifically and politically complex, with requirements for scientists from many different disciplines and cooperation between federal and state workers. PBWEE also involved complex regulatory powers within the experimental zone. Mississippi quarantine officials, for example, had (and exercised) the power to mandate planting dates of cotton, prohibit the transport of seed-cotton and harvesting equipment, and destroy ornamental cotton planted in flowerbeds around homes. Bureaucratic details aside, the experiment was also a tremendously exciting period for the scientists who had sheparded it into existence and developed its concepts over a period of decades. To mention just one example, this was the type of work that had led Davich to switch his employer and field of entomological specialization. He, as well as Knipling, Brazzel, and others, finally had the opportunity to see if their ideas really worked in the field.

THE NOVELTY OF TOTAL POPULATION MANAGEMENT

Uniquely new inventions in any scientific or technical field are frequently difficult to identify, because historical antecedents may give the illusion that a purportedly "new" idea is merely a reworked version of old notions. As noted earlier in Chapter 3, the roots of IPM date back to the emergence in the late nineteenth century of ecology as a specialty among the biological sciences. IPM was a new conceptualization of entomological knowledge but it was solidly based on a tradition of research extending back many years.

Tracing TPM's historical origins is more difficult because of the importance of the sterile male technique in both the development and implementation of the paradigm as a guide to research. Releases of sterile males for insect control were a qualitatively unique invention in entomology. Theories and programs built around sterile male releases therefore became markedly new entities.

Sterile male releases as a component of TPM, however, should not obscure TPM's links to previous entomological developments. Use of insecticides, for example, had a long history predating Knipling's first efforts to forge a new conceptual scheme for entomology. Mass releases of predators and parasites also reflected ideas put forth earlier by Harry

Scott Smith and others. Similarly, attacks against total or near total populations of pest insects, sometimes with the intention of eradication, had been implemented before Knipling and his colleagues made areawide attacks a foundation of TPM. Particularly noteworthy precedents included the campaign against the gypsy moth in Massachusetts (1890–1900), a massive attack costing $10 million on the European corn borer in Ohio and neighboring states (1928), a successful eradication of the Mediterranean fruit fly in Florida (1929), and a successful eradication of the Mexican bean beetle from 3462 acres in Ventura County, California (1946–1955).[71] Entomologists may not have been the instigators of the program against the European corn borers, but their involvement with it and the other actions provided a vivid model and practical experience upon which TPM was constructed in the period after 1955.

Links between TPM and previous, areawide programs were indirect, however, and in any case other elements of the TPM package made this approach novel. Like IPM, the existence of historical antecedents to some parts of TPM in no way diminishes the fact that TPM was a new intellectual entity for the entomological profession. Rivalry between TPM and IPM was also a novel situation for the discipline, and the next chapter outlines the major problems faced by the adherents of each paradigm.

REFERENCE NOTES

1. Most details of Knipling's personal life were gathered in a personal interview, July 13–14, 1976.
2. E. F. Knipling, personal communication, Aug. 18, 1977.
3. Calculated from [E. F. Knipling], Contributions to Literature by E. F. Knipling, unpublished bibliography.
4. Charles G. Scruggs, *The Peaceful Atom and the Deadlly Fly* (San Antonio, Texas: Jenkins Pub. Co., The Pemberton Press, 1975), pp. 25–44, 131 (hereafter cited as Scruggs, *Peaceful Atom*). Scruggs's book is a thorough review of the invention, development, and adoption of the sterile male technique for screwworms. His investigation and mine were undertaken independently of one another. We have no substantial differences in our descriptions of the technique's development, but our interpretations of its significance are radically different.
5. Emory C. Cushing to Sievert A. Rohwer, Feb. 10, 1936, Record Group 7, National Archives (RG7NA) (hereafter cited as Cushing to Rohwer).
6. Ralph Howard Davidson and Leonard Marion Pearis, *Insect Pests of Farm, Garden, and Orchard* (New York: John Wiley and Sons, Inc., 1966), pp. 610–611 (hereafter cited as Davidson and Pearis, *Insect Pests*).
7. Cushing to Rohwer.
8. Davidson and Pearis, *Insect Pests*, p. 610.

9. E. F. Knipling, Screwworm Eradication: Concepts and Research Leading to the Sterile-Male Method, *Smithsonian Report for 1958* (Washington, D.C.: Government Printing Office, 1959), pp. 409–418 (hereafter cited as Knipling, Screwworm Eradication).
10. Cushing to Rohwer.
11. F. C. Bishopp, J. D. Mitchell, and D. C. Parman, Screwworms and Other Maggots Affecting Animals, *Farmers Bulletin 857* (Washington: Government Printing Office, 1917), USDA, Bureau of Entomology and Plant Quarantine (hereafter cited as *Farmers Bulletin 857*).
12. Ibid. The recommendations were continued in 1922 and 1923, see *Farmers Bulletin 857*, revisions of 1922 and 1923.
13. *Farmers Bulletin 857*, revision of 1926; E. W. Laake, D. C. Parman, F. C. Bishopp, and R. C. Roark, Field tests with repellents of the screwworm fly, *Cochliomyia macellaria* Fab. upon domestic animals, *J. of Econ. Entomol.* 19 (1926): 536–539; F. C. Cook, D. C. Parman, and E. W. Laake, Progress report of investigations relating to repellents, attractants, and larvicides for the screwworm and other flies, *J. Econ. Entomol.* 16 (1923): 222–224; Cushing to Rohwer.
14. Cushing to Rohwer; W. E. Dove and D. C. Parman, Screwworms in the Southeastern states, *J. Econ. Entomol.* 28 (1935): 764–772; U.S. Congress, House, Committee on Appropriations, *Department of Agriculture Appropriations Bill for 1950*, Hearings, 81st Congress, 1st sess., 1949, p. 65.
15. Knipling, personal interview.
16. Knipling, Screwworm Eradication, pp. 409–418; idem, personal interview.
17. Jacob Bronowski, *Science and Human Values* (New York: Harper and Row, Pub., 1965), pp. 3–24.
18. Emory C. Cushing and W. S. Patton, Studies on the higher diptera of medical and veterinary importance, *Cochliomyia americana* sp. nov., the screwworm fly of the New World, *Ann. Trop. Med. Parasitol.* 27 (1933): 539–551; Emory C. Cushing, The great imposter, *The Cattleman*, Nov. 1969. Cushing and Patton named their species *C. americana*, but subsequent researchers renamed the screwworm *C. hominovorax* in addition to other names. *C. hominovorax* is the name by which it is currently known.
19. E. W. Laake, E. C. Cushing, and H. E. Parish, Biology of the Primary Screwworm Fly, *Cochliomyia americana* and a Comparison of Its stages with Those of *Cochliomyia macellaria*, *USDA Technical Bulletin 500* (Washington, D.C.: Government Printing Office, 1936); J. M. Brennan, The incidence and importance of *Cochliomyia americana* C. and P. and other wound invading species, *J. Econ. Entomol.* 31 (1938): 646–649; A. L. Brody, Natural foods of the true screwworm, *Cochliomyia americana*, *J. Econ. Entomol.* 32 (1939): 346–347; Knipling, personal interview.
20. Roy Melvin and R. C. Bushland, A Method of Rearing *Cochliomyia americana* C. and P. on Artificial Media, Pub. No. E-88 (Washington, D.C.: USDA, Bureau of Entomology and Plant Quarantine, 1936); Roy Melvin and R. C. Bushland, The nutritional requirements of screwworm larvae, *J. Econ. Entomol.* 33 (1940): 850–852.
21. Arthur W. Lindquist, Myasis in wild animals in South Texas, *J. Econ. Entomol.* 30 (1937): 735–740; idem, Study of the incidence and habits of *Cochliomyia americana* by means of fly traps, *J. Kans. Entomol. Soc.* 11 (1938): 97–104; Knipling, Screwworm Eradication, pp. 409–418; idem, personal interview.
22. Knipling, personal interview.
23. E. F. Knipling to H. J. Mueller, Mar. 6, 1950, and H. J. Mueller to E. F. Knipling, Mar. 10, 1950, both attached to E. F. Knipling to S. A. Rohwer, Mar. 15, 1950; E. F. Knipling to H. J. Mueller, Mar. 17, 1950; RG7NA; Knipling, personal interview.
24. Knipling to Rohwer, Mar. 15, 1950; idem, personal interview.

25. Knipling, personal interview.
26. Raymond C. Bushland and D. E. Hopkins, Experiments with screwworm flies sterilized by X-rays, *J. Econ. Entomol.* 44 (1951): 725–731.
27. Raymond C. Bushland and D. E. Hopkins, Sterilizations of screwworm flies with X-rays and gamma rays, *J. Econ. Entomol.* 46 (1953): 648–656; A. S. Hoyt to E. F. Knipling, Nov. 17, 1950, and R. C. Bushland to E. F. Knipling, Nov. 30, 1950, RG7NA.
28. E. F. Knipling to A. S. Hoyt, Feb. 19, 1952, RG7NA. For Bushland's account of the sterilization work, see R. C. Bushland, "Sterility Principle for Insect Control: Historical Development and Recent Innovations," in *Sterility Principle for Insect Control or Eradication* (Vienna: International Atomic Energy Agency, 1971), pp. 3–14.
29. Knipling, personal interview.
30. Ibid.
31. E. F. Knipling to A. W. Lindquist, Aug. 11, 1953, RG7NA; A. H. Baumhover, Nov. 16, 1953, Special Report K-41, Record Group 310 (Records of the Agricultural Research Service), National Archives (material from this record group is hereafter cited as RG310NA); R. C. Bushland to A. W. Lindquist, Jan. 18, 1954, RG310NA; Knipling, Screwworm Eradication, pp. 409–418. Baumhover was also sent to Puerto Rico to investigate the suitability of that island for the sterile male technique (see W. L. Propham to C. M. Ferguson, Nov. 4, 1953, RG7NA).
32. R. C. Bushland to A. W. Lindquist, Apr. 7, 1954, RG310NA; Second Quarterly Report, 1954, of the Kerrville, Texas Laboratory, Section of Insects Affecting Man and Animals, Entomology Research Branch, Agricultural Research Service, USDA, attached to A. H. Moseman to A. A. M. Struycken, Sept. 9, 1954, RG310NA.
33. A. H. Baumhover, A. J. Graham, B. A. Bitter, D. E. Hopkins, W. D. New, F. D. Dudley, and R. C. Bushland, Screwworm control through release of sterile flies, *J. Econ. Entomol.* 48 (1955): 462–466.
34. Scruggs, *Peaceful Atom*, pp. 89–108, 163–171, 299–300.
35. E. F. Knipling, office memorandum, Sept. 2, 1954, RG310NA. B. A. Porter, head of the Fruit Insects Section of ERD, disagreed with Knipling's list in the above memorandum. He suggested dropping biological control and resistant plant varieties as research lines for deciduous fruits and nuts. Knipling subsequently agreed with Porter's recommendations and asked him to draw up some new ones for crops of his responsibility (B. A. Porter to E. F. Knipling, Oct. 7, 1954 and E. F. Knipling to B. A. Porter, Oct. 14, 1954; both in RG310NA).
36. Index to 1955 Recommendations Relating to Entomology Research of Commodity and Functional Advisory Committees Established Under Title III of the Research and Marketing Act of 1946, unpublished document, RG310NA.
37. Index to 1956–57 Advisory Committee Recommendations and Work Book for Research Budget Preparation for Fiscal 1959, unpublished document, RG310NA.
38. Leo Dale Newsom, personal interview, June 1–2, 1978.
39. C. F. Rainwater and C. R. Parencia, Ky Peper Ewing 1898–1974, *J. Econ. Entomol.* 67 (1974): 568–569.
40. F. C. Bishopp, "Insecticides and Boll Weevils," in *Beltwide Cotton Production Conference, Summary–Proceedings* (Memphis: National Cotton Council, 1955), pp. 19–20; Newsom, personal interview.
41. E. F. Knipling to K. S. Quisenberry, Aug. 31, 1955, RG310NA.
42. E. F. Knipling to Dave L. Pearce, Sept. 29, 1955, RG310NA.
43. For 1955, see Robert E. Stevenson to B. T. Shaw and Harry B. Caldwell, Apr. 19, 1955; for 1956, see Robert E. Stevenson to B. T. Shaw and Harry B. Caldwell, Apr. 24, 1956; both in RG310NA.

44. J. R. Brazzel and O. E. Shipp, The status of boll weevil resistance to chlorinated hydrocarbon insecticides in Texas, *J. Econ. Entomol.* 55 (1962): 941–944.
45. For 1957, see K. P. Ewing to Dr. Knipling, Apr. 4, 1957, and Robert E. Stevenson to B. T. Shaw and Harry B. Caldwell, Apr. 8, 1957; for 1958, see S. E. Jones to R. E. Stevenson, Nov. 5, 1957; all in RG310NA.
46. E. F. Knipling to K. P. Ewing, Feb. 1, 1955, and attached handwritten note to A. H. Moseman, RG310NA.
47. J. Ritchie Smith, Statement on Boll Weevil Eradication, Apr. 4, 1973, 3 pp., mimeo supplied by Smith.
48. The Senate wanted to increase the sum by $100,000, but the House prevailed in Conference. See U.S. Congress, House, Committee on Appropriations, *Department of Agriculture Appropriations for 1959,* Hearings, Part 5, 85th Cong., 2nd sess., 1958, pp. 449–466; U.S. Congress, House, *Department of Agriculture and Farm Credit Administration Appropriation, 1959,* H. Rept. 1584, 85th Congress, 2nd sess., 1958, pp. 12–13; U.S. Congress, House, *Department of Agriculture and Farm Credit Administration Appropriation Bill, 1959,* H. Rept. 1776, 85th Congress, 2nd sess., 1958, p. 4; U.S. Congress, Senate, *Agricultural and Farm Credit Appropriation Bill, 1959,* S. Rept. 1438, 85th Congress, 2nd sess., 1958, pp. 6–7.
49. Working Group on Boll Weevil Research Programs, *The Boll Weevil Problem and Facility Needs to Meet the Problem* (Washington, D.C.: USDA, Dec. 30, 1958), mimeo report.
50. *Proceedings of Boll Weevil Research Symposium* (Washington, D.C.: USDA, 1962), p. 95 (hereafter cited as USDA, *Proceedings*).
51. Theodore B. Davich, personal interview, May 18, 1978.
52. *Ibid.*
53. USDA, *Proceedings,* p. 2.
54. J. R. Brazzel and L. D. Newsom, Diapause in *Anthonomus grandis* Boh., *J. Econ. Entomol.* 52 (1959): 603–611. Previous to Brazzel and Newsom's work, overwintering boll weevils were simply said to "hibernate." Earlier programs for boll weevil control included stalk destruction in the fall so as to make it difficult for the insect to feed enough to "hibernate." Hibernation is now generally confined to overwintering behavior for mammals, and the more precise term of diapause is used for insects. The two states are biologically different in that a hibernating animal can generally be aroused with ease, but an insect in diapause is frequently resistant to reactivation unless precise environmental conditions are met. R-d control was in a sense not radically new because of the earlier programs based on killing "hibernating" boll weevils. Brazzel and Newsom's identification of diapause was probably important in attracting Brazzel's attention to the overwintering period of the insects life.
55. J. R. Brazzel, T. B. Davich, and L. D. Harris, A new approach to boll weevil control, *J. Econ. Entomol.* 54 (1961): 723–730; J. R. Brazzel, Destruction of diapause boll weevils as a means of boll weevil control *Tex. Agric. Exp. Stn. Misc. Pub. 511* (Texas A & M University), 1961, 22 pp.
56. Don R. Rummel, "Reproduction–diapause boll weevil control," in *Boll Weevil Suppression, Management, and Elimination Technology* (Proceedings of a Conference, Feb. 13–15, 1974, Memphis, Tenn.), ARS-S-71 (Washington, D.C.: USDA, 1976), pp. 28–30 (hereafter cited as ARS, *Boll Weevil Suppression.*)
57. Perry L. Adkisson, D. R. Rummel, W. L. Sterling and W. L. Owen, Jr., Diapause boll weevil control: A comparison of two methods, *Tex. Agric. Exp. Stn. Pub.,* Texas A & M Univ., 1966, 11 pp.; Perry Adkisson, personal interview, May 30–31, 1978.
58. O. H. Lindig, "Mass rearing of boll weevils," in ARS, *Boll Weevil Suppression,* pp. 50–52; Erma S. Vanderzant and T. B. Davich, Laboratory rearing of the boll

weevil: A satisfactory larval diet and oviposition studies, *J. Econ. Entomol.* 51 (1958): 288–291.

59. T. B. Davich and D. A. Lindquist, Exploratory studies on gamma-radiation for the sterilization of the boll weevil, *J. Econ. Entomol.* 55 (1962): 164–167.
60. W. Klassen and N. W. Earle, Permanent sterility induced in boll weevils with busulfan without reducing production of pheromone, *J. Econ. Entomol.* 63 (1969): 1195–1198; E. P. Lloyd, J. R. McCoy, and J. W. Haynes, "Release of sterile male boll weevils in the pilot boll weevil eradication experiment in 1972–73," in ARS, *Boll Weevil Suppression*, pp. 95–102.
61. T. B. Davich, J. C. Keller, E. B. Mitchell, Paul Huddleston, Ray Hill, D. A. Lindquist, Gerald McKibben, and W. H. Cross, Preliminary field experiments with sterile males for eradication of the boll weevil, *J. Econ. Entomol.* 58 (1965): 127–131; T. B. Davich, M. E. Merkl, E. B. Mitchell, D. D. Hardee, R. T. Gast, G. H. McKibben, and P. A. Huddleston, Field experiments with sterile males for eradication of the boll weevil, *J. Econ. Entomol.* 60 (1967): 1533–1538; T. B. Davich, "Sterile-male technique for control or eradication of the boll weevil, *Anthonomus grandis* Boh.," in *Sterile-Male Technique for Eradication or Control of Harmful Insects* (Vienna: International Atomic Energy Agency, 1969), pp. 65–72; Davich, personal interview.
62. E. F. Knipling, Some basic principles in insect population suppression, *Bull. Entomol. Soc. Am.* 12 (1966): 7–15 (hereafter cited as E. F. Knipling, Some basic principles). An earlier version of this paper was Knipling's *The Potential Role of the Sterility Method for Insect Population Control with Special Reference to Combining this Method with Conventional Methods*, ARS-33-98 (Washington, D.C.: USDA, Nov., 1964), 54 pp. E. F. Knipling, *The Basic Principles of Insect Population Suppression and Management*, Agriculture Handbook No. 512 (Washington, D.C.: USDA, 1979), 659 pp.
63. Anonymous, Knipling, E(dward) F(red), *Current Biography* 36 (May, 1975): 16–19.
64. Knipling, Some basic principles.
65. E. F. Knipling, Technically feasible approaches to boll weevil eradication, presented at Beltwide Cotton Production–Mechanization Conference, Hot Springs, Ark., Jan. 11–12, 1968.
66. J. Ritchie Smith, personal communication, Sept. 15, 1978.
67. National Cotton Council, Selection of *Locations for Pilot Boll Weevil Eradication Experiments*, unpublished report, Aug. 15, 1969.
68. *Ibid.*
69. Fred Abel to Members of Special Boll Weevil Committee, Sept. 29, 1969, and G. S. Buck to Special Study Committee on Boll Weevil Eradication, May 13, 1970, both from files of Charles R. Parencia; Robert R. Coker to Clifford M. Hardin, Oct. 20, 1969, and Robert R. Coker to Special Study Committee on Boll Weevil Eradication, Dec. 23, 1969, both from files of Perry L. Adkisson.
70. Robert R. Coker to Special Study Committee on Boll Weevil Eradication, Mar. 26, 1971, files of Charles R. Parencia. The USDA's final share of the expenses was $3.61 million, while Cotton, Inc., supplied $1.08 million and the State of Mississippi $0.56 million. See *Overall Plan for a National Program to Eliminate the Boll Weevil from the United States* (Memphis: National Cotton Council, Dec. 4, 1973). p, 22.
71. W. L. Popham and David G. Hall, Insect eradication programs, *Annu. Rev. Entomol.* 3 (1958): 335–354; California Department of Agriculture, Bulletin, *Twenty-Seventh Annual Report*, 35 (1946): 187; idem, *36th Annual Report*, 45 (1956): 149–150; Thomas R. Dunlap, Farmers, scientists, and insects, *Agric. Hist.* 54 (1980): 93–107.

CHAPTER 5

Traumas

Two "mega-experiments," the Pilot Boll Weevil Eradication Experiment (PBWEE) and the Huffaker Project, dominated the politics of entomological research during the 1970s. Both were subject to internal strife and external criticisms, and both weathered the storms to find renewal in the form of new projects. Traumas within the PBWEE were particularly severe, because the results and their significance were subject to radically different interpretations. Evaluation of the PBWEE divided those with primary allegiance to total population management (TPM) against those aligned with integrated pest management (IPM) and thus led to a sharpening of the distinctions between the two approaches to insect control. Individual entomologists were caught in maelstroms of disputes that required them to reexamine their own positions on research directions. It had been possible before the PBWEE to entertain both IPM and TPM as guides to experimentation. After the PBWEE, life in the gray area between IPM and TPM became more difficult but not impossible.

THE PILOT BOLL WEEVIL ERADICATION EXPERIMENT

Design

The PBWEE's genesis from the symbiotic relationship between entomologists and the cotton industry was reflected in its complex administrative structure. Four agencies from the USDA; ten organizations from Mississippi, Louisiana, Alabama, and Texas; and two organizations from the cotton industry pooled their strengths in the efforts. Primary responsibility for executing the experiment fell to the USDA's Animal and Plant Health Inspection Service (APHIS) while supporting research was the responsibility of the Agricultural Research Service (ARS) and state universities.[1] James R. Brazzel as Chief Staff Officer for Methods Development in APHIS and Edward F. Knipling, then Science Advisor to the Administrator of ARS, served as co-chairmen of the Technical Guidance Committee (TGC).[2] The TGC, composed of representatives from the USDA, universities, state departments of agriculture, and the cotton industry, was responsible for setting general policy within the PBWEE. Many members of the TGC took little or no part in the practical operations of the PBWEE, but the TGC was responsibile for interpreting the results. Farrell J. Boyd and Edward P. Lloyd were the leaders for APHIS and ARS, respectively, in the conduct of the work but were not members of the TGC. (See the Appendix for the membership of the TGC.)

Knipling had argued in 1968 that it might be possible to eradicate the boll weevil with insecticides used in reproduction–diapause (r-d) control alone,[3] but the experiment he and his colleagues designed was considerably more complex. The eradication zone, an area roughly within a 25-mile radius of Columbia, Mississippi, was the heart of the exercise. Buffer zones surrounding the eradication area were treated less intensively in order to minimize the number of boll weevils that might migrate into the eradication zone (Fig. 14). Eight suppressive techniques were applied in a coordinated fashion in the core area[4]:

1. *In-season control*—routine insecticide application during the first growing season to kill boll weevils.
2. *Reproduction–diapause control*—application of insecticides at the end of the first growing season to suppress overwintering populations of boll weevils.
3. *Defoliation*—application of a chemical to cotton plants after harvest to deprive boll weevils of food so as to prevent diapause.
4. *Stalk destruction*—physical destruction of cotton plants after harvest to prevent diapause and to deny boll weevils an overwintering haven.
5. *Pheromone traps*—cages baited with boll weevil sex attractant to monitor populations and to destroy those individuals who entered them.
6. *Trap crops*—a few rows of cotton planted at the edge of the fields at least two weeks before the second-year's crop and treated with a systemic insecticide. Trap crops attracted and killed the first boll weevils to emerge from overwintering quarters.
7. *Pinhead-square treatment*—insecticide applications to cotton flower buds in the second year when they were the size of pinheads.

This treatment killed boll weevils not caught in traps or poisoned by trap crops.

8. *Sterile male release*—rearing, sterilizing, and releasing large numbers of sterile insects in the second year so as to block the reproduction of the wild population in the field.

As originally designed, steps 2–8 were to be repeated during the second year and, if needed, during the third year.[5] Due to a shortage of funds, the PBWEE ran only for two years, July 1971 to August 8, 1973. Portions of three growing seasons were included, but the premature curtailment was one of several factors making interpretation of the results difficult.

Had the PBWEE been just a scientific experiment conducted by entomologists, implementing the above treatments at the proper time would not have posed any particular problems. The PBWEE, however, was a field experiment conducted in the midst of commercial cotton production. Southern Mississippi has many farmers producing cotton on small (less than 10 acres) fields scattered among the pine forests. Cooperation from all farmers in the area was essential for the scientific personnel to conduct their work. Southern Mississippi was selected because it was one of the most difficult areas in the country in which to control boll weevils; if eradication could be achieved in this microcosm of the American cotton industry, it was argued that it could be achieved anywhere.[6]

Bringing the many small farmers into the experiment was the responsibility of the extension service. David F. Young, leader of extension entomology at the Cooperative Extension Service of Mississippi State University, directed this aspect of PBWEE. It was his task to organize and instruct the county extension agents in each of the 37 counties and parishes in Mississippi, Alabama, and Louisiana involved in the PBWEE. County agents were responsible for assisting the growers in each county to become effective and knowledgable participants. Young's task was formidable because many of the growers had no cash for insecticides or application equipment and thus could not participate in the in-season control effort of the PBWEE (step 1). In fact, many of the farmers of the area apparently grew the cotton solely to collect the government price support payments and never even bothered to harvest their crop, let alone exercise careful insect control practices on it![7]

A prime requirement of the PBWEE was that every farmer in the experimental zone cooperate with the goals and procedures involved; one grower who did not could jeopardize the entire effort by "raising" boll weevils on his improperly treated cotton.[8] Boll weevils were of course not subject to the law, but farmers were. State departments of agriculture in the three states were therefore involved as executors of the legal dimensions of PBWEE. Mississippi's Department of Agriculture and Commerce had an especially important task to play, as most of the activity of the PBWEE was in that state. A boll weevil quarantine adopted in July 1971 prohibited the growing of noncommercial cotton as ornamental plants. In addition, the movement of boll weevils, seed cotton, gin trash, mechanical harvesting equipment, and any other item that might harbor the insect was strictly regulated to prevent its accidental importation into the eradication area. An amendment to the quarantine was added in early 1972 to prevent the planting of cotton before April 15 in the experimental zone.[9] This regulation allowed the planting of trap crops one or two weeks before the regular crop was planted (step 6). Entrance of the law, courts, and police power into scientific experiments was unusual, and this dimension of the PBWEE sharply distinguished it from most other experiments in entomology and other fields of science. As noted below, land-use control inherent in eradication efforts became one of several stumbling blocks for follow-up efforts to the PBWEE.[10]

PBWEE was designed to answer a seemingly simple question: Was technology available to eradicate the boll weevil from the U.S.? Answering the question, however, involved subtleties not immediately obvious. Clearly eradication would leave zero boll weevils in a particular area, so inability to find the insects would constitute a *prima facie* case that the technology worked. But how does one prove that boll weevils are absent? If no boll weevils were found after treatment, one would still have to answer the challenge, "How do you know you haven't missed finding them?" Such a question was by no means trivial when boll weevil numbers dropped to less than one per acre. A roughly equivalent task would be to find a pea dropped at an unknown point on a football field. Moreover, this "pea" could fly away if disturbed and thus avoid detection.

If boll weevils were present after application of the eradication technology, then suspicions would be raised that eradication had not succeeded. Such boll weevils might, of course, be migrants that entered the test area, a possibility reinforced by the demonstrated ability of the insect to fly at least 45 miles.[11] Unfortunately, it is impossible to distinguish a "native" boll weevil from an "immigrant," so that indirect evidence of migration must support any allegation that boll weevils found in the test area were not indigenuous. Alternatively, one could argue that boll weevils found in the test area, regardless of source, could not reproduce because of the sterile males; therefore their presence was irrelevant because they would soon die without leaving progeny.

Given the difficulties of interpreting the presence or absence of boll weevils at the end of the experiment, ultimate proof of eradication could come only from continued observation of the test area. If eradication had been achieved, then no boll weevils would appear there even after a protracted period of time. (We assume the absence of acts of special creation!) Unfortunately, the eradication zone was within the flight range reported for boll weevils. The PBWEE was therefore unsuited to evaluation by waiting for "ultimate results."

These considerations lead us to conclude that all possible results of the PBWEE were equivocal. Even if no boll weevils were detected in the eradication zone at the termination of the experiment, one could not rest assured that the searching methods had been adequate. In addition, one could not wait to see if boll weevils reappeared in the test zone because they surely would if only by migration from the surrounding areas. Nontrivial assumptions and value judgments were therefore necessary to make any sense of the results, and that is exactly what happened.

Evaluation of the PBWEE, in spite of the difficulties just described, was anticipated by Bayley's appointment of the TGC under the co-chairmanship of Knipling and Brazzel. This group was responsible to the Secretary of Agriculture for guiding and interpreting the experiment. Knipling, however, declined to set strict evaluation criteria in advance of the PBWEE's conclusion. According to his colleague, Waldemar Klassen, "He stated that it was scientifically unsound to draw up criteria in advance of making a cursory examination of the data to be generated in this season."[12]

Generation of hypotheses *ex post facto* from an experiment is a common procedure in science, but final acceptance or rejection of such a hypothesis must always await a second experiment designed independently of the first and capable of producing data allowing a clear-cut distinction between the truth or falsehood of the hypothesis under test. In short, the PBWEE could logically never have been anything but the prelude to a second experiment to test the techniques involved.

A second evaluation mechanism for the PBWEE was created when "certain [unspecified] members" of the TGC requested that Knipling and Brazzel arrange for an outside review by the Entomological Society of America (ESA).[13] ESA President Gordon Guyer agreed and appointed a committee chaired by William G. Eden of the University of Florida in the spring of 1973. Eden's committee met with the TGC in April, June, and August 1973, before issuing their report in December.[14] Undoubtedly, the request for outside evaluation from within the TGC signaled that, even before the final year of the experiment, dissension was present within the TGC and, more importantly, some members were skeptical of the TGC's ability to render an objective judgment.

Both the TGC and Eden's committee were composed primarily of entomologists and assigned specifically to evaluate the PBWEE. Two committees assigned the same task was enough to raise the specter of confusion should they disagree, but to make matters even more complex a third committee emerged and played an important role in the evaluation of the PBWEE. Donald Kennedy of Stanford University became chairman in 1971 of a committee at the National Academy of Sciences (NAS) to perform a general technology assessment of past control methods. I served as the principal staff officer for the effort. Eradication came into the Kennedy committee's purview as a technological concept of insect control.

The primary task of evaluating boll weevil eradication fell to a subgroup known as the Cotton Study Team chaired by Stanley D. Beck, an insect physiologist from the University of Wisconsin. The Cotton Study Team also included as its only other entomologist Perry Lee Adkisson, who at the time was involved with both the TGC and the Huffaker Project. Adkisson served on the parent body to the Cotton Study Team as well. Although the report of the Cotton Study Team was influential in the Congress because of its comments on the PBWEE, it should be noted that neither Beck's team nor Kennedy's parent committee ever formally evaluated the detailed data of the PBWEE; their comments were instead more general and dealt with some of the underlying assumptions of eradication as a concept of insect control.

Results

Perhaps only one result of PBWEE was not disputed: techniques used to suppress boll weevils in the test area dramatically lowered the numbers of the insect. Dickey D. Hardee (ARS) and Farrell J. Boyd (APHIS) published data indicating that the number of adult boll weevils per acre dropped from 807 to 0.2 between 1971 and 1973.[15] It was impossible to ascribe precise shares of the killing to any particular control technique, but use of r-d control undoubtedly claimed a large share of the victims. Moving beyond this simple "body count," however, entangles one in a morass of (1) copious data presented in a confusing, unintelligible manner, (2) conflicting data, (3) possibly unreported data available only to a few persons, and (4) diametrically opposed conclusions based on more or less the same data.

Part of the problem lay in the multiple detection methods used for surveys. Intense visual and machine surveys were the primary methods, but another, the use of pheromone traps, proved to have pivotal results in the squabble over the PBWEE's meaning. Substantial improvements in trapping increased sensitivity during the course of the PBWEE, and during the last months of work, traps were undoubtedly the most sensitive detection method available. Particularly efficient were in-field traps, simple devices placed directly on cotton plants in a farmer's field.[16]

Visual and machine surveys detected no boll weevils in the southern two-thirds of the eradication zone during the last month of the experiment, but the northern part was infested.[17] Pheromone traps, however, detected boll weevils in some northern fields that were "clean" by visual and machine surveys.[18] Moreover, a few boll weevils were found in the traps placed in the southern part of the eradication zone during the last month.[19]

Conflicts between the reports of visual or machine surveys, on the one hand, and pheromone trap data, on the other, resulted in a bewildering array of statements in the formal publication of the data from the PBWEE. For example, Boyd stated: "Out of a total of 1,817 acres in 236 fields, boll weevil infestations were detected [visually] in 34 fields (14.4%) amounting to 167 acres (9.2%). . . . No infestations were detected in [the southern two-thirds of the eradication zone]."[20] Boyd's data referred to the time period from July 11 to August 8, 1973, the last month of the experiment. Simultaneously, Hardee and Boyd presented pheromone trapping data for the period July 1–August 3 indicating that approximately 17 boll weevils were trapped in the southern two-thirds of the eradication zone.[21] Despite the obvious inconsistency between these two reports involving a common author (Boyd), researchers in the PBWEE offered, for the public record, no explanation other than "immigration." Yet the published migration data lent scant or no support to such a hypothesis.

Failure to resolve obvious inconsistencies in the data probably reflected a fundamental problem from the conduct of the PBWEE. Careers were at stake because of the heavy commitment of the National Cotton Council and key federal and state entomologists to the eradication concept. One entomologist, whose name must still remain confidential, reported "unofficially" to Adkisson on the TGC that the visual surveys might have missed some infestations because inexperienced personnel were involved. Adkisson received these reports even before the pheromone trapping data from Hardee were available. They led him to become highly skeptical of all data reported in the PBWEE and ultimately to his conclusion that boll weevils had not been eradicated. The informal reports were not widely discussed at the time because of apprehension that careers could be damaged by pressing the issue.[22]

The TGC had met periodically over the course of the experiment, and on August 30, 1973, it gathered in Starkville, Mississippi, at the Boll

Weevil Research Laboratory (BWRL) for its last session. Knipling had prepared in advance of the meeting a draft statement declaring that the experiment demonstrated the technical feasibility of eradicating the boll weevil.[23] After considerable discussion, Adkisson's and others' skepticism about the feasibility of eradication led to an impasse in which it was clear that several of the TGC members would not agree to Knipling's draft statement. Adkisson was the reluctant leader of this group and recollects that his stance was one of the most difficult tasks he had ever faced in his professional life: "I had to screw up all the courage I had to be a minority member, and mainly for my respect and friendship for Knipling, which I still have. . . . I hated to be put in a position of being in opposition to a man I admired and still do."[24]

Adkisson's position also represented a profound change for him. He had been one of the early pioneers in developing the r-d method of control, a technique that by all accounts, including data from the PBWEE, caused nearly incredible reductions in boll weevil populations. He had been optimistic about the prospects for eradication until as late as April 1973, a mere four months earlier.[25]

Tensions within the TGC ran high, but dissidents were reluctant to force an angry confrontation over the results. Adkisson therefore suggested a compromise wording for Knipling's draft statement in which the phrase "eliminate as an economic pest" was substituted for "eradicate." His language was acceptable to Knipling and J. Ritchie Smith of the National Cotton Council, two of the major proponents of eradication on the TGC, and also to those members who were doubtful that the PBWEE had demonstrated adequate technology for such an effort. It avoided the possibility of a minority report, which neither Knipling nor Smith wanted, and allowed an honorable exit for members of the TGC who were in a difficult position politically. Fowden G. Maxwell, for example, passed Adkisson a note stating "This saves my hide" after the compromise was accepted.[26] Maxwell was a former staff entomologist under Davich at the Boll Weevil Research Laboratory and then chairman of Mississippi State University's Department of Entomology. He had been a leader in obtaining money from the Mississippi State Legislature for the PBWEE, a factor undoubtedly contributing to his reluctance to see an open battle within the TGC over the interpretation of the PBWEE.

Adkisson's compromise language was the only way to end the meeting with a semblance of order, but its ambiguity made subsequent policy-making contentious. Robert Coker, Ritchie Smith, Knipling, Brazzel, Davich, and other proponents of eradication simply went on behaving as though "eliminate as an economic pest" was entirely synonomous with "eradicate" as they launched a movement for a national "elimination" program. Adkisson used the language in an entirely different vein: he believed technology could eliminate economic damage by the insect, but any program based on it would be open-ended. It would have to be used year after year because it wouldn't really reduce the boll weevil population to zero. He felt that as long as cotton growers understood the difference between open- and closed-ended programs, then they were well served.[27]

A major question is why Adkisson and Knipling reached such diametrically opposed interpretations from ostensibly the same data of the PBWEE. A number of factors were the foundation for Adkisson's stance. First, Adkisson's suspicions about the reliability of the visual surveys for boll weevils were aroused by the informal reports he received and then compounded by Hardee's evidence that pheromone traps could detect low-level infestations with greater sensitivity than the visual or machine surveys. Hardee's data further indicated that boll weevils were present during July in portions of the southern two-thirds of the eradication zone. Finally, data available at the meeting on August 30 indicated that "sterile males" released in the eradication zone were neither all sterile nor all male. Adkisson believed that r-d control could reduce boll weevil populations to almost undetectable levels, but that eradication would require a more effective sterile male release program. Otherwise allegedly sterile males might simply reinfest an area, even if all other suppression techniques succeeded in eradicating the insect. We return to this point shortly.

Knipling agreed with Adkisson that the sterile male technique needed improvement in order to play its proper role in an eradication effort, but he was fully confident that the necessary improvements would be made during the course of an all-out campaign. He also believed that the PBWEE had demonstrated no reproduction of boll weevils for two generations in 170 fields 25 miles or more from heavily infested cotton, a fact that was sufficient in his mind to conclude that the PBWEE had indicated the technical feasibility of eradicating the insect.[28] Knipling's assertion that the PBWEE data demonstrated such a fact may be correct, but neither the unpublished final report from APHIS nor the published final report from ARS presents data such that Knipling's assertion can be checked by an outsider to the experiment. It is interesting to note therefore that neither Adkisson's nor Knipling's pivotal evidence was available for general discussion.

Had no boll weevils been found in the eradication zone, the only question that would have been germane was the adequacy of the detection methods. Boll weevils were present, however, so Adkisson's and Knipling's stand off centered around (1) were the pests migrants from somewhere else, or (2) were they immaterial, as sterile males prevented their reproduction in the eradication zone?

First we examine the question of migration. William H. Cross of the PBWEE operated lines of pheromone-baited traps radiating out from near the center of the eradication zone. His data for 1973 indicated that during the period June 6–13, boll weevils were at a peak in their emergence from overwintering grounds and were dispersing over wide areas in search of new cotton. Wide dispersal patterns were inferred from capture of weevils at trap sites one or more miles from cotton fields. Trapping data for the periods July 4–11 and July 25–August 1 indicated that few boll weevils were migrating, because only five weevils were captured away from cotton fields in the entire eradication zone. All five were captured in the earlier period. Boll weevils migrated again after the first of August, but substantial migration was not detected until August 15, after the PBWEE ended. During periods when migration was evident, boll weevils were caught in a "gradient" of increasing numbers as trap distance from the center of the eradication zone increased.[29]

What did these data mean? Surprisingly little formal discussion surrounded them. Boyd argued for APHIS that they indicated "that the majority of the infestations found in 1973 were caused by migrant, gravid females,"[30] and Cross of the ARS applied a similar interpretation to his results.[31]

Such an interpretation may be correct, but it requires some assumptions. First, no significant migration was observed between July 4 and the termination of the experiment on August 8. Therefore if one is to interpret the data of Cross as demonstrating that weevils found in the eradication zone were migrants, then one must assume that they migrated in during June and that they or their progeny were the individuals detected in traps located in cotton fields. One must also assume that the "gradient" in the number of weevils captured (higher numbers further from the center of the eradication zone) reflected a *direction* of migration toward the eradication zone. Perhaps it did, but it is possible that the gradient merely reflected the fact that higher numbers of weevils were living at greater distances from the eradication center. No direction of migration was necessarily implied by the existence of the so-called "gradient." Adkisson did not believe that the Cross data proved that weevils caught in the eradication zone were migrants from outside, so he did not accept the assumptions necessary for such an interpretation. We have then an extremely interesting example of different people looking at the same data and interpreting it in radically different ways because the assumptions they brought to the analysis were different.

Second, we turn to whether boll weevil reproduction was blocked in the eradication zone becaue of the sterile male releases. Data gathered at the BWRL and at the Baton Rouge Cotton Insects Research Laboratory indicated that boll weevils reared, sterilized, and released in the PBWEE were neither completely nor permanently sterile; nor were they completely male as some females were inadvertantly released due to errors in sexing the insects before release. The quality of the "sterile males" produced declined even more as the termination of the experiment on August 8 approached, and temporary personnel in the mass-rearing facility began to lose morale due to impending layoffs. Presence of some fertile males and females in "sterile male" releases were not necessarily fatal to the success of the sterile male technique as a method of suppression, but they lowered its efficiency.[32] Their presence may have been fatal to an eradication attempt because large numbers of genuinely sterile males would be essential until frost or starvation killed all weevils—wild, released–fertile, and released–sterile. Should released–fertile insects survive beyond the period of "sterile male" releases, they could provide the nucleus of reinfestation that would negate any "eradication" effort.

That the "sterile male" releases were perhaps fatally flawed was evident early in August when hybrid offspring from matings of released and wild insects were found in the field.[33] Subsequent discoveries of hybrid individuals after the TGC meeting of August 30[34] added further confirmation to the notion that "sterile male" releases probably could not have provided an eradicatory *coup de grace* to the remnants of the boll weevil population still in the area.

Adkisson firmly believed that a better sterile male technique was essential to a successful eradication attempt. He looked at the evidence available on August 30 and concluded the sterile male technique simply wasn't ready to go. Knipling was aware of the same data, but his assumptions were different from Adkisson's. He, too, acknowledged the need for improvement in the sterile male technique, but he believed that such refinements could and should come in the course of a massive eradication exercise. Several months later he argued in a letter to Hardee that sterile male releases, insecticides, and traps virtually stopped reproduction in the eradication zone.[35]

Members of the TGC were closest to the PBWEE, yet they had numerous problems in interpreting its data. It was not surprising, therefore, that others who looked at the experiment also had trouble. What was unfortunate was that the ambiguity and confusion created by the language of the TGC report was only slightly alleviated by the report from the ESA committee under Eden. Eden's group was sure that eradication meant reduction of a specified population in a particular area to zero, and therefore "eradication" and "elimination as an economic pest" might be different. They could not, however, agree on whether there was any significant difference between "accomplishing eradication" and "demonstrating feasibility of eradication." Furthermore, the committee was divided over whether or not technical feasibility of eradication was demonstrated in the experiment. They expressed "reservations" about undertaking any massive program of eradication until further research had improved the techniques used in the PBWEE, especially the sterile male technique. Eden's committee was of no help on the major question of the day: should a Beltwide eradication effort be attempted? Rather, they threw up their hands and said the matter was a sociopolitical decision that should be made "objectively."[36]

Political matters were indeed heavily involved in the PBWEE, but such matters were inherently subjective because politics reflects values. Science, too, is subject to nonobjective factors, as will be discussed in Chapters 6 and 7. The undoing of the ESA Review Committee was their failure to consider where values played a role in the science they were supposed to judge. In a sense they heaped the burden of objective decision making on the Congress, possibly the most nonobjective body to be found anywhere on the face of the Earth.

Beck's Cotton Study Team at the NAS fared little better than Eden's group but for different reasons. In late 1974, their draft report expressed severe doubt about the technical feasibility of eradicating the boll weevil. Such a conclusion was not surprising because Adkisson was the only cotton entomologist on the committee; Beck had kept himself informed of the developments in the PBWEE and clearly sympathized with Adkisson's interpretation of the data. Given the fact that the PBWEE had already been argued and discussed nearly to death, the Cotton Study Team made no effort to recapitulate all the evidence once again. Rather they relied on Adkisson's and Beck's judgments and confined their largely negative comments to a few paragraphs. Their treatment would have been justified and passed review in almost any other situation. Emotional heat and quirk of circumstances in the NAS review process, however, quickly snared them.[37]

All NAS reports were subjected to a peer review process by the Report Review Committee. Knipling, one of the few applied entomologists in the NAS, was asked to serve as a reviewer of the Cotton Study Team report. His appointment to serve in this capacity was as justified as the appointment of Adkisson to the Cotton Study Team; after all, both were eminent entomologists clearly recognized as leaders in their field. Past events had already cast the issue, however, and Knipling's review with its predictable rebuttal shed no new light on the subject. It was largely a reenactment of the disputes in the TGC meeting.

Knipling was of course in disagreement with the Cotton Study Team's briefly presented conclusions on boll weevil eradication, but he was outraged by what he considered the heavily biased manner in which it was presented. He considered Beck a long-time opponent of eradication efforts and that his appointment to chair an NAS committee was bound to lead to predetermined conclusions.[38] He may have been right about Beck's inclinations, but clearly he was in no position to argue about somebody else's predispositions. Furthermore, he questioned whether Adkisson adhered to a consistant position on eradication.[39] Again, Knipling was correct, because Adkisson had undergone a change in 1973.

A flurry of negotiations resulted in a compromise by late 1975,[40] and the revised Cotton Study Team report was released in early 1976.[41] Its toned-down statement continued to express strong reservations about the feasibility of eradicating the boll weevil, but it went along with the eradication proponents by approving a new trial eradication program in North Carolina.[42] The concept of continuing large-scale eradication experiments was thus legitimized but with the caveat that they would probably fail.

THE TRIAL BOLL WEEVIL ERADICATION PROGRAM

The NAS endorsement of a trial in North Carolina was not an original suggestion but an endorsement of a proposal that came from extensive discussions held before and in the wake of the PBWEE. Coker appointed a committee to develop a plan for a national program in early 1972, over a year before the end of the PBWEE.[43] Knipling chaired the group, which included Brazzel and Adkisson among its ten members. The committee recommended on December 4, 1973, that a national "elimination" program be started in 1975 in western Texas and proceed eastward. All boll weevils were to be eliminated by the end of the eighth year (1982).[44] Coker and others from the cotton industry met in Washington on December 12 to discuss the subcommittee's report with Secretary of Agriculture Earl Butz, other USDA administrators, and a number of Congressmen.[45] Congress had in the meantime passed a law for the National Cotton Council directing that the Secretary of Agriculture carry out such a program if he believed it was technically feasible (P.L. 93-86).[46]

Proponents of eradication, however, could not organize a sufficiently strong base of support for a national eradication program begun in Texas. The transition began during conferences held in Memphis during February, 1974; vigorous opposition surfaced during the sessions.[47] J. R. Phillips (University of Arkansas) presented a statement from himself and seven other southern entomologists who had severe doubts about the technology then available.[48] Charles Lincoln (University of Arkansas), Dale Newsom (LSU), and Dan Clower (also LSU) expressed similar opinions independently.[49]

Fowden G. Maxwell, chairman of the entomology department at Mississippi State and a member of the TGC, proposed a compromise in April, 1974, for a limited trial eradication program that, if successful, could be expanded to a national program. He also recommended that a research team be established to evaluate the effort and recommend appropriate follow-up including options to abort, hold, or expand.[50] Maxwell's proposal was quickly adopted by university and cotton industry people in Mississippi and by the directors of the southern agricultural experiment stations.[51] Adkisson completed the transition by explaining to key Texas cotton growers why he felt a national program was premature.[52] His opposition was probably influential in the judgment made by Assistant Secretary of Agriculture Robert W. Long on June 6, 1974, that a trial program should be held in North Carolina.[53] In October, the limited, experimental program received sufficient endorsement to proceed from federal and state entomologists, regulatory personnel, and the cotton industry.[54] The National Cotton Council's original proposal for a national program had discussed and dismissed the proposition of beginning in Virginia and North Carolina.[55] A complex of political and scientific considerations led to the adoption of a limited trial in the east.

Problems of coordinating legal and financial arrangements between the federal and state governments and cotton growers proved to be time-consuming. Congressman Jaime Whitten (D., Miss.), chairman of the Agricultural Appropriations Subcommittee, raised a series of objections to the program between 1974 and September, 1977. They included (1) concerns that the regulatory powers essential to the program amounted to federal land-use control,[56] (2) insufficient grower and state cooperation with the program,[57] and (3) lack of technical feasibility of the eradication technology.[58] The delay until October 1974 of agreement on the size and

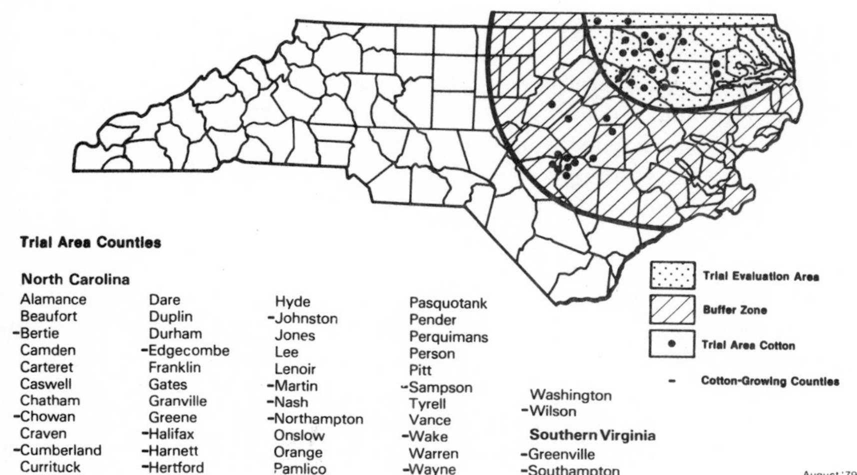

FIGURE 15. Area of Three-Year Boll Weevil Eradication Trial in North Carolina and southern Virginia, showing evaluation area and buffer zone. [Source: USDA/APHIS.]

location of the trial precluded the USDA's request for funds for the trial for the fiscal year 1976 budget[59]; the Senate provided an appropriation of $3.5 million anyway, but acceded to Whitten's position for delay in conference.[60]

Secretary Butz arranged a meeting of cotton industry people, the governors of North and South Carolina, and high USDA officials with President Gerald Ford on January 9, 1976, and Ford allowed the USDA to request $1.7 million for an eradication trial for fiscal year 1977.[61] The Senate in 1976 urged immediate implementation of the trial, but Whitten again prevailed in conference and refused to allow the expenditure of the $1.7 million until all states had passed and implemented legislation authorizing their participation and the Director of the BWRL certified a technical breakthrough that justified trying eradication again. Whitten in 1976 specifically cited the doubts raised by the recently released report of the Cotton Study Team as justification for his skepticism on the adequacy of the technology.[62]

The stalemate lasted until 1977 when Whitten agreed to the USDA's argument that the required technical developments had been achieved with improved mass-rearing and sterilization techniques.[63] The Trial Boll Weevil Eradication Program began in 1978 (Fig. 15).

THE HUFFAKER PROJECT

Just as a certain amount of trauma surrounded the PBWEE, so, too, did the Huffaker Project generate controversy among its participants and between the participants and funding agencies. Unlike the PBWEE, however, disagreements surrounding the Huffaker Project centered more on the *emphasis* given different research lines rather than on the *interpretation* of specific research results. This difference is not surprising because the PBWEE was one experiment in which the results were the key issue; the Huffaker Project on the other hand, was a coordinated series of hundreds of experiments on many insect pests of six crops, the outcome of any one of which was not key to the overall success of the endeavor.

Internal debate emerged from a sense of frustration at the difficulties of meeting extraordinarily complex goals, particularly in the areas of economics and agroecosystem modeling. Carl Huffaker proposed, in 1971 before funding had been secured, that economic analysis and reasoning had to be based on the realities of the private market economy: "Crop pest control in this country rests fundamentally on a system of free enterprise in which a profit to the grower *must be our primary objective.*" He went on to note that benefits to society through lower food and fiber costs and improved quality of the environment were secondary but intertwined with the first. Clarity of thinking demanded that the two be separated, especially if modeling were to include economic factors, but Huffaker believed the amalgamation of the two objectives up to that point had done no harm. He argued that the two were compatible because the long-term interests of growers were moving closer to those of "society and the environment." In addition to placing the profitability of new techniques as the foremost criterion of success, Huffaker argued that it was not their responsibility to plan optimal land-use strategies for the farmer or society, the one exception to this rule being in pest control for forests, in which public ownership and multiple-use potential might warrant optimal land-use studies. For the agricultural crops, profitable pest control for the given crop was the only legitimate objective of their research.[64]

Over two years later, Joseph Charles Headley, an economist on the project's steering committee, revived the question of what economists were supposed to provide in the research. He was concerned about the validity of the continued assumption that what is good for the farmer is also good for society. He also raised another point that had not been formally discussed in the Huffaker Project. Would criteria for economic success of new techniques center upon returns to some individual farmers or also upon effects on the farm population as a whole?[65] Headley's latter question dealt with the fact that farmers are heterogeneous in their abilities to adopt new techniques. Those who can't adopt are frequently less educated and undercapitalized individuals. They have frequently been left behind as their more prosperous neighbors changed production practices and received the benefits of the new research results. Most agricultural scientists have traditionally not been concerned with these problems.

Headley's concerns did not disrupt work in the Huffaker Project, but neither were they ever answered in a particularly satisfactory way. Yet, the inability of the entomologists in the Huffaker Project to handle the most serious questions of their social science colleagues was a source of frustration to at least some of the latter.[66] It relegated them to dealing simply with crop production economics on the individual farm level. Such studies were important, but confining social questions to that level implicitly meant that farmer profitability was all important and that it was acceptable to ignore unequal impacts of new technology. These same issues were also implicit in the PBWEE but received even less attention there.

Headley's concerns were closely connected to another source of problems generated by the Huffaker Project in the area of agroecosystem modeling. What comprises an agroecosystem? A subsidiary question centered on the emphasis given to systems analysis and modeling in the research effort. Headley, in raising questions about possible differential impacts of new techniques on farmers and society, was arguing that any holistic model of an agroecosystem must include a more complete view of the political economy of agriculture. Huffaker and the other entomological investigators involved in the Project had no quarrels with the gist of Headley's questions, but they were unable to deal with the complexities in such research tasks. Modeling plant–insect interactions alone was an extremely difficult task. Thus, the implicit answer given to Headley was that only the most simple aspects of bookkeeping on the farm level were to be included in the modeling efforts; by implication, agroecosystems contained people but without any details of behavior and social organization.

No major rancor was associated with the simplification of agroecosystems, but some irritation was generated over the relative slowness of some crop subprojects, particularly citrus, to develop modeling.[67] A suggestion was even made in 1975 that the citrus work he eliminated from the Huffaker Project, but Huffaker stoutly disagreed.[68] Citrus researchers were more concerned with introducing biological control agents into the U.S. than with mathematical descriptions of the relationships between citrus trees, their pests, and natural enemies of the pests. Paul DeBach, director of the citrus work until health problems forced him to diminish his efforts, argued that regardless of the sophistication in modeling, biological control was in the end an empirical matter. In his view one could have all the equations in the world, but if the biological facts were of poor quality any model based on them would be worthless.[69] One good natural enemy could eliminate or reduce any need for chemicals regardless of whether one had equations to "explain" how it worked.

Debate over the sophistication of economics and the role of modeling in the Huffaker Project was largely an internal matter that only occasionally threatened the ability of the participants to continue working together. Indeed, such disagreements as there were served primarily as centers of lively debate that was stimulatory rather than inhibitory to fruitful collaboration. Less benign were a series of negotiations between leaders of the Huffaker Project and the National Science Foundation (NSF) over the funding level and length of the Project's existence. At the center of the disagreements lay different perceptions of the role of modeling in the research.

The NSF had an uneasy relationship with the applied agricultural scientists because they continued to operate on the premise that the NSF's mission was to support "basic" science. So long as systems analysis and modeling were emphasized, the NSF was content.* Other aspects of the research tended to interest the Foundation less. These divergences of interests on the two sides created a near impasse in early 1974 as the NSF Board temporarily withheld further funds from the project. The crisis lasted only a day, but its very occurrence was a trauma for the Huffaker Project. In order to understand how it came to pass we must review some of the prior events.

We noted in Chapter 3 that the Huffaker Project began as a component of the International Biological Program (IBP) and that the NSF

*The NSF staff must be credited with the initial impetus that launched the Huffaker Project into the research line of systems analysis and modeling. Ironically, the perspective on modeling that eventually dominated work in the Huffaker Project may have been a profound shift away from the original notions intended by the NSF staff. Biome studies predominated over ecosystem-modeling efforts in other U.S. components of the IBP in the late 1960s and probably were the type of modeling studies envisioned by the NSF. Time-varying life-table studies developed initially from work by R. D. Hughes in Australia, however, were the *modus operandi* adopted in the Huffaker Project. The intellectual history of this subtle but important shift has not yet been described or analyzed. (I thank Andrew P. Gutierrez for bringing this distinction to my attention. Dr. Gutierrez is currently preparing a review of developments in ecosystem modeling.)

became the lead funding agency for IBP projects within the U.S. Hence, Huffaker and his colleagues had submitted their original proposal to the NSF rather than to the USDA, the latter having been the traditional source of support for agricultural science. The NSF at the time was receptive to such projects, especially those which were components of the IBP. We also noted that NSF's Charles Cooper, who had jurisdiction over the original Huffaker proposal, took an active role in reformulating the organization of the proposal away from specific pests to crop systems. Heavy pressure for the use of systems analysis and modeling in the research also originated at the NSF. New patterns of funding and of research were thus strong characteristics of the Huffaker Project, and a mismatch of interests was thus possibly to be expected. This became evident approximately one year after the work had begun.

Cooper left the NSF, and was replaced by William E. Hazen. Hazen along with other project officers from the USDA and the EPA attended the steering committee meeting of the project in November 1972 and the first conference of modelers in January 1973. His "memorandum to the files," written in April, summarized his first assessment of the Huffaker Project's progress with special emphasis on the role, or lack thereof, of modeling.[70] Hazen and his fellow project officers believed that in general good progress was being made, but he pointed to a number of areas he thought weak:

1. Project managers were not devoting enough attention to modeling as a method of managing research, i.e., using simple models to identify data gaps, filling the gaps, generating a more complex model, and identifying further data gaps.
2. Components of each of the six agroecosystems had not been identified. Were they to consist simply of crop and pest, or were economy and the general environment to be added as well? Here, Hazen was pointing out the problem of lack of economic sophistication that was later amplified by Headley, as noted earlier.
3. How was the central management of the project, i.e., Huffaker, Ray Smith, the subproject directors, and the executive committee, going to exercise control over the research directions and accomodate the constraints imposed by "level funding"? Here, Hazen was alluding to the notion that increased levels of support were not likely to be forthcoming, a preview that was born out in fact within the year.
4. No "modeling coordinator" had at that time appointed with a defined set of tasks to encourage and unify modeling efforts among the six agroecosystems.

Hazen was clearly concerned that modeling was not playing the role he expected it to play in the research. Was he generally negative about the prospects for improvement? Hazen's memorandum to the files certainly made no such pessimistic judgment, but Carl Huffaker reacted strongly as if the entire project were under attack. Huffaker believed it was a "scorching indictment of our uses of modeling." Moreover, he felt the NSF misunderstood the program as a whole and its managerial methods for coordination and communication. He requested that the subproject leaders and executive committee members outline responses and needed changes in the operations of the research.[71] In May, Hazen visited with Huffaker, Smith, and Andrew P. Gutierrez (a modeler at Berkeley), and managed to smooth some of the ruffled feathers that had been raised by his memorandum.[72] A factor of more practical importance was Hazen's news that the NSF definitely would not increase its funding level for the third year of operation of the Huffaker Project. The foundation had alloted $1.3 million for the year 1973, and that was where the figure would stay for 1974.[73] The EPA would probably match the NSF's contribution, so the total would be $2.6 million for 1974. In their original proposal, Huffaker and his colleagues had requested $3.7 million for 1974, so Hazen's word on the funding situation was seen as a major setback. In the year following the May meeting with Hazen, relationships between the NSF and the project continued to deteriorate and this exasperated the patience of Huffaker and other project leaders.

Huffaker began planning for 1974 operations on an optimistic note. Even though the Ecosystems Analysis Division at the NSF had no capacity for increased funding for 1974, he believed that new funds might be made available by a different NSF program, Research Applied to National Needs (RANN). Therefore, he directed his subproject leaders to draw up budgets totaling $3.6 million rather than $2.6 million as suggested by Hazen.[74] In July, Huffaker went a step further and asked his subproject leaders to submit *three* budgets for 1974: one for $3.6 million, one for $2.6 million, and one for $1.0 million specifically designed for RANN. He planned to submit the first but anticipated falling back to the second.[75] Spirits were still high among project leaders as they met in Chicago in September and were joined by Hazen's replacement at the NSF, Jerry F. Franklin.[76] Passage of summer brought the dark clouds of fall, winter storms, and uncertainty in the Huffaker Project. We turn first to the negotiations Huffaker and his associates had with the NSF.

By October, little hope prevailed for funding at any level beyond $2.6 million from the NSF and the EPA. Moreover, organizers of the Huffaker Project became convinced that continued tenure of their project at NSF beyond 1974 was in doubt. In early October, Ray Smith called on Warren Muir, a staff member of the President's Council of Environmental Quality (CEQ). Muir told Smith that some people in the Office of Management & Budget (OMB) thought the Huffaker Project was to last three years, not five years.[77] Smith explained otherwise, and Huffaker followed up with statements to Muir and the NSF outlining the verbal understanding he had reached with Cooper in 1971 that their work had to proceed for five years if it was to produce significant results.[78] Muir's contacts in OMB enabled him to report to Huffaker in December that arguments for a five-year tenure had been persuasive, but that the funding level to be expected would not rise above $2.6 million per year. If more money was to be had, then the USDA had to be the source.[79] Overtures to the USDA began in October, a thread we will pick up shortly.

Huffaker submitted the formal proposal for 1974 in October with a budget total of $3.6 million. Not unexpectedly, both the NSF and EPA refused to process it and demanded a reduced figure of $2.6 million. Huffaker instantly complied with his stack of already prepared alternative budgets, and the proposal again began its path through the NSF peer-review system.[80] Results of that review reinitiated a sense of dismay among the leaders of the Huffaker Project because they felt their project was not receiving an adequate or fair hearing at the NSF.

James Thomas Callahan, Franklin's assistant program director at the NSF, had the unpleasant duty of summarizing the NSF's views for Huffaker.[81] Focusing on agroecosystems was acknowledged to be the best organizing device for the project, but reviewers questioned whether adequate exchange between crop systems was being achieved. They particularly objected to the fact that models between projects were incompatible. Publications were judged as "unimpressive" or "scant," and the management expenses* were seen as excessive and of little productivity. Callahan noted that the reviewers found little to criticize in the alfalfa and cotton work, but all others (citrus, pome and stone fruits, soybeans, and pine bark beetles) were criticized either for lack of modeling, too narrow a focus on particular pests species rather than a whole-ecosystem approach, or insufficient efforts to develop adequate sampling techniques for estimating the sizes of pest populations.

* Management expenses consisted of three-fourths of Huffaker's salary, one-fourth of Ray Smith's, and additional funds for an administrative assistant (Jane Clarkin) and secretary (Nettie Mackey). Management also bore expenses for importation of foreign predators and parasites and coordinating modeling. The proposal also had a request for an "executive scientist" to help Huffaker manage the Project.

Callahan's letter, mailed December 20, was a poor Christmas present. After the holidays, Huffaker took up the task of preparing a defense of the Project's work. He thanked Callahan for the detailed comments and asked for a meeting between the NSF and Huffaker Project leaders in early February.[82] He asked leaders of the subprojects to respond in detail to the complaints.[83] Most researchers react with some pique to criticisms of their efforts, and responses to Huffaker from his research colleagues were in keeping with this tradition. By the time Huffaker left for Washington in early February, he was armed with a sheaf of letters defending the project's efforts. Perhaps one of the most universally attacked criticisms was that of insufficient publications. Justifiably, the workers argued that at the time their report was prepared, they had been working only 16 months; complaints of few publications were, they felt, unwarranted at that time.

Huffaker's conversations with Callahan in Washington on February 6 served largely to increase his sense of unease over the NSF's handling of the project. Not only was the level and duration of funding at issue, but an old issue was raised once again: was the NSF justified in supporting "applied" science when its mission was to support "basic" science? It appeared to Huffaker and his close associates that the NSF was seriously reconsidering its commitment to sponsoring research on the creation of nonchemical methods of insect control. As Perry Adkisson so aptly put it later in April, "There is some funny business in the NSF over our project."[84] Yet the NSF may not have been of a single mind, as so often happens in large bureaucracies. H. Guyford Stever, director of the NSF, had in early January assured Jarvis E. Miller (Adkisson's boss at Texas A & M University) that the NSF was still interested, which elicited from Adkisson the comment, "Dr. Stever apparently has more interest in the project than do the project managers."[85] "Funny business" at the NSF became distinctly unhumorous in late February when the NSF withheld its approval of funds ($1.3 million) for 1974 on the grounds that the project had insufficient basic science to warrant NSF participation.[86] Huffaker and Smith prepared in less than 24 hours a summary of basic science in the project and transmitted it via telephone to NSF project officers.[87] Their arguments emphasized their investigations of ecological relations between crop plants, pests, natural enemies, and physical factors. Unfortunately they were always in a box because in the conventional wisdom agricultural research was applied research by definition.

Funds were awarded for 1974, but Haffaker realized that their position at the NSF was precarious. He launched a flurry of activities to resurrect the project's financial security. First, he urged his investigators to couch their results in more traditional ecological language and to publish in such journals as *Ecology* or *Ecological Monographs* rather than the more applied agricultural journals such as the *Journal of Economic Entomology*.[88]

Second, Huffaker responded in detail to the criticisms Callahan had given in his December letter and in his conversations in February; Huffaker also used this opportunity to respond in detail to the criticisms voiced over a year earlier in Hazen's memorandum to the files of April 3, 1973.[89] His spirited defense, buttressed by letters he had received from his project associates, focused on (1) the fact that the NSF was attempting to change the orientation of the research away from that which had originally been worked out with Charles Cooper, and (2) the likelihood that NSF project officers and reviewers were not familiar enough with the work of the project to render useful criticims. Huffaker was particularly upset that NSF personnel had not made enough site visits to learn the intricacies of agricultural research, a telling complaint because none of the NSF officers had an agricultural research background.

Finally, Huffaker and Ray Smith requested a meeting with Eloise Clark, NSF's director of the Biological and Medical Science Division with jurisdiction over Callahan and Franklin in Ecosystems Analysis.[90] In May, Huffaker, Smith, Newsom, and Adkisson met with Clark and her staff to iron out their differences, but important correspondence preceded that session.

Huffaker had intended that his barrage of letters about the state of the project would open the way for frank discussions with the NSF. Franklin responded in kind with his view of the situation.[91] He insisted that NSF's objectives for the research had not changed and that "biological control" was of great importance. Moreover, Franklin argued that the NSF had never envisioned that the Huffaker Project could completely analyze six agroecosystems; NSF urgings had been designed to encourage the use of modeling as a tool in the development of new control techniques, not to see modeling as the end result of a research project.

Franklin also delved into his difficulties of trying to function as a staff person obligated to serve both the Huffaker Project and the NSF Board. The latter matter was being particularly difficult because of the basic versus applied science issue. Board members asked why the USDA wasn't participating in or totally supporting this project because it was agricultural research. As an addition, Franklin noted that no chance existed for increased funding during 1975 and that if funded at all, the NSF might have to cut its contribution from $1.3 million to about one million dollars. Only the USDA could rescue the Huffaker Project from financial disaster.

It is at this point we must pick up the thread leading to the USDA, which had played an important role by providing the majority of the funds to launch the Huffaker Project in 1972. At the outset, however, the USDA had stated that its contributions were for one year only (as discussed in Chapter 3). The department's prominence in the first year of the project's funding was thus matched by its thunderous absence in the second and subsequent years. We can thus easily sympathize with those members of the NSF Board who kept asking where was the USDA in this quintessential agricultural work.

The USDA's absence was surely not due to any lack of invitation for their participation in the Huffaker Project. Selected personnel had participated on a voluntary basis from the beginning as investigators and as members of the steering committee. E. F. Knipling was a member of the steering committee until his full retirement from the USDA in 1973.[92] Huffaker and other leaders of the project had always wanted participation and funding from the USDA, and they continued their discussions with high-level USDA personnel in late 1973 and early 1974.[93] Yet, these pleas were to no avail, and the USDA never became involved in the Huffaker Project, other than in minor ways, after its initial contribution of funds.[94] Why did the primary agricultural research agency in the U.S. refuse to participate in one of the major efforts to supplant the Nation's overdependence on insecticides with nonchemical control techniques?

Two closely related factors underlay the USDA's steadfast refusal to join. The first was essentially bureaucratic, the other essentially philosophical, but neither could be totally separated from the other. First, the Huffaker Project, ostensibly a research program based in the state universities and a few USDA labs, was in reality a new "shadow" research administration on a quasi-national basis. Entomological research up to 1972 had been done either in the relatively centralized laboratories of the USDA under guidance from Washington or in the relatively decentralized state universities under much looser guidance from experiment station directors and department heads. The Huffaker Project established a new research directorate in which scientists who voluntarily associated themselves with the Project could work under a guidance system directed from Berkeley with strong input from the executive committee of the project. Huffaker strongly believed in the principle that the best scientific creativity came from voluntary participation by researchers, but continued participation required a researcher to adhere to the basic goals of the overall research effort.

The NSF compounded the image of a new bureaucracy by its insistence at the project's inception that Huffaker serve as the locus for approval of all changes in research direction, a prerogative usually reserved for NSF staff members.[95] Thus, Huffaker, officially an employee of the University of California, became for all intents and purposes a major research administrator for the NSF and the EPA.

Administrative arrangements within the Huffaker Project were sufficient to threaten the USDA's established turf. The specter of bureaucratic competition was compounded by the deliberate exclusion of USDA people from important decision-making roles within the Huffaker Project:

- In 1971, extensive conversations and meetings were held to plan cooperation among USDA and state researchers in Huffaker's proposal. The USDA suggested a dual university–USDA administrative steering committee for guiding the work on a national basis. Huffaker and his close associates desired close cooperation with the USDA, but they were extremely leery of any shared administrative responsibilities that might diminish research conducted according to the IPM paradigm.[96] As a result, no lasting, high-level coordination of research ever developed.
- No member of USDA ever served on the executive committee, the group Huffaker and Smith referred to most often for guidance.
- No member of the USDA ever served as a subproject director.
- During 1972 and 1973, the first two years of operation, the steering committee did have some USDA representatives, but they were nonvoting members. Voting privileges were extended to them only in 1974, when more USDA personnel were added.[97]

Exclusion of USDA personnel from the halls of power within the Huffaker Project in effect made the project unwelcome at the USDA. Complaints about budgetary constraints notwithstanding, the USDA could have found money to put into the project after 1972 if its research leaders had chosen to do so. At the very least, the USDA could have put up a stronger show of moral support. That they chose not to was partly to protect their own abilities to set research directions rather than let the Huffaker Project take some of that responsibility from them.

Bureaucratic concerns alone, however, cannot explain the USDA's position. Philosophical considerations also played a role and are the key to understanding the tension between the USDA and the Huffaker Project. Both organizations were searching for alternatives to the reliance on insecticides. The problem was that a different paradigm for guiding research had emerged and matured in the USDA under the leadership of Knipling (see Chapter 4).

Knipling's TPM paradigm for seeking a way out of the insecticide dilemna was best exhibited in the PBWEE. The approach involved massive campaigns against selected single species when technology was judged adequate to warrant an eradication effort. Even though both Knipling and other USDA staff served at different times on the steering committee of the Huffaker Project, they were not major contributors to it. Many USDA personnel regarded the research efforts of the Huffaker Project as worthy but only a fall-back position from more ambitious eradication schemes. Huffaker and Ray Smith, as proponents and architects of IPM, believed that eradication schemes, however sophisticated, were usually wrongheaded and doomed to costly failure because they were ecologically naive.

Leading entomologists in the USDA and the Huffaker Project were thus miles apart on the philosophical foundations for guiding new research efforts. Under the best of circumstances, it would have been difficult or impossible on philosophical grounds for the USDA to contribute significantly to the Huffaker Project even if no bureaucratic threat had been present.

A peculiar juxtaposition of events made an already difficult situation even more difficult. At the very time that Huffaker and his colleagues came under severe pressure from the NSF (April 1973–May 1974), Adkisson, a leading participant in the Huffaker Project, threw a monkey-wrench into the USDA's and the National Cotton Council's plans to launch a national boll weevil eradication program. Recall that it was the end of August, 1973, that Adkisson took his stand against judging that the PBWEE had demonstrated the capacity for boll weevil eradication. Anger and dismay at the embarrassment of having such an expensive experiment judged a failure could only have exacerbated any sense of unease that USDA officials had about dealing with the Huffaker Project. Ill will combined with a continuing strong drive for trying another expensive eradication experiment made an impenetrable wall around any discretionary money that the USDA might have put into the Huffaker Project.

Failure to gain major USDA support led leaders in the Huffaker Project on a frustrating search for backing in many other places. Approaches to the Congress led largely by the TEXARLAM (Texas, Arkansas, Louisiana, and Mississippi) group produced some support but ultimately were not productive in securing the funding levels sought by the project.[98] Some moral support was gained from the directors of the Agricultural Experiment Stations in the Western Region and from the National Association for State Universities and Land Grant Colleges.[99] Warren Muir on the staff of the CEQ continued his quiet behind-the-scenes support as well. Efforts to direct overhead expenditures into direct research outlays were partially successful.[100]

Despite the setbacks, the bits and pieces of moral support gathered by the project leaders were probably important in pursuading the NSF to continue their funding beyond the growing season of 1974. Huffaker, Smith, Adkisson, and Newsom achieved this concession in May, 1974, during their meeting with Clark, Callahan, and Franklin.

A full review of the project by the NSF, EPA, USDA, and a special panel of basic ecologists was conducted in October 1974. Strong endorsements by the ecologists assured NSF's continued support of the project.[101] The EPA's support was never seriously in jeopardy because their regulatory stance against insecticides made it politically useful for them to be involved in the creation of alternatives to chemicals. Their only concern was that they put no more than 50% of the total funds into the project's budget, thus limiting them to matching NSF contributions. The Huffaker Project continued operating through the growing season of 1978.

CONCLUDING REMARKS

It should be abundantly obvious at this point that efforts to create alternatives to the reliance on insecticides were simultaneously scientific and political activities. Both the PBWEE and the Huffaker Project were founded upon philosophical assumptions within the scientific community and upon the political support of diverse elements from the general society. In their operations, both were subjected to criticism on scientific grounds, and their continued viability depended upon the maintenance of at least a modicum of political support from circles outside the entomological profession. Searching for salvation from the dilemmas posed by insecticides was therefore in its very essence a cultural phenomenon dependent upon both scientific creativity and the mustering of nonscientific social support. We turn in the next part to an analysis of the cultural dimensions of this scientific enterprise.

APPENDIX

Technical Guidance Committee, Pilot Boll Weevil Eradication Experiment

P. L. Adkisson
Department of Entomology
Texas A & M University

F. S. Arant
Department of Zoology and Entomology
Auburn University

Richard Carlton
State Department of Agriculture
Louisiana

T. B. Davich
Boll Weevil Research Laboratory
Agricultural Research Service
U.S. Department of Agriculture

C. C. Fancher
Mississippi Department of Agriculture and Commerce

O. T. Guice
Mississippi State Plant Board
Mississippi State University

W. F. Helms
Plant Protection Division
Animal and Plant Health Inspection Services
U.S. Department of Agriculture

F. G. Maxwell
Department of Entomology
Mississippi State University

R. C. Riley
Cooperative State Research Service
U.S. Department of Agriculture

J. S. Roussel
Louisiana State Agricultural Experiment Station

W. A. Ruffin
Department of Agriculture and Industries
Alabama

D. R. Shepherd
Animal and Plant Health Inspection Service
U.S. Department of Agriculture

George Slater
Cotton Incorporated

Ritchie Smith
National Cotton Council of America

D. F. Young
Mississippi State University

C. R. Parencia (secretary)
Agricultural Research Service
U.S. Department of Agriculture

J. R. Brazzell (co-chairman)
Animal and Plant Health Inspection Service
U.S. Department of Agriculture

E. F. Knipling (co-chairman)
Agricultural Research Service
U.S. Department of Agriculture

REFERENCE NOTES

1. Evaluation of the Pilot Boll Weevil Eradication Experiment, USDA, Animal and Plant Health Inspection Service, p. 1 (hereafter cited as USDA, Evaluation). This unpub-

lished report bears no date but was prepared by late 1973. It contains 60 pages plus three appendices: Intensive Field Sampling in Eradication and First Buffer Areas, Pilot Boll Weevil Eradication Experiment, 1973, by E. P. Lloyd; Relative Populations and Suggested Long-Range Movements of Boll Weevils Throughout the Area of the Pilot Boll Weevil Eradication Experiment as Indicated by Traps in 1973, by W. H. Cross; and Use of In-Field Traps Baited with Grandlure in the Pilot Boll Weevil Eradication Experiment in 1973, by D. D. Hardee. This document was the only written summary of the PBWEE until 1976 when the USDA published the proceedings of a symposium held in Feb., 1974 (note 2).

2. E. F. Knipling, "Report of the Technical Guidance Committee for the Pilot Boll Weevil Eradication Experiment," in *Boll Weevil Suppression, Management, and Elimination Technology* (Proceedings of a conference, Feb. 13–15, 1974, Memphis Tenn.), ARS-S-71 (Washington, D.C.: USDA, 1976), pp. 122–125 (hereafter cited as ARS, *Boll Weevil Suppression*). This volume is the only official publication of the results of the PBWEE, issued approximately two and one-half years after USDA, Evaluation.
3. E. F. Knipling, Technically Feasible Approaches to Boll Weevil Eradication, presented at Beltwide Cotton Production–Mechanization Conference, Hot Springs, Ark., Jan. 11–12, 1968, pp. 6, 11.
4. A detailed description of the PBWEE can be found in F. J. Boyd, "Operational plan and execution of the Pilot Boll Weevil Eradication Experiment," in ARS, *Boll Weevil Suppression*, pp. 62–69.
5. The original experimental design was described in National Cotton Council, Selection of Locations for Pilot Boll Weevil Eradication Experiments, Aug. 15, 1969, pp. 5–9, unpublished report by a subcommittee of the Special Study Committee on Boll Weevil Eradication.
6. USDA, Evaluation, pp. 1–2.
7. ARS, *Boll Weevil Suppression*, pp. 70–72.
8. For those with a jaundiced sense of humor, one grower in the PBWEE area did not let the whereabouts of one of his cotton fields be known, and experimenters did not find it until Sept. 21, 1972, more than a year after the PBWEE began. This field was in fact a heavy producer of boll weevils. See USDA, Evaluation, p. 17.
9. O. T. Guice, Jr., "Regulatory activities carried on under the Pilot Boll Weevil Eradication Experiment," in ARS, *Boll Weevil Suppression*, pp. 73–74. Guice was Director, Division of Plant Industry, Mississippi Department of Agriculture and Commerce, and a member of the TGC.
10. For a discussion of regulatory problems in a national eradication effort, see H. L. Bruer, "Regulation aspects of boll weevil eradication in the cotton belt" (hereafter cited as Bruer, Regulation), in ARS, *Boll Weevil Suppression*, pp. 159–160.
11. T. B. Davich, D. D. Hardee, and Jesus Acála M., Long-range dispersal of boll weevils determined with wing traps baited with males, *J. Econ. Entomol.* 63 (1970): 1706–1708.
12. Waldemar Klassen to T. W. Edminster, May 31, 1973, files of C. R. Parencia.
13. E. F. Knipling and J. R. Brazzel to Gordon E. Guyer, Feb. 27, 1973, files of C. R. Parencia.
14. Entomological Society of America Review Committee, The pilot boll weevil eradication experiment, *Bull. Entomol. Soc. Am.* 19 (1973): 218–221 (hereafter cited as ESA Review Committee, The pilot).
15. D. D. Hardee and F. J. Boyd, "Trapping during the Pilot Boll Weevil Eradication Experiment, 1971–73" (hereafter cited as Hardee and Boyd, Trapping), in ARS, *Boll Weevil Suppression*, pp. 82–89; data cited are in Table 3, p. 83.

16. D. D. Hardee, "Development of boll weevil trapping technology," in *ibid.*, pp. 34–40.
17. F. J. Boyd, "Boll weevil population levels during the in-season and reproduction–diapause control phases of the Pilot Boll Weevil Eradication Experiment," pp. 75–81 (hereafter cited as Boyd, Boll weevil population levels); and E. P. Lloyd and W. P. Scott, "Intensive sampling of twenty-five selected fields in eradication and first buffer areas of the Pilot Boll Weevil Eradication Experiment in 1973," pp. 108–112; both in ARS, *Boll Weevil Suppression*.
18. Hardee and Boyd, Trapping, data from Table 9, p. 86.
19. *Ibid.*, data from Table 6, p. 84.
20. Boyd, Boll weevil population levels, p. 79.
21. Hardee and Boyd, Trapping, data calculated from Table 6, p. 84.
22. Perry Lee Adkisson, personal interview, May 30–31, 1978.
23. *Ibid.;* C. R. Parencia to Participants [of Technical Guidance Committee, PBWEE], September 13, 1973, files of Charles R. Parencia.
24. Adkisson, personal interview.
25. *Ibid.;* J. Ritchie Smith to Individuals Listed on Attached Statement, Apr. 11, 1973, files of C. R. Parencia.
26. Handwritten note in files of Perry L. Adkisson.
27. Adkisson, personal interview.
28. E. F. Knipling, *The Basic Principles of Insect Population Suppression and Management*, Agriculture Handbook No. 512 (Washington, D.C.: USDA, 1979), pp. 537–538. I have been unable to locate any more precise statement Knipling made connecting his conclusions about the PBWEE with the data generated in the PBWEE.
29. W. H. Cross, "Relative populations and suggested Long-range movements of boll weevils throughout the area of the Pilot Boll Weevil Eradication Experiment as indicated by traps in 1973" (hereafter cited as Cross, Relative populations), in ARS, *Boll Weevil Suppression*, pp. 103–107.
30. Boyd, Boll weevil population levels, p. 81.
31. Cross, Relative populations, p. 104.
32. E. P. Lloyd, J. R. McCoy, and J. W. Haynes, "Release of sterile male boll weevils in the Pilot Boll Weevil Eradication Experiment in 1972–73," in ARS, *Boll Weevil Suppression*, pp. 95–102; E. F. Knipling, Suppression of pest Lepidoptera by releasing partially sterile males, *BioScience* 20 (1970): 465–470.
33. *Ibid.* The bodies of released insects were "ebony," a phenotype caused by two recessive alleles. Matings between ebony and wild weevils produced the "bronze" phenotype, the genotype of which was the heterozygote.
34. M. E. Merkl, "Postexperiment developments of the Pilot Boll Weevil Eradication Experiment," in ARS, *Boll Weevil Suppression*, pp. 119–121.
35. D. D. Hardee to J. R. Brazzel through T. B. Davich, Feb. 1, 1974; E. F. Knipling to D. D. Hardee through T. B. Davich, Feb. 5, 1974; both letters in files of J. R. Brazzel.
36. ESA Review Committee, The pilot.
37. Although I was not deeply involved with the writing of the Cotton Study Team report, I accept as a staff member for that effort an equal share of the responsibility for any of the report's shortcomings. I believed at the time the report was released that it was fully adequate as a policy study. I continue to believe that the biological reasoning underlying the report's skepticism on eradication is sound. The shortcomings became clear to me only after the passage of several years and lay in our inability at the time to comprehend the socio–political dimensions of the eradication movement. I continue to believe that the five-volume set from the Kennedy Committee

is still one of the finest studies ever done on the problems associated with pest control.

38. E. F. Knipling, personal interview, July 13–14, 1976.
39. *Ibid.*
40. E. F. Knipling to Sterling Hendricks, Dec. 16, 1974; Robert E. Green to Reviewers of the Pesticide Study, Dec. 30, 1974; Robert E. Green to E. F. Knipling, Apr. 24, 1975; E. F. Knipling to Robert E. Green, Apr. 29, 1975; E. F. Knipling to Philip Handler, June 25, 1975; E. F. Knipling to Philip Handler, July 18, 1975; E. F. Knipling to Philip Handler, Aug. 27, 1975; E. F. Knipling to John Coleman, Aug. 28, 1975; and Philip Handler to E. F. Knipling, Sept. 23, 1975. All of above supplied by E. F. Knipling, July 13–14, 1976.
41. *Pest Control: An Assessment of Present and Alternative Technologies, Vol. 3, Cotton Pest Control* (Washington, D.C.: National Academy of Sciences, 1975), 139 pp.
42. *Ibid.*, pp. 4–5.
43. Robert R. Coker to Perry Lee Adkisson, May 26, 1972, files of J. Ritchie Smith.
44. *Overall Plan for a National Program to Eliminate the Boll Weevil from the United States* (Memphis: National Cotton Council, Dec. 4, 1973), pp. 5, 6, 57 (hereafter cited as NCC, *Overall Plan*).
45. T. B. Davich to R. J. McCracken, Dec. 13, 1973, files of J. R. Brazzel.
46. Bruer, Regulation, in ARS, *Boll Weevil Suppression*, p. 159.
47. J. Ritchie Smith, personal interview, June 5, 1978.
48. J. R. Phillips, [comments], in ARS, *Boll Weevil Suppression*, p. 169.
49. Charles Lincoln, [comments], in ARS, *Boll Weevil Suppression*, p. 172; L. D. Newsom, "The elimination concept and its alternative," in *Ibid.*, pp. 149–153; Dan F. Clower, A Statement Regarding the Plan to Eradicate the Boll Weevil from the United States, presented to the American Farm Bureau Cotton Advisory Committee, Apr. 9, 1974.
50. Fowden G. Maxwell to Louis N. Wise, Apr. 17, 1974, files of J. Ritchie Smith.
51. W. L. Giles to John C. Stennis, June 25, 1974, files of J. Ritchie Smith; Louis N. Wise to Jamie L. Whitten, July 16, 1974, files of J. R. Brazzel; R. Dennis Rouse to Robert W. Long, 3 June 1974, files of J. Ritchie Smith.
52. P. L. Adkisson to L. D. Anderson, June 5, 1974, files of P. L. Adkisson; idem, personal interview.
53. F. J. Boyd to J. R. Brazzel, June 6, 1974, files of J. R. Brazzel.
54. Albert R. Russell to Earl L. Butz, Feb. 14, 1975, files of J. Ritchie Smith.
55. NCC, *Overall Plan* pp. 56–57.
56. U.S. Congress, House, *Agriculture–Environmental and Consumer Protection Appropriation Bill, 1975*, H. Rept. 1120, 93rd Congress, 2nd sess., 1975, p. 28.
57. U.S. Congress, House, *Making Appropriations for Agriculture and Related Agencies Programs for the Fiscal Year Ending June 30, 1976, and the Period Ending September 30, 1976, and for Other Purposes*, H. Rept. 528, 94th Congress, 1st sess., 1976, p. 9; U.S. Congress, House, Committee on Appropriations, *Agriculture and Related Agencies Appropriations for 1977*, Hearings, Part 3, 94th Congress, 2nd sess., 1976, p. 458; U.S. Congress, House, Committee on Appropriations, *Agriculture and Related Agencies for 1978*, Hearings, Part 2, 95th Congress 1st sess., 1977, pp. 346–347; U.S. Congress, House, *Agriculture and Related Agencies Appropriations Bill, 1978*. H. Rept. 384, 95th Congress, 1st sess., 1977, pp. 46–47.
58. U.S. Congress, House, *Making Appropriations for Agriculture and Related Agencies Programs for the Fiscal Year Ending June 30, 1976, and the Period Ending September 30, 1976, and for Other Purposes*, H. Rept. 528, 94th Cong. 1st sess., 1976, p. 9; U.S. Congress,

House, Committee on Appropriations, *Agriculture and Related Agencies Appropriations for 1978*, Hearings, Part 3, 94th Cong., 2nd sess., 1976, pp. 453–456; U.S. Congress, House, Committee on Appropriations, *Agriculture and Related Agencies Appropriations for 1978*, Hearings, Part 2, 95th Cong., 1st sess., 1977, p. 385; U.S. Congress, House, *Agriculture and Related Agencies Bill, 1978*, H. Rept. 384, 95th Cong., 1st sess., 1977, pp. 46–47.

59. U.S. Congress, Senate, Committee on Appropriations, *Agriculture and Related Agencies Appropriations, Fiscal Year 1976*, Hearings, Part 1, 94th Congress, 1st sess., 1975, pp. 92–94, 130–132.
60. U.S. Congress, Senate, *Agriculture and Related Agencies Appropriation Bill, 1976*, S. Rept. 293, 94th Cong., 1st sess., 1976, p. 18; U.S. Congress, House, *Making Appropriations for Agriculture and Related Agencies Programs for the Fiscal Year Ending June 30, 1976, and the Period Ending September 30, 1976, and for Other Purposes*, H. Rept. 528, 94th Cong., 1st sess., 1975, p. 9.
61. Albert R. Russell to Beltwide Action Committee, Jan. 22, 1976, files of J. Ritchie Smith.
62. U.S. Congress, House, *Agriculture and Related Agencies Appropriation Bill, 1977*, H. Rept. 1224, 94th Cong., 2nd sess., 1976, pp. 41–42.
63. Robert R. Coker to Boll Weevil Action Committee on Boll Weevil Eradication, September 30, 1977, files of J. Ritchie Smith. Attached to this memorandum are press releases from the USDA and the National Cotton Council plus a summary prepared by the USDA of improvements in technology.
64. C. B. Huffaker to Proposed Ad Hoc Committee to consider "The Role of Economic and Systems Analysis in the IBP–Biological Control–Crop Ecosystems Project," quotes on pp. 1 and 3, files of C. B. Huffaker.
65. J. C. Headley to Carl Huffaker, Sept. 21, 1973, files of C. B. Huffaker.
66. Richard B. Norgaard to J. C. Headley, Nov. 8, 1973, files of C. B. Huffaker.
67. F. N. David to C. B. Huffaker, Nov. 22, 1972, files of C. B. Huffaker.
68. Carl B. Huffaker to Christine Shoemaker, July 2, 1975, files of C. B. Huffaker.
69. Paul DeBach, personal interview, Mar. 22–23, 1977.
70. William E. Hazen, Memorandum to the Files, Apr. 3, 1973, 3 pp., files of C. B. Huffaker.
71. Carl Huffaker to Subproject Leaders, Executive Committee, Apr. 17, 1973, files of C. B. Huffaker.
72. C. B. Huffaker to P. L. Adkisson, S. D. Beck, G. E. Guyer, R. F. Smith, E. J. Armbrust, R. W. Stark, S. C. Hoyt, L. D. Newsom, P. DeBach, May 3, 1973, files of C. B. Huffaker.
73. *Ibid.*
74. C. B. Huffaker to Subproject Leaders, June 29, 1973, files of C. B. Huffaker.
75. Carl B. Huffaker to Principal Investigators and Subproject Leaders, July 23, 1973, files of C. B. Huffaker.
76. L. D. Newsom, Minutes of Steering Committee Meeting, Integrated Pest Management Project, Palmer House Hotel, Chicago, Sept. 11, 1973, files of C. B. Huffaker.
77. Ray F. Smith, [Notes of] Wednesday, Oct. 3, 1973, Washington, D.C., files of C. B. Huffaker.
78. Carl B. Huffaker to Warren Muir, Oct. 18, 1973; Carl B. Huffaker, Statement Concerning Tenure of the Integrated Pest Management Project (National Science Foundation Grant GB-34718), Nov. 8, 1973, 2 pp.; both in the files of C. B. Huffaker.

79. C. B. Huffaker, Notes on a talk with Warren Muir, Dec. 10, 1973, files of C. B. Huffaker.
80. C. B. Huffaker, IPM Project, Minutes of Executive Committee Meetings, Nov. 25–26, 1973, and subsequent related matters (no date but presumably written in late Nov. or early Dec. 1973), files of C. B. Huffaker.
81. James T. Callahan to Carl B. Huffaker, Dec. 20, 1973, files of C. B. Huffaker.
82. Carl B. Huffaker to J. T. Callahan, January 3, 1974, files of C. B. Huffaker.
83. Carl B. Huffaker to P. L. Adkisson, E. J. Armbrust, Paul DeBach, T. W. Fisher, E. H. Glass, S. C. Hoyt, L. D. Newsom, R. W. Stark, and R. F. Smith, Jan. 4, 1973 [*sic,* should be 1974], files of C. B. Huffaker.
84. P. L. Adkisson to C. B. Huffaker, Apr. 29, 1974, files of C. B. Huffaker.
85. H. Guyford Stever to Jarvis E. Miller, Jan. 4, 1974; P. L. Adkisson to Carl Huffaker and Ray Smith, Jan. 14, 1974; both in files of C. B. Huffaker.
86. Jerry F. Franklin to Carl B. Huffaker, Apr. 15, 1974, files of C. B. Huffaker.
87. Carl B. Huffaker and Ray F. Smith, "Some Scientific and Ecological Advances of the IBP Pest Management Project," memo, Feb. 22, 1974, 7 pp., files of C. B. Huffaker.
88. Carl B. Huffaker to All Participants in IPM Program, Mar. 1, 1974, files of C. B. Huffaker.
89. Carl B. Huffaker to James T. Callahan, Mar. 12, 1974, files of C. B. Huffaker.
90. Carl B. Huffaker and Ray F. Smith to Eloise Clark, Mar. 11, 1974, files of C. B. Huffaker.
91. Jerry F. Franklin to Carl B. Huffaker, Apr. 15, 1974, files of C. B. Huffaker.
92. C. B. Huffaker and Ray F. Smith, The Principles, Strategies and Tactics of Pest Population Regulation and Control in Major Crop Ecosystems, Progress Report and Renewal Proposal, Vol. 1, Integrated Summaries, Dec., 1972, mimeo, pp. 5–13, 28–32.
93. P. L. Adkisson to Robert W. Long, Oct. 11, 1973; Carl B. Huffaker to Robert C. Riley, Jan. 14, 1974; both in files of C. B. Huffaker.
94. Robert W. Long to Eloise E. Clark, June 17, 1975, files of C. B. Huffaker. Long, assistant secretary of the USDA, had agreed to contribute $267,000 of USDA funds to the Huffaker Project in May, 1974. His letter to Clark listed the projects they supported and said their commitment had been fulfilled.
95. C. B. Huffaker to Principal Investigators, IBP Project, Apr. 19, 1972, files of C. B. Huffaker.
96. The USDA's suggestion was summarized by Huffaker in a memorandum to the steering committee, IBP/NSF Proposals, Oct. 14, 1971, files of C. B. Huffaker. Particularly strong negative reactions to the USDA's suggestion came in letters to Huffaker from Robert L. Rabb (N.C. State Univ., Oct. 21, 1971), T. W. Fisher (Univ. of Calif., Riverside, Nov. 9, 1971), H. T. Reynolds (Univ. of Calif., Riverside, Oct. 22, 1971), and Ray F. Smith (Univ. of Calif., Berkeley, Oct. 25, 1971), all in the files of C. B. Huffaker.
97. C. B. Huffaker and Ray F. Smith, Integrated Pest Management, The Principles, Strategies and Tactics of Pest Population Regulation and Control in Major Crop Ecosystems, Progress Report and Renewal Proposal, Vol. 1, Integrated Summaries," Nov., 1973, mimeo, pp. 25–26.
98. C. B. Huffaker, IPM Project, Minutes of Executive Committee meetings, Nov. 25–26, 1973, and subsequent related matters (no date but presumably prepared in late Nov. or early Dec., 1973); F. G. Maxwell to Carl B. Huffaker, Dec. 11, 1973; both in the files of C. B. Huffaker.

99. J. B. Kendrick to Chairman Swindale, Regional Director Browning, Regional Director Fortmann, Regional Director Halpin, Assistant Secretary Long, Aug. 13, 1974; Ray F. Smith, [Notes], Aug. 2, 1974; both in the files of C. B. Huffaker.
100. Carl B. Huffaker to A. G. Manza, Mar. 12, 1974; J. B. Kendrick to C. B. Huffaker, Aug. 10, 1974; both in the files of C. B. Huffaker.
101. Carl B. Huffaker to Principal Investigators, Executive Committee, Steering Committee of the IPM Project, Oct. 29, 1974, files of C. B. Huffaker; C. B. Huffaker, personal communication, 1979.

PART III

Entomology in Its Cultural Context

Creation of expert entomological knowledge is the central problem in this study. Specific events involving particular individuals were the focus of the historical drama reconstructed in the previous five chapters. At the heart of the action lay decisions on research lines, articulation of general theories and strategies, interpretation of data, and a series of developments in the political life of the U.S. It would be impossible to understand the major trends within the discipline without an understanding of these intimate details. Nevertheless, larger cultural forces also had important impacts on the growth of entomological knowledge.

In this section, we turn to a general analysis of the interactions between American culture on the one hand and entomological expertise on the other. General principles are illustrated with examples from the previous section, but the focus will be on considerations that transcended the activities of individual scientists. Chapter 6 outlines a general conceptual framework, and Chapter 7 covers the philosophical problems underlying entomology. Chapter 8 highlights the technological revolution in agriculture, a social transformation that, above all other factors, guided the creation of entomological expertise. Personal and professional impacts of the agricultural revolution on entomologists are the subject of Chapter 9. The study concludes (Chapter 10) with a discussion of how entomological expertise fits into contemporary agricultural production.

CHAPTER 6

A Conceptual Framework

ENTOMOLOGY IS BOTH SCIENCE AND TECHNOLOGY

Understanding the relationships between science and technology has long been a central problem for those who have studied the generation of expertise. The fundamental questions focus on (1) What is the relationship between changes in the two, i.e., does technological change depend upon scientific change or vice versa, are the two best seen as independent ventures, or is a more complex relationship based upon mutual interactions involved? (2) How do the two areas compare in their modes of work, social organizations, motivations, and personnel? (3) What relationship does each bear to the reality of the natural, material world that exists independently of human society?

Little uniformity has arisen from the various analyses of science and technology except for the general conclusion that the two types of activities have been separable since the mid-nineteenth century; each proceeds under different rules and poses different problems for comprehension and management. Simultaneously, the two fields are related, but the relationship is a dynamic one that fluctuates according to time period, geographic region, culture, and subject matter.[1] Tremendous overlap between scientists and technologists exists in some fields, but not others. Science is an activity that generates models of the natural world that are seen variously as truth, ever-closer approximations of truth, or at least partially a reflection of the cultural roots and organization of scientists.[2] Technology, on the other hand, is a system for manipulating the material world in order to satisfy physical wants and needs. Generators of technology deal directly with material reality, but their expertise may depend as much on the social and political organization of the economy as upon their use of theoretical models of nature.

Entomology is a field of expert knowledge in which both science and technology are intimately intertwined and virtually inseparable for analytical purposes. Entomologists frequently find themselves simultaneously performing functions that can be seen as "science" on the one hand and "technology" on the other. Certainly over a period of years, virtually every economic entomologist has performed both types of activity. Indeed, the close association and frequent confounding of scientific and technological modes of activity in entomology is a source of some of the disputes that have racked the field in the years since 1945. Even though it is difficult to disentangle the two types of activity from one another, it is essential to try insofar as possible.

We begin by noting that technological expertise can be separated into four component parts, using a scheme outlined by Carl Mitcham: (1) knowledge, (2) process, (3) artifact, and (4) volition.[3] Technology-as-knowledge has two components: theoretical or scientific knowledge and practical or technical knowledge. For entomology, the former comprises our ability to describe and predict how pest populations change in response to natural and human processes that alter their habitat. It is based upon our knowledge of insect physiology, insects as organisms, and insects as evolving species. The latter includes our ability to modify insect habitats so that pest populations reach a desired level.

Entomology-as-scientific-knowledge is closely related to other biological sciences, and many entomologists think of themselves as biologists who work with insects. Entomology-as-technical-knowledge is a heterogeneous body of practices, some of which are explicitly based on scientific theories. Some of the simplest insect control measures did not originate from scientific concepts but rather from folk customs. For example, the first selections of resistant varieties of crop plants undoubtedly came from the intuitive use of the least damaged plants as the source of seeds for the following year's crop. Entomology since its professionalization in the nineteenth century has been more complex because of its attempt to be a scientific, as well as useful, art. The use of mathematical models in the design of practical control technique, for example, is the current leading device for creating technology solidly based on science. Both the Huffaker Project and the Pilot Boll Weevil Eradication Experiment were efforts of this type despite their many differences.

Mitcham suggests that technology-as-process includes the diverse activities of invention, design, making, and using.[4] He points out that the first two, invention and design, are closely related to technology-as-knowledge, which is where we shall consider them. For our purposes, the most important point is the fact that invention and design of insect control practices have been done since 1945 primarily by those we have identified as the professional entomologists.

Entomology-as-making and -using, on the other hand, is generally done by persons who are not professional entomologists. Chemical manufacturing is perhaps the most obvious example of entomology as a process of making: research chemists, chemical engineers, and many others in the chemical industry are all essential parts of making insecticides. Similarly, the manufacturing of spray equipment and insect traps plus the production of insect-resistant crop seeds can also be seen as part of the making of insect control devices. Our focus has not been on the activities performed by these auxillary troops of the insect control enterprises, but fostering change in insect control practices is decidedly affected by those connected with the chemical industry.

Using insect control practices is also not the province of the professional entomologists but belongs to those who suffer pest problems in the course of their other activities. We have been primarily concerned with the insect control problems of agriculture, but farmers use only about half the insecticides used in all of the U.S. If we accept use of insecticides as a surrogate measure of all insect-control practices, we can conclude that farmers perform about half of the insect control work of this nation. Others who suffer from insects are an extremely heterogeneous group including homeowners, governments, retail establishments such as restaurants, industrial firms, and public health officials charged with control of disease-bearing insects. Generation of expertise on insect control has been closely tied to the insect problems in agriculture, but it should not be forgotten that considerable use of this knowledge has been adapted for use on different kinds of problems by people other than farm businessmen. As with entomology-as-making, we will return to some of the political aspects of entomology-as-using in subsequent chapters.

Entomology-as-artifact, continuing with Mitcham's terminology, helps us focus on a central element of our analysis of insect control practices: the tools by which the job is done. Two levels of "tools" can be distinguished. First, conceptual schemes or paradigms designed by entomologists provide the basis for organizing the multitude of activities performed by farmers in their efforts to control pests. Second, each of the component activities called for in the schemes can be seen as a tool in its own right for performing a specific part of the insect control effort in the production of food and fiber. Examples would include particular insecticides, spray machines, sterile males, attractants and repellants, fertilizing practices, irrigation techniques, selection of plant variety, times and techniques for planting and harvesting, post-harvest preparations for the following crop, systems analysis, and computer simulations. Each of these component tools has important aspects of engineering design, relationships to human bodily functions, aesthetics, environmental impact, and impact on human social structures and values. Their use in coordinated schemes, however, makes it more economical to discuss them as they serve as components rather than individually.

Entomology-as-knowledge, -as-process, and -as-artifict each refers to components of insect control practices that are relatively easy to identify as published literature, overt behavior, and tools, respectively. One is nonetheless still left with the question, Why does a given individual choose to act in a particular way? More specifically for our study, why does a professional entomologist decide to engage in a particular line of research or advocacy of a specific public policy on insect control research or practices? A subsidiary question that we must consider even though it is not central to our examination of the professional entomologists is, Why does an individual farmer or group of farmers act in a particular way toward insects? Surely we must provide some sort of answer to these questions if we are to ameliorate the crises that have beset insect control in the years since 1945. We must deal, in other words, with the question of volition or will to perform specific actions that are part of the insect control technologies.

Volition is unfortunately, as Mitcham points out, perhaps the most difficult of all of the elements to understand. It involves questions of inferring motive from overt behavior and of inquiring into the nature of humans and the natural environment. It is an open question whether we can know our own motivations as individuals, let alone the motivations of others. Similarly, little agreement comes from discussions about the properties of human and natural systems. All such inquiries inevitably collide with metaphysical considerations, and the inquiring scholar's own metaphysical assumptions and presuppositions color the vision that results. We are left, therefore, with the dangerous enterprise of attempting to solve the problem of volition in entomology based on imperfect and subjective evidence.

Evaluation of the evidence must include examination of the metaphysical visions of the various participants, socioeconomic organization of insect control, politics affecting research and regulation, and dynamic interactions between entomology-as-science and entomology-as-technology. Behavior reflecting volition is in other words, embedded within a historical drama, which puts a premium on our ability to understand who did what, and when, before we venture to speculate why. Part II of this book was devoted to unraveling many of the personal interactions, but we are still not prepared to venture conclusions about the nature of volition in entomology. We first need a more refined theoretical sense of the philosophical, political, and economic bases of entomology before we return to the question of volition in Chapter 9.

THE CONFOUNDING OF SCIENTIFIC AND TECHNOLOGICAL EXPERTISE IN ENTOMOLOGY

We began our analysis of the generation of expert knowledge in entomology by dissecting the elements of the field from one another: the scientific from the various technological aspects. We now turn to the reasons for the confounding of entomology-as-science with entomology-as-technology. The high overlap between the scientific and technological dimensions of entomological expertise in professional organization, employment, and individuals underlies the problem. Furthermore, scientific and technological aspects of the field have exhibited a complex and dynamic interaction.

American entomologists originally organized themselves into two different societies that reflected a split between applied and nonapplied aspects of their work. The American Association of Economic Entomologists (AAEE, organized in 1889) consisted primarily of those interested in the technology of insect control, and the Entomological Society of America (ESA, organized in 1906) contained those more interested in the strictly scientific description and analysis of insects, but considerable cross membership existed. In 1949, efforts were begun to merge the two groups into one organization. Merger was readily approved by the members of the AAEE, but sufficient opposition to amalgamation existed in the ESA to require two ballots before the requisite majority for merger was obtained.[5] Unification began in 1953 under the name of Entomological Society of America, a scientific and professional society devoted to all aspects of the study and control of insects.

Cross-membership before unification plus the publication of applied articles in the old ESA's journal had always made the distinction hazy between the scientific and technological aspects of entomology. After unification, one could determine a particular entomologist's location along the spectrum between the scientific and technological poles of entomology only by an examination of an individual's interests. As exemplified below, many members of the new ESA simply can't be dichotomously categorized in terms of scientific versus technological interests.

Surveys of entomologists have distinguished ESA members by their current activities and by their memberships in other societies. For example, 19% indicated in 1972 that they spent most of their time in basic research while 24% were primarily occupied with applied research.[6] Similarly, about 6% of ESA members belonged to the Ecological Society of America, which probably indicates individuals with strong interests in basic science.[7] Despite these differences, the fact that entomologists themselves chose to merge all practitioners, basic and applied, into one profession means entomology as a discipline must be seen as a melding of scientific and technological dimensions.*

Place of occupation likewise gives little clue to an entomologist's interests or work activities. Forty-seven percent work for a college or university and 28% work for the federal government, the two largest loci of employment for the profession. It would be impossible to distinguish the scientific aspects of entomology from the technical within this large group of the profession as both the universities and the federal government perform both basic and applied research. Private industry employs 12% of the profession, and state and local governments absorb about 5%.[8] These two types of employers contain entomologists primarily concerned only with applied aspects of the discipline.

We may lament that it is difficult or impossible to distinguish the entomologist-as-scientist from the entomologist-as-technologist on the basis of professional societies and employer, but can we distinguish the two by looking at specific individuals? Here, too, we are forced to acknowledge that particular entomologists alternate their modes of operation. Consider, for example, the diverse works of a few entomologists who figured so prominently in the historical drama unfolding since 1945:

Edward Fred Knipling was a careful observer of the behavior of the screwworm flies in the late 1930s, and began constructing models of insect populations in the mid-1940s.[9] Neither of these dimensions of his work led immediately to control techniques; rather they were systemically organized pieces of information about the natural world and efforts to articulate a model of it, respectively. In this type of activity, Knipling

* Motivations for merging the AAEE and the old ESA were based primarily on a desire for a stronger professional image. The new ESA was large enough to support a full-time executive officer, which neither predecessor had. Efforts to enhance professional stature have been a perennial theme in entomology since the nineteenth century.

was generating what we usually call scientific expertise. In the 1950s and 1960s, Knipling was the primary designer of programs to eradicate the screwworm fly from Curaçao and Florida and the boll weevil from southern Mississippi, respectively. Design of practical technique is the hallmark of technological expertise, and Knipling was therefore a technologist as well as a scientist.

Ray Fred Smith had a similar heterogeneity in his activities. He and A. E. Michelbacher systematically gathered data on the population dynamics of the alfalfa caterpillar in order to understand the ecology of the insect in the central valley of California. Smith in 1959 was a coauthor of a paper that presented a general theory of insect pest populations as they were affected by natural enemies and insecticides.[10] In both of these efforts, Smith is best described as a scientist. In contrast, Smith's work to establish pest control districts to control the alfalfa caterpillar in the late 1940s contained the crucial element of design. He was clearly acting as a technologist in that case.

James Roland Brazzel offers yet another example of the difficulty of distinguishing scientist from technologist in the field of entomology. In 1959, he and Leo Dale Newsom published a paper on the basic physiology of diapause in boll weevils.[11] Within a few years, Brazzel had taken that information and used it in the design of the reproduction–diapause control method. Once again we see that entomologist-as-scientist is confounded in the same person with entomologist-as-technologist.

Some entomologists have less diversity in their career patterns and behave more consistently either as a scientist or as a technologist. Extension entomologists, for example, are virtually pure technologists as they take expertise generated by researchers and help farmers design practical insect control schemes for particular situations. Some research entomologists function strictly as scientists without a thought given to the design of control practices, but they have for the most part been excluded from this story on economic entomology. It is worth noting, however, that one of the most eminent of basic entomologists, Carroll Williams of Harvard University, gave careful attention to a quintessential technological problem, the design of insect hormones for control practices.[12] We must conclude therefore that individual entomologists generally bind together both scientific and technological knowledge. Our models for the generation of that expertise must therefore accommodate both elements.

Generation of entomological expertise has involved a dynamic interplay between the scientific and technological elements. No simple formula exists to relate changes in entomological science and entomological technique to one another because the relationship changed with time and subject matter, among other factors. A few examples will demonstrate this complexity.

Technology can precede science in the generation of entomological expertise. Control practices in this case are adopted either intuitively or on pragmatic grounds with no underlying foundation of how the technique works in terms of abstract models of the material world.

- Albert Koebele's introduction in 1888 of the vedalia beetle to control cottony cushion scale in California ignited a flurry of interest in comparable importations of other natural enemies to control different pests.[13] Knowledge of secondary parasites (parasitic insects that attack the predators or parasites of pest insects), however, was rudimentary, and thus the danger of inadvertant importations of secondary parasites was high. Only a few entomologists had the skills needed to avoid introductions of secondary parasites. Leland O. Howard of the USDA almost forbade further importations of natural enemies into California, but in 1913 Harry Scott Smith assumed responsibilities for such work in the state. Howard trusted Smith's skills.[14] Technological enthusiasm for biological control had run ahead of its scientific foundations before Smith's appointment.
- DDT was adopted for use in Switzerland, the U.S., and elsewhere before molecular details of its mode of action were known. It was known to poison nerves, but how remains unknown even to this day. Technological expertise that provided the justification for its adoption lay primarily in the uncontested fact that it killed a wide variety of insects and had a long duration of action in the field. Unknown and possibly unimaginable at the time of its adoption were its abilities to cause eggshell thinning in some species of birds and its propensity to concentrate in the fatty tissues of species occupying high trophic levels in the biosphere.[15] As in the previous example on biological control, technological expertise in the absence of scientific knowledge can lead to the adoption of practical techniques that might otherwise not be adopted if all of their attributes in the natural world were known.

Science can precede technology in the entomological game. This will be an obvious statement when one considers the voluminous information and theories generated systematically by entomologists on evolution, behavior, cellular and reproductive physiology, and genetics, few of which have been used to design practical control methods. Science leading technology generally becomes of interest only when a particular piece of basic knowledge is thought to have important implications for design, but the efforts to transfer it into a technology are frustrated. The nature of the barrier varies, but a few examples will indicate that they may be many and complex.

- Hormones controlling insect development such as ecdysone and juvenile hormone have been known for decades, but only two registrations for juvenile hormone have been accepted. High expectations for the "third-generation" insecticides have not yet materialized in the form of significant alternative control technologies. A recent policy study lamented this sad state of affairs but suggested that both biological and social considerations might in principle confine hormonally based insecticides to minor uses.[16]
- Mathematical models depicting the interactions of host and parasitic insects have appeared in the basic scientific literature since the 1930s and before (albeit accompanied by a stream of criticism and debate even to this day). Strategies of integrated pest management based upon biological control as the core suppression technique are founded upon those theories from basic ecology. Despite immense hopes and the considerable efforts exhibited in research, much of the basic knowledge remains unused. Robert van den Bosch estimated that only 10% of California's cotton acreage was under integrated pest management despite his judgment that the knowledge base was adequate to bring all of it under such control technologies.[17] Socioeconomic barriers are the primary hindrances to translation of this science into practical technologies, as we will discuss in more detail later.

Science and technology can interact rapidly to effect more rapid change in each compared to rates of change that would exist in the absence of interactions. Most applied scientists, regardless of specialization, earnestly hope they are always working in an environment in which such symbiotic effects will occur. Mutual enhancement can generally occur only when the research environment encourages or demands it. Specific efforts must be made to overcome the barriers of discipline, research organization, and geography. Some prominent events from entomology exemplify the idea.

- Studies on the natural history and basic population dynamics of velvetbean caterpillar, soybean looper, green cloverworm, corn earworm and stink bug on soybeans in the South resulted in the design of new, generally higher economic thresholds for insecticidal treatments.[18] These studies were conducted as part of the Huffaker Project and its efforts to understand agroecosystems in a holistic fashion. More accurate economic thresholds are perhaps the simplest of all technological advances in entomology because of their potential ease of implementation. They require only that the farmer count insects present in the field and spray less often; major shifts in farm production technology are not required.

- Studies led by Erma Vanderzant and others on the basic nutrition of the pink bollworm (*Pectinophora gossypiella* Saunders) were conducted in the late 1950s. They were closely coordinated with efforts to develop mass-rearing and sterilization procedures for the insect. By the early 1960s, Vanderzant's basic studies had been incorporated into the design of mass-rearing methods, and by 1970 they were in use in efforts to control the moth by the sterile male technique.[19]

Our detailed dissection of entomology to this point was intended to identify the intellectual and social elements of the field. We are now in a position to offer some interim conclusions about entomological expertise. Economic entomology must be seen as a continuum of diverse activities.[20] First, entomologists acting as *technologists* emphasize the element of design. Will a suppression technique or a coordinated set of them actually work in socioeconomic and biological contexts? If not the technology fails, and the entomologist as "engineer" must return to the drawing board. Second, the entomologist as an *applied scientist* emerges in efforts to formulate the rules governing the behavior of agroecosystems. Such theories must include both socioeconomic factors as well as those limited to the biology of the crops, pests, and other species involved. This aspect of entomology is applied rather than basic because agricultural systems themselves are human artifacts rather than natural systems.* Third, entomologists are sometimes *basic scientists*. In this mode, they are indistinguishable from other biologists who have no applied interests.

* A peculiarity surrounding our concept of "natural" must be noted here. If humans are seen as *not* part of the natural world, then clearly everything we do, such as agriculture, is somehow not "natural." In this case, applied science must be rigorously distinguished from basic science on the grounds that the latter studies only "natural systems" (i.e., without human involvement). If, on the other hand, we include humans in nature, then clearly everything we do, including agriculture, is "natural." If such a meaning is accepted, the differences between applied and basic science disappear. Given the strong tradition of distinguishing the two types of science, we have continued the language. Our use of the term *natural* is one strictly of historical convenience at this point.

Understanding entomology as a continuum ranging from the strictly technological to the strictly scientific immediately allows us to make a fundamental observation that helps explain why entomology has been such a controversial field: criteria for truth of entomology-as-technology are not the same as criteria for truth of entomology-as-science. Practical suppression techniques must in some way relate to both the biological relam and the socioeconomic world. Entomologists as designing engineers must therefore be as savvy in their instincts for the sociopolitical as they are for the biological. Science, on the other hand, requires entomologists to relate to the community of other biologists, and the standards for judging excellence of research may be quite different from those used in judging technological adequacy. A different way of outlining the dilemma faced by entomologists is that they as individuals slide back and forth on a continuum of activities from the technological to the scientific. Yet when they are at opposite ends of the spectrum (a position they frequently occupy simultaneously) their expertise is judged by different rules. They have accommodated to the tension as an integral part of their intellectual life.[21]

KNOWLEDGE IN ENTOMOLOGY

The historical narrative presented in Part II was implicitly based upon an epistemology that now needs to be made explicit. Two reasons demand such as effort. First, our presentation of the history of entomology since 1945 was shaped by presuppositions derived from a theory of knowledge that is in its own right problematic and controversial. Use of other epistemological concepts was possible and, had they been adopted, the history presented would have been quite different. The reader needs to share the insights I can offer into my own presuppositions in order to judge my historical narrative. Second, different sides in the controversies about insect control technologies appealed to "expert knowledge," "objective facts," and ultimately to a conception of entomological science as "truth" in order to bolster their own viewpoints and destroy those of their opponents. Entomologists of different persuasions frequently entered intellectual slugfests to defend particular concepts, especially those relevant to policy issues on insect control. The epistemology adopted here has substantial implications for the use of "scientific knowledge" in the articulation of public policy.

Thomas S. Kuhn and Harold I. Brown, both inspired by insights from the history of science, heavily influenced the epistemological basis for this study.[22] Kuhn chose to regard both discovery and justification of scientific theories as important and relevant to our understanding of that knowledge.[23] Brown extended Kuhn's assertion by proposing a scheme by which discovery can be understood as a rational process. Both Kuhn and Brown moved substantially away from the more traditional positivism stemming from August Compte. A detailed examination of the differences between the empiricist-based philosophy of science and the historicist philosophy need not be given here; interested readers can better pursue the argument in the works of Kuhn, Brown, and others.[24] Instead, a short resume of the epistemology proposed by Brown will suffice as a guide for this book.

Brown argues that all perceptions of the natural world ("empirical data" in the language of the working scientist) are seen as meaningful only in terms of some theory, which in turn was the mental device guiding the collection of the data in the first place.[25] Put another way, no such thing as theory-free evidence exists in the daily research activities of science. No researcher can pursue the gathering of all facts in a Baconian fashion in an effort to articulate inductively scientific laws or theories: "we require some basis for deciding what research problems are worth pursuing. It is our accepted theories, the systems of presuppositions to which we are already committed, which provide this basis."[26]

Brown argues that the concepts of a particular science and the network of relationships between them form a web; the entire net of relationships and concepts constitutes the working propositions or presuppositions that guide the collection and interpretation of data by research workers. He adopts Kuhn's notions of normal science and revolutionary science by arguing that in revolutions the contents of the relationships and concepts change.[27] During nonrevolutionary periods, researchers use the network of concepts and relationships as a guide for the collection and interpretation of data deemed to be important.[28]

Brown's metaphor of a web is derived from Kuhn's notion of a paradigm that guides research designed to solve some puzzle that is itself defined by the paradigm. For Kuhn, puzzle-solving is the essence of normal science. A scientist ordinarily assumes that if he cannot solve the puzzle, the fault lies in himself and his methods rather than with the paradigmatic proposition guiding his work. Only in the face of repeated "anomalies" (data that solve no puzzles and remain uninterpretable in the framework of the existing paradigm) will efforts be made to invent new paradigmatic propositions.[29] Articulation of a new, competing paradigm establishes the problem of theory choice for the concerned scientific community. Kuhn and Brown believe that the traditional maxims for deciding between competing theories (accuracy, consistency, breadth, simplicity, and fruitfulness) give ambiguous rules for making such choices.[30] No algorithm exists for making a mechanical choice between competing paradigms. The only recourse, Brown argues, is to human judgment.[31] The collective judgment of a scientific community is the foundation upon which paradigms continue in use or are discarded.

Kuhn explicitly excluded technological developments from his purview on the development of scientific knowledge,[32] and Brown, in his efforts to formalize a Kuhnian epistemology, did not venture into the realm of technological expertise either. Edward W. Constant used the concept of paradigmatic change in his study of the turbojet revolution in aircraft propulsion.[33] Entomology is a field of expertise that is simultaneously scientific and technological, so we will follow Constant in expanding the concept of paradigmatic change to the study of insect control technologies (Chapter 9). For the moment, we note that a historicist epistemology requires an understanding of new meanings for some old words that are central to scientific and technological creativity. The utility and meaning of language, as argued by D. L. Phillips, surely rests upon socially accepted conventions.[34] A major problem in the politics of insect control is that conventions concerning language collapsed (Chapter 7) so it is essential to make clear the meanings of fundamental ideas.

Rationality, long cited as a hallmark of the scientific enterprise, has frequently been interpreted as the use of or search for an algorithm or set of rules that scientists apply when making decisions. If the algorithm is correct, then anyone who knows how to use it will achieve the same decision in a question of theory choice. Kuhn and Brown argue that such an algorithm cannot be found; rationality instead consists of trained scientists, working within a paradigmatic framework, making judgments based on a set of values. Accuracy, consistency, breadth, simplicity, and fruitfulness for further research constitute some of the most important of these values; Kuhn adds that social utility could be added to this list, a value that in entomology looms high in importance.[35]

Objectivity is a casualty of the new concept of rationality, but only in terms of the positivistic notion of science establishing true theories of nature. Brown argues that objectivity must instead be understood as a process in which theory choices are made. The process depends upon scientists making reasoned judgments, that is, decisions tied to observation, theory, and values. He does not envision objective decision-making as the arbitrary selection of theories without reason. In Brown's sense, objectivity is a property of knowledge that comes only after substantial testing of competing theories by different researchers. He argues that multiple testing has always been included as part of the process of positivistic science, but largely to correct for the mistakes in the use of rational rules seen as algorithms. Because algorithms do not exist in Brown's epistemology, multiple testing is even more important, because it provides the experiences necessary for reasoned judgments by a community of research workers.[36] At the foundation of Brown's (and Kuhn's) concept of objectivity is the reality of the material world that exists independently of any theory. As a materialist, Brown believes that despite all of the errors that might be made individually and collectively by scientists, ultimately we can anticipate that stimuli from nature will force the correction of erroneous theories.

Scientific knowledge in the positivistic sense of infallible truth does not exist in Brown's epistemology. Rather, he suggests that "truth" needs to be understood in two senses: Truth_1 is the reality that exists in nature. Truth_2 is the reality described in paradigmatic propositions currently held by a collection of reaearchers working in a particular area. Scientific knowledge is the best collective judgment made by a particular community of researchers in a particular time period and is therefore truth_2.[37] Truth_2 may be synonymous with truth_1, but it may not be. Furthermore, we cannot tell the difference. A group of scientists will always believe that their particular version of truth_2 is in fact as close to truth_1 as anyone has ever gotten and is a good approximation of truth_1.

Brown's concept of scientific knowledge as truth_2 may be outrageous, even dangerous, to many. For example, scientists arguing for a particular research pattern over another will frequently let their argument lapse into language suggesting that the paradigm they hold is truth_1 and ought to command the respect of all other researchers. Similarly, policy debates using scientific expertise have an enormous tendency to use that knowledge as if it were truth_1 instead of truth_2. After all, what better way is there to defeat a political opponent than to have infallible knowledge about the nature of the material world?

Scientific knowledge demoted to the status of truth_2 from its privileged position of truth_1 raises the potential for a series of ugly charges against Brown's epistemology: historicism, psychologism, relativism, and subjectivism. It is beyond the scope of this book to explore each of these issues other than to note that Brown's major reply is that all of these terms become derogatory only on the presupposition that the scientific method can achieve infallibly the positivistic goal of articulating truth_1.[38] Neither Brown, Kuhn, nor I would argue that science is forever incapable of achieving truth_1, but the historical record suggests that truth_1 is a most elusive entity to capture. For two hundred years, for example, physicists took Isaac Newton's mechanics as truth_1. Yet Albert

Einstein's relativistic mechanics displaced Newton's scheme in the community of physicists and showed his mechanics to have been at a level of $truth_2$. The record of scientific progress over the past 300 years is sufficient for this writer to accept the notion that what we have at any particular moment in time from a group of scientists is an articulation of $truth_2$.

Provisional acceptance of Brown's epistemology and the outlines of Kuhn's model for scientific change opens up an avenue of approaching the analysis of developments in entomology. Specifically, it indicates that we can understand the tumultous events in the discipline as efforts to establish paradigms for guiding research. We need to understand the meaning of both the concepts and the relationships between them for each of the major paradigms invented. Further, we need to understand how different entomologists made their choices between competing paradigms and the effect such choices had upon the profession of entomology. Inquiry into the nature of theory choice takes us into the "reasoned judgments" that Brown argues constitute scientific rationality. In particular it allows us to search for the values that particular individuals exercised in their decision making. Elucidation of values underlying scientific research choices will in turn lead us to the other aspect of entomology, technological expertise. Before we begin, however, we need further to refine the notion of paradigm and how it can be applied in an analysis of entomology.

PARADIGMS REFINED

Kuhn's original concept of paradigms that guided scientific research was based on the notion that they had two characteristics: (1) an ability to attract an enduring community of researchers, and (2) an ability to generate problems or puzzles plus the conceptual tools for their solution.[39] Subsequent criticism of Kuhn's notion of paradigms and his theory of scientific change forced Kuhn to modify his views, and, some suspect, possibly to abandon them.[40] Kuhn's ambiguous status vis-à-vis his own concepts of scientific change are interesting in their own right but need not overly concern us here. We will simply adopt his more mature articulation of the concept of paradigm and use it to elucidate the events in entomology.

Kuhn's refined concept of paradigm led him to suggest the term *disciplinary matrix* for the set of notions that he originally designated by the word *paradigm*. Disciplinary matrix refers to the set of elements possessed by the practicing members of a discipline that allows them to discuss professional matters unproblematically and to achieve a degree of unanimity in their scientific undertakings that would otherwise be blocked by each scientist's different historical experiences. The elements most central to Kuhn's notion of disciplinary matrix are symbolic generalizations, models, and exemplars, each of which requires some description.

Symbolic generalizations are statements that summarize the major, accepted findings of the profession in an easily understood, shorthand notation. Kuhn suggests that equations such as f = ma and statements such as "chemical composition is in fixed proportions by weight" or "all cells come from cells" are major symbolic generalizations for physics, chemistry, and biology, respectively. Researchers learn these generalizations during their training and begin their own research careers with efforts to apply them to the solution of new and yet unsolved puzzles. In Brown's terms, Kuhn's symbolic generalizations would be part of the concepts tied together by relationships and which during normal science elicit little or no critical scrutiny.

Models are a complex set of baggage in Kuhn's refined concept of paradigm. They range from preferred analogies to deeply held, metaphysical commitments giving ontological status to some entity. Models serve as heuristic devices; for example, an analogy may suggest a way of looking at some phenomenon in terms of an already understood event. Research paths toward a solution of an unknown event may then be suggested by the research paths that led to the solution of the earlier event. Models containing metaphysical commitments define the entities needing investigation and the criteria for judging success. Differing metaphysical commitments may therefore demand different research programs that in turn will be subject to different notions of excellence.

Exemplars are the third element of Kuhn's refined sense of paradigm and the element that originally led him to propose the use of the term paradigm. They are the set of concrete problems that a discipline had already solved and which usually constitute the examples of success presented in textbooks. Students and researchers, Kuhn argues, learn how to do their science by studying past exemplars of practitioners in their field. Mastery of these exemplars allows the researcher to incorporate the symbolic generalizations and models of the discipline into his own mind for use in attacking new and unsolved puzzles.

Brown was less interested in the criticism that attended Kuhn's original concept of paradigm and his subsequent modification of it. Instead, he roughly equated *paradigm* with "theory that guides research" and which is composed of concepts tied by relationships. Both concepts and relationships undergo change during paradigm shifts or, in Kuhn's language, revolutionary science. For our purposes, we can accept Brown's notion of concepts related to each other in a theory as equivalent to Kuhn's notion of symbolic generalizations. Brown's presuppositions involving concepts and relationships are like Kuhn's models, especially when the concepts and relationships involve metaphysical commitments. Kuhn's exemplars have no exact counterpart in the language of Brown's epistemology, but clearly are included in Brown's use of the term *paradigm*.

SUMMARY REMARKS

All conceptual frameworks for the analysis of expert knowledge are problematic in the sense that the study of expert knowledge is at this point a disputed process. Another way of putting it is that no one paradigm dominates the historical and philosophical analysis of science and technology. In this chapter, we have outlined the major features of the analytical scheme underlying this book. It begins with the notion that entomology is both a science and technology. The technological aspects of entomology are complex and consist of elements we know as knowledge, process, artifact, and volition. Of these elements, volition is the most difficult to analyze, and we will use Chapters 7 through 9 to establish the philosophical and sociopolitical basis for an explanation of why entomologists engaged in their particular activities. For the moment, we note that the scientific and technological aspects of entomological expertise are intimately intertwined and thereby provide a tension to the discipline: criteria for truth in scientific studies differ from criteria for excellence in technology. Understanding truth in scientific knowledge requires an epistemology. We have adopted for this book a theory of knowledge that was articulated by Thomas Kuhn and Harold Brown. Articulation of paradigms and choice among paradigms are the central activities of entomologists-as-scientists in this epistemology. In the next chapter, we reconstruct the major paradigms that have been articulated in American economic entomology in the years since 1945.

REFERENCE NOTES

1. Industrialized societies of the twentieth century can make a sharp distinction between scientist and technologist on the basis of separate professional organizations. Distinctions between the two modes of activity were more difficult to make before the mid-nineteenth century, and contrasting interpretations of their relationships have

been presented. R. A. Buchanan argues that science and technology before 1850 are both reflections of a single "Promethean Revolution" that began in Medieval Europe. The distinctions we see today have been the result of professionalization ["The Promethean Revolution: Science Technology and History" in *History of Technology 1976*, A. Rupert Hall and Norman Smith, eds. (London: Mansell, 1976), pp. 77–83]. Otto Mayr argues that a search for one relationship between science and technology is bound to fail because there have been many [The science–technology relationship as a historiographic problem, *Technology and Culture* 17 (1976): 663–673]. Edwin Layton has argued that science and technology were separate before the nineteenth century but came into closer relationships afterward; they still can be distinguished, however, by professional organization and the element of design in technology, among other factors [American ideologies of science and engineering, *Technology and Culture* 17 (1976): 688–701].

2. The nature of scientific knowledge and how it is created has been a lively field of study since the appearance of Thomas S. Kuhn's *The Structure of Scientific Revolutions* in 1962. A convenient collection of some of the important papers surrounding Kuhn's work is in Imre Lakatos and Alan Musgrave, eds., *Criticism and the Growth of Knowledge* (Cambridge: Cambridge Univ. Press, 1970), 282 pp.
3. Carl Mitcham, "Types of Technology," in *Research in Philosophy and Technology*, Paul T. Durbin, ed., 1 (Greenwich, Connecticut: JAI Press, 1978): 229–294.
4. *Ibid.*, p. 242.
5. E. G. Linsley, Consolidation of the Entomological Society of America and the American Association of Economic Entomologists, *Ann. Entomol. Soc. Am.* 45 (1952): 359.
6. Betty Hardee and Kazuo Tomita, "A Survey of Scientific and Professional Characteristics of the General Membership of the Entomological Society of America," Report No. 25, Johns Hopkins University, Center for Research in Scientific Communication, July, 1973, p. 6.
7. *Ibid.*, p. 9.
8. *Ibid.*, p. 6.
9. See for example, E. F. Knipling and B. V. Travis, Relative importance and seasonal activity of *C. americana* C. and P. and other wound-infesting blowflies, Valdosta, Ga., 1935–36, *J. Econ. Entomol.* 30 (1937): 727–735; E. F. Knipling, personal communication, Nov. 10, 1978.
10. A. E. Michelbacher and Ray F. Smith, Some natural factors limiting the abundance of the alfalfa butterfly, *Hilgardia* 15 (1943): 369–397; V. M. Stern, Ray F. Smith, R. van den Bosch, and K. S. Hagen, The integration of chemical and biological control of the spotted alfalfa aphid: The integrated control concept, *Hilgardia* 29 (1959): 81–101.
11. J. R. Brazzel and L. D. Newsom, Diapause in *Anthonomus grandis* Boh., *J. Econ. Entomol.* 52 (1959): 602–611.
12. C. M. Williams, Third-generation pesticides, *Scientific American* 217 (July, 1967): 13–17.
13. Richard L. Doutt, "The historical development of biological control," in *Biological Control of Insect Pests and Weeds*, Paul DeBach, ed. (New York: Reinhold Pub. Corp., 1964), pp. 21–42.
14. L. O. Howard, *A History of Applied Entomology*, Smithsonian Miscellaneous Collections, Vol. 84, Nov., 1930, pp. 155–156; L. O. Howard to Harry S. Smith, June 20, 1921, copy supplied by Harold Compere.
15. U. S. Environmental Protection Agency, *DDT* (Washington, D.C.: EPA, 1975), 300 pp.
16. *Pest Control: An Assessment of Present and Alternative Technologies* (Washington, D.C.: National Academy of Sciences, 1975), pp. 343–344.

17. Robert van den Bosch, *The Pesticide Conspiracy* (Garden City, New York: Doubleday & Co., Inc.), p. 173.
18. L. D. Newsom, M. Kogan, F. D. Miner, R. L. Rabb, L. G. Turnipseed, and W. H. Whitcomb, "General accomplishments toward better pest control in soybean," in *New Technology of Pest Control*, Carl B. Huffaker, ed. (New York: Wiley and Sons, 1980), pp. 74–75, Table 3.11.
19. P. L. Adkisson, Erma S. Vanderzant, D. L. Bull, and W. E. Allison, A wheat germ medium for rearing the pink bollworm, *J. Econ. Entomol.* 53 (1960): 759–762; Milton T. Ouye, Effects of antimicrobial agents on micro-organisms and pink bollworm development, *J. Econ. Entomol.* 55 (1962): 854–857; Clyde A. Richmond and Carlo Ignoffo, Mass rearing pink bollworms, *J. Econ. Entomol.* 57 (1964): 503–505; Agricultural Research Service, *Plant Protection Division 1970* (Washington, D.C.: USDA, 1971), pp. 18–19.
20. The continuum described here is adapted from a general scheme proposed by Edwin T. Layton, American ideologies of science and engineering, *Technology and Culture* 17 (1976): 688–701.
21. Charles E. Rosenberg has written extensively on the tension impinging upon applied sciences. See *No Other Gods* (Baltimore: Johns Hopkins Univ. Press, 1976), 273 pp., for a convenient summary of his work. Chapter 9, "Science, technology, and economic growth," is particularly important.
22. Thomas S. Kuhn, *The Structure of Scientific Revolutions*, 2nd ed. (Chicago: University of Chicago Press, 1970), 210 pp. (hereafter cited as Kuhn, *Structure*); idem, *The Essential Tension* (Chicago: The University of Chicago Press, 1977), 366 pp. (hereafter cited as Kuhn, *Tension*); Harold I. Brown, *Perception, Theory, and Commitment* (Chicago: Precedent Publishing, Inc. 1977), 203 pp. (hereafter cited as Brown, *Perception*).
23. Kuhn, *Tension*, p. 326.
24. Karl R. Popper's *The Logic of Scientific Discovery*, 2nd ed. (New York: Harper and Row, 1968), 480 pp., is frequently contrasted with Kuhn's work. Popper acknowledged that historically science frequently developed with irrational elements, but he believed that an empiricist-derived logic enabled scientists to construct ever closer approximations of truth. A standard compendium of the issues involved is Imre Lakatos and Alan Musgrave, eds., *Criticism and the Growth of Knowledge* (Cambridge: Cambridge University Press, 1970), 282 pp. Recent articles exploring the epistemological issues include John Krige, Popper's epistemology and the autonomy of science, *Social Studies of Science* 8 (1978): 287–307, and Michael Mulkay, Knowledge and utility: Implications for the sociology of knowledge, *Social Studies of Science* 9 (1979): 63–80. Current literature on the philosophy of science can be traced through the "Critical Bibliography," an annual publication of the History of Science Society in *Isis;* e.g., for 1979 see *Isis* 70 (1979), "*Critical Bibliography 1979,*" pp. 21–25.
25. Brown, *Perception*, p. 81.
26. *Ibid.*, p. 101.
27. *Ibid.*, pp. 111–116.
28. *Ibid.*, pp. 95–101.
29. Kuhn, *Tension*, pp. 266–292.
30. *Ibid.*, pp. 320–339.
31. Brown, *Perception*, pp. 147–148.
32. Kuhn, *Tension*, pp. 237–239; Margaret Masterman, "The nature of a paradigm," in *Criticism and the Growth of Knowledge*, Imre Lakatos and Alan Musgrave, eds. (Cambridge: Cambridge University Press, 1970), p. 71.

33. Edward W. Constant, A model for technological change applied to the turbojet revolution, *Technology and Culture* 14 (1973): 553–572.
34. Derek L. Phillips, *Wittgenstein and Scientific Knowledge: A Sociological Perspective* (London: The Macmillan Press, Ltd., 1977), p. 47.
35. Brown, *Perception,* pp. 145–151; Kuhn, *Tension,* pp. 330–331.
36. Brown, *Perception,* pp. 154–155.
37. *Ibid.,* p. 153.
38. *Ibid.,* pp. 145–154.
39. Kuhn, *Structure,* p. 10.
40. Kuhn, *Tension,* pp. 293–319; Martin J. Klein, Aber Shimony, and Trevor J. Pinch, Paradigm lost? A review symposium, *Isis* 70 (1979): 429–440.

CHAPTER 7

The Philosophical Foundations

We are now ready to reconstruct the philosophical foundations of entomology since 1945. Of particular importance are the presuppositions and concepts that were fundamental components of each of the major paradigms: Integrated Pest Management (IPM), Total Population Management (TPM), and chemical control.

PRESUPPOSITIONS

Presuppositions provide the background for all scientific work. Some of the most common include such tightly held beliefs as "every effect has a cause" and "the material world is real." These particular metaphysical presuppositions are in fact so basic that it is impossible to conceive of science without them. Entomologists shared these particular notions with all other natural scientists, so distinctions within the field lay elsewhere than with such fundamentals.

Presuppositional differences between the three paradigms lay in fundamental notions about the presumed role of man in the natural world. Implicit and explicit answers given to the following questions provide the major demarcations:

- What is the relationship between humans and the natural world?
- Do intrinsic limitations attend human abilities to manipulate the natural world?
- If so, what are the limitations?

The published record of the entomological literature is nearly devoid of serious attention to these difficult questions.[1] A complex range of implicit answers, however, can be found in the literature and from unpublished correspondence and interviews.

Entomologists performing normal science with the chemical control paradigm were not inclined to voice a great deal of sentiment about their attitudes toward the natural world or about the relationship of humans to it. Rather, they focused on the practicality of their mission: find the cheapest and most efficient chemical to control insects and deliver the information to those people who need to control.[2] Implicitly, they accepted the following assumptions:

- The natural world was complex in terms of how insects cause damage, but many of those complexities could be safely ignored if effective poisons were used properly.
- Man's manipulation of nature was necessary for his own well-being. The needed manipulations included the usual agricultural practices of plowing and planting. Once effective insecticides were available, they, too, became part of the "needed" manipulations. Humans were, in short, the stewards of the natural world and both could and should do what was needed to protect their interests.
- Intrinsic limits to man's ability to manipulate nature, if they existed, were far removed from the questions of controlling insects with chemicals. Insecticides had to be used with care because they were poisons, but in using them man was not treading into a situation in which they could result in a deleterious "backfire" on man's welfare.

Entomologist Clay Lyle (Mississippi State University) provided an enthusiastic vision of the chemical future in his presidential address to the American Association of Economic Entomologists in 1946. He believed that the effectiveness of the new insecticides such as DDT and BHC was high and that the general public was eager to follow the lead of entomologists in attacking insect problems. "Is this not an auspicious time," he asked, "for entomologists to launch determined campaigns for the complete extermination of some of the pests which have plagued man through the ages?" He then suggested targets for eradication such as the gypsy moth, housefly, horn fly, cattle grubs, cattle lice, screwworm fly, and Argentine ant. He closed with the exhortation, "In the words of Daniel Hudson Burnham, let us 'Make no little plans. They have no magic to stir men's blood.' "[3]

Lyle's attempt to rouse the troops for a concerted chemical campaign against insect pests was successful, but not in terms of leading to any eradications. Indeed, E. F. Knipling, who later spoke eloquently for eradication attempts against certain key pests, recalled that Lyle's remarks had little impact on the development of his own thoughts.[4] Instead, Lyle's exhortations are important to note because he gave a vision of man's dominant role in the natural world that was a general reflection of the implicit assumptions operating within the largest segment of the entomological community. Lyle's vision was also shared by many farmers.

It is difficult today to find an unabashed adherent to the chemical control paradigm among research entomologists. Even though research papers are still published in which the research design is to find how best to use particular chemicals,[5] researchers generally acknowledge that the use of chemicals carries with it a series of associated problems. Research in entomology, however, is a different activity from the complex work of farmers. The demise of a research community that once stoutly defended the design of research on the basis of the chemical control paradigm has not yet been reflected in a transformation of pest control practice in the farm community.

The research community that developed around the IPM paradigm developed a set of assumptions about the natural world and man's role within it that was different from that implicitly held in the chemical control paradigm. Moreover, the theoreticians of the IPM school were more explicit about the nature of those assumptions.

The most important assumptions made in the IPM school were that (1) humans are a biological species firmly embedded in a complex ecosystem, (2) anything they do to control insects competing with them for resources must be based on the presupposition of man as an ecological entity, (3) man changes the environment with technology to meet his needs, and (4) those technologies are subject to limitations due to human ignorance about the complexity of the environment. The first formal presentation of the IPM paradigm in 1959 stated these assumptions as follows:

> All organisms are subjected to the physical and biotic pressures of the environments in which they live, and these factors, together with the genetic makeup of the species, determine their abundance and existence in any given area. . . . Man is subjected to environmental pressures just as other forms of life are, and he competes with other organisms for food and space.
>
> Utilizing the traits that sharply differentiate him from other species, man has developed a technology permitting him to modify environments to meet his needs. Over the past several centuries, the competition has been almost completely in favor of man. But . . . he changed the environment . . . [and]

> a number of species, particularly among the Arthropoda, became his direct competitors. . . . Today. . . his population continues to increase and his civilization to advance . . . [and] he numbers his arthropod enemies in the thousands of species. . . .
>
> In the face of this increased number of arthropod pests man has made remarkable advances in their control, and economic entomology has become a complex technical field. Of major importance have been new developments in pesticide chemistry and application. . . . Without question, the rapid and widespread adoption of organic insecticides brought incalculable benefits to mankind, but it has now become apparent that this was not an unmixed blessing.[6]

The IPM paradigm was thus firmly based upon fundamental assumptions about the natural world and man's role in it. As the paradigm matured in the 1970s, some important additions were made. First, an explicit sense that man would achieve sound and safe pest control measures by mimicking nature was articulated. Consider the following two statements:

> . . . biological control, together with plant resistance, forms *nature's* principal means of keeping phytophagous insects within bounds in environments otherwise favorable to them. *They are the core around which pest control in crops and forests should be built*. Biological control in practice . . . is . . . often possible only within the framework of integrated control, which itself usually depends upon a core of biological control and plant resistance.[7][my emphasis]
>
> Scientific pest control has always required a knowledge of ecological principles, the biological intricacies of each pest, and the natural factors that tend to regulate their numbers. Today, it is more necessary than ever before to take a broad ecological overview concerning these problems. . . . We cannot afford any longer to disregard the considerable capabilities of pest organisms for countering control efforts. . . . *It is for this prudent reason that we must understand Nature's methods of regulating populations and maximize their application*.[8][my emphasis]

The second addition of note—hinted at in the second quotation, "We cannot afford any longer to disregard the considerable capabilities of pest organisms for countering control efforts"—suggests that man's technological powers may be limited by intrinsic biological factors. Scientists in general and applied scientists in particular are ever reluctant to concede the existence of intrinsic limits to man's knowledge and power. Nevertheless, Robert van den Bosch, one of the foremost theoreticians of the IPM paradigm, moved to such a concession in 1978. He may not have represented a majority opinion within the IPM school, but his criticisms of chemical control were explicitly based on his sense of man's inability to dominate Nature:

> Our problem is that we are too smart for our own good, and for that matter, the good of the biosphere. The basic problem is that our brain enables us to

> evaluate, plan, and execute. Thus, while all other creatures are programmed by Nature and subject to her whims, we have our own gray computer to motivate, for good or evil, our chemical engine. Indeed, matters have progressed to the point where we attempt to operate independently of Nature, challenging her dominance of the biosphere. This is a game we simply cannot win, and in trying we have set in train a series of events that have brought increasing chaos to the planet.[9]

It is important to note that those entomologists such as van den Bosch who had doubts about the ability of man to dominate the natural world based their pessimism on the ills associated with insecticides: resistance, resurgence, secondary-pest outbreaks, environmental damage, and health hazards. To these observations they added their convictions about the complexity of ecosystems and the evolutionary successes of the arthropods over the past 300 million years. In their own literature, they seldom resorted to explicit philosophical considerations about the nature of the man–environment relationship. Rather, they presented their conclusion that man was subject to domination as one derived from an objective consideration of empirical facts. I submit, however, that such images are really metaphysical presuppositions that are not subject to empirical proof. I share this assumption with the members of the IPM school, but that in no way diminishes the importance of recognizing the presupposition for what it is. More importantly, not all entomologists who were upset about the problems associated with insecticides shared this notion about man's relationship to nature, and the type of research they pursued was markedly different as a result.

As noted earlier, Knipling of the USDA was the major theoretician of TPM. An examination of Knipling's works over the period 1955 to the present indicates that he, too, operated on the basis of a series of presuppositions and assumptions that are metaphysical in nature. He shared many assumptions with his colleagues in the IPM school: (1) humans are a biological species firmly embedded in an ecosystem, (2) anything they do to control insects competing with them must be based on the realization that man is an ecological entity, (3) man changes the environment with technology to meet his needs, and (4) sound pest control will come from mimicking natural processes. The overlap of the assumptions of the two paradigms gives them some features in common. Knipling did not accept, however, the notion that technological advances were subject to intrinsic limitations. He readily agreed that ignorance of the complexity of ecological systems was a cause of the failure of some pest control practices, particularly those based on insecticides, but he was a profound optimist who believed that hard work and dedication could solve exceedingly difficult problems in mastering natural processes.

Knipling argued in 1965 that eradication of certain key pests was a legitimate goal for entomological research. His dramatic sense of optimism was shown in his conclusion:

> The development of procedures for achieving and maintaining complete control of specific insect populations will not be easy. A satisfactory solution to each major insect problem will require imagination and the best scientific talent that we can muster. Research costs will be high. . . . The high cost of control, the high losses in spite of control efforts, and the undesirable side effects of current methods of control obligate us to take an entirely new look at some of the most costly and most troublesome of our insect problems. There is ample justification for taking bold and positive steps in our research efforts. . . . These are the reasons for my interest, my confidence, and my enthusiasm. . . .[10]

In 1978, Knipling again reiterated his supreme confidence in the prospects for successful research. He outlined three levels of control: eradication when technically feasible and economically justified; area-wide or ecosystem-wide management of some major pests; and critical monitoring of pest populations and application of control measures when needed. The three strategies are listed in decreasing order of difficulty, and Knipling acknowledged that the eradication notion was "probably the most controversial among members of the entomological community." Nevertheless, he argued that continual improvements in technology required a continual reappraisal of the technical feasibility of eradication efforts. His sense of optimism, indeed his faith in the forthcoming fruits of technological innovation were again articulated:

> I have a great confidence in the ingenuity of our young scientists to perfect the technology necessary to put sound principles of insect suppression into practice in future years. . . . I see real opportunities for relegating many of the more persistent and costly pests to a status of minor importance economically, and in an ecologically sound manner, by reducing total populations on an ecosystem basis in an organized and coordinated way, using some of the approaches and principles of suppression discussed.[11]

Knipling's confidence that technology could be developed to the point of totally managing an insect pest, even to the point of eradication, must not be interpreted to mean that the adherents of the IPM paradigm were mere pessimists who doubted the ultimate successes of their own creative research efforts. Far from it, they were just as confident of their chances of success as adherents of the TPM paradigm were.

Ray Smith, Carl Huffaker, Perry Adkisson, and Dale Newsom exhibited a powerful optimism in a 1974 address to the European Plant Protection Organization on the progress of the Huffaker Project:

> How well has the [Huffaker Project] applied this ecological containment strategy? . . . The amount of progress that has been made after only two

> years of cooperative interdisciplinary research has had a marked, beneficial effect on agricultural research throughout the country. . . . The stimulus of research being done in the IPM project has convinced numerous administrators that the approach being followed is the proper way for doing agricultural research. . . . A highly significant development has been the attraction of personnel from many other disciplines to work on the project without any financial support from the project. . . . This has come about because of the intellectual excitement being generated by this new approach to agricultural research. The method is now being adopted for the whole area of crop production.[12]

The differences between the two schools of thought rest on more subtle points. Most adherents of the IPM paradigm (1) saw no particular need to reduce a pest population to zero, (2) viewed eradication efforts as diversionary from better avenues of research, and (3) believed eradication efforts would almost invariably prove unworkable, expecially for well-established and widely distributed insects. The IPM school was content, in other words, to suppress a pest species below economically damaging numbers and then do no more than necessary to keep it there.

The issue of eradication, therefore, is the heart of the difference between the two schools. Eradication is the ultimate in ecosystem management in that once a species is removed from an area, the ecosystem is qualitatively different in perpetuity. The reduction in numbers of a pest species resulting from manipulations derived from the IPM school also changes the ecosystem, but the continued presence of the animal in the area means the change is reversible. The high reproductive capacities of insects would cause the pest to regain high population densities if suppression techniques were removed.

The change in the ecosystem resulting from eradication has profound implications for human behavior in that fewer constraints remain on human activities. Specifically, a farmer who is freed from ever having to worry about a pest can alter his production practices without having to consider the implications of the change for its effect on the former pest insect. A pest control scheme in which eradication is never attempted or achieved is destined to be needed in perpetuity because the insects will always be a potential problem. A farmer thus has no hope of ever being freed from the constraints imposed by the presence of the insect. Knipling was highly conscious of this limitation of the IPM paradigm and was unwilling to accept it.

A related difference between the paradigms centers on the problems of the legal and moral rights of other species. Before 1950, only a few authors, such as Aldo Leopold in *Sand County Almanac*, gave any attention to the rights of other species. The emergence of the environmental movement in the late 1960s, however, brought the notion of such "rights" into the arena in which debates on insect control were fought.[13] Eradication came to be seen by a few entomologists as a concept posing serious questions for their discipline in terms of the rights of other species. The recent advent of such questions makes it impossible to do more than briefly summarize the current hazy state of the debate.

Proponents of eradication (TPM or chemical) implicitly assumed that the target of annihilation had no rights in the treatment area; since these entomologists seldom seriously considered the global eradication of an insect, there was some ambiguity surrounding their implicit assumptions of rights outside the targeted eradication zone. Knipling believed eradication of a native species might be ecologically damaging, but his concern was for deleterious consequences for the ecosystem, not the target insect.[14]

Proponents of IPM had mixed reactions about the rights of other organisms. Newsom believed no moral principle was involved; he would, for example be glad to eradicate the boll weevil, but he doubted the effectiveness of the proposed technology.[15] Paul DeBach, one of the foremost advocates of classical biological control, was not opposed to eradication on moral grounds because extinction is a natural process. He, like Newsom, raised questions of practicality and the effect of eradication on the ecosystem as a whole.[16] Robert Rabb moved closer to a principled objection to eradication: "The use of the [technological] power is a tremendous responsibility and must be done without arrogance and with a subtle sensitivity, if not a reverence, for the value of all life."[17] Entomologist Robert L. Metcalf, who converted to IPM sometime after *Silent Spring* was published, occupied the polar position with an explicit, metaphysical assertion: "I do firmly believe that species should be regarded as sacred and man indeed has no right or reason to destroy them."[18]

ENTOMOLOGICAL THOUGHT AND GENERAL INTELLECTUAL TRENDS

It should not be supposed that the philosophical differences between the different paradigmatic visions in entomology had no counterpart in the intellectual world outside the profession of entomology. On the contrary, each of the schools reflected or became part of intellectual currents among nonentomologists. Some lay authors articulated the presuppositions upon which entomological ideas were based better than the entomologists.

Rachel Carson's *Silent Spring* was an attack on the chemical control paradigm as well as a major contribution to contemporary environmental philosophy. It contained explicitly metaphysical elements:

> The "control of nature" is a phrase conceived in arrogance, born of the Neanderthal age of biology and philosophy, when it was supposed that nature exists for the convenience of man. The concepts and practices of applied entomology for the most part date from that Stone Age of science. It is our alarming misfortune that so primitive a science has armed itself with the most modern and terrible weapons, and that in turning them against the insects it has also turned them against the earth.[19]

Carson explicitly denied any human right to treat the natural world as a mere commodity "for the convenience of man." She implicitly endorsed the principle that some moral limits might attend the level of affluence to which humans could rise. Some human behavior, she argued, must be subordinated to the rights of nature. Carson's vision of nature as an entity with rights were present in her earlier works and clearly served as the foundation of *Silent Spring*.[20]

Man's need to live in harmony with nature is part of a long-standing romantic tradition in Anglo-American philosophy. Historian Donald Worster identified the first major articulation of this "arcadian" view of nature with the works of Gilbert White in 1789.[21] Henry David Thoreau perhaps more than anyone else brought a romantic ecological thought into the mainstream of American literature, where it has resided to this day.[22] More recent reflections of nature as entity include Theodore Roszak's *Person/Planet*.[23] Roszak's book is one of the most explicit manifestations of the metaphysical notion that the earth may be a sentient being.

Carson wrote before either IPM or TPM were sufficiently mature to recognize them as alternative and competing strategies for guiding entomology away from its infatuation with insecticides, so she had no explicit thoughts on them. Instead she pointed enthusiastically to all sorts of alternative control techniques including biological control and the sterile male technique.[24] Her beliefs in nature-as-being, however, were continued in the writings of van den Bosch in *The Pesticide Conspiracy*.[25] Van den Bosch believed in a nature that man could not dominate. It is interesting to note that those entomologists who regarded Carson's work as a positive contribution, such as Carl Huffaker, DeBach, and Reece Sailer, were those associated with biological control in the "classical" sense. In general, it appears that those who worked in biological control and later IPM were the least antagonistic to *Silent Spring*. Entomologists who were most annoyed by Carson's work had a deeper affinity for the chemical control paradigm. IPM is based upon the presupposition that nature ought not to be endlessly violated with ignorantly applied insecticides. Furthermore, the vision of natural enemies and host-plant resistance providing natural control transforms nature into a partial ally rather than a total adversary of human interests. Thus a concept of nature-as-being enters into the IPM at a fundamental level. IPM of all the paradigms in entomology is the closest to Carson's philosophy.

Other lay writings were in hot disagreement with Carson, and philosophy more than any other factor appears to lie at the base of the separations. Congressman Jaime Whitten (D., Miss.) wrote perhaps the most eloquent and heartfelt of all the rebuttals to Carson in his *That We May Live*.[26] Undoubtedly Whitten's origins near the insect-infested cotton lands of Mississippi and his bout with malaria as a youngster led him to appreciate the short-term economic and health benefits of insecticides. Just as Carson was transfixed with the potential of disaster from the use of chemicals, Whitten was repelled by any attack on the agricultural economy. He feared Carson's ideas would resurrect a labor-intensive agriculture, to him a specter of poverty. Their conclusions were diametrically opposed and reflected a difference in philosophical predilections. Just as Carson ended her book with a glimpse into her philosophical assumptions, so too did Whitten:

> The general public must be made to realize that man's environment is a combination of everything that has gone before and that it will continue to be changed. For as I stated in the beginning, as man has gone along, day by day, year by year, throughout history, he has continued to change and build for himself a synthetic environment—his clothing, his housing, his food, in fact, almost everything about him is the result of converting natural elements into products of use to him.[27]

Carson was repelled by industrial man's use of nature; Whitten celebrated it as the source of prosperity in his defense of the chemical control paradigm.

The TPM paradigm was designed to guide research away from total reliance on the use of insecticides, but its adherents maintained a higher enthusiasm for the benefits from insecticides than did adherents of the IPM paradigm. Somewhat paradoxically, Whitten as the principal lay defender of chemicals did not develop much enthusiasm for the experiments generated under guidance from TPM. He at first opposed, for example, the Trial Boll Weevil Eradication Program, and only after several years did he allow his Agricultural Appropriations Subcommittee to release funds for the trial.

Popular support for TPM came from another person, Charles G. Scruggs, an editor for the *Progressive Farmer*, a farming magazine widely circulated in the southern states. When he spoke to a national conference on boll weevil eradication, Scruggs went to the heart of the matter while exhorting the entomologists to pursue the eradication program:

> You will succeed! Why do I know this? I have a good authority on which to base the statement. Genesis, Chapter 1, Verse 28, says this: "And God blessed them, and God said unto them, Be fruitful, and multiply, and replenish the earth, and subdue it: and have dominion over the fish of the sea, and over the fowl of the air, and over every living thing that moveth upon the earth."
>
> This is the basis for our will to win! This is the correct view—not the statements of Rachel Carson who wrote: "The 'control of nature' is a phrase conceived in arrogance, born in the Neanderthal age of biology and philosophy, when it was supposed that nature exists for the convenience of man."
>
> Nature *does* exist for the convenience of man, for the Bible tells us so. That's why you will win![28]

Many entomologists, even proponents of eradication, may have been embarrassed by Scruggs's Bible-thumping, because the secular norms of contemporary science give little sanction to such an explicit appeal to metaphysics. "Objectivity" is the hallowed goal, and few scientists want to be cornered with the Bible as the basis of their beliefs. Scruggs was not a scientist, however, so he was freed from the constraints of the professionals, and he, like Carson, articulated his deeply held beliefs. The irony of Scruggs's position is that he took a deliberate slap at Carson despite the fact that she, like Scruggs, became involved in the search for alternatives to insecticides and even extolled the virtues of the sterile male technique, which was the foundation of most eradicatory schemes articulated by the TPM school. Scruggs disdained her views based on his correct interpretation that their philosophies differed. Unfortunately, agreement of the need to move away from total reliance on insecticides became totally obscured in a battle over the correct metaphysical foundation on which to stand.

We can only speculate that, had Carson lived, she would have endorsed what we now recognize as IPM, but other groups who shared many of her presuppositions became strong lay advocates for IPM. Of particular importance was the Sierra Club, founded upon the work and philosophy of John Muir.[29] Consider the Club's testimony in support of a congressional appropriation to finance the Huffaker Project:

> Conservationists have long protested the exorbitant use of chemical pesticides. . . . Not only has the reckless use of chemical pesticides wrought ecological havoc and decreased biological diversity—a condition which is necessary to the quality of our environment—but, as testimony has shown, such overdependence and reckless use also threatens production of vital food and fiber crops, forest products, and endangers human health. . . . We welcome the promise held out by successful development of integrated biological–cultural pest control methods.[30]

Pressures for pragmatism always force congressional testimony to emphasize the practical aspects of legislation, but the club's clear disdain for upsetting an ecological order and decreasing biological diversity provides a glimpse of their underlying philosophy of nature. Just as John Muir celebrated the intrinsic value of wilderness as sacred and rejuvenating because of its natural order and diversity, so too does the modern Sierra Club argue for IPM on the grounds that pesticides have disrupted that order and diversity.[31]

Connections between the philosophical assumptions of professional entomologists and their lay supporters were necessary for development of political support for the different schools of entomology. Similarly, such assumptions were necessary for the conduct of scientific work under each of the three different paradigms. Intrusions of metaphysical presuppositions into entomological work were therefore not to be regretted; however, the inability of the various partisans to articulate and discuss their different assumptions was unfortunate.

NATURALISM AND HUMANISM IN ENTOMOLOGY

The above discussion on the presuppositions contained within contemporary efforts to innovate in entomology began with the assertion that two related but in some ways rival paradigms were developed during the late 1950s and 1960s. If the philosophical discussion just presented is accepted, then clearly one source of differences between adherents of the two paradigms is philosophical in nature. Succeeding sections will discuss other differences. The importance of metaphysical presuppositions in entomology appears so strong, however, that it is worth venturing some labels in order to facilitate discussion about the issues raised. Labels can both obscure and illuminate, so their use is not an unmixed blessing. Nevertheless, I will propose some with the hope they will help, not hinder, further thinking.

Both the IPM and TPM paradigms are embedded in a matrix of ecological theory. Both see man as an element of the natural world and both articulate their visions in terms of ecosystems and learning how to mimic nature in controlling insects. The crucial differences between the two lie in the position accorded man: The IPM paradigm stops short of venturing for total mastery of nature as epitomized in the notion of eradication. The TPM paradigm makes that step beyond IPM and argues that total mastery of ecosystems, up to and including qualitative adjustments of the species composition, is the vision toward which entomologists should bend their efforts. The crucial difference between them thus is the position of man within the biosphere: he is not the total master in IPM; he dares to be so in TPM. It is for this reason that I propose "naturalistic" as a name for the underlying presuppositions of IPM and "humanistic" for TPM. The meanings of each term are as follows:

Naturalistic—A belief system that man is a part of the biosphere but that he cannot be the total master of it. He may manipulate for his own benefit, but there are intrinsic limits to his manipulative powers that reside in the properties of the material world.

Humanistic—A belief system that man is part of the biosphere and that he can be master of it. He may manipulate it for his benefit, and there are no intrinsic limits to his manipulative powers that reside in the properties of the material world. The limits, such as they are, stem from his current ignorance of natural processes.

CONCEPTS

Concepts held by working scientists define the entities forming the subject matter of the science. They can usually be hierarchically ordered into major concepts and various subordinates. Entomologists have borrowed many from other areas of biology such as taxons, evolution, development, and so forth. A few concepts, however, have special importance to entomology and provide a means of distinguishing the major paradigms. The ones considered here are pest, control and economic threshold, environmental quality, ecosystem, and integrated control.

Pest

The purpose of economic entomology has always been to alleviate the damage and annoyance caused by insects. To be a pest, therefore, was to be an insect that bothered people. Entomologists have for over a century explicitly realized that the concept of *pest* had no connection to taxonomic status as an insect. Thaddeus William Harris stated this principle most eloquently in the mid-nineteenth century:

> Destructive insects have their appointed tasks . . . ; they are exposed to many accidents through the influence of the elements, and they fall a prey to numerous animals, many of them also of the insect race, which, while they fulfill their own part in the economy of nature, contribute to prevent the

> undue increase of the noxious tribes. Too often, by our unwise interference with the plan of Providence, we defeat the very measures contrived for our protection.[32]

Harris's notion that there are both useful and destructive insects was echoed continuously by entomologists who followed him. William Luckmann and Robert Metcalf later expanded Harris's notion by denying that *pest* had any meaning in terms of ecological theory.[33]

Pest, therefore, has always been an entirely anthropocentric concept that requires for its understanding ideas from the behavioral sciences and the humanities as well as the natural sciences. Economics and questions of human values are particularly important. Perhaps one of the greatest ironies of economic entomology has been that until the late 1960s no economist devoted serious attention to the problems of the discipline.[34] Entomologists approximated overall dollar values of losses from insects, but these efforts were for the most part unsophisticated in terms of economic theory.[35] A variety of economists, sociologists, and others have begun to make contributions to the problem of defining *pest*,[36] but the discipline of entomology is still not united on even an economic definition let alone a more comprehensive social one.

The concept of *pest*, the very heart of economic entomology, thus must be seen as problematic. Some adherents of IPM endow a pest with rights, e.g., the right not to be annihilated. More generally, a pest in IPM is a part of nature, over which man will never achieve total power. Furthermore, in IPM a particular species is a pest only when its numbers are greater than an economic threshold. When its numbers are reduced, it is no longer a pest; indeed it might even have beneficial properties if it serves as food for the preservation of its natural enemies.

Chemical control and TPM, in contrast, book no rights for creatures dubbed as pests and admit no limitations in principle on technological prowess. People, according to these two schools, exercise supreme authority for the stewardship and dominion of nature. Some adherents of the chemical control paradigm included the notion of economic threshold, which implied that pest status was lost at low population levels. A species targeted for eradication under TPM, however, remains a pest until its population level drops to zero. TPM designed solely to suppress a population over a large area acknowledges that a species loses pest status when its numbers became sufficiently low.

Control and Economic Threshold

Textbooks in economic entomology have for many years articulated the concept that the damage done by an insect must in some way be commensurate with the costs of controlling it, regardless of what practices were used. Dwight Isely, for example, one forerunner of the IPM paradigm, led his introductory students through a step-by-step analysis of an insect problem beginning with the direction to determine the economic importance of the damage before attempting to do anything about it.[37] Similarly, Clell L. Metcalf and W. P. Flint in 1939 noted that as all applied means of control were expensive, some estimate of the savings expected must be made.[38] Their concept of balancing costs and benefits was made in the context of the chemical control paradigm before the advent of DDT. In more recent years, advocates of the eradication of specific insects have always couched their arguments in terms of the long-term savings that would balance the high, short-term costs of such efforts.[39]

All three paradigms, therefore, conceive of control in an economic context; no action against the offender need be initiated unless the damage level becomes sufficiently great. The chemical control paradigm contained the concept of threshold level for action but advanced no theory or methods for determining it. Automatic spray schedules usually abandoned all pretense of using the concept of economic threshold. Furthermore, the concept was usually buried in a mass of details on how chemicals were to be used. Metcalf, Flint, and Metcalf's textbook, for example, presented in 1951 about 80 pages of detailed discussion on the various insecticides, and an additional 26 pages described application machines. Although the authors analyzed the various ways insects were damaging crops and estimated the aggregate amount of loss in dollar values, they made no effort to explain how an entomologist should estimate when to take action. Instead only one paragraph informed the reader not to apply control unless it was economically worthwhile.[40] The overall impression from the book was therefore an exhortation to use a chemical if intuitively it seemed worthwhile.

Early architects of the IPM paradigm defined the term *economic threshold*, tying it directly to the quantitative population level at which action needed to be taken: "The density at which control measures should be determined to prevent an increasing pest population from reaching the economic-injury level."[41] J. C. Headley of the University of Missouri was one of the first economists to devote serious attention to the economic aspects of insect control, and he offered a refined definition of economic threshold in 1972: the population level at which the rate of change of the value of the production (yield) was equal to the rate of change of the cost of control (both value and cost were depicted as functions of the population levels). He also argued that his economic threshold was the optimal population level to maintain in terms of returns to the grower.[42]

Economist Richard B. Norgaard and his colleagues at the University of California, Berkeley, refined Headley's conceptualization of *economic threshold*. First, Norgaard and Alexander Davidson distinguished between *damage threshold* and *economic threshold*.[43] The former was the population level at which the farmer began to suffer losses in yield, but the losses were not high enough to justify any control activities. The latter was the population level at which control activities were justified, i.e., the economic threshold as Headley had defined it. Second, Norgaard and Darwin C. Hall expanded Headley's definition of *economic threshold* to include consideration of the timing and dose level of applied insecticide.[44] Headley's model had included only one application of poison per year at an unspecified dose and time.

Stimulated by the Huffaker Project, other economists continued to increase the level of detail in models of the economic threshold. D. Hueth and U. Regev brought in the notion of changes in the economic threshold during the growing season.[45] H. Talpaz and I. Borosch added the possibility of multiple applications of insecticide per year; they also brought in the factor of application costs in their model for calculating the timing and dosages of insecticide applications.[46] Norgaard summarized the work on economic thresholds in 1976 by arguing that although it had been a fundamental part of the efforts to develop integrated pest management, its use in the design of crop protection systems might decline as pest management slowly became crop management.[47] The myriad of details that affected economic thresholds made them virtually incalculable in practical terms.

Researchers working within the TPM paradigm have not yet attracted many economists to their problems, and thus only a general framework for their economic thought can be identified. Wide-area attacks on a pest species are central to the TPM school, rather than suppression efforts for individual fields or for individual farm enterprises. Enlargement of the reference frame was particularly important if eradication was the goal of TPM-guided research. For example, the requirement for 100% cooperation from all citizens in the eradication zone had economic implications. Nevertheless, researchers within TPM tended to present economic analyses much as was done in the chemical control paradigm and in IPM before economists such as Headley entered the scene: estimate the losses from a pest, calculate the value of the losses based on current prices of the lost commodity, estimate costs of control, and proceed with the control strategy if the cost figure is greater than the control value.[48] This method of economic analysis totally ignored the political questions inherent in spending public funds for the benefit of private farm businesses. It also evaded the problem of amortizing large initial costs that were to be "repaid" with a stream of benefits stretching over a period of years. TPM ideas, in other words, generally ignored the requirement for discounting benefits that will be returned over a long period of time, a fundamental feature of cost–benefit estimation methodologies that have been in vogue for many years.[49] Only in 1974 did the USDA develop an analysis of eradication experiments that included discounting.[50]

Concepts of *control* and *economic threshold* in economic entomology are still in a state of flux at this time. Clearly IPM has been the paradigm to attract significant input from professional economists working within the framework of welfare economics. Political aspects of the economic dimensions of IPM have not been effectively explored, and almost no economic analysis has yet been done for TPM. The earliest generation of economic concepts within the chemical control paradigm are now generally seen as too simplistic by all economic entomologists, but a fully articulated theory of entomology in the political economy of agriculture has not yet emerged. We will return to this subject in Chapter 10.

Environmental Quality

Economic entomologists in the days before Rachel Carson seldom if ever used the expression *environmental quality*. Indeed, virtually no one did. As a reflection of this, textbooks and other literature written before the 1960s simply contained no reference to such a concept. Instead, entomologists made the implicit argument that the control of noxious insects improved what we would now call the environment. Most entomologists today would still argue that most if not all control operations improved our environment, and the majority of citizens would undoubtedly agree. Only the strongest opponents of insect control, for example, would not acknowledge that excluding mosquitoes from our presence made our environment better! The difference now, however, is that entomologists explicitly acknowledge the existence of environmental damage from insecticides and other forms of insect control practices. Robert Metcalf and his colleagues, writing in 1975 from the IPM perspective, maintained that environmental quality must be incorporated as an active working concept in the design of new insect control technologies:

> It seems clear that if we are to preserve for future generations some semblance of the biological order of the world of the past and hope to improve on the deteriorating standards of urban public health, environmental science and technology must quickly come to play a dominant role in designing our social and industrial structure for tomorrow. . . . What is urgently needed is a total

> systems approach to modern civilization through which the pooled talents of scientists and engineers, in cooperation with social scientists and the medical profession, can be focused on the development of order and equilibrium to the presently disparate segments of the human environment. . . . Surely a technology that has created such manifold environmental problems is also capable of solving them.[51]

Overtones of an engineered society for the purpose of protecting the environment may not appeal to all readers, but it is important to note that the language represents a major change for Robert Metcalf. Robert, the son of entomologist C. L. Metcalf, revised his father's textbook, *Destructive and Useful Insects*, in 1951 and 1962. He continued the overwhelmingly chemical orientation of the 1939 edition, and his own research was predominantly oriented toward the solution of problems under the chemical paradigm, namely what chemical, used when and how, to control a pest problem. In neither the 1951 nor the 1962 version did he discuss problems of environmental pollution, even though by that time a literature was available that would have at least enabled him to inform the beginning student that environmental quality was one of the concepts that a new economic entomologist should think about. Yet by 1975, as evidenced by the quotation above, Metcalf was deeply concerned about the problems of environmental quality, and his personal research had taken a turn toward the investigation of pesticide degradation and transport in the environment. In a televised interview he acknowledged that Rachel Carson's reference to economic entomology as a "stone-age science" was particularly discomforting to him because of his family's long involvement in entomology.[52]

The changes in Metcalf's concept of environmental quality and its incorporation into economic entomology was reflected by many other workers in the IPM paradigm.[53] Workers in the TPM tradition have not to this point produced textbooks articulating fundamental concepts of their school, but it is clear from the work of researchers like Knipling and Brazzel that they, too, were motivated by the notion of environmental pollution in the creation of their research strategies.[54] The demise of the chemical control paradigm within the entomological research community was, therefore, partially conditioned by the articulation of a new concept of environmental quality.

Ecosystem

Textbooks written under the guidance of the IPM paradigm are strongly oriented toward a concept of pest control based upon ecosystems analysis, and we discussed in Chapter 5 how differing concepts of agroecosystems were problematic in the research of the Huffaker Project. Similarly we noted in Chapter 4 that the TPM paradigm was oriented toward an ecological notion of pest control, especially one based on a knowledge of the population dynamics of the pest. No concept of *ecosystem* was expressed in connection with the chemical control paradigm.

Given that IPM and TPM both espoused a concept of *ecosystem* as a fundamental notion, why did they differ so in their judgments? The answer lies partly in the differing concepts of "ecology" that the two research strategies utilized. IPM emphasized the interactions between the pest, its natural enemies, the plant, potential pests, and their natural enemies. IPM was clearly related to the notion of *synecology*, in which emphasis is given to the processes governing communities of organisms.[55]

Smith and van den Bosch added an even more complex dimension to their concept of agroecosystems in 1967: ecosystems have a history of evolutionary development. They illustrated their notion with a discussion of the emergence of the agroecosystem of the San Joaquin Valley in California.[56] Prior to the entry of the Spanish in 1772, a large population of Yokuts Indians lived on the elk, antelope, fish, tule roots, acorns, pine nuts, and other seeds in the Valley. Insects now known as crop pests, such as alfalfa caterpillar and cotton bollworm, existed in the Valley, but were of little or no importance to the hunting–gathering culture of the Yokuts. Spanish cattle and, later, Anglo-American wheat radically changed the ecological nature of the Valley. Irrigation, the introduction of many new crops, and the unintended immigration of alien pest species into the Valley completed its transformation into the twentieth-century agribusiness empire that is now heavily dependent upon insecticides.

Smith and van den Bosch clearly believed that an entomologist without an appreciation for the historical evolution of the Valley's agroecosystem would be prone to suggest unrealistic or unwise research programs for insect control: "Successful integrated pest control must be sensitive to these changes that occur both on the short-term dynamic basis and the long-term evolutionary basis."[57] Their point was that entomologists needed to recognize the full complexity of ecosystems, and a historical–evolutionary perspective helped develop the needed sensitivities.

In contrast, TPM stems from the notion of *autecology*, in which great emphasis is placed upon understanding the population dynamics of one species, especially as it is affected by the abiotic environment.[58] IPM searches for the multiple interactions of many species, but TPM explores one species, the pest, in great detail in order that an all-encompassing control technique can be created, one that might even drive the species to oblivion. Differing concepts of ecology thus distinguished the two paradigms.

Integrated Control

Perhaps no other word in contemporary economic entomology so exquisitely exhibits both the powers and frailties of language as does the term *integrated*. As we have traced, it began its residence in the vocabulary of the discipline with the work of A. E. Michelbacher and later that of Stern, van den Bosch, Smith, and Hagen. In its original incarnation, it symbolized the notion of combining classical biological control and chemicals so that they mutually reinforced each other. Later developments added by Smith, Reynolds, van den Bosch, and others enlarged the concept to mean a system of insect control based on an understanding of the population dynamics of the pest species, potential pest species, natural enemies of pests, and the phenology of the crop plant's development. Host plant resistance, cultural methods, and other suppressive techniques were added to biological control, to be integrated with the use of chemicals if they were needed. The goal of entomology in this use of *integrated* was the containment of pest species below an economic threshold. IPM as a paradigm was thus founded on a concept of *integrated* that developed over a period of years and subsumed a synecological meaning and a goal of containment rather than annihilation of the pest.

Integrated as a term was also extensively used by Knipling in his articulation of the principles of the TPM paradigm. On the surface, his use of the word was parallel to that of the framers of the IPM paradigm, namely, the combination of a variety of techniques in ways that they became mutually reinforcing rather than destructive. The fact that Knipling's interests lay in the integration of chemicals, parasitic and predatory insect releases, and sterile male releases distinguishes him somewhat from the California researchers, whose interests were more aligned with classical biological control. What most differentiated the TPM use of *integrated* from that of IPM, however, were underlying concepts not immediately visible in the definition of that term. TPM's sense of ecology as autecology and its goal of eradication (at least for a few species) provided a context for the word *integrated* that was markedly different from that of IPM. As a result, we have been faced with two radically different nuances surrounding the word *integrated*.

People unfamiliar with the intricate details of professional entomology might well be confused over disputes between adherents of the different paradigms when both of them refer to "integrated control" as the proper research path! Only when the underlying context of the word is examined does it become clear that two words were needed in place of one in order to describe the situation unambiguously. Confounding of the meaning of *integrated* was in fact the reason for the adoption in this essay of the terms *integrated pest management* and *total population management* as labels for the major paradigms developed in response to the crisis with chemicals. Priority for use of the word *integrated* clearly belongs to the work done by the California entomologists. TPM, the paradigm developed by Knipling and his associates, is associated with terms that occur frequently in Knipling's writings and appear to symbolize accurately TPM's unique elements.

Knipling was conscious that his use of the word *integrated* was different from that of the IPM school:

> [Carl B. Huffaker and Ray F. Smith] are not thinking integrated control in the sense that I am. I'm thinking integrated control in the sense that you're taking advantage of the characteristics of different systems and putting them together for total management of a population. They're looking at integrated control . . . [as being] based on assessment of economic threshold levels and not to use control measures until they reach that goal. . . . Now, I maintain that we'll never solve some of these insect problems that way.[59]

Once the outsider to entomology understands the difference, then rational discussion of the debates between the two paradigms can begin.

For many years, the chemical industry made no public comments upon either IPM or TPM as efforts to develop technology less dependent upon the use of insecticides. Efforts by the EPA to use the concepts of IPM as part of the regulatory scheme for pesticides, however, stimulated in 1979 a formal position statement by the National Agricultural Chemicals Association (NACA) on the concept of integrated control.[60] The NACA's use of the term *integrated* indicates that the poor, battered word has been assigned yet a third context that makes it acquire nuances different from its meaning in both IPM and TPM. The NACA defines integrated pest management as "an approach in which principles, practices, methods, materials, and strategies are chosen to control pests, while minimizing undesirable results." Explicitly, the NACA maintains that pest control methods must be suitable for the farmer, rancher, and other users and that government should neither subsidize nor regulate the use of integrated control practices as a way to reduce the use of chemicals. The NACA's use of the term is totally devoid of any reference to the population dynamics of pest species but endorses the concept of economic threshold as articulated in the IPM paradigm.

Given the long history of efforts to base "integrated control" on ecological theory, the NACA's efforts can only be seen as an insipid perversion of language rather than as a serious contribution to the design of more effective pest control techniques. They have reduced the concept of integrated pest management to a process of "choice" based on no meaningful criteria. Further, they maintain that the economic interests of the farmer, rancher, or other user are the ultimate arbiter in any evaluation of alternative control practices. All previous efforts to account for economic externalities in the use of pesticides are thus discarded. Finally, they oppose any use of regulation to encourage integrated pest management, presumably because they fear possible adverse effects on the sale of their wares. The use of law to foster technological change among pest controllers may be problematic, but the NACA rejects the notion of even thinking about it. If care is not exercised in understanding the meaning of *integrated*, the NACA's qualified "endorsement" of IPM will be the kiss of death for the concept because it reduces the language to meaningless gibberish.

CONCLUDING REMARKS

We have examined the philosophical foundations of entomology in some detail as we sought explanations for the differences between different research strategies and for the differences that have divided researchers belonging to different paradigmatic schools. An epistemology based upon a Kuhnian notion of scientific change proved to be a fruitful tool in the search for intellectual order underlying the chaos of postwar American economic entomology. Indeed, the argument to this point can be summarized by noting that the different paradigms with their varying presuppositions and concepts were the cause of at least one of the major disputed questions within the profession: should efforts be made to eradicate or merely to control an insect pest? IPM and TPM gave different answers to this question because the detailed structure of their paradigms subsumed different answers. Disputes between them were unresolvable in terms of concepts common to both. They used the same words but intended different meanings and one could not understand the argument without a dictionary to translate from one to the other. These difficulties existed despite the fact that both emerged from and repudiated the chemical control paradigm.

Our progress toward sense of the problem of innovation within entomology, however, is not sufficient for placing this scientific/technical field in its total social and political context. In particular, we have not dealt with one of the elements of entomology-as-technology that we identified earlier: volition. More specifically, we have offered no explanation for either the origin of the philosophical notions that we have just dissected or the reasons that chemical control technologies continue to dominate the technology of insect control in the field of practical agriculture. Entomologists of course do not make all of the decisions for farmers about the pest control techniques that will be used. We must thus turn to an examination of the relationships between the entomologists and the two groups with whom they interact most regularly: their farmer clients and the chemical industry. In this exploration we will find clues both to the sources of entomological philosophy and to the dominance of insecticides in the practical world of agricultural businesses.

REFERENCE NOTES

1. Robert L. Zimdahl, a weed scientist at Colorado State University, has given some thought to the value questions implicit in the use of pesticides [Pesticides—a value question, *Bull. Entomol. Soc. Am.* 18 (1972): 109–110]. He has also argued independently of this work that a "pesticide paradigm" was operative in the pest control sciences after World War II [The pesticide paradigm, *Bull. Entomol. Soc. Am.* 24 (1978): 357–360]. Zimdahl's "pesticide paradigm" is similar to what I call the "chemical control paradigm." Boysie E. Day, a weed scientist at the University of California, Berkeley, has also noted that value judgments have heavily influenced the argument over pesticides and pest control [The axiology of pest control, *Agrichemical Age* (June, 1976): 5–6].
2. An excellent statement of the mode of operation of entomologists working within the chemical control paradigm can be found in C. L. Metcalf, W. P. Flint, and R. L. Metcalf, *Destructive and Useful Insects*, 3rd ed. (New York: McGraw Hill Book Co., Inc., 1951), pp. 1–76, 255–386.
3. Clay Lyle, Achievements and possibilities in pest eradication, *J. Econ. Entomol.* 40 (1947): 1–8.
4. E.F. Knipling, personal communication, Nov. 10, 1978.
5. For example, see J. J. Linduska, Evaluation of soil systemics for control of Colorado potato beetle on tomatoes in Maryland, *J. Econ. Entomol.* 71 (1978): 647–649; C. R. Harris, H. J. Svec, and R. A. Chapman, Potential of pyrethroid insecticides for cutworm control, *J. Econ. Entomol.* 71 (1978): 692–696; R. W. Staub and A. C. Davis, Onion maggot: Evaluation of insecticides for production of onions in muck soils, *J. Econ. Entomol.* 71 (1978): 684–686.
6. V. M. Stern, R. F. Smith, R. van den Bosch, and K. S. Hagen, The integrated control concept, *Hilgardia* 29 (1959): 81–85.
7. F. Wilson and C. B. Huffaker, "The philosophy, scope and importance of biological control," in *Theory and Practice of Biological Control*, C. B. Huffaker and P. S. Messenger, eds. (New York: Academic Press, 1976), p. 4.
8. R. F. Smith, J. L. Apple, and D. G. Bottrell, "The origin of integrated pest management concepts for agriculatureal crops," in *Integrated Pest Management*, J. L. Apple and R. F. Smith, eds. (New York: Plenum Press, 1976), p. 12.

9. Robert van den Bosch, *The Pesticide Conspiracy* (Garden City, New York: Doubleday and Co., Inc., 1978), p. 12 (hereafter cited as van den Bosch, *Pesticide Conspiracy*).
10. E. F. Knipling, Some basic principles in insect population suppression, *Bull. Entomol. Soc. Am.* 12 (1966): 7–15.
11. E. F. Knipling, Eradication of plant pests—pro, *Bull. Entomol. Soc. Am.* 24 (1978): 44–52.
12. R. F. Smith, C. B. Huffaker, P. L. Adkisson, and L. D. Newsom, Progress achieved in the implementation of integrated control projects in the USA and tropical countries, *EPPO Bull.* 4 (1974): 221–239.
13. For examples of recent discussions on the question of the rights of nature see E. F. Murphy, Has nature any right to life, *Hastings Law J.* 22 (1971): 467–484; Charles Hartshorne, The rights of the subhuman world, *Environ. Ethics* 1 (1979): 49–60; J. Baird Callicott, Elements of an environmental ethic: Moral considerability and the biotic community, *Environ. Ethics* 1 (1979): 71–81; Richard A. Watson, Self-consciousness and the rights of nonhuman animals and nature, *Environ. Ethics* 1 (1979): 99–129. See also Footnote 20.
14. E. F. Knipling, Advances in technology for insect population eradication and suppression, *Bull. Entomol. Soc. Am.* 24 (1978): 44–52.
15. L. D. Newsom, Eradication of plant pests—con, *Bull. Entomol. Soc. Am.* 24 (1978): 35–40; idem, Personal interview, June 1–2, 1978.
16. Paul DeBach, Some ecological aspects of insect eradication, *Bull. Entomol. Soc. Am.* 10 (1964): 221–224.
17. Robert L. Rabb, Eradication of plant pests—con, *Bull. Entomol. Soc. Am.* 24 (1978): 40–44.
18. Robert L. Metclaf, Personal communication, Sept. 22, 1978.
19. Rachel Carson, *Silent Spring* (Boston: Houghton Mifflin Co., 1962), p. 297 (hereafter cited as Carson, *Silent Spring*).
20. Carson's three earlier works (*Under the Sea-Wind, The Sea Around Us,* and *The Edge of the Sea*) were collected into one volume, *The Sea* (London: MacGibbon and Kee, 1964), 611 pp. In this volume see p. 20 for Carson's notion that man could not dominate the oceans, in contrast to his behavior on land. She had an appreciation for the eternal duration of the oceans that approached an eschatological mood (see p. 200). Carson viewed life in and around the sea as an indomitable, purposeful force (pp. 400, 576).
21. Donald Worster, *Nature's Economy* (Garden City, New York: Anchor Books, 1979), p. 5 (hereafter cited as Worster, *Nature's Economy*).
22. Henry David Thoreau, *Walden and Other Writings* (New York: Modern Library, 1937), pp. vii–xx, introduction by Brooks Atkinson; Worster, *Nature's Economy*, p. 58–111.
23. Theodore Roszak, *Person/Planet* (Garden City, New York: Anchor Press, 1979), 347 pp.
24. Carson, *Silent Spring*, pp. 277–296.
25. van den Bosch, *Pesticide Conspiracy*.
26. Jaime L. Whitten, *That We May Live* (Princeton: D. van Nostrand Co., Inc., 1966), 251 pp. See especially pp. 46–47, 55–56.
27. *Ibid.*, p. 215.
28. Charles G. Scruggs, "The will to win," in *Boll Weevil Suppression, Management, and Elimination Technology* (Proceedings of a conference, Feb. 13–15, 1974, Memphis, Tenn.) ARS-S-71 (Washington, D.C.: USDA, 1976), p. 129 (hereafter cited as ARS, *Suppression*). Scruggs also wrote a book celebrating the triumph of the sterile male technique over the screwworm fly [*The Peaceful Atom and the Deadly Fly* (Austin, Texas: Jenkins Pub. Co., The Pemberton Press, 1975), 311 pp.]. Scruggs took an active role in launching a sterile male program in Texas and its later expansion to all of Mexico.

29. Worster, *Nature's Economy*, pp. 185, 274.
30. Testimony of Linda M. Billings, U.S. Congress, Senate, Committee on Agriculture and Forestry, *Pest Control Research*, Hearings, on S. 1794, 92d Cong., 1st sess., 1971, p. 163.
31. See, for example, John Muir, *Our National Parks* (Boston: Houghton Mifflin Co., 1901), pp. 1–36.
32. Thaddeus William Harris, *A Treatise on some of the Insects of New England which Are Injurious to Vegetation*, 2nd ed. (Boston: White and Potter, 1852), pp. 1–2.
33. William H. Luckmann and Robert L. Metcalf, "The pest-management concept," in *Introduction to Insect Pest Management*, Robert L. Metcalf and William H. Luckmann, eds. (New York: John Wiley & Sons, 1975), p. 4 (hereafter cited as Metcalf and Luckmann, eds., *Introduction*).
34. J. C. Headley and J. N. Lewis, *The Pesticide Problem: An Economic Approach to Public Policy* (Baltimore: The Johns Hopkins Press, 1967), 141 pp. Headley and Lewis approached the problem of pesticides from the point of view of welfare economics. They touched on the problem of pest control as a component of a technological production system but did not delve deeply into the social and political implications of altering the system by changing public policy on pesticides. Headley later elaborated on the problems of measuring cost/benefit ratios in pest control [Economics of agricultural pest control, *Annu. Rev. Entomol.* 17 (1972): 273–286]. Earlier he had estimated that farmers receive $4 for every $1 invested in pesticides. Gerald A. Carlson and Emery N. Castle presented a theory for evaluating environmental externalities in "Economics of pest control," in *Pest Control Strategies for the Future* (Washington, D.C.: National Academy of Sciences, 1972), pp. 79–99.
35. See, for example, C. L. Metcalf, W. P. Flint, and R. L. Metcalf, *Destructive and Useful Insects*, 3rd ed. (New York: McGraw-Hill Book Co., Inc., 1951), pp. 39–40. Lack of sophistication in efforts of entomologists to quantify damages centered on two problems: (1) no effort was made to account for likely drops in price if destroyed commodities were suddenly to appear on the market (i.e., entomologists failed to use the economists' concept of elasticity), and (2) no effort was made to relate the economic aspects of insect control to the social structure of the agricultural economy (i.e., entomologists failed to use the concept of political economy).
36. David Pimentel and John H. Perkins, eds., *Pest Control: Cultural and Environmental Aspects*, AAAS Selected Symposium No. 43 (Boulder, Colorado: Westview Press, 1980), 243 pp.
37. Dwight Isely, *Methods of Insect Control*, Part 1, 2nd ed. (Minneapolis: Burgess Pub. Co., 1942), 121 pp.
38. C. L. Metcalf and W. P. Flint, *Destructive and Useful Insects*, 2nd ed. (New York: McGraw-Hill Book Co., Inc., 1939), p. 240.
39. Robert R. Coker, "Economic impact of the boll weevil," in ARS, *Suppression*, pp. 3–4.
40. C. L. Metcalf, W. P. Flint, and R. L. Metcalf, *Destructive and Useful Insects* 3rd ed. (New York: McGraw Hill Book Co., Inc., 1951), pp. 257–336, 360–386.
41. Vernon M. Stern, Ray F. Smith, Robert van den Bosch, and Kenneth S. Hagen, The integrated control concept, *Hilgardia* 29 (1959): 81–101.
42. J. C. Headley, "Defining the economic threshold," in *Pest Control Strategies for the Future* (Washington, D.C.: National Academy of Sciences, 1972), pp. 100–108.
43. Alexander Davidson and Richard B. Norgaard, Economic Aspects of Pest Control, delivered to the Conference on Plant Protection Economy, European and Mediteranean Plant Protection Organization, May 15, 1973, Brussels, 22 pp.

44. D. C. Hall and R. B. Norgaard, On the timing and application of pesticides, *Annu. J. Agric. Econ.* 55 (1973): 198–201.
45. D. Hueth and U. Regev, Optimal agricultural pest management with increasing pest resistance, *Annu. J. Agric. Econ.* 56 (1974): 543–552.
46. H. Talpaz and I. Borosch, Strategy for pesticide use: Frequency and applications, *Annu. J. Agric. Econ.* 56 (1974): 769–775.
47. Richard B. Norgaard, The economics of improving pesticide use, *Annu. Rev. Entomol.* 21 (1976): 45–60.
48. E. F. Knipling, Eradication of plant pest—pro, *Bull. Entomol. Soc. Am.* 24 (1978): 44–52.
49. For a review of cost-benefit methodologies see Deborah Lee Williams, Benefit–cost analysis in natural resources decision making: An economic and legal overview, *Nat. Resour. Lawyer* 11 (1979): 761–796. (I thank Richard J. Daum for bringing this article to my attention.) Efforts were made by the USDA in 1974 to perform a cost–benefit analysis for boll weevil eradication that included the discounting factor. This study had no effect on the decision-making about an eradication experiment, because it occurred *after* commitment to eradication was firm (Richard J. Daum, personal communication, 1979).
50. The Boll Weevil: A Preliminary Evaluation of Three Alternative Federally Supported Programs [USDA, APHIS], unpublished paper, Nov., 1974, 36 pp. plus figures and tables.
51. Robert L. Metcalf and James N. Pitts, Jr., Series preface, in Metcalf and Luckmann, eds., *Introduction*, pp. ix–x.
52. Robert L. Metcalf, Model ecosystem approach to insecticide degradation: A critique, *Annu. Rev. Entomol.* 22 (1977): 241–261; *Nova: The Insect Alternative* ([Boston]: WGBH Educational Foundation, 1978), pp. 4–5.
53. See, for example, the three editions of Van Allen Little's *General and Applied Entomology* (New York: Harper and Brothers, Pub., 1957, 1963, 1972). The earliest is a straightforward presentation of the chemical control paradigm, but his orientation was clearly converted to the IPM school by 1972. His latest version offers much discussion on ecological theory.
54. Knipling, personal interview; J. R. Brazzel, personal interview, May 26–27, 1978.
55. Robert P. McIntosh, "Ecology since 1900," in *History of American Ecology*, Frank N. Egerton, ed. (New York: Arno Press, 1977), p. 360 [pagination reflects numbering of the original publication, Benjamin J. Taylor and Thurman J. White, eds., *Issues and Ideas in America* (Norman: Univ. of Oklahoma Press, 1976)] (hereafter cited as McIntosh, Ecology since 1900).
56. Ray F. Smith and Robert van den Bosch, "Integrated control," in *Pest Control*, Wendell W. Kilgore and Richard L. Doutt, eds. (New York: Academic Press, 1967), pp. 312–315.
57. Ibid., p. 312.
58. McIntosh, Ecology since 1900.
59. Knipling, personal interview.
60. *The Integrated Pest Management Issue* (Washington, D.C.: National Agricultural Chemical Association, 1979), 11 pages plus appendix.

CHAPTER 8

Revolutionary Farmers

Culturally derived philosophical assumptions were not the only factors influencing the development of entomological thought in the years after World War II. Socioeconomic and political considerations also played a role in the creation and adoption of new entomological expertise. Most importantly, American agriculture continued a long-term trend of substituting capital* for labor. Domestic agricultural production also became a part of strategic international planning in the U.S. In periods of open warfare, the food of American farmers assumed a role comparable to combat weapons. During times of peace, food came to play a role in diplomatic maneuvering and negotiations.

It is easy to state that agricultural production "changed" over a period of time. In fact, the transformation of agriculture was a revolutionary change in ways of living for farmers and all other Americans. The U.S. has gone the farthest of any society toward reducing labor requirements in agriculture and utilizing food production as a tool in foreign policy. American farmers of the late twentieth century are seldom considered "revolutionary," but it must be understood that the technological changes they endured and welcomed transformed the social and intellectual significance of food production. Obliterated was the

* In this essay *capital* includes machinery and structures such as tractors and irrigation works; purchased inputs such as fertilizers and pesticides; and knowledge as exemplified by college degrees and other specialized training. Each of these different types of capital requires a farmer to expend money in order to gain access to it. Use of capital inputs in farming implies a more pronounced social division of labor compared to earlier farming that was more dependent upon a farmer's individual actions. Most forms of capital are based upon technological and scientific expertise.

myth of America as a Jeffersonian democracy based upon a class of yeoman farmers. The fading of a romanticized rural landscape has not yet been reflected in an alteration of the place of farming in the American mind. Disputes about insect control technologies have been entrapped in the conflict between farming perceived with a Jeffersonian mythology and farming in its industrialized reality. This chapter reviews the transformation of agriculture since 1861. It is intended to dispel the myths so that we can more precisely understand the forces shaping the development of entomology.

AGRICULTURAL REVOLUTION: THE PERCEPTIONS AND CAUSES

Technological innovations allowed the substitution of capital for labor, and they were the preeminent trend in American agriculture since the 19th century. Statistics demonstrate the gross feature dramatically: in 1800, 373 hours of work were required to produce 100 bushels of wheat; in 1950 only 28 hours were required. By 1973–1977, the figure had dropped to 10 hours. Corn production required 344 hours per 100 bushels in 1800, 39 hours in 1950, and 4 hours in 1973–1977. The story in cotton was much the same. One bale required 601 hours in 1800, 126 hours in 1950, and 12 hours in 1973–1977.[1] Cheap energy, improved machinery, fertilizers, pesticides, new plant varieties, irrigation, and other technological developments were necessary for improved labor productivities.[2] Virtually every innovation that came into use required the farmer to expend capital (money) for the technology that increased his own output per hour of labor invested. Some of the innovations improved yields per hectare as well.

One consequence of the substitution of capital inputs for labor was a decrease in the number of farms and the number of people engaged in farm work. Expansion of European settlement into the North American continent was not complete until after 1900, so the trend toward fewer farms and farmers did not become evident until the 1930s. The peak year for number of farms was 1935 when 6.8 million were in operation.[3] By 1978, this number had dropped to an estimated 2.68 million.[4] Peaking of the total labor force engaged in agriculture occurred in 1916, somewhat earlier than the peak for numbers of farms, when 13.6 million people were employed on farms.[5] The farm population dropped steadily after the 1930s: 30.5 million lived on farms in 1940 compared to 9.7 million in 1970.[6] In 1977, 7.8 million people lived on farms, 3.6% of the

U.S. population.[7] Total farm employment dropped to 4.2 million, representing 31% of the level in 1910–1914.[8] The period 1954–1963 was particularly momentous in terms of change as 6 million residents and 2.1 million workers left farming; 1.2 million farms disappeared, or about 300 per day.[9]

As fewer people engaged in farming on fewer farms, the average acreage of each farm rose steadily. Whereas the average farm had only 151 acres in 1930, it had an estimated 400 acres in 1978.[10] Correlated with the rise in average acreage per farm was the transformation of the type of farm supplying most of the produce reaching the market. After the 1960s, large farms captured a majority of the sales of farm products. Farms selling over $100,000 worth of goods constituted 1.7% of all farms in 1964 and sold 25.1% of all products. By 1974, 9.0% of the farms had gross sales this large and sold 54.2 percent of all farm products. Average annual sales from this class of farm in 1974 were $286,000.[11]

Technological change in agriculture transformed the social meaning of farming as an occupation. Land ownership and operation of a farm were always one way to prosperity and membership in the elite of American society, even in colonial days. Until the 1960s, however, only a minuscule portion of farmers ever achieved much wealth. Technology that allowed one person or family to operate hundreds or even thousands of acres permitted a farm family entry into the small fraction of families with net incomes in excess of $50,000 per year. For example, if the 9.0% of farms selling in excess of $100,000 worth of goods in 1974 each had an average gross income of $286,000, then we could expect each of them to have an annual net income of between $29,000 and $57,000 (based on production expenses equal to 89–90% of gross income). Such a net income clearly placed these people far above the average income of $11,434 for 1974.[12] A net family income of $32,000 in 1974 was sufficient to place the family in the top 5% in terms of income.[13] Nearly 18% of farm families had incomes in excess of $25,000 in 1976, far above the median income of about $15,000 for that year.[14]

The technological revolution in agriculture has also made the socioeconomic structure of the farming industry far more complex than it was in the past. First, persons operating large farms can now expect to enter the income classes previously achieved only by a small group of businessmen, executives, and some professionals such as doctors and lawyers. Many of these individuals are the descendents of families who have farmed for a living for many generations, and we can think of them as "traditional" farmers. That these individuals are still engaged in farming is generally a sign that they have expanded the size of their operations and the intensity of capital use in it. Second, by the early 1960s, vertical integration, or the combining of farm production units into the decision-making framework of farm-input or farm-output industries, made the distinction hazy between rural-based farming and urban-based manufacturing activities. Investment from nonfarm firms has become a source of capital for agriculture.[15] Third, in a somewhat ironic twist, wealthy "nonfarmers" have also taken to investing in farming. Frequently they plan to farm at a level of no profit or even losses so as to use the tax laws to offset their high nonfarm incomes.[16]

Regardless of the route into farming, the continuing trend toward consolidation of farms into larger operating units means that the people in the farming business are increasingly members of the elite of American society in terms of their income, wealth, and power. They are increasingly well educated and active in a variety of public and private affairs.[17] Former President Jimmy Carter was perhaps the emerging prototype of the new farmer for whom interests in agricultural production, related agribusiness services, and politics are tightly interwoven.[18]

Technological change transformed the social meaning of farming from an occupation in which only a few could reach prominence to one in which a majority occupied positions of high prestige. Economist R. G. Bressler of the University of California at Berkeley stated in 1958, "Science made agriculture a business, not a relatively low-paying way of life. . . . Science saved the American farmer from agrarian peasantry."[19]

Bressler's statement was accurate in terms of the farmers remaining in business, but he neglected to say that those forced out may have wondered from what they were being saved. Rural sociologists in Louisiana concluded that many farmers did not have a well-articulated vision of what had happened to them as a result of technological change.[20] Economist G. E. Brandow of Pennsylvania State University noted that inequity among farmers and between farmers and nonfarmers was potentially a problem in American society.[21]

Writers from a number of disciplines have analyzed the changes in agriculture over the past century, and it is clear that a human drama lay behind colorless statistics and notions of economic mobility. Personal triumphs and tragedies were involved as the majority of American people changed their daily work patterns from farming to something else.

Some authors have celebrated the sharp, hardworking farm entrepreneurs who took the first risks in the adoption of new practices at the farm level.[22] These early adopters tended to be those who profited most from the innovations and who continued in farming over the long term.

Their less innovative peers found the farming "game" less and less rewarding. Some individuals were delighted to leave agriculture for better opportunities in the cities and towns. Others, however, were forced out of farming by economic pressures.[23] For them, technological revolution meant dejection and defeat. One of the most vivid descriptions of the unhappiness associated with the technological revolution was provided by novelist John Steinbeck in *The Grapes of Wrath*. The "tractor man" may have been the harbinger of reduced drudgery for those who remained to run the machines, but those who left felt as though they had been pushed out by a technology they had no part in controlling.[24] Wendell Berry's eloquent book *The Unsettling of America* presents a general condemnation of agricultural technology that depopulated the ranks of farmers.[25]

Social scientists have joined in the attempt to understand what happened. Rural sociologists used the tools of positivist science in searching for means to "improve" rural communities as they searched for better ways of informing farmers about new technology. Concepts of improving rural communities rested upon the assumption that new farming practices were necessary to the maintenance of pleasant, prosperous, and morally strong rural areas. Practical efforts to foster innovation led to the creation of a subdiscipline within rural sociology known as adoption–diffusion research.[26]

Rural sociologists were undoubtedly correct that improved farming practices could lead to higher prosperity and stronger rural communities for some, but unfortunately few of them studied the obverse side of the coin. Innovation also disrupted farm families and rural communities, as it required millions to seek alternative employment. A prominent exception to this generalization was a 1973 study, *Hard Tomatoes, Hard Times* by James Hightower, who concluded that the agricultural revolution was systematically biased against farm workers, blacks, small farmers, and consumers.[27] William Friedland and his associates at the University of California, Santa Cruz, are perhaps the only group to have studied a *prospective* innovation. They argue that mechanical lettuce harvesting could displace many workers. It may be adopted if (1) labor becomes too costly or difficult to control, (2) technical improvements dramatically increase the effectiveness of current harvesters, or (3) transportation costs increase dramatically.[28]

Agricultural economists became enchanted with the study of "efficiency" as seen in terms of higher productivity per hour of labor exerted on the farm. Enormous attention was given to helping farm operators plan the best use of technology for their particular farm situation.[29] In the 1950s, economists turned to studies of innovation *per se* because they recognized it as a major source of dynamism in agriculture. Zvi Ghriliches was one of the first in his treatment of the adoption of hybrid corn. He argued that different times, rates, and levels of adoption could be explained on the basis of its profitability compared to traditional varieties.[30] Moreover, the returns to the public investment in research on hybrid corn were large.[31]

More recently, economists Yujiro Hayami, Vernon Ruttan, and their colleagues argued that the agricultural technology created in different countries was precisely that required to use most efficiently the production factor that was most scarce in the country. Innovation was, in other words, induced by shortages in factors of production. They illustrated their theory with an examination of farming in the U.S. and Japan between 1880 and 1960.[32] U.S. farmers were highly receptive to technologies that economized on the use of labor, which historically was in a state of chronic shortage; Japanese farmers were much more attuned to the adoption of technologies that increased the productivity of land, which was in short supply in Japan. This situation reflected the relative abundance of land compared to labor in the U.S. and of labor compared to land in Japan.

Economists, just as was true for sociologists, recognized but tended not to dwell on the economic problems of the faceless multitude who could not continue farming in a context of capital-intensive technology.[33] The lack of interest shown by agricultural economists in the plight of individuals, however, in no way lessened the economic hardships that were faced by those who left direct agricultural production. It is possible that the rapid decline in labor on farms might have created an inefficient social use of resources, but only a few studies have been conducted regarding this problem.[34]

Regardless of perspective, all who have examined the nature of contemporary American agriculture have concluded that it is now quite a different operation than it was a century or more ago. Capital-intensive technology was substituted for labor in response to the relatively high cost of labor compared to land and energy. Econometric arguments alone, however, do not fully explain why or how the switch took place. Social, political, and philosophical factors also favored the demise of labor, and together with economic considerations constituted a cultural milieu for technological change. Specifically, attitudes toward labor and the sociopolitical origins of agricultural science and technology were such that substitution of other inputs for labor was invariably the choice made.

ATTITUDES TOWARD LABOR

Agriculture in American society has always suffered from a bewildering and paradoxical collage of characterizations, which reflected powerful myths about the role of farming in American democracy. Farming has been called the most important occupation, the source of rugged individualism, and the foundation of American democracy.[35] If one wanted to achieve virtue as a citizen, farming was the surest and perhaps only route to take. Yet it was farming, especially of tobacco and cotton, that provided the foundation for slavery in America and the near eclipse of any American claim to democratic virtue. Similarly, the "noble farmer" has also been referred to by an assortment of names that connote anything but respect: *bumpkin, hayseed, clod-hopper,* and *hick* being just a few of the less-endearing terms.[36] Agriculture has been cited as the foundation of American financial prosperity, yet rural America has consistently been the location of a higher level of poverty, deprivation, poor housing, illiteracy, malnutrition, and reduced occupational opportunity than have the urban centers. Economists have long lamented the source of the problem, the historic trend for average farm incomes to lag behind urban incomes.[37]

Evidently farming occupies an ambiguous place in the American mind, and it enjoys the dubious distinction of being both loved and hated with a great deal of passion, even vitriol. Farmers are glorified yet at the same time ridiculed and debunked. Ironically, those farmers who achieved the most positive fame in the popular mind are precisely those who did the least *manual* work as part of their activities. George Washington and Thomas Jefferson, for example, are both frequently referred to with pride as farmers, yet each owned slaves and made them do most of the labor. Moreover, both Washington and Jefferson were noted as much or more for their efforts to innovate in farming than for their farming *per se.*[38] The celebrated farmer now is almost invariably the progressive farm businessman operating hundreds of thousands of dollars worth of equipment on large tracts of land.[39] He is celebrated for his labor-saving devices rather than his manual work in raising food, fiber, and livestock.

These contradictory images of farming lead me to suggest that Americans in fact despised manual farm work and rejected as backward those who invested high amounts of human labor in agriculture. Americans celebrated the great masters of slaves or of complicated machines and chemicals, but the celebration was directed at managerial and technological prowess, not physical labor. An individual who persisted in not using the most modern practices was regarded as a fool, demented, and possibly even evil.

SOCIOPOLITICAL ORIGINS OF AGRICULTURAL SCIENCE AND TECHNOLOGY

Public policy conducive to the invention, refinement, and adoption of new farming technologies originated over a period of many years dating back to the founding of the nation. The patent law was authorized in the Constitution but did not receive much debate at the Constitutional Convention. In theory it was designed to encourage invention by granting inventors monopoly powers for a defined period. Publication combined with a specific time limitation of patent rights was supposed to improve the public welfare.[40] The extent to which the patent law was necessary to foster inventiveness or to which it improved the public welfare is a matter of debate. Earl W. Hayter argued that abuses of patent rights were a source of agrarian discontent in the latter half of the nineteenth century. Inventors of agricultural implements went to great lengths to protect the financial privileges guaranteed by the patent laws, and it was easier to collect royalties from farmers than from manufacturers.[41] A great flurry of patenting of agricultural inventions between 1855 and 1870 was strongly correlated with increased values of agricultural output and increased investments in agriculture.[42]

Agriculture was assigned a special status among American industries because, in addition to inducements for private invention through the patent law, an elaborate public-sector research establishment was created to invent, develop, and adapt new practices for farmers. The foundation for this system consisted of the land grant colleges, the agricultural experiment stations, and extension services run cooperatively by the colleges, counties, and the federal government. Provisions for these institutions were made, respectively, by the Morrill Acts of 1862 and 1890, the Hatch Act (1887) and Adams Act (1906), and the Smith–Lever Act (1914).[43] Land grant colleges provided a high level of education in the scientific aspects of agriculture, while experiment stations performed research on new techniques. The extension service helped transfer the new techniques from the universities and experiment stations to every county.

Later enlargement of this system came with the organization of the Bureau of Agricultural Economics (BAE) in 1922 and its entry into social and economic studies. Ultimately the BAE's efforts in social planning were sharply curtailed due to opposition from the American Farm Bureau Federation and some southern Congressmen, who believed the BAE was stirring up race hatred.[44] The BAE's tasks of gathering economic data have remained as a supplement to the major efforts in agricultural research, which are in the physical and biological sciences. In 1946, the Research and Marketing Act increased funds for utilization research and other research areas, and established a set of public (mostly farmer) advisory committees to set priorities for research.[45]

Why and how was the agricultural research network established? Hope for private gain and an ideological commitment to free enterprise on the part of early American leaders presumably account for the existence of the private research efforts. More problematic is the case of the public research establishment. Unabashed enthusiasts for public research efforts would like to believe that the benefits of the research to both farmers and the general public were so large that it is obvious why the public network was established and maintained.[46] Such reasoning is too simple, however. Considerable controversy accompanied the creation of each element of the teaching–research–extension complex in the nineteenth and early twentieth centuries. The Morrill Act was vetoed by President James Buchanan in 1859 during the political turbulence of the pre-Civil War years. It was passed again by the Congress and signed by President Abraham Lincoln in 1862 after both Lincoln and Stephen Douglas had supported it during the campaign of 1860.[47]

Similar controversies surrounded efforts to launch research on a sustained basis. For example, Evan Pugh, president of Pennsylvania's new agricultural college, devoted great but futile efforts in 1861 to persuade the state legislature to finance research at the college.[48] Similarly, John Pitkin Norton and Samuel William Johnson both encountered apathy from farmers and state legislators in New York and Connecticut, respectively, in their efforts to establish European-like experiment stations between 1850 and 1875. Johnson's ideas finally succeeded as the Connecticut legislature granted $2800 to Wesleyan University in 1875 for establishment of an agricultural experiment station. Success came, however, only after Orange Judd, a trustee of Wesleyan and editor of *American Agriculturalist*, had arranged the Wesleyan connection and offered personally to match state funds with $1000.[49] When the Hatch Act was passed in 1887, the constitutional legitimacy of its state grants was a bone of contention.[50] Moreover, considerable ambiguity surrounded the roles of the experiment stations. Were they to conduct practical research of immediate utility on the farm, or basic research?[51] Passage of the Adams Act was blocked in Congress for two years due to opposition from Speaker of the House Joseph Gurney Cannon.[52]

Extension activities, too, emerged in a cloud of controversies over who should operate them and how. Agricultural colleges were nervous that a federal extension service would cause them to lose influence within their own states. Federal officials were concerned that local colleges would not pursue farm demonstration work with any vigor and thus extension work would fail to take research results beyond the confines of academe.[53] The idea of working with black farmers in the South was objectionable to some white members of Congress.[54]

Clearly the creation of a system for generating and transmitting expert knowledge in agriculture did not come without serious arguments. Most of the disputes did not reflect direct opposition to the development of a scientific agriculture *per se*, but the fact that opposition was serious and sustained indicates that the putative benefits of better agricultural technology did not instantly win the hearts and minds of all policy makers and citizens. Whatever might be thought about the agricultural research network now, it must be understood that its perceived benefits did not overwhelm all other considerations when the system was created. Who, then, wanted a concerted and continual effort to innovate in agriculture and why? A number of different groups supported the notion of progress in farming through scientifically based technology.

First, a growing cadre of professional scientist–administrators appeared in America in the nineteenth century and lobbied long hours for the creation of agricultural research.[55] Their motives were complex. Many of them had come from farm backgrounds, but they sought career fulfillment via intellectual work rather than farming. In some cases, a desire to excell in science was closely intermingled with a sense of religious duty to serve mankind through promoting the efficiency of agriculture. Johnson, a leading proponent of the public experiment stations, for example, was a devout Congregationalist who believed he served God through science.[56]

Second, farm journalists and publishers were frequent allies in the efforts to gain a higher capacity for using science in agriculture. Judd's efforts in Connecticut, for example, were crucial to the founding of the first experiment station in 1875.[57] Later, in the twentieth century, the Wallace family of Iowa was highly influential through experimentation on their own farms and through the popular magazine *Wallace's Farmer* in efforts to improve the agricultural technology of the U.S. They also turned out Secretaries of Agriculture in great profusion: Henry C. Wallace served Warren G. Harding (1921–1924) and his son, Henry A. Wallace, served Franklin D. Roosevelt (1933–1941).[58] [Henry A. Wallace later served as Vice President (1941–1945) and Secretary of Commerce (1945–1946). He was unsuccessful in his bid for the presidency in 1948.]

Third, commercial interests related to agriculture, such as banking, railroads, and retail merchants, backed scientific and technological innovation in agriculture. Seaman A. Knapp, generally considered the founder of extension work, was explicitly aware of the power of nonfarm commercial interests in forcing technological change. Knapp utilized this power in 1904 during the Texas boll weevil emergency by persuading bankers to make credit contingent upon adoption of technical practices that Knapp endorsed.[59] Efforts of nonfarm commercial interests were especially important in the National Soil Fertility League, which helped launch the extension service in 1914.[60] Undoubtedly their interests lay in the higher economic activity their firms would have if farm output were more plentiful.

Finally, some farmers participated actively and crucially in the efforts to launch scientific agriculture. Legends abound of farmers averse to "book farming" by professors and scientists, but it is important to realize that not all farmers were filled with antipathy toward science and technology. Quite the converse, in fact; if no farmers had risen in favor of science and education, those institutions surely would have failed. The expertise had to be adopted to keep the scientific establishment viable. Farmer support of agricultural science and technology included the larger and more prosperous farmers who saw that improvement of their operations through innovation was a major route to prosperity for them.[61] This class of farmers became through time a larger and larger proportion of all farmers. As their strength in the farming community increased, farmer support of scientific and technological institutions was consolidated.

Technologically sophisticated farmers now completely dominate agricultural production in the U.S. Science and technology were the foundation for their rise to preeminence in their industry and to the income elite of America. Despite its high income potential, farming is still frought with paradox, as political scientist Don F. Hadwiger has so eloquently stated:

> As theologians are grateful for the Trinity, historians and political scientists should be grateful for the American farmer, because paradox is his most abundant product. The farmer, whose independence, self-respect, and condition of equality were called the "most precious part" of this Republic, was the first citizen to rebel against the Republic, and the second to do so, and so on. Farmers were an outraged majority, and later a satiated minority. They were rural pragmatists who bit hardest for third parties, conservatives who provided the most votes for Socialist and Populist platforms. And when our noblest citizens developed a sound progressive program, these farmers lacked the social stature to lead. Farming, glorified as the most humanizing and satisfying of occupations, recently ranked second from the bottom on

a ten-point occupational prestige scale, just below serving as deckhand, just above peddling and taking in ironing.[62]

Farming is no longer a working man's occupation and the birthplace of working-class revolts. It is based on capital and its practitioners are thoroughly capitalist in their behavior and values. They may not yet have achieved a social status comparable to their incomes, but the return of a farmer, Jimmy Carter, to the White House indicated that social status, too, is now within reach.

AGRICULTURAL REVOLUTION: THE COURSE OF EVENTS

An analysis of the perceptions and causes of the agricultural revolution provides an understanding of what the revolution meant in the abstract, but only an examination of its course of events can unfold a sense of the existential experience. Technological transformation of American agriculture took approximately a century, so that any one individual had only a partial glimpse of the forces of change at work. Four generations of farm families watched labor being slowly squeezed out of agriculture, but it is only with the perspective of hindsight that we can get a sense of the overall magnitude of the changes. The course of events was slow in terms of an individual farmer's operations. In some cases it was a question of whether a part-time hired hand would continue to work on the farm or go to work full-time in a factory. Often the question was whether a son would choose to take over the family farm as his father neared retirement. In cases such as these, relatively little trauma was involved; rather, events just seemed to work out that way, but the direction of change was always such that in the end fewer people were left in farming. In some cases, of course, the phenomenon of labor leaving agriculture was the consequence of bankruptcy, forced sale, and tremendous stress on a distraught family. Whatever the circumstances, however, the coveted prize was always the opportunity to attain prosperity as a farm owner–operator. Only a few made it.

War and depression strongly influenced the rate of adoption of new farm technologies, and the pace of the agricultural revolution was thus uneven. Likewise, cyclical changes in weather and climate patterns added their influence to the course of events. Politicoeconomic and physical factors thus compounded the difficulties a farmer encountered in dealing with the stream of new inventions. Moreover, war conditions emphasized the strategic importance of agriculture as a source of strength for government leaders. The Janus-faced specter of nationalism was thus frequently present as a background motif to farming. This section explores the highlights of how the agricultural revolution unfolded so that we may better understand the complexities of the cultural milieu in which insect control decisions were made.

1861–1914

In the years before the Civil War, many Americans lived in rural areas and most working people earned their livelihood from farming. In 1860, 59% of all gainfully employed persons were engaged in agriculture.[63] The war brought unparalleled prosperity to northern farmers but economic and political defeat to the agricultural South.[64] Prosperous northerners, plagued by a shortage of labor, used the opportunity provided by high prices to intensify the capital inputs on their farms, especially the adoption of horse-drawn machinery for the harvest of small grains.[65] Private research, particularly by farm implement manufacturers,[66] provided much of the new technology, but passage of the Morrill Act in 1862 established the first component of the public research network. After the war, the new land grant universities came to be prominent in the enhancement of technological change in agriculture.

New farm practices in the nineteenth century included the adoption of new plant varieties[67] and new animal stock, some use of chemicals such as Paris green (to kill Colorado potato beetles and other insects) and sodium nitrate fertilizer, and a host of changes in the infrastructure that made commercial farming feasible in areas previously too remote from markets. The opening of the Erie Canal in 1825, for example, heralded a new era in transportation technologies for bulky commodities such as wheat. The development of an effective refrigerated railroad car in the 1870s allowed more efficient transportation of valuable meats from the West to eastern markets.[68]

Overwhelming all other inventions in terms of ultimate impact on the agricultural economy, however, was the continual progress made during the nineteenth century toward the replacement of human labor with machines run by animals and later by steam or gasoline engines. Improved cast iron plows developed early in the century, for example, allowed a man to plow 1.5 to 2.0 acres per day instead of the customary 1.0.[69] This was a 50–100% increase in his efficiency in getting a crop started. Similarly, the development of combines for the reaping and threshing of grain crops, plus improvements in the steam and gasoline engines, allowed similar leaps in labor productivity in the late nineteenth century.[70] Displacement of animal power from the farm did not come until after World War I, but the largest and most well-capitalized farms began the substitution of mechanical power for animal power well before that time.[71]

Federal policies opened the western lands of the U.S. for settlement and dispersal to private hands in the latter part of the 19th century. At the same time, increasing industrialization in both the U.S. and Europe created a greater demand for agricultural goods in the developing urban centers. That demand was met by the expansion of farm production into the new lands and the use of new machinery. Increases in output outdistanced the capacity of U.S. and European consumers to purchase food, so American agriculture experienced a virtually continual farm depression from 1867 to 1898.[72] The rise of the Patrons of Husbandry (Grange, 1867), the National Independent (Greenback) Party (1876), the National Farmers' Alliance (1877), the Populists (1891), and the Farmers' Educational and Cooperative Union (National Farmers' Union, 1902) was a prominent political response of farmers to their economic difficulties.[73] Particularly hard-pressed were those individuals who were deeply in debt or who had insufficient land and capital to take advantage of the new inventions. It must be remembered that, even in the days of homesteading, farmers were a heterogeneous lot divided by relative levels of prosperity. Fortunes could be made on highly capitalized bonanza wheat farms in North Dakota after 1875,[74] for example, but in 1880 one-fourth of all farmers were tenants, frequently a sign of low income and status.[75] The proportion of tenant farms continued to rise until it reached a peak of 42% in 1930–1935.[76]

Prices relative to production costs rose after 1898, and American agriculture entered what some have called the "Golden Age," lasting through World War I.[77] Consumers in urban America may have suffered in this period of high food prices, and exports to Europe dropped somewhat.[78] The fire-breathing radicalism of the populist period mellowed but did not disappear as prosperity brought middle-class incomes in sight for many farmers.[79]

The problems of farmers in the period 1861–1914 can be seen to stem from a variety of sources. Profiteering railroad owners, middlemen, financiers, and other businessmen seeking a share of the farmer's wealth created part of the problem. Similarly, government policies that led to the opening of western lands for settlement as well as those favoring creditors over debtors were important elements of the picture. What is less widely recognized, however, is that the advances in farming technology that occurred during and after the Civil War were also at the base of many farmers' frustrated efforts to achieve prosperity. Well-capitalized, progressive farmers frequently were in a position to take advantage of new labor-saving machinery on large tracts of land and thereby to earn enough income to belong to the middle-class. Farmers heavily in debt or without any hope of acquiring enough land to use the new machines were left with a more marginal existence.

Farmers' problems during this period were, in short, partially attributable to the growing use of science and technology on the farm. Most of the inventions had come from the genius of private inventors, but the period 1861–1914 also saw the establishment of the public network of agricultural research stations with their associated colleges and extension services. In the decades following 1914, the outpouring of innovations from the public research network was added to that from private inventors. What is ironic is that although the common image of science and technology is one of the promoters of well-being, the very farmers who most needed assistance in the years before 1914 were precisely the ones who were unable to take advantage of the new inventions.

1914–1954

All major pieces of the agricultural research network (teaching–research–extension) were in place by 1914. World War I caused high farm prices and a declining availability of farm labor, which enabled and required farmers to increase their mechanization. In 1914, only 17,000 tractors were in use on farms, but 246,000 were in use by 1920.[80] Total farm employment reached a peak of 13.6 million in 1916 and then began to drop, a trend that has continued to this day. By 1954, only 8.6 million people were employed on farms.[81] Technical advice from the public and private research establishments aided the transition to a higher level of capital-intensive agriculture.

Price declines for farm produce began in 1919 and by 1920 American farmers had entered a period of serious depression.[82] Farm implement sales reached $471 million in 1920 but dropped to $223 million in 1923.[83] The total value of farm machinery and implements reached $3.6 billion in 1920 but had dropped to $2.8 billion by 1923; values rose (with intermittent declines) after 1923, but did not match the 1920 level until 1942, when they reached $4.0 billion.[84] Despite the fluctuations in expenditures for and values of farm machinery and implements, the total amount of mechanization increased throughout the 1920s. The number of tractors on farms rose from 246,000 in 1920 to 920,000 in 1930. Motor trucks increased from 139,000 to 900,000, and automobiles jumped from 2.1 million to 4.1 million. Grain combines increased more than 15-fold during the decade, from 4000 to 61,000. Similarly, corn-pickers rose from 10,000 to 50,000, and farms with milking machines increased from 55,000 to 100,000.[85] The fact that the value of the machinery fell or rose only slowly while the number of machines steadily increased probably reflected a tendency for farmers to use a machine longer during the period of low food prices. It can be reasonably concluded that some farmers continued to mechanize in spite of, indeed in response to, the low prices and fierce competition in the agricultural enterprise. Only through such efforts to innovate could a farm operator hope to cut production costs and achieve prosperity.[86]

The realization that farmers bought farm inputs in a tariff-protected market but sold in an unprotected market led to efforts to bring the protection of tariffs to capitalistic agriculture. The McNary–Haugen movement of the 1920s called for the federal government to absorb the exportable surplus of farm production for sale in the world markets at a low price. Domestic prices would be higher and thus bring prosperity to farmers.[87] Farmers with a strong financial base, however, tended to oppose the MacNary–Haugen bills and continued to increase their use of innovations from science and technology to maintain their prosperity.[88] Farm journalists helped fuel the continued trend toward capital-intensive farming through, for example, the "Master Farmer" movement launched in 1925 by Clifford V. Gregory, editor of *Prairie Farmer*.[89] Simultaneously, of course, labor continued to leave agriculture, and one economist noted in 1927 that many people, rural and urban, assumed one lived on a farm only as a last resort.[90]

Although the various McNary–Haugen bills never became law, low farm prices remained a serious election issue in 1928. The newly inaugerated President, Herbert Hoover, convened a special session of Congress to pass the Agricultural Marketing Act and establish the Federal Farm Broad. Voluntary cooperation among farmers helped them to adjust their marketing so as to avoid seasonal gluts on the market, but this maneuver did not end their serious depression.[91]

The onset of the worldwide depression in 1929 further increased the problems farmers faced. Enactment of the Hawley–Smoot Tariff in 1930 had been intended by President Hoover to help farmers, but as enacted it probably hurt them by decreasing their abilities to export farm produce and increasing the prices they paid for farm inputs and other consumer items.[92] Farm prices were also forced down as the wages of urban consumers were curtailed by large jumps in unemployment. President Franklin Roosevelt's efforts to aid farmers resulted in the Agricultural Adjustment Act (AAA) of 1933, a law passed with the support of major farm groups like the American Farm Bureau Federation. Direct government payments to producers for reducing acreage was the major mechanism of the policy to boost farm income.[93] Creation of the Commodity Credit Corporation in October 1933 made possible the introduction of nonrecourse loans for cotton, corn, and later other crops.[94] The Supreme Court's Hoosac Mills decision in 1936 ended the first AAA, but it was replaced by the Soil Conservation and Domestic Allotment Act of 1936 and the AAA of 1938. Government support of prices at specified parity ratios together with control of acreage planted was the foundation on which the Roosevelt administration hoped to keep prices up and unusable farm surpluses down. The former goal was met with some success, but large government stocks of wheat, cotton, and corn were embarrassing until the outbreak of World War II transformed the "surplus" into crucial "military reserves."[95] The AAA of 1938 with high price supports remained the pattern for American farm policy into and beyond World War II, despite efforts by the Republican party and, later, Secretary of Agriculture Charles F. Brannan's efforts to introduce some element of flexibility into the levels of price support.[96]

A second thrust of Roosevelt's farm relief efforts is less well known today because, in contrast to the price support programs, it ended in the 1940s under a hail of criticism and controversy. The Emergency Relief Act of 1933 created the Federal Emergency Relief Administration, in which administrators began a program of planned, rural farm communities that would help poor families acquire productive farms. These cooperative communities suffered from poor management in some cases, unrealistic economic expectations in others, and from resistance to cooperation by residents. Moreover, they were divided into family tracts that were too small to take advantage of the revolution in mechanization sweeping American agriculture. These problems were enhanced by hostility against alleged "socialism" or "communism" from well-capitalized farmers represented by the National Cotton Council and the American Farm Bureau Federation. Internal problems and external opposition ended what should be seen as the last government-backed effort to foster a yeoman agrarian democracy.[97] A loan program for tenants under the Bankhead–Jones Farm Tenant Act of 1937 was equally limited in effectiveness, in that no loans were large enough to establish a tenant on a farm sufficiently well-capitalized to survive without protection from the competition of larger farms. Again, the limitations on the act came from Congressmen not wanting to see the government help tenant farmers become "better" than those who were already established as farm owner–operators.[98]

Lack of employment opportunities in the cities, and the ability to subsist on a farm, probably accounted for an increase in the number of farms and the farm population in the 1930s.[99] In the long run, however, the New Deal legislation enhanced the attractiveness of capital-for-labor substitutions. Direct payments to farmers plus supported prices gave them the means to finance the adoption of new practices. Moreover, restrictions on the numbers of acres planted, but no restrictions on the capital inputs to those acres, encouraged farmers to use land-saving technologies such as fertilizers and insecticides. Guaranteed prices provided a stable situation in which they could reliably calculate their expected returns for adopting new technology. Continued improvements in machinery, plant varieties (especially hybrid corn), and fertilizers resulted in increased labor and land productivities, thus leading to an ever-lessened need for people in agriculture.[100] Tractors numbered 920,000 in 1930 and rose slowly to 1.05 million in 1935. Between 1935 and 1940, tractors numbers rose more rapidly, to 1.55 million. Expenditures for machinery fell sharply in 1932 and 1933, but picked up again in the late 1930s. Similarly, expenditures for fertilizer and lime fell from $288 million in 1930 to $125 million in 1932, but by 1940 the total had climbed back to $261 million.[101]

World War II drew workers from agriculture by the development of industrial opportunities and by inducting men into the armed forces.[102] High prices also returned with the outbreak of hostilities.[103] Wartime conditions both demanded that farmers economize on labor and gave them the prosperity to do so. Continued advances in mechanization during and after the war offered farmers the potential to plow, plant, harvest, and store ever-increasing amounts of produce for each hour of labor they invested.

Although mechanization had been the major source of capital-intensive innovation up to 1940, chemical inventions became increasingly important after that date. Advances in fertilizer production, particularly the introduction of anhydrous ammonia as a nitrogen fertilizer,[104] enabled a single individual, working with sophisticated machinery, to raise and collect higher yields. Other chemicals, such as the herbicide 2,4-D and antibiotics added to swine feed, further increased production for the technologically advanced farmer and thereby reduced the time needed to produce a given unit of crop or animals.[105] Insecticides were also a part of the chemical revolution in agriculture.

In the aggregate, the productivity of labor in agriculture grew at a rate of 1.8% per year between 1889 and 1957. Most of the growth, however, occurred in the latter part of the period. The years 1937–1948 saw labor productivity grow at 3.8% per year; in 1948–1957 growth had reached 5.7% per year. Growth of the productiveness of labor in agriculture was consistently higher than that of nonfarm industries.[106] Improved productivity came not only from adoption of new machines and chemicals but also from improved education of farm workers and expansion-of-scale on the average farm.[107]

Not only were machinery, chemicals, and education changing the domestic social importance of farming, but American agriculture became a permanent part of the international cold war strategy in the 1950s. The chemical industry itself supported the turn of events. In the words of E. I. DuPont de Nemours & Co., "The whole scientific fraternity works with the farmer in this struggle."[108] Herbert Thomasek of the Pittsburgh Chemical Co. commented, "we will [make] this a greater, healthier, stronger, impregnable America, God grant that this be true."[109]

1954–Present

President Dwight Eisenhower and his Secretary of Agriculture, Ezra Taft Benson, brought a number of changes into office with them in 1953. Eisenhower, in keeping with his campaign pledge, maintained his backing of high price supports through 1954. Both Eisenhower and Benson, however, were ideologically committed to a free market in agriculture and wanted a more flexible system of farming legislation.[110] Benson firmly believed as a matter of religious and political principle that abundance and national security would come from free-market conditions that favored technologically progressive entrepreneurs in agriculture. In addition, he believed that the price support system was useless in helping low-income farmers. The only route for them was to expand their farm acreage and use of capital or find more income outside of farm work.[111] As he put it,

> With faith in our ability to move forward we can continue to achieve miracles of production. Without that larger view we are doomed to fasten more chains upon our economy, and finally to reduce ourselves to the level of the socialized systems of the world.[112]

Congress agreed to some of Benson's plans for flexible price supports in the Agricultural Act of 1954, but the Secretary was not able to force a return to a true free market. Political opposition from farm constituencies countered Benson's thinking.[113] Continued price supports assisted further technological change, and 18% of U.S. farms went out of business between 1956 and 1962.[114] It is quite likely that the continuation of price supports had the paradoxical effect of enabling farmers to make further investments in capital-intensive technology (which made large farms more competitive than small farms) while at the same time it enabled poorly capitalized farmers to eke out a living. Ultimately, of course, the well-capitalized farmers prevailed.

Surpluses relative to consumer demand continued, and three management programs were used to control or dispose of them.[115] Two were familiar from earlier years. First, weak acreage controls helped repress production. Second, a large amount of produce moved into government ownership: $8 billion by December 1959.[116] The third method of handling the surplus was through the formal integration of agricultural policy with foreign affairs. Public Law 480 was passed in 1954 as a domestic agricultural program to sell excess food supplies abroad.[117] Enhanced foreign disposal of American produce helped maintain prices much as had the Marshall Plan after World War II.[118]

Senator Hubert Humphrey's efforts in the late 1950s, led to a transformation of P. L. 480 from merely a surplus-disposal program to one in which agricultural production was a conscious part of American foreign policy.[119] The name of the revised program was "Food for Peace," but its operation contained important political implications. John F. Kennedy's Secretary of Agriculture, Orville Freeman, argued in 1966 that P. L. 480's requirement for recipient countries to have a free enterprise economy was not an effort to force capitalism on them—he maintained only that free enterprise worked better.[120] The fruits of American agricultural technology were thus endowned with significant ideological overtones.

Regardless of one's political values, it is clear that government involvement in agriculture during the Kennedy–Johnson years (1960–1968) was necessary for the prosperity of many farmers. Higher prices induced by government activities gave farmers the incomes necessary to continue expansion, mechanization, and adoption of chemicals in their operations. At each step of the way, their use of human labor decreased in favor of increased use of capital-intensive technology. The research establishment assisted the transformation on a continuing basis. Moreover, food production was rationalized within a policy framework encompassing both domestic and foreign strategic goals.

Little change in agricultural or foreign policy came with the change of administration to Richard Nixon. Nixon's second Secretary of Agriculture, Earl L. Butz, was less inclined to worry about the fate of poor farmers than had Freeman under Kennedy and Johnson, but the distinctions were ones of style and rhetoric. Butz fundamentally believed that the future of farming belonged to those who could utilize new technologies.[121] Transfer of the presidency from the Republicans under Gerald Ford to the Democrats under Jimmy Carter brought a new interest in the course of change in the farming economy. Carter's Secretary of Agriculture, Bob Bergland, was, like Carter, a working farmer before his entrance into public life.[122] He was also seriously concerned that "bigness" in agriculture was a threat to values formerly resident in the "family farmer" and the social fabric of rural life.[123] The sentiment for helping small farmers was expressed in some of the provisions of the Food and Agriculture Act of 1977,[124] and Bergland used this opportunity to launch a new initiative in examining the structure of American agriculture. He presented the idea that the pace of technological and economic change had slowed in the 1970s compared to the three previous decades, and this slow-down provided an opportunity to examine the past and make adjustments for the future.[125] Bergland called in March 1979 for a new initiative in setting goals on who could and should control the food production system of the U.S. He was explicit in urging, in an address to the National Farmers' Union, that "a handful of giant operators" should *not* gain complete control of American agriculture.[126] The reports *Status of the Family Farm*[127] and *Structure Issues of American Agriculture*[128] were issued in 1978 and 1979. Underlying Bergland's efforts was the notion that the technology that fueled the changes in American agriculture may have had some highly undesirable social features in that they increased class antagonisms and disparities of income, degraded environmental quality, and posed a threat to the long-term health of the natural resource based on which food production depends.[129]

The ultimate impact of the Carter/Bergland initiatives is uncertain, especially in the new administration of Ronald Reagan. Nevertheless a few observations can be made that are relevant to an understanding of insect control technologies within the current context of agricultural production:

1. Concern over the deleterious effects of the technological revolution in agriculture is to be welcomed, because social inequality and environmental hazard have been hallmarks of the changes in agriculture. Unfortunately both the timing and the foundations upon which the concerns are based may be such that any policy initiatives resulting from them will be little or no useful consequence. It is possible that Bergland's concerns were an effort to "shut the barn door after the horse had left." After all, the technological revolution in agriculture is a *fait accompli,* and the conditions necessary to reverse it might be extremely painful for everyone. Amelioration, of course, might be possible.

Probably more important than the late timing was the inadequacy of the philosophical foundation on which the concerns were based. Bergland, like many Americans, was infected with the Jeffersonian myth that somehow the farmer's work is uniquely virtuous in a social sense. Therefore the "family farm" is a precious element to be preserved in our society. Full consideration of this myth is beyond the limits of this study, but this writer considers the Jeffersonian ideology to be so much twaddle. Farmers are neither more nor less virtuous than other classes of citizens. Focusing upon the family farm as a particularly valuable institution is misleading. The real questions that ought to occupy the minds of policy makers are (a) How are the resources for agricultural production to be controlled and used in a global society? (b) How are the benefits of the agricultural industry to be distributed? Any preconceived notion about the virtuosity of "family farmers" that intrudes into efforts to answer these important questions will result in a contradictory, muddled policy.

2. Technological change is generally acknowledged to be the major factor resulting in larger, specialized farms.[130] Two other factors are less well recognized. First, many other "problems" seen in the structure of farming are related to increased size and specialization. For example, barriers to entry into farming and environmental degradation are both partially attributable to the use of the new technologies by large farms. Second, it was no accident that researchers produced the types of technologies they did. Scientists in both the public and private sector responded to the demands of the well-capitalized farmers and produced inventions that "worked" in the context of these producers.

Given (a) the preeminence of technological change in affecting the structure of agriculture and (b) the existence of an agricultural science community accustomed to meeting the needs of a particular class of farmer, one might suppose that deliberate efforts to eliminate the economic and social attractiveness of large-scale farming and to remold the research community would be prominent pieces of the administration's concerns. They are not. Therefore, future changes in agriculture are likely to be directed by the same forces that have been operating for the past century and more. Well-capitalized farmers will continue to set the pace in demanding and using the outputs of the research community. Researchers in turn will meet those demands and not pursue alternative research pathways producing less capital-intensive technology.

As an example, the private farm implement manufacturers spent $204 million on research and development in 1975.[131] One particular firm, Deere & Co., was reported in early 1980 to have had a growth rate faster than that of Xerox and nearly twice that of IBM and Texas Instruments during the 1970s. Deere & Co. spent 4% of its sales income on new product development.[132] The continued research and development efforts in both the public and private sectors mean that the future for

American agriculture probably holds much the same elements as the past. Large operations will further consolidate their position within agriculture; the size of operations will depend primarily on the technology available and the ability of farmers to muster the capital requirements for its adoption. Only social or economic revolutions that are unexpected and of an unforeseeable nature will alter this course of events.

CONCLUDING REMARKS

In Chapter 10 we will turn to a more detailed discussion of future directions for insect control in the light of what has happened in American agriculture since 1861. For the moment we will simply summarize the situation as it was at the end of the 1970s. Agriculture was a capital-intensive operation engaged in by a small part of the population. In 1979, 2.33 million farms were in operation; but in 1974, only 825,000 of them accounted for 90% of all agricultural sales. Probably fewer than 100,000 farms accounted for over 50% of all production in 1979. A middle class income from farming ($18,500 per year) required a capital investment of $461,900 in 1977. Entry into farming was accordigly more difficult than it had been in 1940 and before.[133] As a result, farming was tending to become a closed profession. The course of technological change made it difficult to farm except for those born into and inheriting an established farm firm. Those successful in farming could expect to earn an income far above the national median. They might not have been the wealthiest people in America, but they were far from the poorest.

The trappings of wealth and power that go with operating a major farm, however, are plagued with a potentially fatal irony. Operating expenses as a proportion of gross farm income rise with the size of the gross income. For example, in 1977 a farm with sales of over $100,000 had operating expenses of 88%, while farms selling less than $100,000 had expenses of 75%. One economist argued hypothetically that a decrease in the gross income would affect the net income of the smaller farms less than a similar percentage decrease in the gross income of larger farms. The smaller difference between net and gross incomes on the larger enterprises were the cause of this heightened sensitivity to changes in net income.[134]

Large farms—the type which American farms are tending to become—are thus potentially lucrative, but perhaps also highly vulnerable enterprises. Farmers may be able to guard themselves against disastrous price declines through political action leading to government price support programs. Their vulnerability to loss of income from price declines is mirrored, however, by a similar sensitivity to any factor that decreases yields, such as insects. The trends of American agriculture that led to larger farms may thus be creating businesses particularly sensitive to damage from insect pests.

From this vantage point, we can begin to see through the fog of rhetoric surrounding insect control technologies: The purpose of insect control technology is only secondarily to protect crops from damage; its primary purpose is to protect farm firms, especially large ones, from bankruptcy. Moreover, this protection occurs in a context in which food has important strategic as well as domestic uses. Insects threaten national security as well as domestic tranquility under the American system of capital-intensive agriculture. Once the paradox of wealth with vulnerability is understood, the motivating forces underlying change in entomology can be comprehended.

REFERENCE NOTES

1. Data for 1800 and 1950 are from Bureau of the Census, *Historical Statistics of the United States, Colonial Times to 1957* (Washington: Government Printing Office, 1960) series K 83–97, p. 281 (hereafter cited as *Historical Statistics, Colonial–1957*). Data for 1973–1977 are from USDA, *Agricultural Statistics 1978* (Washington: Government Printing Office, 1979), Table 642 (hereafter cited as *Agricultural Statistics 1978*).
2. William L. Cavert, The technological revolution in agriculture, 1910–1955, *Agric. Hist.* 30 (1956): 18–27; John C. Ellickson and John M. Brewster, Technological advances and the structure of American agriculture, *J. Farm Econ.* 29 (1947): 827–847; A. N. Johnson, The impact of farm machinery on the farm economy, *Agric. Hist.* 24 (1950): 58–62; Wayne D. Rasmussen, The impact of technological change on American agriculture, *J. Econ. Hist.* 22 (1962): 578–591.
3. Bureau of the Census, *Statistical Abstrct of the United States 1977* (Washington D.C.: Government Printing Office, 1978) p. 674, Table 1134 (hereafter cited as *Statistical Abstract 1977*).
4. *Agricultural Statistics 1978,* Table 601.
5. *Historical Statistics, Colonial–1957,* series K 73–82, p. 280.
6. *Statistical Abstract 1977,* p. 675, Table 1135.
7. *Agricultural Statistics 1978,* Table 619.
8. *Ibid.*, Table 621.
9. Willard W. Cochrane, *The City Man's Guide to the Farm Problem* (Minneapolis: Univ. of Minn. Press, 1965), p. 29 (hereafter cited as Cochrane, *City Man's Guide*).
10. *Agricultural Statistics 1978,* Table 601.
11. *Statistical Abstract 1977,* p. 678, Table 1143.
12. *Statistical Abstract 1976,* p. 378, Table 605. The average income for all domestic industries was $9994, and average annual supplements amounted to $1440. Total average income was $11,434.
13. *Ibid.*, p. 406, Table 652.
14. *Agricultural Statistics* 1978, Table 661.

15. Lawrence A. Jones and Ronald L. Mighell, "Vertical integration as a source of capital in farming," in *Capital and Credit Needs in a Changing Agriculture*, E. L. Baum, Howard G. Diesslin, and Earl O. Heady, eds. (Ames, Iowa State Univ. Press, 1961), pp. 147–160; Harold R. Jensen, "Farm management and production economics, 1946–1970" (hereafter cited as Jensen, Farm management), in *A Survey of Agricultural Economics Literature, Vol. 1*, Lee R. Martin, ed. (Minneapolis: Univ. of Minn. Press, 1977), pp. 3–88.
16. Jensen, Farm management, p. 49; Donald K. Larson and Thomas A. Carlin, Income and economic status of people with farm earnings, *South J. Agric. Econ.* 6 (Dec., 1974): 73–79.
17. A fundamental connection between education and an ability to use capital in farming was noted by Roger C. Woodworth and J. W. Fanning, "Relationships between capital and education," in *Capital and Credit Needs in a Changing Agriculture*, E. L. Baum, Howard G. Diesslin, and Earl O. Heady, eds. (Ames: Iowa State Univ. Press, 1961), pp. 337–344. James D. Tarver and C. Shannon Stokes document the increased educational achievements of farm youth in Georgia between 1940 and 1960 (Educational Trends of Rural and Urban Population of Georgia, *Coll. of Agric. Exp. Stn. Res. Report 130*, University of Georgia, May, 1972, Tables 16–18. Wayne D. Rasmussen argues that technical change in agriculture has changed farming from an occupation to a profession that requires substantial educational support. At the same time, the decreasing number of farmers has created both an intellectual and fiscal crisis for the agricultural colleges (Liberal Education and Agriculture, Institute of Higher Education, Columbia Univ., mimeo, [1958], 49 pp.).
18. Carter's business interests were begun by his father, Earl Carter, who ran a farm supply store in Plains, Georgia. Earl expanded his operations to include (1) purchasing peanuts on contract for oil processing, (2) 4000 acres of peanut production, and (3) fertilizer merchandising. The varied business interests were kept in the family after Earl Carter's death in 1953. See *Current Biography Yearbook 1977* (New York: H. W. Wilson Company, 1978), pp. 100–101.
19. R. G. Bressler, The impact of science on agriculture, *J. Farm Econ.* 40 (Dec., 1958): 100.
20. Adriann K. Constandse, Pedro F. Hernandez, and Alvin L. Bertrand, Social implications of increasing farm technology in rural Louisiana, *Agric. Exp. Stn. Bull. No. 628*, La. State University and Agricultural and Mechanical College, Aug. 1968, 39 pp.
21. G. E. Brandow, "Policy for commercial agriculture, 1945–71," in *A Survey of Agricultural Economics Literature, Vol. 1*, Lee R. Martin, ed. (Minneapolis: Univ. of Minn. Press, 1977), pp. 212, 276.
22. Keith C. Barrons of the Dow Chemical Co. presents a positive image of the new farming technologies in *The Food in Your Future* (New York: Van Nostrand Reinhold Co., 1975), 173 pp. He balances his presentation with frank acknowledgements of the pressures under which contemporary farmers work. A particularly enthusiastic endorsement of capital-intensive farming is Edward Higbee, *Farms and Farmers in and Urban Age* (New York: The Twentieth Century Fund, 1963), pp. 3–4, 45–75 (hereafter cited as Higbee, *Farms and Farmers*). Wheeler McMillen was a fan of the progressive farmer before World War II, as expressed in *Too Many Farmers* (New York: William Morrow & Co., 1929), pp. 295–297. See also Lowry Nelson, *American Farm Life* (Cambridge: Harvard Univ. Press, 1954), p. 31.
23. The clearest articulation of technological change as the source of dynamism in agriculture is Willard W. Cochrane, *Farm Prices: Myth and Reality* (Minneapolis: Univ. of Minn. Press, 1958), pp. 96–107 (hereafter cited as Cochrane, *Farm Prices*). An earlier

articulation of the same theory is in Carl T. Schmidt, *American Farmers in the World Crisis* (New York: Oxford Univ. Press, 1941), pp. 31–37, 60–80. Frederic C. Flegel gathered evidence from Wisconsin farmers in 1951 that demonstrated (1) high farm incomes were associated with innovation, and (2) farmers consider other farmers with higher incomes to be the best farm operators; see Farm incomes and the adoption of farm practices, *Rural Sociology* 22 (1957): 159–162. Olaf F. Larson and Everett M. Rogers summarized a large body of sociological research on changes in farming in "Rural society in transition: The American setting," in *Our Changing Rural Society: Perspectives and Trends,* James H. Copp, ed. (Ames: Iowa State Univ. Press, 1964), pp. 39–67. Increased inequality in agriculture as a result of innovation was reviewed by Willis Peterson and Yujiro Hayami, "Technical change in agriculture," in *A Survey of Agricultural Economics Literature, Vol. 1,* Lee R. Martin, ed. (Minneapolis: Univ. of Minn. Press, 1977), pp. 528–532. A recent article justifying innovation despite painful displacement is Richard E. Just, Andrew Schmitz, and David Zilberman, Technological change in agriculture, *Science* 206 (1979): 1277–1280 (hereafter cited as Just, Schmitz, and Zilberman, Technological change).

24. John Steinbeck, *The Grapes of Wrath* (New York: The Viking Press, 1939), pp. 47–53.
25. Wendell Berry, *The Unsettling of America: Culture and Agriculture* (New York: Avon Books, 1977), 228 pp.
26. A classic study of this type was on the adoption of two important inventions, 2,4-D and antibiotic supplements in swine feeds, prepared by George M. Beal and Everett M. Rogers, The Adoption of Two Farm Practices in a Central Iowa Community, *Special Report No. 26,* Iowa State Univ. of Science and Technology, Agric. and Home Econ. Exp. Stn., June, 1960, 20 pp. A general summary of adoption–diffusion research is provided by Joe M. Bohlen, "The adoption and diffusion of ideas in agriculture," in *Our Changing Rural Society: Perspectives and Trends,* James H. Copp, ed. (Ames, Iowa: Iowa State Univ. Press, 1964), pp. 265–287.
27. James Hightower, *Hard Tomatoes, Hard Times* (Cambridge, Mass.: Schenkman, 1973), 268 pp.
28. William H. Friedland, Amy E. Barton, and Robert J. Thomas, Conditions and consequences of lettuce harvest mechanization, *Hort. Science* 14 (Apr., 1979): 110–113.
29. Jensen, Farm management, pp. 55–56.
30. Zvi Griliches, Hybrid corn: An exploration in the economics of technological change, *Econometrica* 25 (1957): 501–522.
31. Zvi Griliches, Research costs and social returns: Hybrid corn and related innovations, *J. Polit. Econ.* 66 (1958): 419–431. For a general review of studies on rates of return see Willis Peterson and Yujiro Hayami, "Technical change in agriculture," in *A Survey of Agricultural Economics Literature, Vol. 1,* Lee R. Martin, ed. (Minneapolis: Univ. of Minn. Press, 1977), pp. 505–523. Robert E. Evenson and Yoav Kislev studied rates of return to agricultural research on a global basis and concluded that rates of return were far higher than "normal" returns, in *Agricultural Research and Productivity* (New Haven: Yale Univ. Press, 1975), p. 157.
32. Yujiro Hayami and Vernon Ruttan, *Agricultural Development: An International Perspective* (Baltimore: Johns Hopkins Press, 1971), pp. 55–59, 129–133. For a general argument on how imbalances in technology, labor unrest, and shortage of materials can force technological change in particular directions, see Nathan Rosenberg, *Perspectives on Technology* (New York: Cambridge Univ. Press, 1976), pp. 108–125.
33. G. E. Brandow, "Policy for commercial agriculture, 1945–71," in *A Survey of Agricultural Economics Literature, Vol. 1,* Lee R. Martin, ed. (Minneapolis: Univ. of Minn. Press, 1977), p. 276.

34. Just, Schmitz, and Zilberman, Technological change.
35. Wilson Gee, *The Place of Agriculture in American Life* (New York: The Macmillan Co., 1930), p. 22.
36. *Ibid.*, p. 5.
37. Don Paarlberg, *American Farm Policy* (New York: John Wiley and Sons, Inc., 1964), pp. 90–91.
38. For a brief account of Washington, see Cecil Wall, George Washington: Country Gentlemen, *Agric. Hist.* 43 (1969): 5–6. Thomas Jefferson's activities as a farmer have been reviewed by E. Merton Coulter, Southern agriculture and southern nationalism before the Civil War, *Agric. Hist.* 4 (1930): 77–91; August C. Miller, Jefferson as agriculturalist, *Agric. Hist.* 16 (1942): 65–78; Henry A. Wallace, Thomas Jefferson's *Farm Book:* A review essay, *Agric. Hist.* 28 (1954): 133–138. Wallace, Franklin Roosevelt's first Secretary of Agriculture, was particularly strong in his endorsement of Jefferson as an outstanding American.
39. For two popular articles about modern farming, see Jules B. Billard, The revolution in American agriculture, *National Geographic* 137 (1970): 147–185; and James A. Sugar, The family farm ain't what it used to be, *ibid.* 146 (1974): 391–411.
40. U.S. Congress, Senate, Temporary National Economic Committee, *Patents and Free Enterprise Monograph No. 31* (Washington, D.C.: Government Printing Office, 1941), 179 pp.
41. Earl W. Hayter, The western farmers and the drivewell patent controversy, *Agric. Hist.* 16 (1942): 16–28; idem, The patent system and agrarian discontent, 1875–1888, *Miss. Val. Hist. Rev.* 34 (1947): 59–82.
42. Irwin Feller, Inventive activity in agriculture, 1837–1890, *J. Econ. Hist.* 22 (1962): 560–577.
43. For an early review of the entire agricultural teaching and research establishment, see Edward Wiest, *Agricultural Organization in the United States* (Lexington: Univ. of Ky. Press, 1923), pp. 187–289.
44. Gladys L. Baker and Wayne D. Rasmussen, Economic research in the Department of Agriculture: A historical perspective, *Agric. Econ. Res.* 27 (1975): 53–72.
45. E. A. Meyer, Developments under the Research and Marketing Act of 1946—finance, administrative organization, procedure, and policy, *J. Farm Econ.* 29 (1947): 1378–1382; Edward C. Banfield, Planning under the Research and Marketing Act of 1946: A study in the sociology of knowledge, *J. Farm Econ.* 31 (1949): 48–75.
46. See, for example, "Statement from the South Carolina Agricultural Experiment Station, October 24, 1977," in U.S. Congress, Senate, Committee on the Judiciary, *Priorities in Agricultural Research of the U.S. Department of Agriculture—Appendix*, Appendix to Hearings, Part 2, 95th Congress, 1st sess., 1977, pp. 56–61. A quote gives the flavor: "Agricultural research benefits people. . . . And that is what agricultural research is all about: producing food and fiber economically to benefit all segments of society. Agricultural research is designed to improve the quality of life of all people."
47. Earl D. Ross, "Father" of the land-grant college, *Agric. Hist.* 12 (1938): 151–186.
48. Charles Rosenberg, *No Other Gods* (Baltimore: Johns Hopkins Univ. Press, 1976), p. 145 (hereafter cited as Rosenberg, *No Other Gods*).
49. H. C. Knoblauch, E. M. Law, W. P. Meyer, B. F. Beacher, R. B. Nestler, and B. S. White, Jr., State Agricultural Experiment Stations, *USDA Misc. Publ. No. 909*, May, 1962, pp. 12–22.

50. *Ibid.*, pp. 50–52; Rosenberg, *No Other Gods*, p. 173.
51. Rosenberg, *No Other Gods*, pp. 146–151.
52. *Ibid.*, pp. 180–182. Blair Booles argues that Cannon's philosophy of government was antagonistic toward federal intervention in the affairs of the people. He became the antithesis of the Progressive era as symbolized by Robert La Follette and Theordore Roosevelt. See *Tyrant from Illinois* (New York: W.W. Norton & Co., Inc., 1951), 248 pp.
53. Joseph C. Bailey, *Seaman A. Knapp, Schoolmaster of American Agriculture* (New York: Columbia Univ. Press, 1945), pp. 260–276 (hereafter cited as Bailey, *Knapp*).
54. Roy V. Scott, *The Reluctant Farmer: The Rise of Agricultural Extension to 1914* (Urbana: Univ. of Ill. Press, 1971), pp. 307–313.
55. Rosenberg, *No Other Gods*, pp. 135–177.
56. *Ibid.*, p. 138.
57. *Ibid.*, p. 148.
58. Edward L. and Frederick H. Schapsmeier, *Henry A. Wallace of Iowa: The Agrarian Years, 1910–1940* (Ames: Iowa State Univ. Press, 1968), pp. 53, 88.
59. Bailey, *Knapp*, pp. 177–183.
60. *Ibid.*, pp. 260–276.
61. Rosenberg, *No Other Gods*, pp. 163, 176–177; Higbee, *Farms and Farmers*, pp. 49–51, 60–61; Cochrane, *Farm Prices*, pp. 105–107. For a study of how the West Virginia Grange wanted an experiment station to their liking, see William D. Barns, Farmers *versus* scientists: The Grange, the Farmer's Alliance, and the West Virginia Agricultural Experiment Station, *W. V. Acad. Sci. Proc.* 37 (1965): 197–206.
62. Don F. Hadwiger, Farmers in politics, *Agric. Hist.* 50 (1976): 156.
63. Bureau of the Census, *Historical Statistics of the United States, 1789–1945* (Washington, D.C.: Government Printing Office, 1949), series D7, p. 63 (hereafter cited as *Historical Statistics, 1789–1945*).
64. John Schlebecker, *Whereby We Thrive* (Ames: Iowa State Univ. Press, 1975), pp. 154–161 (thereafter cited as Schlebecker, *Whereby*).
65. Leo Rogin, *The Introduction of Farm Machinery in Its Relation to the Production of Labor in the Agriculture of the United States During the Nineteenth Century* (Berkeley: Univ. of Calif. Press, 1931), p. 91 (hereafter cited as Rogin, *Introduction of Farm Machinery*); Wayne D. Rasmussen, The impact of technological change on American agriculture, 1862–1962, *J. Econ. Hist.* 22 (1962): 578–591; idem, The Civil War: A catalyst of agricultural revolution, *Agric. Hist.* 39 (1965): 187–195.
66. Inventors were in some cases part-time farmers as well as implement makers. For example, the first McCormick reapers (1840–1844) were made as a sideline on the McCormick farm in Rockbridge County, Virginia. After 1844 Cyrus McCormick began manufacturing in Ohio and New York. After 1847, McCormick's reapers were made exclusively in Chicago (Rogin, *Introduction of Farm Machinery*, pp. 74–75).
67. Knowles A. Ryerson, History and significance of the foreign plant introduction work of the USDA, *Agric. Hist.* 7 (1933): 110–128.
68. Schlebecker, *Whereby*, pp. 89–91, 171.
69. *Ibid.*, pp. 100–101.
70. Rogin, *Introduction of Farm Machinery*, pp. 213–241.
71. Wheat harvesting in California, for example, changed from animal power to steam power in the 1890s (*ibid.*, p. 147). Technological change was an uneven process, however; practices changed at different rates in different crops and regions [Earle D. Ross, Retardation in farm technology before the power age, *Agric. Hist.* 30 (1956): 11–18].

72. Schlebecker, *Whereby*, pp. 157–163.
73. John D. Hicks, *The Populist Revolt* (Minneapolis: Univ. of Minn. Press, 1931), pp. 54–95, 97, 209–215; William P. Tucker, Populism up-to-date: The story of the Farmers' Union, *Agric. Hist.* 21 (1947): 198–208; William D. Barns, Oliver Hudson Kelley and the genesis of the Grange: A reappraisal, *Agric. Hist.* 41 (1967): 229–242.
74. Stanley N. Murray, Railroads and the agricultural development of the Red River Valley of the North, 1870–1890, *Agric. Hist.* 31 (1957): 57–66.
75. *Historical Statistics, 1789–1945* (Washington, D.C.: Government Printing Office, 1949), series E 24, p. 96. For an argument that tenancy, at least in nineteenth-century Iowa, was both a useful and necessary economic institution, see Donald L. Winters, *Farmers without Farms: Agricultural Tenancy in Nineteenth Century Iowa* (Westport, Connecticut: Greenwood Press, 1978), pp. 106–108.
76. *Historical Statistics, 1789–1945*, series E 24, p. 96.
77. James H. Shideler, *Farm Crisis 1919–1923* (Berkeley: Univ. of Calif. Press, 1957), pp. 4–10 (hereafter cited as Shideler, *Farm Crisis*).
78. Schlebecker, *Whereby*, pp. 159–160.
79. Theodore Saloutos and John D. Hicks, *Agricultural Discontent in the Middle West 1900–1939* (Madison: Univ. of Wis. Press, 1951), p. 31.
80. *Historical Statistics, Colonial–1957* series K 150, p. 285.
81. *Ibid.*, series K 73, p. 280.
82. Shideler, *Farm Crisis*, pp. 46–52; *Historical Statistics Colonial–1957*, series K 122, p. 283.
83. Shideler, *Farm Crisis*, p. 79.
84. *Historical Statistics, Colonial–1957*, series K 158, pp. 284–285.
85. *Ibid.*, series K 150–155, p. 285.
86. This conclusion is a restatement of the "agricultural treadmill" argument advanced in Cochrane, *Farm Prices*, pp. 105–107.
87. John Philip Gleason, The attitudes of the business community toward agriculture during the McNary–Haugen period, *Agric. Hist.* 32 (1958): 127–138.
88. Darwin N. Kelley, The McNary–Haugen bills, 1924–1928: An attempt to make the tariff effective for farm products, *Agric. Hist.* 14 (1940): 170–180.
89. See Clifford V. Gregory, The Master Farmer movement, *Agric. Hist.* 10 (1936): 47–58.
90. T. N. Carver, Rural depopulation. *J. Farm Econ.* 9: (1927) 1–10.
91. Alice M. Christensen, Agricultural pressure and governmental response in the United States, 1919–1929, *Agric. Hist.* 11 (1937): 33–42.
92. Murray R. Benedict, *Farm Policies in the United States, 1790–1950* (New York: The Twentieth Century Fund, 1953), pp. 250–252 (hereafter cited as Benedict, *Farm Policies*); Allan Rau, *Agricultural Policy and Trade Liberalization in the United States, 1934–56; A Study of Conflicting Policies* (Geneva: Droz, 1957), pp. 46–50.
93. Wayne D. Rasmussen and Gladys L. Baker, A short history of price support and adjustment legislation and programs for agriculture, 1933–65, *Agric. Econ. Res.* 18 (1966): 69–78 (hereafter cited as Rasmussen and Baker, A short history); Christiana M. Campbell, *The Farm Bureau and the New Deal* (Urbana: Univ. of Ill. Press, 1962), pp. 188–195.
94. Rasmussen annd Baker, A short history.
95. *Ibid.*
96. Benedict, *Farm Policies*, pp. 472–477, 484–490.
97. Donald Holley, *Uncle Sam's Farmers* (Urbana: Univ. of Ill. Press, 1975), pp. 25–26, 261–278.
98. Edward C. Banfield, Ten years of a Farm Tenant Purchase Program, *J. Farm Econ.* 31 (1949): 469–486.

99. Number of people on farms dropped from 32 million in 1910 to 30.5 million by 1930. The number rose to 32.4 million in 1933, but dropped again by 1940 to 30.5 million. The farm population continued to drop after 1940. The number of farms was 6.37 million in 1910. It rose unevenly to 6.81 million in 1935 and thereafter dropped. [Bureau of the Census, *Historical Statistics of the United States, Colonial Times to 1970* (Washington, D.C.: Government Printing Office, 1975), series K-1 and K-4, p. 457].
100. E. O. Heady and L. Auer, Imputation of production to technologies, *J. Farm Econ.* 48 (1966): 309–322; A. Richard Crabb, *The Hybrid Corn Makers: Prophets of Plenty* (New Brunswick: Rutgers Univ. Press, 1947), 331 pp.
101. *Historical Statistics, 1789–1945,* series E 106, 108, 115, p. 100.
102. Albert A. Blum, The farmer, the army, and the draft, *Agric. Hist.* 38 (1964): 34–42.
103. The parity ratio rose from 80 in 1940 to 117 in 1945. It was above 100 in 1942–1945. Cash receipts rose from $9.1 billion in 1940 to $22.3 billion in 1945. (*Historical Statistics, 1789–1945,* series E 88, p. 99).
104. Synthetic ammonia production based on the work of Fritz Haber began in Germany in 1913. Both World War I and World War II stimulated the production of ammonia as an intermediate in the manufacture of explosives. Improvements in production technology during the 1950s and 1960s allowed the construction of plants producing over 1000 tons per day. Much of the ammonia was used in agriculture as a fertilizer. For example, in the U.S. 89% of the ammonia produced in 1968 was used for fertilizer. Anhydrous ammonia is the major supplier of nitrogen fertilizer in the U.S. See A.V. Slack and G. Russell James, eds., *Ammonia,* Vol. 2, Part 1 (New York: Marcel Dekker, Inc., 1973), pp. 2–30.
105. Gale E. Peterson, The discovery and development of 2,4-D, *Agric. Hist.* 41 (1967): 243–253; George M. Beal and Everett M. Rogers, The adoption of two farm practices in a central Iowa community, *Special Report No. 26,* Agric. and Home Econ. Exp. Stn., Iowa State Univ. of Science and Technology, June, 1960, 20 pp.; U.S. Congress, Senate, Committee on Labor and Public Welfare, *Manpower, Chemistry, and Agriculture,* Senate Document 103, 82nd Congress, 2nd sess., 1952, 45 pp.
106. John W. Kendrick, Productivity trends in agriculture and industry, *J. Farm Econ.* 40 (1958): 1554–1564.
107. Zvi Griliches, The sources of measured productivity growth: United States agriculture 1940–1960, *J. Polit. Econ.* 71 (1963): 331–346.
108. *The Story of Farm Chemicals* (Wilmington, Delaware: E.I. DuPont de Nemours & Co., [1954]), 32 pp.
109. Herbert Thomasek, Chemical industry in farm management, *J. Am. Soc. Farm Managers and Rural Appraisers* 18 (1954): 11–16.
110. Edward L. Schapsmeier and Frederick H. Schapsmeier, Eisenhower and Ezra Taft Benson: Farm policy in the 1950s, *Agric. Hist.* 44 (1970): 369–378 (hereafter cited as Schapsmeier and Schapsmeier, Eisenhower).
111. Ezra Taft Benson, *Freedom to Farm* (Garden City, New York: Doubleday and Co., Inc., 1960), pp. 222–223, 231, 233–235.
112. *Ibid.,* p. 37.
113. Schapsmeier and Schapsmeier, Eisenhower.
114. Cochrane, *City Man's Guide,* p. 29; Bureau of the Census, *Historical Statistics of the United States Colonial Times to 1957, Continuation to 1962 and Revisions* (Washington, D.C.: Government Printing Office, 1965), series K 1, p. 41. 4.514 million farms were reported in 1956 but only 3.688 million in 1962.
115. Cochrane, *City Man's Guide,* pp. 29–30.
116. *Ibid.*

117. Peter A. Toma, *The Politics of Food for Peace* (Tucson: Univ. of Ariz. Press, 1967), pp. 39–45 (hereafter cited as Toma, *Food for Peace*).
118. For a discussion of U.S. food aid to Europe and elsewhere after 1945, see Allen J. Matusow, *Farm Policies and Politics in the Truman Years* (Cambridge: Harvard Univ. Press, 1967), pp. 145–169; Harry B. Price, *The Marshall Plan and Its Meaning* (Ithaca New York: Cornell Univ. Press, 1955), pp. 29–38; and Toma, *Food for Peace*, pp. 25–28.
119. Toma, *Food for Peace*, pp. 39–45.
120. Orville L. Freeman, *World Without Hunger* (New York: Frederick L. Praeger, 1968), p. 99.
121. Earl Lauer Butz served as an Assistant Secretary of Agriculture under Ezra Taft Benson, where he became identified with Benson's goal to lower price supports. As Nixon's Secretary, Butz was instrumental in raising price supports in order to win farmer support for the 1972 elections, Butz, despite his political realism, remained ideologically committed to a free market and to larger farm units replacing smaller ones. See *Current Biography Yearbook 1972* (New York: H. W. Wilson Co., 1973), pp. 65–67.
122. Bob Selmer Bergland served as a representative of the Minnesota Farmers' Union between 1948 and 1950. He then began operation of a commercial farm, which still continues. He entered the 92nd Congress, where he served until becoming Secretary of Agriculture in 1977 [*Who's Who in America 1978–1979*, Vol. 1 (Chicago: Marquis Who's Who, Inc.), p. 257.]
123. Bob Bergland, "Foreword," in *Structure Issues of American Agriculture*, Agricultural Economic Report 438, Economic, Statistics and Cooperative Service, USDA, 1979, p. i (hereafter cited as Bergland, Foreword).
124. 91 *Stat*. 1005–1006; Sections 1440–1443; Title 14, subtitle F, of the Food and Agriculture Act of 1977, P.L. 95–113.
125. Bergland, Foreword.
126. Bob Bergland, speech prepared for the National Farmers Union Convention, Kansas City, Mo., Mar. 12, 1979, Office of the Secretary, USDA 571–79, 13 pp.
127. *Status of the Family Farm*, Agricultural Economics Report No. 434, Second Annual Report to the Congress, Economic, Statistics and Cooperative Service, USDA, 1979, p. i (hereafter cited as USDA, *Status*).
128. *Structure Issues of American Agriculture*, Agricultural Economics Report 438, Economics, Statistics and Cooperatives Service, USDA, 1979, 305 pp. (hereafter cited as USDA, *Structure Issues*).
129. Bergland, Foreword.
130. Yao-Chi Lu, "Technological change and structure," in USDA, *Structure Issues*, pp. 121–127.
131. *A Survey of U.S. Agricultural Research by Private Industry* (Washington, D.C.: Agricultural Research Institute, 1977), p. 5.
132. Bob Tomarkin, The country slicker, *Forbes*, 125 (Jan. 21, 1980): 39–42, 44
133. USDA, *Status*, pp. 4–6.
134. David Lins, The financial condition of U.S. agriculture: Past, present, implications for the future, Economics, Statistics and Cooperative Service, Staff Report, June, 1979, pp. 4–5, 20–21.

CHAPTER 9

Entomologists and the Revolution

ENTOMOLOGY AND PROFESSIONALISM

Economic entomology as a distinct field of study began in the last half of the nineteenth century. Its crystallization into a discipline and a profession was contemporaneous with the emergence of mechanized, capital-intensive agriculture. Indeed, professionalism for entomologists was analogous in a socioeconomic sense to the transformation of agriculture. Just as farmers gained social status and better incomes by substituting capital for labor, entomologists gained status and higher incomes by organizing themselves into a strong professional association. The development of economic entomology was also an integral part of the growth in American government and universities as major loci for research and teaching. By 1900, entomologists were an identifiable scientific group with intellectual and social roots extending to other academics, farmers, and colleagues in the civil service.

Entomologists to this day have continually sought to demonstrate their utility, integrity, and competence to their agricultural clients, and this behavior was the major source of dynamism in the profession. After 1888, entomology's niche within government and academia was generally secure, and entomologists used governmental and academic bases as springboards for participation in the agricultural revolution. In this chapter we explore how entomologists consolidated themselves into a stable profession that was both part of and influenced by technological change in agriculture. Entomologists individually and collectively cannot be understood if they are abstracted from the cultural events that led to the substitution of capital for labor in the production of food and fiber. Moreover, the shape of their theories and ideas, it will be argued, strongly reflected the imperatives of the agricultural revolution.

Professionalism as a general phenomenon was aptly described by Magali Sarfatti Larson as "for the middle classes a novel possibility of *gaining status through work*"[1] (her emphasis). Larson further noted that "the professions first had to create a market for their services. Next, and this was inseparable from the first task, they had to gain special status for their members and give them respectability."[2] In their relationships to agricultural interests, entomologists found the market for their expertise and the source of their political support for research funds. Professionalism in entomology entailed capturing this market implicit in farmers' needs for protection from insect damages. In their relationships with other scientists, entomologists found conceptual and methodological tools, as well as philosophical legitimacy for their claims equating their expertise with objective truth. Professionalism also entailed establishment of a niche within the university whereby entomologists alone could control the production of expertise and of new entomologists. They could thereby offer to client agriculturalists a reasonably standardized product for which claims of superiority to all other forms of "expertise" about insect control could be defended.

Monopoly control of the processes of creating and certifying expertness in entomology combined with a market outlet for that expertise was the route through which entomologists achieved "status through work." The highlights of the professionalization process can be briefly sketched. We turn first to the capturing of the agricultural market and then to the establishment of entomology as an academic discipline. Finally, we note that many entomologists prominent in the years after 1945 were personally and professionally affected by the events of the agricultural revolution.

CAPTURING THE AGRICULTURAL MARKET

Farm operators were the ultimate recipients of entomological expertise, but in the initial stages of professionalization, they never directly contracted with entomologists for services. Farmers in the nineteenth century were generally far too small to warrant hiring their own insect experts, even if the latter had been available. Mediation of the state in the transactions between professional entomologists and farmers was the only way in which the market for expertise could be developed into a stable occupation.

Thaddeus William Harris, the first professional entomologist, worked on the geological surveys of Massachusetts during the 1830s, but his efforts were supplemental to his major job as librarian at Harvard College.[3] The federal government and the state of New York appointed full-time entomologists beginning in 1853–1854 when they, respectively, hired Townend Glover and Asa Fitch. Glover's responsibilities included many tasks other than the control of insect pests; Fitch achieved greater influence by establishing the model for professional entomologists in the civil service.[4]

More vigorous efforts to create scientifically based methods of insect control in the federal government came as a result of devastating outbreaks of migratory locusts [especially *Caloptenus* (now *Melanoplus*) *spretus*] in 1873–1876 west of the Mississippi River.[5] Locusts had plagued American farmers at intervals just as they had done to Old World farmers since Biblical days and before. Locust outbreaks causing severe hardships on the Great Plains had been reported in 1855–1857 and 1864–1867.[6] Outbreaks in the 1870s, however, coincided with farmers making their first tentative adjustments to the use of expensive machines. In the Dakota Territory, for example, good weather and wheat prices between 1867 and 1873 had led many new settlers to expand their capital investments and acreages despite their previous losses to locusts in the 1860s.[7] Thus, the seriousness of the losses of the 1870s were perhaps intensified by a heavier debt load resulting from recent investments. Moreover, the locusts came on the heels of the Panic of 1873, thus further heightening the calamity. The foreclosure of farms was the inevitable result.[8]

Swarms of grasshoppers, drought, and financial collapse left many farmers at or below the level of destitution. Charles Valentine Riley, then state entomologist for Missouri, argued effectively for federal action, and Congress appropriated $18,000 in 1876 for the establishment of a three-man Entomological Commission. Riley as chairman of the panel vigorously led the development of scientific information on the malady. Locust problems diminished through natural causes in the decade after 1877, but the Commission's publication helped establish the scientific reputation of entomology in the U.S. More important, Riley won sufficient attention to be appointed entomologist in the Department of Agriculture in 1878. He succeeded Glover and proceeded to increase the scope and quality of the work in the federal government.[9] Riley and his successor, Leland Ossian Howard, had the energy, dedication, and skills fundamentally important in making the USDA the major source of employment for entomologists in later years.

Establishment of the land grant universities, state agricultural experiment stations, and extension services created additional professional opportunities in each state of the union. These positions, combined with those with the federal government, became the major market place in which entomologists could sell their knowledge to farmers. Entomology passed from an amateur's hobby to full-time professional work. By the beginning of the twentieth century, it was clearly possible for a young man (occasionally a young woman) to contemplate making a living by studying insects and their control. Development of a large insecticide industry and the emergence of consulting entomologists later served as a supplementary market for entomological expertise,[10] but these developments were confined largely to the years after 1945. Service in the federal government, in state universities, and in state departments of agriculture continue today as the work places for the vast majority of entomologists.

Employment of entomologists by the government was an important step in the efforts of entomologists to establish their authority and prestige as *the* group to whom the lay public should turn for help with their insect problems. A few positions, however, did not by any means establish control over the market for entomological expertise within the hands of specialists. Many other people, most of whom claimed no special knowledge about insects, were quite willing in the late nineteenth century to offer their own opinions and methods whenever an insect malady struck. Perhaps the most vivid examples of the continuing pressure of amateurs were visible when new insects appeared and caused devastating losses. Boll weevils entering Texas elicited an offer of a $50,000 reward from the state legislature for practical remedies, and thousands of ideas flooded in from many parts of the country. A similar set of events occurred in France when the grape phylloxera [*Phylloxera vitifoliae* (Fitch)] caused disastrous losses in the French wine industry. A reward of 300,000 francs elicited thousands of suggestions, all apparently worthless.[11]

L. O. Howard, director of entomology for the USDA from 1894 to 1927, remarked in 1930 that these two instances demonstrated the futility of putting hopes for practical insect control methods in any hands but those competent by training to deal with insects.[12] Howard was clearly piqued at the diversion of attention caused by the lingering notion in government that useful knowledge could come from persons who were not certified as "experts." The failure of practical remedies against either the boll weevil or the grape phylloxera solidified the claim professional entomologists could make that they were the ones to whom society should turn for help.

Nineteenth- and early twentieth-century successes against boll weevils and phylloxera included alteration of farming practices and use of resistant host plants, respectively. Entomologists had a variety of other successes by 1925 that further consolidated their claims to legitimacy through efficacy. The most notable examples included:

- *1888–1889:* biological control of cottony-cushion scale by the vedalia beetle, in California
- *1890–1912:* partial suppression of gypsy moth with lead arsenate, sanitation, and biological control, in Massachusetts
- *1916–1920:* control of boll weevil with calcium arsenate, in the South[13]

These and other developments were reflected in the ability of entomologists to articulate by the late nineteenth and early twentieth centuries a systematic outline of numerous general suppression technologies. A. S. Packard, for example, noted the use of fertilizers, crop rotation, burning or removing crop residues, insecticides, and parasitic insects in his *Entomology for Beginners* (1888).[14] Similarly, E. Dwight Sanderson emphasized crop rotation, time of planting, fertilization, sanitation, burning, plowing, trap crops, and insecticides in his textbook, *Insect Pests of Farm, Garden and Orchard* (1913).[15]

Despite these advances, entomologists continued to worry until after World War II that farmers and the general public did not appreciate the need for their expert knowledge. A recurring theme of presidential addresses at the annual meetings of the American Association of Economic Entomologists in the years before 1945 was the need for entomologists both to serve farmers and the public and to impress on their clients the need for entomological expertise. George A. Dean's address in 1921, for example, stressed the need for entomologists to cooperate with each other, with other agricultural scientists, and with private concerns like the Farm Bureau in the development of insect control measures.[16] Similarly, A. F. Burgess in his address of 1924 stressed the fragility of the acceptance of entomological expertise when he argued that the future for entomologists looked grand but that they could not let the "undisciplined and careless . . . participate with us [or] our cause may be weakened."[17] Discovery of the organic, synthetic insecticides like DDT allayed their sense of unease, but that period of calm lasted only a decade. Contemporary pronouncements on the need for quality and excellence in entomology are highly reminiscent of the period before 1945.

Entomologists of the early twentieth century may have worried about the security of their discipline in the public mind, but their fears by that time were not about being supplanted by a rival source of expertise. Rather, they worried about being ignored as irrelevant. The only serious scientific challenge to the adequacy of entomological expertise came from physicians and toxicologists who were worried about the safety of arsenical and lead residues on sprayed produce, especially apples.[18] At stake was not whether insecticides such as lead arsenate were effective against insect pests but whether the residues left were safe for human consumption. A similar challenge to entomological expertise came from the physicians, toxicologists and environmentalists in the years after 1945 (Chapter 2).

ENTOMOLOGY AS AN ACADEMIC DISCIPLINE

Consolidation of control over the market for entomological expertise could not come in the absence of some device for distinguishing a "certified" expert in the subject from the lay person. University education became that device by the end of the 1880s, and employment as an entomologist after that time became increasingly rare without a college degree at least in the biological sciences and, increasingly, in the specialty of entomology itself.

Course offerings in entomology were the prerequisite for such a development. Lectures on natural history, sometimes including the insects, were available before the Civil War, but no courses specifically devoted to the study of economic entomology were offered until afterwards. Land grant colleges established under the Morrill Act in 1862 were the loci for the development of the academic discipline of economic entomology. A. J. Cook (Michigan Agricultural College, 1867), T. J. Burrill (University of Illinois, 1868), and Charles Valentine Riley (Kansas State College, 1870) were the pioneer teachers in the field. Herman August Hagen began offering entomological instruction in 1873 at Harvard; his first student, John Henry Comstock, began teaching the subject at Cornell the same year. C. H. Fernald first taught entomology at the Maine Agricultural College in 1872 and in 1886 moved to found the department at the Massachusetts Agricultural College. B. F. Mudge followed in Riley's footsteps at Kansas State College in 1871–1872.[19]

First offerings of courses were eventually followed by majors and graduate programs. By 1918, 24 land grant colleges offered majors. In 1928, 36 American and 7 Canadian institutions offered majors in entomology. In the U.S., graduate work in economic entomology could be pursued in 37 different places.[20]

The period 1875–1925 can thus be identified as the time in which economic entomology coalesced into a recognizable discipline whereby formal training and a degree were required to become a practitioner. Individuals with master's and doctorate degrees were clearly in leadership roles by 1925, but for many years after that time a bachelor's degree could suffice to gain entry into the lower echelons of entomological service.

By 1948 some entomologists complained about the inadequate training of many members of the discipline. Roger C. Smith, for example, found that only 31% of entomologists registered with the National Roster possessed the Ph.D. degree. He believed that entomology as a field thus compared poorly with fields in which Ph.D.'s were more common. Zoologists (46%), botanists (56%), plant pathologists (56%), anatomists (73%) and plant physiologists (74%) all had higher proportions of their ranks in possession of the highest academic degree. Smith believed that the problems of entomology were no simpler than those in other fields and that more entomologists could benefit themselves and their profession with advanced work.[21] In a similar vein, the USDA's Sievert A. Rohwer raised the question of whether entomologists were trained sufficiently broadly; he was especially conscious that mission-oriented work in the USDA allowed little opportunity for an entomologist to broaden himself through on-the-job training.[22] Inadequate training undoubtedly was one problem underlying the crisis atmosphere of entomology in the years following 1945. As noted in Chapter 10, however, one must not put an undue emphasis on training alone in efforts to resolve the crisis in entomology.

Somewhat before and concomitantly with the emergence of economic entomology as an academic discipline, the practitioners of the subject organized themselves into a variety of local and national professional societies. The first groupings were local and not focused on applied entomology. The Entomological Society of Pennsylvania, for example, was founded in 1842. It folded in 1852 after publishing the species in a major collection of insects. Taxonomic work on North American species was for the first time appropriated by U.S. entomologists from the Europeans.[23]

The first national organization, the Association of Economic Entomologists (AAE), was established in 1889 under the inspiration of Riley and his assistant L. O. Howard. "American" was added to their title in 1908. The Entomological Society of America (ESA), a second national organization formed in 1907, was dedicated primarily to nonapplied questions.[24] The AAEE merged in 1953 with the ESA and kept the latter's title. Economic entomologists far outnumbered their nonapplied colleagues, and thus dominated the one national society. No significant rivals have ever challenged this group for authority in the design of control practices for insects.

One further note is of interest in the rise of the economic entomologists as a professional group. In contrast to many fields of science, economic entomology as an organized discipline originated as much or more in the U.S. than in Europe. It thus stands in contrast to some of the other subjects of agricultural science, such as soil and fertilizer chemistry,[25] and to virtually all of the basic sciences that originated in the nienteenth century or before.

Entomology in the form of nonapplied studies in natural history, however, originated in Europe. An example of influential writings of this type was four volumes by William Kirby and William Spence, entitled *An Introduction to Entomology,* and published between 1822 and 1826.[26] Kirby and Spence described some applied aspects, but their emphasis was on compiling all knowledge then in existence.

A few Europeans engaged in applied entomological studies before 1860. Prominent examples included John Curtis' *Farm Insects* (1859),[27] which was in many respects the forerunner of the twentieth-century textbook on economic entomology. Especially important was Curtis' organization of his material by crop rather than by taxonomic class of insect. Also significant as an important European contribution to economic entomology was *Die Forst-Insekten* published by Julius Theodor Christian Ratzeburg in three volumes between 1837 and 1844.[28]

Such works as Curtis' and Ratzeburg's were probably important influences on scientifically trained European immigrants who made important contributions to the development of applied entomology in America. Foremost among these were Benjamin Dann Walsh and H. A. Hagen.[29] Walsh came from England in 1838 after training at Cambridge as a contemporary with Charles Darwin. Walsh went on to have a heavy influence on C. V. Riley, another English immigrant but one without formal education. Hagen was brought from German by Louis Agassiz to the Museum of Comparative Zoology at Harvard in 1870, and he in turn had a powerful influence on the education of J. H. Comstock. As already noted, Comstock went on to found the entomology department at Cornell, where he had a powerful effect on the training of subsequent generations of American entomologists.

Despite these important early European contributions to economic entomology, most Americans who made their reputations in economic entomology in the last half of the 19th century were native born and received all of their training in the U.S. Moreover, few, if any, Americans found it necessary to travel to Europe for advanced training in the field.

Howard noted in 1894 that despite early European leadership in basic entomology, Europeans in general found little need for insect suppression measures until the last half of the 19th century or after. Howard ascribed the lack of the science to a number of factors:

> A climate much less favorable to the undue multiplication of injurious insects than that of North America, and which, moreover, seems to act as a barrier against the importation of foreign destructive species; the actually smaller number of injurious species and the vastly greater familiarity with all phases of the life-history of these species by all classes of the people—partly resulting from the older civilization, partly from educational methods, and partly from the abundance of elementary and popular literature on questions of this character; *the denser population and the resulting vastly smaller holdings in farms, the necessarily greatly diversified crops, the frequent rotation of crops, together with the clean and close cultivation necessitated by the small size of the holdings; and the cheaper and more abundant labor, have all resulted in a very different state of affairs regarding the damage which may be done by injurious insects.* . . . [T]he Chief of the Agricultural Section of the Ministry of Agriculture of Prussia, in conversation with the writer last summer, argued that Germany does not employ general economic entomologists; that its experiment stations seldom receive applications for advice on entomological topics. . . . European nations, therefore, can afford to let the insect problem alone to a much greater extent than the United States, for the reason that it is of infinitely less importance with them than with us.[30] [emphasis added]

Europe's cooler climate may indeed have been important in lessening the need for insect control compared to the generally warmer climate of the United States. Probably of more importance, however, was the fact that Europe's agriculture remained less specialized and less capital-intensive than that of the U.S. until well into the 20th century. Less dependence on capital gave European farmers more flexibility in withstanding the fluctuations of yield resulting from insect pests. Economic entomology was therefore an "uninteresting" subject in the European context.

Further evidence of America's lead in developing the subject comes from some statistics gathered in Britain at the onset of World War I. From 1913–1915, the Imperial Bureau of Entomology counted 1089 papers published in America. Only Russia (582) and Great Britain (531) had even half as many. Germany and France were next, but the war had begun to limit their productivity sharply by 1915.[31]

That professional economic entomology, westward expansion, and the mechanization of agriculture began simultaneously in the U.S. was thus not a coincidence. Insect problems encountered in the new agricultural lands west of the Mississippi River, particularly grasshoppers, combined with an increasing capitalization of agricultural enterprises, demanded and received attention. The new western states, in turn, spawned some of the earliest workers who shaped the field. After economic entomology was professionally consolidated, the close relationships between the discipline and farming interests became ironclad. In addition, the technological revolution in agriculture as it continued into the twentieth century had an effect on the personal lives of entomologists. Especially significant were career decisions made by individuals who were prominent in innovative efforts after 1945. Congruence between developments in entomology and agriculture also influenced entomologists' perceptions of the problems in insect control.

ENTOMOLOGISTS AND THE AGRICULTURAL REVOLUTION

Entomologists active after 1945 came from both urban and farm backgrounds, and their socioeconomic class origins ranged upward from abject poverty. Personal interviews with a few of the most innovative scientists revealed that some individuals became entomologists at least partially because of the technological transformation in agriculture. Indeed, it appears that one reason some of the rural men entered the profession was that the consolidation of land into larger farms made farming itself an impossible or undesirable personal option.

Consider the following examples briefly. E. F. Knipling was raised on a small farm in east Texas, but left it to his brothers because the effort required for farming on a small scale simply didn't pay what it was worth.[32] L. D. Newsom of Louisiana also was raised on a farm—one so small that his family supplemented their income with nonfarm sources. All four Newsom brothers achieved advanced degrees, and his generation left farming altogether.[33] C. B. Huffaker was never particularly interested in farming, and the loss of the family farm during the depression of the 1930s merely confirmed his decision to seek his fortune elsewhere.[34]

The events in a few lives warrant a lengthier discussion. Charles Gatewood Lincoln was raised on an apple farm in northwestern Arkansas, but pursued training in entomology under Dwight Isely at the University of Arkansas and then at Cornell University for his Ph.D. He joined the staff of the University of Arkansas as extension entomologist in 1942, and spent his entire career there giving particular attention to cotton insect problems. His family's efforts to raise apples were fraught with difficulties, as he later recounted:

> My dad was the best apple grower in northwest Arkansas. It just wasn't possible to be good enough to survive. Everything happened, the Depression, the Food and Drug Administration, codling moth out of control, the wrong varieties, overage orchards. Name it, it happened and it all happened at once. I guess it's to his credit that he faced the tidal wave longer and went broke worse than anybody else.[35]

Lincoln saw his father's problems to have resulted from general economic depression, government regulations on insecticide residues, a chronic severe pest, and high capital costs to establish an orchard in a variety that could compete in the large urban markets located far from Arkansas. It must be understood, though, that these problems were really symptomatic of a larger set of changes in apple production. As we recounted in Chapter 1, apple growers suffered from overproduction relative to demand all thrugh the 1920s. Further declines in consumer purchasing power in the 1930s made it impossible for all but the most sophisticated growers operating in the most favored locations to survive. Arkansas' warm climate permitted three and sometimes four generations of codling moth per year, but in the Pacific Northwest and the Northeast growers generally had to contend with only one or two generations per year. Efforts to produce codling-moth-free apples in Arkansas required six or seven applications of lead arsenate, which undoubtedly increased the potential for growers' conflicts with the Food and Drug Administration.[36] Arkansas growers were further disadvantaged compared to northeastern producers by their greater distance from large markets. What Lincoln experienced, therefore, was a brutal and changing set of circumstances that simply made it impossible for some growers to stay in business.

Perry Lee Adkisson experienced a similar set of experiences, but the circumstances were changed in that he made his decision to enter entomology after World War II. He grew up on a medium-sized Arkansas cotton farm in the rich land of the Mississippi delta. Adkisson completed his undergraduate studies at the University of Arkansas in 1950, where Isely showed an interest in him. Adkisson was not yet ready to make a career commitment, and he was drafted into the army for the Korean War. It was not until his release in 1953 that he was faced with the need to consider seriously his future work. As he recounted:

> Meantime, some events had happened in my family which made it impossible for me to go back to the farm because of some deaths and division of land.

> There was not enough land for me and my brother both to farm. So he was already a farmer and had a family. I made the decision that there was not enough land to support both of us in the style in which either one of us would like to be supported and that he should take the farm and I'd go ahead and do something else. I was single and did have a college education, which he didn't have.[37]

Adkisson decided to return for graduate training at the University of Arkansas, where he received his master's degree in agronomy. He then completed his Ph.D. in entomology at Kansas State University (1956) and entered into the ranks of the professional entomologists.

The return of higher prices and farmer prosperity in the post-World War II years made Adkisson's decision-making process somewhat more flexible than Lincoln's, but the underlying role of the technological transformation of agriculture should not be missed. Adkisson could have entered farming by splitting his family's land with his brother. Both of them recognized, however, that the increasing mechanization of cotton production made it economically unrewarding to farm unless one had a sufficiently large acreage. The Adkisson family farm may have been large enough to yield a middle-class income for one family when operated with tractors and other equipment, but it was not large enough to support two middle-class life styles. In addition, rising land prices would have made it difficult or impossible for two young farmers to purchase the additional land needed for a modern operation. Adkisson's decision to seek his fortune within the ranks of the professional scientists serving the new, mechanized farmer was undoubtedly one of the wisest economic decisions he ever made.

Consider the final example of the interaction between the agricultural revolution and the personal decisions men made to enter professional entomology. James Roland Brazzel was born and raised in Lincoln Parish, Louisiana, an area of small farms (100–200 acres) in the northeastern part of the state. Cotton was the cash crop, and his family had lived in the area since the Civil War. He entered Louisiana State University (LSU) in 1938 with uncertain future plans, but World War II and postwar military service in occupied Japan interrupted his education. He left the armed forces in early 1950 to complete his bachelor's degree at LSU. Before his entrance to school in the fall he bought a tractor and grew a crop of cotton. The summer of 1950 turned out to be one of the worst boll weevil years on record, and he was unable even to meet his production expenses. Upon his arrival in Baton Rouge that fall, Brazzel went to the entomology department to tell them of his experiences; Newsom encouraged him to enter entomology as a career. Brazzel earned his bachelor's and master's degrees in entomology at LSU and then went to Texas A & M for his Ph.D.

He never regretted his choice, but the appeal of farming never left his blood:

> And I always, even though I'd grown up and worked like heck and plowed mules and so forth on the farm, I still liked the farm. I thought farming was the thing. . . . What I would really have rather been and would rather be right now is a farmer. But I didn't have the opportunity. That hill section of Louisiana is not economic row-crop land, it's timber land. And you know it's awfully hard to break into the field of farming nowadays. But I feel like I got the next best thing. I'm very closely associated with agriculture in the field that I'm in, and I think it's worked out very nicely for me. It's been good to me.[38]

Brazzel's departure from active farming was in some ways like Lincoln's and Adkisson's. In the years before the 1930s, his home parish in Louisiana had supported people on small farms growing cotton with mules. His own family had been prosperous enough to send him to LSU and even wanted him to pursue medicine as a career. Mechanization, consolidation of farms into larger units, a host of other capital-intensive technologies, and the low productivity of land in the hill sections compared to the richer Mississippi delta lands changed the situation entirely. Middle-class life styles could seldom be achieved on small farms in the hill country. Brazzel's misfortune to try his hand at farming in precisely the year the boll weevil was at its worst was the final blow to persuade him to seek his fortune elsewhere. Brazzel, like Lincoln and Adkisson, found a more congenial life as an entomologist than he would have as a farmer. The ranks of farmers diminished as the ranks of professional entomologists grew.

It would be unwarranted to make general conclusions about how entomologists decided to enter their profession based upon the small number of interviews conducted for this study. What is nevertheless clear is that the competition in the farming industries during the transition from low-capital/high-labor to high-capital/low-labor influenced the growth of the entomological profession. Undoubtedly other agricultural sciences were affected as well, as they also recruited some of their new members from the ranks of the young men leaving agriculture. If the spill-over consisted simply of people leaving one occupation to enter another and nothing more, then the relationships between the development of agriculture and the development of entomology might not be particularly significant. The mutual interactions, however, went far beyond a transfer of personnel.

THE SHAPING OF ENTOMOLOGICAL EXPERTISE

Professional entomologists, whether they came from farm or urban backgrounds, entered into an occupation to serve those farmers who had the managerial skill, capital, and luck to survive a technological revolution that drove most of them out of business. Whether an individual entomologist was recruited from the ranks of those leaving agriculture or not made no difference; as a group, they realized that their profession's support in government and the university depended upon the satisfaction of their clients. Their farmer clients in turn knew that lowering production costs through the adoption of new technology was the only way to survive in the business of being a farmer. A never-ending cycle was thus established in which entomologists designed insect control practices that reduced production costs; those farmers that adopted them were the individuals who remained in business. Continuing competitive pressures among farmers remaining in business led them to seek new processes to reduce their production costs; entomologists responded with new innovations; and a new round of adoptions ensued.

An important corollary follows from this theory of entomological advance. Entomologists became socialized into a subgroup of society that viewed the world from the perspective of a farmer operating in a highly competitive industry. Contacts with peer scientists were also important to the prestige of an individual entomologist, but entomologists never forgot the nature of their primary clients. They believed that the agricultural revolution meant improvement for human life, and they celebrated their own contributions to its progress. They seldom if ever made critical comments about the direction of change in farming.[39] If they had, it would undoubtedly have made it difficult to keep the attention and support of their clients who were leading the change. Entomology became a conservative profession in the sense that it saw the world through the eyes of an increasingly wealthy class of farmers.

Entomologists shaped their research to fit the socioeconomic situation of their technologically progressive clients. Allegiance to the interests of their clients even superseded differences resulting from the various paradigms, integrated pest management (IPM), total population management (TPM), or chemical control.

Consider Huffaker's comments on the fundamental facts of life in the design of IPM schemes:

> Crop pest control in this country rests fundamentally on a system of free enterprise in which profit to the grower *must be our primary objective.* Other secondary objectives involving benefit to our society accrue indirectly as

> reduced cost to the consumer or through improved quality of the environment.[40] [his emphasis]

Brazzel was also heavily motivated to mold his research choices toward the interests of his clients as he advocated an eradication effort inspired by TPM against boll weevils. In a personal interview he related:

> BRAZZEL: If we ended up here with a program that we considered successful and it was proposed to go across the [cotton] belt with an eradication program, if we couldn't get grower referendums to support it, I wouldn't want any part of it. . . . If we're not doing something that the grower out there, the majority of them, feel is the thing that they need, I think we're misplaced and fooling them. . . . I'd rather have the growers' support for something that we're trying to do than to have the entomological profession's support. No doubt in my mind as to who I'd take.
>
> PERKINS: Why is that?
>
> BRAZZEL: Because that's who I work for, I don't work for the entomological profession.[41]

Adkisson, who in the period 1968–1973 was deeply involved with both the IPM and TPM paradigms, viewed his job as one of keeping the farmers of Texas in business. He was repelled, for example, by the very thought that one solution to the crisis of the cotton growers in the lower Rio Grande Valley was to have them switch from cotton to another commodity. He believed such a "solution" would upset the agricultural economy of the entire region and was therefore simply not to be entertained as a viable guideline.[42] Instead, he and his associates sought a way for cotton growers in the area to maintain a competitive position within the context of U.S. and world cotton production.

A particularly vivid example of the close cooperation among entomologists and their clients is the sequence of events surrounding the development of the sterile male technique for screwworm fly control. The technical aspects of the story were detailed earlier, but biological considerations were by no means sufficient for perfecting such a complex technology. Knipling and other USDA entomologists also had to marshall the social support necessary for the development of their ideas.

Most important was the active support of the livestock growers in areas infested with screwworms. The work was expensive: estimated costs in 1954 of the Curaçao work alone were almost $20,000.[43] Congress would not have been likely to allocate research funds without pressure from their livestock-growing constituency. In fact, Knipling had to be very careful during the years before Curaçao about letting Congressmen know the USDA was investigating the sexual behavior of screwworms for fear of ridicule by legislators.[44] Business interests, particularly Southern cattlemen, however, pressured their representatives for relief from the dangers caused by the fly, especially between 1949 and 1952. The appropriations that flowed to the USDA were crucial to the experiments on Sanibel and Curaçao, but the dollars came only after concerted lobbying efforts.

The year 1949 was particularly bad for screwworms, and numerous members of Congress received requests for help from their constituents. Frank P. Samford, President of the Alabama Chamber of Commerce, for example, wrote every member of the Alabama delegation and requested their assistance.[45] At the time, Knipling had no evidence that the screwworm could be controlled by the sterile male technique. Even so, he was sufficiently optimistic about controlling the insect that he outlined the requirements for a program to eradicate the flies to William Howard Smith, president of the Alabama Cattlemen's Association.[46]

South Carolina's Senator Burnet R. Maybank and Congressman L. Mendel Rivers requested information from the USDA in 1950 for their constituents plagued with screwworms. In the case of one request to Senator Maybank, the Charleston Chamber of Commerce wanted the Senator to "pressure" the USDA into controlling screwworms.[47]

Senator Lister Hill of Alabama had several interchanges with USDA personnel during 1951. In response to a request from cattleman Smith, Hill requested information in March on screwworm control. Between March and August, Hill took an increasingly active interest in Knipling's work. Knipling outlined a detailed research proposal to Hill and estimated that a sum of $20,000 for the first year and $40,000 for each of two succeeding years would be adequate to finance pilot studies on the sterile male technique. After the conclusion of the formal Senate hearings on the fiscal year 1952 agricultural appropriations bill, Hill inserted language to provide $20,000 for Knipling's research on sterilization. Walter Randolph, president of the Alabama Farm Bureau Federation, told the Senate Appropriations Subcommittee on Agriculture during the following year's hearings that Hill had made the insertion at Randolph's request.[48]

Why were the cattlemen of the southeastern states so upset about screwworms in the period 1949–1952? Part of the reason stems from the weather patterns of the period. For example, screwworms were usually only a small problem as far north as South Carolina, but the warm weather of the winter of 1948–1949 allowed them to overwinter further north than usual and thus cause more than normal problems. Thus the cries for help were partly the result of weather patterns creating an unusual situation. Of more fundamental importance was the fact that before Knipling's sterile male technique, the only control of screwworms came through wound treatments, which required considerable labor in the form of cowboys searching for infested animals. Cattlemen, just as all other agricultural producers, were constantly attempting to reduce their labor costs. Hence the very idea of the sterile male technique appealed to them because it was intrinsically labor-saving. Knipling's work, therefore, was entirely consonant with the dominant theme of American agriculture—the substitution of capital inputs for labor whenever possible. Both scientists and ranchers were aware of this factor and it was part of their motivation to cooperate in the search for a technological solution to screwworm problems.[49]

ECONOMIC ENTOMOLOGISTS AND BASIC SCIENCE

What can be said abut the sense of legitimacy economic entomologists gathered from their status as natural scientists? Did that position count for nothing? Were the judgments of other peer scientists not important motivating factors for entomologists? A few examples easily demonstrate that a sense of belonging to a scientific community was important to them. Knipling realized tremendous satisfaction from his election to the National Academy of Sciences, in which he was one of the few applied scientists.[50] Paul H. DeBach noted with pleasure that one of his papers received considerable attention from basic biologists. It was on competitive displacement among species of the genus *Aphytis*, parasites on California red scale [*Aonidiella aurantii* (Maskell)].[51] The work was of interest to applied entomologists, but its greater importance lay in the demonstration of a process fundamental to evolutionary and ecological theory. Huffaker also felt a strong sense of accomplishment when basic biologists reviewing his IPM proposal at the National Science Foundation gave it their wholehearted endorsement because of its solid foundation in ecological theory.[52]

Despite the fact that some economic entomologists won recognition and respect among nonapplied scientists, relations with that peer group were not always easy. Many of the entomologists interviewed for this study noted that basic scientists tended to regard their applied colleagues as second-rate workers. L. O. Howard made a similar comment in 1930.[53] Adkisson articulated the ambiguous nature of the economic entomologist's role in the larger community of scientists:

> I also wanted the professional recognition of [basic] scientists. . . . Once I began to do some work in the field and feel like . . . my work in the basic aspects would be at least acceptable, I began to publish it . . . outside the economic entomology journals. . . . I began to correspond and go to meetings . . . with people in the more basic sciences. And that's not an easy thing

> to do. I can tell you from my own experience, if you're an agricultural scientist, it is very difficult to earn the respect of peers in the so-called basic sciences. *It becomes somewhat even an emotional situation of being torn between wanting to do basic research that really whets your curiosity and is gaining you attention by academicians and at the same time maybe have to let that kind of work go to take care of practical responsibilities that you have to meet a problem in the state with a producer group. . . .* It's a real problem that plagues agricultural scientists all over the country. And as a result, somewhere along the line, agricultural scientists in my opinion were looked down on. They may have an inferiority complex. But I believe this in general that agricultural scientists do not get due recognition. There's a snobbery, academic snobbery, it's on this campus as on every campus. And some of the people over in the College of Science or somewhere else think they're doing super-science, and the people in agriculture are a bunch of cowboys.[54] [emphasis added]

Uncertain as their status was among other scientists, entomologists were seen by the general public simply as "scientists." They derived prestige from that identification and used it to ward off attacks on insect control science and technology. By far the strongest challenge was Rachel Carson's *Silent Spring.* She essentially called entomologists incompetent, corrupt, and unworthy of holding special privelege within society because the knowledge they espoused was a menace both to the farmer and to the general public.[55] Entomologists felt beleaguered by the attack, but they had sufficient strength as an organized profession with political support in the farming industries to survive (Chapter 2).

Political decisions to curtail uses of insecticides represented partially successful challenges to entomological expertise by people outside the profession. To the extent that such incursions continue in the future, entomologists will have failed at what Magali Saffarti Larson called the "Professional Project." Larson argued that all professional groups attempt to consolidate their power over the market for their expertise and the production of that knowledge.[56] No evidence suggests that entomologists would not like to speak with absolute authority on matters of insect control, but it is unlikely they will achieve a monopoly position in the near future.

Even if economic entomologists were to achieve monopoly power over insect control technology via their roles as trained scientists, most would probably feel that prestige as scientists could never replace the sense of status derived from their role in capital-intensive farming. Their ties to the farming industries made them a part of the agricultural revolution. What was good for the industry was perceived as acceptable and good by the economic entomologists. The vast majority of these scientists would now probably reject any opportunity to enter farming for themselves, but their hearts and minds lie with the capital-intensive farmer and his problems.

ENTOMOLOGISTS AND THE CHEMICAL INDUSTRY

Critics of insecticidal control technologies have at various times implied or charged that entomologists as a profession were corrupted or "bought off" by the insecticide industry. Rachel Carson, as noted above, was perhaps the most widely read critic of this persuasion:

> It was reported in 1960 that only 2 per cent of all the economic entomologists in the country were then working in the field of biological control. A substantial number of the remaining 98 per cent were engaged in research on chemical insecticides.
>
> Why should this be? The major chemical companies are pouring money into the universities to support research on insecticides. This creates attractive fellowships for graduate students and attractive staff positions. Biological-control studies, on the other hand, are never so endowed—for the simple reason that they do not promise anyone the fortunes that are to be made in the chemical industry. These are left to state and federal agencies, where the salaries are far less.
>
> This situation also explains the otherwise mystifying fact that certain outstanding entomologists are among the leading advocates of chemical control. Inquiry into the background of some of these men reveals that their entire research program is supported by the chemical industry. Their professional prestige, sometimes their very jobs depend on the perpetuation of chemical methods. Can we expect them to bite the hand that literally feeds them? But knowing their bias, how much credence can we give to their protests that insecticides are harmless?[57]

Although the precise mechanisms by which the insecticide industry was alleged to have "captured" the work of the professional entomologist were frequently not spelled out, provision of grant support was usually the suspected route. Under this hypothesis, entomologists were led to perform research on insecticides and then argue for the efficacy and safety of the chemicals, presumably to procure grants for future work. Furthermore, entomologists advocated public policy favorable to the chemical industry and to the use of insecticides for the same reason.

The "corruption" hypothesis of the dynamics of entomology undoubtedly has some truth in it. A few entomologists were perhaps so swayed by the lure of research funds from the chemical industry that they abandoned research pathways to alternative types of control technologies. Certainly the fact that the chemical industry channeled grant money to university and government researchers created the possibility for the industry to "purchase" whatever expertise it needed in order to merchandise its wares better. *It is nevertheless my belief that to attribute overriding importance to any such corrupting effect represents a serious and complete misreading of the dominant forces motivating creative work in entomology.*

Entomologists and their expertise were indeed purchased, and in some ways "corrupted" by forces outside of the profession, but the "purchasing agents" were capital-intensive farmers and their representatives in Congress and state houses. Economic entomologists frequently were derived from farm families and had close ties to farmers. Their political support was based in the farming interests of the nation. Allegiance to farmers and their problems was the dominant motivating force driving their creative energies. The chemical industry with its products and research grants were merely handmaidens to the entomological purpose of providing their usefulness to those farmers surviving the holocaust of the technological revolution in agriculture.

As explained more fully in Chapter 10, chemicals won the battle for supremacy among insect control technologies precisely because they were the technology that best fit the needs of the farmers who were battling to stay in business as two-thirds of their peers were forced into other lines of work. Chemicals could be purchased in amounts precisely fitted to each farmer's individual needs. A farmer had no reason to cooperate or coordinate his insect control technologies with other farmers when chemicals were the weapon of choice.[58] Chemicals were capital-intensive and they required little labor to apply. Chemicals also provided the illusion of complete mastery over nature: spray and your enemy was dead, usually before your very eyes. Indeed, without resistance, resurgence, secondary pests, and the problems of health and environmental safety, little incentive would exist even now for farmers or entomologists to alter their methods for suppressing pest populations. Neither IPM nor TPM would exist as intellectual constructs or in experimental design without the crisis associated with the insecticides. *It was the entomologists' loyalty to the farmer and his problems that led first to the chemical control paradigm and then to the new paradigms.*

CONCLUDING REMARKS

It is now possible to join two considerations raised in earlier chapters with a suggestion for the nature of creativity in insect control technology: First, volition among entomologists was the one aspect of insect control that could not profitably be discussed earlier. Second, we used the concept of paradigms in the study of entomology-as-science, but Thomas Kuhn, the most influential scholar in using the notion of *paradigm,* avoided using paradigms in the study of technology.[59] I believe the concept of paradigms can usefully be expanded to the study of technological change, and the process of expansion leads us directly to the problem of volition.

As noted earlier, Edward W. Constant extended the concept of paradigmatic change to technology in his study of the replacement of propeller-driven airplanes by turbojets.[60]

Constant noted that his scheme did not allow an explanation of why one person became involved in a new research line and another did not. My device for expanding the concept of paradigm suggests the source of volition in the behavior of entomologists taken collectively. Like Constant, I, too, cannot claim to offer an explanation of why some individuals became involved in articulating new paradigms and others did not.

Kuhn's mature notion of paradigms in science can be expanded to cover technology by supplementing his notion of the *disciplinary matrix,* which was composed of (1) symbolic generalizations, (2) models, often with metaphysical dimensions, and (3) exemplars. For studies of technology, the disciplinary matrix is as developed by Kuhn plus one additional element: (4) a sense of the social context in which the technology, if successful, will be used.

"Sense of the social context" requires some elaboration. By this term I mean some sort of appreciation, either intuitive or explicit, of who wants the fruit of innovative labor and under what conditions they will be able or inclined to use it. A well-developed "sense of the social context" gives directions to the technological innovator on the types of research to perform, the interpretations of data from experiments, and the choice of overarching theories to rationalize a pattern of research in a career or in a research institution. Without any "sense of the social context," an innovator in the scientifically based technologies has no particular incentive to go one way or another in his daily routine. With it, he can pattern his creative work along lines that have maximum possibilities of producing useful expertise that will eventually be adopted.

Paradigms thus understood operate to guide research in scientifically based technologies. A failure of a paradigm to yield solutions to particular technological puzzles can create a crisis in the research operations of a scientifically based technology. Practitioners will then seek changes in either the symbolic generalizations, models, or sense of the social context so as to create a new paradigm to guide research. Success of the newly articulated paradigm will be judged by its ability to foster research that solves the crisis and thus becomes a new exemplar inspiring subsequent research.

Briefly recapitulating the argument made earlier, the chemical control paradigm underwent a crisis because it could not successfully handle the problems of resistance, resurgence, secondary pests, and environmental and health hazards. IPM and TPM were articulated as rival alternatives to the chemical control paradigm. Each of the three paradigms had different symbolic generalizations, models and exemplars. All shared essentially a common sense of the social context, namely that entomology primarily serves the needs of capital-intensive agriculture.

"Sense of the social context" is the key component to understanding volition. A technological innovator understands the social context of his work and uses it as the ultimate legitimation of his creativity. He comes explicitly to understand that service to the clientele is his motivation to do the work. He molds his scientific and technological creativity so that it meets the needs of those who will use it. The clientele, of course, often reinforce the researcher's sense of the social context by supporting the research designed to serve them. A researcher cannot shift his research without considering the effect of the shift on the clients. Similarly, a change in the status or identity of the clients can be disorienting to the researcher.

Entomologists knew that their primary clients were the technologically innovative farmers who, as the twentieth century progressed, were surviving the massive exodus of people from agricultural production. As a profession they geared their work to serve this ever-diminishing group. Moreover, they *willed* themselves to serve this group because it was the social reference frame for their creative work and for their status within the community of entomologists. Service to technologically sophisticated farmers was also the source of their political support for further work.

The entomological mind was thus part of a social complex in which creativity, professional standing, and means to further research dollars were all tied intimately to a group of clients, who in turn were constantly buffeted by the continuing fruits of scientific research. Intellectual turmoil and crisis in entomology under such conditions were not surprising.

REFERENCE NOTES

1. Magali Sarfatti Larson, *The Rise of Professionalism, A Sociological Analysis* (Berkeley: Univ. of Calif. Press, 1977), p. 5 (hereafter cited as Larson, *Rise of Professionalism*).
2. *Ibid.*, p. 8
3. L. O. Howard, A brief account of the rise and present condition of official economic entomology, *Insect Life* 7 (1894): 55–108 (hereafter cited as Howard, A brief account).
4. L. O. Howard, *A History of Applied Entomology*, Smithsonian Misc. Collection, Vol. 84, 1930, pp. 35–50 (hereafter cited as Howard, *History*).

5. U.S. Entomological Commission, *First Annual Report* (Washington, D.C.: Government Printing Office, 1878), pp. 1, 34.
6. John T. Schlebecker, Grasshoppers in American agricultural history, *Agric. Hist.* 27 (1953): 85–93.
7. Harold E. Briggs, Grasshopper plagues and early Dakota agriculture, 1864–1876, *Agric. Hist.* 8 (1934): 51–63.
8. *Ibid.*
9. Howard, *History*, pp. 54–55, 78–83.
10. Mortimer D. Leonard, The development of commercial entomology in the United States, *Proceedings Tenth International Congress of Entomology, 1956*, Vol. 3, (Ottawa[?], 1958), pp. 99–106.
11. Howard, *History*, p. 215.
12. *Ibid.*
13. For a review of the work on gypsy moth and boll weevil, see Thomas R. Dunlap, The triumph of chemical pesticides in insect control, 1890–1920, *Environ. Rev.* No. 5 (1978): 38–47. See Chapter 4 for discussion on biological control.
14. A. S. Packard, *Entomology for Beginners* (New York: H. Holt, 1894 [c. 1888]), pp. 221–222.
15. E. Dwight Sanderson, *Insect Pests of Farm, Garden and Orchard* (New York: John Wiley and Sons, 1913), pp. 32–78.
16. George A. Dean. How we may increase the effectiveness of economic entomology, *J. Econ. Entomol.* 15 (1922): 44–53.
17. A. F. Burgess, Our Association, *J. Econ. Entomol.* 18 (1925): 47.
18. James Whorton, *Before Silent Spring* (Princeton: Princeton Univ. Press, 1974), 288 pp.
19. Howard, *History*, pp. 27, 70–78.
20. Paul Knight, The development and present status of entomological courses in American colleges and universities, *J. Econ. Entomol.* 21 (1928): 871–877.
21. Roger C. Smith, The doctor's degree, *J. Econ. Entomol.* 41 (1948): 843–845.
22. S. A. Rohwer, Are entomologists too specialized?, *J. Econ. Entomol.* 41 (1948): 995–996.
23. Conner Sorensen, American entomologists organize the Entomological Society of Pennsylvania, 1842–1852, unpublished paper presented to the West Coast History of Science Society, Dec. 27, 1978, 9 pp.
24. Howard, *History*, p. 69; American Association of Economic Entomologists, Constitution, and Report of the Joint Committee on Legislation, *J. Econ. Entomol.* 2 (1909): 4–8.
25. Margaret Rossiter, *The Emergence of Agricultural Science* (New Haven: Yale Univ. Press, 1975), 275 pp.
26. William Kirby and William Spence, *An Introduction to Entomology* (London: Longman, Hurst, Rees, Orme, and Brown, 1822–1826), 4 vols.
27. John Curtis, *Farm Insects* (London: John Van Voorst, 1883), 528 pp. Curtis dated the introduction of the first edition as Jan., 1859.
28. F. Schwerdtfeger, "Forest entomology," in *History of Entomology*, Ray F. Smith, Thomas E. Mittler, and Carroll N. Smith, eds. (Palo Alto, California: Annual Reviews, Inc., 1973), pp. 367–369.
29. Howard, *History*, pp. 51, 61–63.
30. Howard, A brief account, pp. 73–74.
31. Anon., Editorial, *Rev. Appl. Entomol.* 4 (1916): 1; see also Howard, *History*, pp. 542–543.
32. Edward F. Knipling, personal interview, July 13–14, 1976.
33. L. D. Newsom, personal interview, June 1–2, 1978.
34. Carl B. Huffaker, personal interview, March 17–18, 1977.
35. Charles G. Lincoln, personal interview, June 6–7, 1978.

36. Dwight Isely and A. J. Ackerman, Life history of the codling moth in Arkansas, *Agric. Exp. Stn. Bull. No. 189*, University of Arkansas, Dec., 1923, 57 pages; E. J. Newcomer and W. D. Whitcomb, Life history of the codling moth in the Yakima Valley of Washington, *USDA Bull. No. 1235*, Nov. 28, 1924, 76 pages; F. E. Brooks and E. B. Blakeslee, Studies of the codling moth in the central Appalachian region, *USDA Bull. No. 189*, Apr. 12, 1915, 49 pp.
37. Perry L. Adkisson, personal interview, May 30–31, 1978.
38. James R. Brazzel, personal interview, May 26–27, 1978.
39. An important exception was Robert van den Bosch's *The Pesticide Conspiracy* (Garden City, New York: Doubleday and Co., Inc., 1978), 226 pp. Van den Bosch's book, however, is so recent that its effect cannot yet be judged.
40. C. B. Huffaker to Proposed Ad Hoc Committee to Consider "The Role of Economic and Systems Analysis in the IBP–Biological Control–Crop Ecosystems Project," June 25, 1971, files of C. B. Huffaker.
41. Brazzel, personal interview.
42. Adkisson, personal interview.
43. A. H. Moseman to A. A. M. Struycken, Jan. 8, 1954, Record Group 310, National Archives (RG310NA).
44. Knipling, personal interview.
45. See, for example, Frank P. Samford to George Andrews, Sept. 28, 1949, RG7NA.
46. Percy N. Annand to William Howard Smith, Nov. 22, 1949, RG7NA (letter prepared by Knipling).
47. Ashmead F. Pringle, Jr., to Burnet R. Maybank, Sept. 22, 1950, RG7NA.
48. William Howard Smith to Lister Hill, Feb. 28, 1951; Avery S. Hoyt to Lister Hill, Mar. 14, 1951; W. L. Popham to Lister Hill, May 4, 1951 (letter prepared by Knipling); M. E. H., Office Memorandum, Aug. 17, 1951; all from RG7NA. U.S. Congress, Senate, Committee on Appropriations *Agricultural Appropriations for 1953*, Hearings, 82nd Congress, 2nd sess., 1952, p. 839.
49. For anecdotes on Texas ranchers' use of labor to handle problems with screwworms, see Charles G. Scruggs, *The Peaceful Atom and the Deadly Fly* (Austin, Texas: Jenkins Pub. Co., The Pemberton Press, 1975), pp. 128–131.
50. Knipling, personal interview.
51. Paul H. DeBach, personal interview, March 22–23, 1977; Paul DeBach and Ragnhild A. Sundby, Competitive displacement between ecological homologues, *Hilgardia* 34 (1963): 105–166.
52. Carl B. Huffaker to Principal Investigators, Executive Committee of the IPM Project, Oct. 29, 1974, files of C. B. Huffaker; idem, personal communication, 1979.
53. Howard, *History*, p. 540.
54. Adkisson, personal interview.
55. Rachel Carson, *Silent Spring* (Boston: Houghton Mifflin Co., 1962), especially pp. 258–259.
56. Larson, *Rise of Professionalism*, pp. 104–135.
57. Carson, *Silent Spring*, pp. 258–259.
58. J. C. Headly, The economic milieu of pest control: have past priorities changed?, in *Pest Control: Cultural and Environmental Aspects*, David Pimentel and John H. Perkins, eds. (Boulder, Colorado: Westview Press, 1980), pp. 81–97.
59. Thomas Kuhn, *The Structure of Scientific Revolutions*, 2nd ed. (Chicago: Univ. of Chicago Press, 1970), pp. 19, 69.
60. Edward W. Constant II, A model for technological change applied to the turbojet revolution, *Technology and Culture* 14 (1973): 553–572.

CHAPTER 10

Entomology and Agricultural Production

Integrated pest management (IPM) and total population management (TPM) resulted from the convergence of a complex array of factors. Developments in each school of thought were prompted by a series of crises associated with insecticides (Chapter 2), were guided by the changing capital structure of agriculture (Chapter 8), and were aimed at maintaining for entomologists a degree of monopoly power over the expertise concerning insects and their control (Chapter 9). Yet the end products of these intellectual endeavors were markedly different. Why?

Some of the distinguishing features can be accounted for by assimilation of different philosophical traditions (Chapter 7). Moreover, each school of thought had its theoretical origins in efforts to control specific insects in particular agricultural situations (Chapters 3–5). Each paradigm also had its origins in different bureaucratic structures (Chapters 3–5).

Knowledge of philosophical and historical context is necessary but not sufficient to understand the differences between the new competing schools in entomology. Moreover, merely tracing the origins of IPM and TPM leaves unexplored the fact that chemical control strategies still dominate the insect control practices of farmers, even though the chemical control paradigm now has little influence among research entomologists. To account for the disparity between research and practice it is necessary to understand that the suppression techniques generated from each of the paradigmatic schools had different socioeconomic, political, philosophical, and biological characteristics. These new practices were not immediately or easily substituted for the older chemical control techniques, nor were IPM and TPM interchangeable with each other. This chapter considers the functions of insect control expertise in contemporary agriculture and examines how the technology from each of the major paradigms is compatible with the needs and habits of farmers and ranchers.

INSECT CONTROL AND AGRICULTURAL PRODUCTION

Pest insects by definition have the potential to reduce yields. Unfortunately, generalizations about the magnitude, frequency, location, and significance of insect damage are subject to a bewildering array of assertions, allegations, and accusations. As a result, the function of pest control is difficult to assess in an unambiguous fashion.

Part of the problem stems from the fact that measurement of losses to insects is an intrinsically difficult task. Ideally one would like to know the precise level of loss at a particular time as a function of a specific level of infestation.[1] Unfortunately, accurate measurements of yields and infestation levels are difficult on test plots and even more difficult under the conditions of commercial farming. Moreover, many other factors can affect yields, such as weather, weeds, plant pathogens, fertilizer levels, timing of planting and other operations, irrigation levels, the cropping history, neighborhood cropping patterns, and soil types. Other variables thus compound the effects of insects, and experimenters as well as farmers have difficulty placing an accurate "blame" on insects for suspected losses of yield. Added to the biological complexities of measuring physical loss are even more complex variables that determine the economic and social significance of losses to farmers and to the general society.

Precise measurement and interpretation of insect losses may well be an impossible task, but intuitive, judgmental assessments have been made by farmers and entomologists for many years. Yield loss is the foundation for farmers' efforts to control insects, and producers know that losses can occur either as reductions in physical quantities or in quality.

Estimates of quantitative losses have been made for most crops in the U.S.[2] and for many major crops on a global basis.[3] Most of the estimates are really nothing but educated guesses by knowledgeable people working in the field, but in a few instances measurements have been made through experimentation. Cotton yields, for example, were 22–34% higher when treated with inorganic insecticides (primarily calcium arsenate) and 41–54% higher when treated with synthetic, organic insecticides. These estimates were made in central Texas, Louisiana, and South Carolina between 1928 and 1958.[4] EPA's proposed cancellation of aldrin prompted a study of insect losses in corn from soil insects in 1974. Entomologists in the Corn Belt estimated yield losses of 10–30% from wireworms and cutworms (many species in the families Elateridae and Noctuidae, respectively) when the insecticide aldrin was not used. Use of alternative insecticides in place of aldrin would result in estimated losses of 0–15% compared to those with aldrin.[5] Control of lygus bugs in clover and on lima beans with insecticides increased yields by 79% and 198%, respectively, in California.[6]

Farmers worry not only about the quantity of their yields but also about the quality. Apples, for example, are subject to attack by the codling moth and other insects plus a number of fungal diseases. Although these pest organisms can sometimes damage trees and thus reduce the tonnage of apples produced annually, the more important problems stem from the fact that the highest returns to apple production come from fruit marketed as fresh produce. Such fruit must ordinarily be free from insect damage to enter the high-priced market. Economic loss is estimated to occur in some areas if greater than 1% of the fruits are culled because of pest damage.[7]

A similar situation exists in contemporary California citrus production. Thrips [*Scirtothrips citri* (Moulton)] feed on the developing fruits and leave a scar on the rind once the orange is ripe. Orange production, too, is more profitable when the fruit enters the market for consumption as fresh fruit. Thrips' scars reduce the grade of oranges and thus lower the price that can be obtained for them. As a result, growers tend to treat heavily for thrips even though the insect does not appreciably reduce the yield in tons per acre nor harm the interior quality of the fruit. Surveys conducted with a limited number of growers indicated they were aware they treated for thrips in order to avoid cosmetic damage.[8] Economist Darwin C. Hall argued that California citrus growers might be hampered in efforts to switch from heavy chemical controls to an IPM-derived control strategy based on stringent, cosmetic quality standards.[9]

A particularly interesting case of cosmetic spraying involved the use of chlorobenzilate to control citrus rust mite [*Phyllocoptruta oleivora* (Ashmead)] on grapefruit in Florida. Chlorobenzilate causes tumors in mice, and the Environmental Protection Agency (EPA) began examining it as a potential carcinogen in 1976. In 1978, the EPA decided to continue its registration on the grounds that the chemical was selective in its toxicity and therefore useful in IPM programs.[10] Ironically, however, citrus rust mite is primarily cosmetic, as the result of feeding on the fruit produces "russeted" produce. Russeted grapefruit generally brings a lower price, but sometimes they attract a premium. Russeted fruit may be sweeter than unscarred grapefruit, because water loss from the mite's feeding may cause an increased sugar content.[11] The EPA has therefore allowed the continued use of a possible human carcinogen in order that Americans can eat cosmetically perfect but possibly less sweet grapefruit. That this case is justified on the grounds of chlorobenzilate's demonstrated usefulness in IPM programs is a particularly tragic piece of logic. Revamping quality standards for grapefruit might be a far preferable course of action from the view of the general public.

Some controversy erupted over the allegation that cosmetic standards resulted in a higher level of insecticide use.[12] Certainly those who defended contemporary chemical treatments could reasonably fear that the notion of "cosmetic spraying" tended to make such efforts appear trivial in the eyes of the public. To a farmer, of course, it matters little whether his yields are reduced in quantity or in quality. In either case, his revenues are reduced and he is economically worse off. Moreover, no single farmer can decide unilaterally to abandon either quantitative or qualitative criteria in judging production methods. Competition in capital-intensive agriculture encourages each individual grower to strive for maximum returns; those who don't risk losing their businesses.

Insect control plays important indirect roles as well as directly influencing quantity and quality of yield. One of the most important indirect functions is to serve as insurance against disastrous losses from pests. Two factors were responsible for increasing the importance of the insurance function. First, increasing use of capital, frequently obtained on credit, placed a premium on farmers maintaining a reliable, adequate cash flow to repay loans.[13] To the extent that insect control practices increased the size and reliability of yields, they reduced the risk carried by a farmer and his creditors and thereby increased his ability to procure capital inputs through credit. Second, the increasing specialization in agriculture that accompanied the technological revolution simultaneously increased the propensity for pest outbreaks. This effect was due partially to increased monocultures of a single crop over wide, contiguous areas.[14] Reliable insect control became a blanket of protection for agricultural production made more vulnerable through socioeconomic and biological changes.

The concept of insect control technology as insurance in capital-intensive agriculture is well accepted, but it has proven difficult to estimate its magnitude. Studies by the National Academy of Science (NAS) in 1975 estimated that both corn and cotton production had evolved a heavy use of insecticides that were "insurance" in nature. In corn, for example,

> There is some agreement that perhaps 50–60% of the corn acreage treated with insecticides in the Corn Belt annually represents unneeded application—unneeded, that is, in hindsight. In the early stages of each growing season, it is difficult for growers to predict whether treatment is going to be needed on a given field or farm. Recommendations from the extension services and the private trade often vary, and nontreatment can be financially disastrous in a pest outbreak. Therefore, since pesticides do not harm the crop directly, since they are cheap in relation to crop value, and since information is imperfect, the theory of production economics and common sense both suggest insurance-type applications will be made by prudent growers, even though they are clearly a misuse of insecticides from the broader perspective.[15]

Closely related to insurance treatments was the ability of reliable insect control to allow technological innovations that were otherwise impossible. Examples of this were given earlier, such as the adoption of profitable fertilization, irrigation, and harvesting practices by cotton farmers in the 1950s, all of which increased the propensity for outbreaks of boll weevils (Chapter 2). Only the protection offered by the chlorinated hydrocarbon insecticides permitted the adoption of such cultural practices. When resistance to these insecticides developed, cotton farmers were suddenly faced with the potential for disaster. An enormous part of the technology that made cotton farming profitable suddenly became unusable unless new means of suppressing boll weevils were developed. Breakdown of insecticidal control practices for boll weevils thus became a prime motivator for efforts to innovate. Development of new insecticide treatments and the origins of both IPM and TPM drew much inspiration from the specific problems in boll weevil control and their relationship to a total package of farm production practices.

Freedom to innovate in agriculture continues to be a substantial and important desire among farmers, and every indication suggests that entomologists will continue to be called upon for an umbrella of protection under which farmers can continue their relentless path of innovation. A prominent example of new technology that will likely demand innovations from entomologists is known as no-till farming (NTF). NTF is a heterogeneous set of practices in which herbicides are substituted for soil tillage and plowing operations that have been relied upon for millenia as a means of controlling weeds. NTF has many advantages that are attractive to farmers or the general society. Foremost are reductions in the requirements for labor, energy, and machinery in farm production. Moreover, substantial decreases in soil erosion can be achieved with NTF. Unfortunately, NTF leaves a residue of crop refuse on the ground, which provides a breeding ground for both insect and fungal pests. NTF has been extensively adopted only in a few crops and areas, but trends in adoption suggest that by the year 2000 substantial acreages may be farmed with NTF technology. If the predictions are true, entomologists (and plant pathologists) may find that the problems with which they work are substantially altered by NTF.[16] They will be called upon to develop effective insect control practices in the context of NTF operations.

A final indirect function of insect control technology is its ability to reduce labor requirements for food and fiber production. As losses to insects are reduced, a farmer is able to produce more. Increased supplies will tend to depress the price of the commodity, and some growers will cease producing the crop. Decreased capital resources might also be used in the crop's production, but the relative cheapness of capital compared to labor up to 1980 has meant that farmers have almost uniformly reduced labor rather than capital inputs. The end result is that insect control practices play an indirect role in the reduction of labor in agriculture. Farmers will continue to seek enhanced yields from insect control methods so as to further reduce their input of labor per unit of output.

COMPATIBILITY OF TECHNOLOGY AND PRODUCTION

Insect control increases quantities and qualities of yields, insures against catastrophic losses, allows freedom to innovate in other production practices, and reduces the amount of labor needed in agriculture. Clearly, agricultural producers will not voluntarily abandon their current reliance on insecticides unless the alternatives are economically advantageous and reliable. Moreover, the prospective new insect control technologies must be congruent with the social, political, and philosophical attributes of contemporary agricultural production.

Chemical control, TPM, and IPM each have a unique mix of features that affects their ability to be used in commercial agriculture. Each also reflects its historical origins as control practices for particular insects. Understanding the cultural and biological parameters of each major strategy is essential for any efforts to foster change of insect control technology.

Chemical Control

It is difficult to pinpoint with any precision when the chemical control strategy became dominant. Some have argued that insecticides were firmly entrenched by the 1920s,[17] but this book emphasizes their rise to dominance in the decade ending about 1950. It is less important, however, to quibble over precise dates than it is to understand the cultural and biological bases for the success of insecticides. Chemicals replaced other methods of dealing with insect pests because certain advantages were provided by the toxic materials. Entomologists and agriculturalists became enthusiastic about insecticides only because the chemicals "worked" in terms of both biological and cultural criteria.

Biological circumstances were less important to the emergence and structure of the chemical control paradigm than they were to the development of IPM and TPM. Toxic chemicals used as insecticides tended to have broad-spectrum activity against many species, and their success obscured subtle but important differences in the biological properties of different organisms. Economic returns to farmers were universally the characteristic cited as the fundamental reason for which the materials should be adopted. Estimates in the late 1960s and early 1970s of aggregated monetary returns for pesticide expenditures were $3–5 for each $1 invested.[18] Differences among farmers, crops and regions, however, limit the usefulness of aggregated cost–benefit ratios as a tool for understanding the attractiveness of insecticides to the farming industries. Other factors in the social and political organization of agriculture were also highly important. Particularly important considerations were the political, social, and philosophical attributes of the insecticidal techniques.

Insecticides were compatible with the political divisions of responsibilities in agricultural production. Both the farming and chemical industries matured under a political philosophy in which government set the rules for economic activity but did not become an active participant. Farmers were considered atomistic entrepreneurs who owned or leased land and proceeded to use it in almost any way they saw fit. Similarly, the decentralized chemical industry could perform such research as they found in their interest, manufacture products based on their expertise, and sell them in any way they could so as to turn a profit on their investment. Government intervened only by establishing land-distribution policies, agricultural research institutions, farm subsidy programs, and rules under which chemicals could be manufactured, sold, and used. More importantly, government did *not* own and operate farms or chemical manufacturing and distribution facilities. Nor, in the American political framework, was it assumed that insect control was fundamentally a public responsibility. Exceptions were made for disastrous outbreaks of introduced species such as the gypsy moth and European corn borer, but in general the assumption was that each individual would handle his own insect problems.[19] Insecticides suited these assumptions in political philosophy perfectly, because everyone with a problem could "solve" it with a chemical precisely suited to their own specific circumstances.

Socially, too, insecticides were compatible with the organization of the American agricultural production system. Each farmer was an individual entrepreneur competing with all other farmers for a share of the market. Although cooperation among farmers has a long and honorable place in American history, coordination of farming activities remained in a contradictory relationship to the fundamental fact of American agriculture, which was that farmers competed with each other. Competition through technological advance, rather than cooperation, was the hallmark of American farming.

Insecticides as one component of technological change in agricultural production were admirably suited to the social nature of agricultural production. Each farmer could purchase and apply a chemical at precisely the right time for his operations without informing or cooperating with his neighbor. Farmers were thus enabled to continue their competition with each other via chemical techniques of insect control.

Philosophical considerations, also, favored the adoption of insecticide-based control practices. A socially atomized, competitive production system using many capital inputs encouraged the image of the farm as a machine. In the words of *Farm Journal*, describing the heavy yields of 1979, "these tremendous totals reinforce the fact that *the American family farm is a well-oiled, production machine that hums with almost unlimited potential*"[20] (emphasis added). Machines are attractive because they are rational and predictable, i.e., they overcome the vagaries of nature in a way that gives man more complete control over certain process. The image of farms as "machines" is meant to convey the notion that despite the unpredictable events of the natural world, farmers are in control to the maximum extent feasible.

Insecticides in theory are congruent with the image of farms as machines. They are purchased inputs, designed to be used in an algorithmic manner, in order to make a farmer's operations predictable. Resistance, resurgence, secondary pests, and environmental hazards destroyed the concept of insecticides as reliable mechanistic cogs in the production of some crops in some regions. Where the chemicals remain effective, they continue to function as a simple, cheap, reliable tool that fits easily into a production process perceived as mechanistic.

The economic, political, social and philosophical desiderata of the "ideal" insect control technique (from the farmer's viewpoint) undoubtedly accounts for the tremendous success of the chemicals. This is not to say that other suppression strategies and techniques did not also provide some match with the characteristics of agricultural production, as will be pointed out shortly. As a strategy, however, chemical control still fits into the agricultural production system better than its rivals, TPM and IPM.

TPM and IPM were both articulated as alternatives to the chemical control strategy, but their individual relationships to the latter paradigm were entirely different. In addition, both TPM and IPM were developed from a series of successes in the control of specific insects. The biological habits of those species were radically different from each other, a factor of considerable importance in the acceptance and attractiveness of each of the new paradigms. Also of importance was the fact that TPM was developed largely in the USDA while IPM originated in the land grant universities. Finally, the compatibility of both TPM and IPM with agricultural production trends was not as high as their predecessor, the chemical control strategy.

Total Population Management

TPM's relationship to the chemical control strategy was friendly rather than adversarial. E. F. Knipling appreciated both the strengths and limitations of insecticides as he sought ways of combining various suppression techniques into effective strategies for suppression or eradication of target populations. Depending upon the situation, insecticides were either central or peripheral. It is important to note, however, that in the largest experiments inspired by TPM, those connected with boll weevil eradication, insecticides played a central role in reducing boll weevil populations—to the extent that sterile male experiments were designed as the *coup de grace.*

The importance of insecticides in TPM arises partly from theoretical considerations: they are a highly effective tool when pest populations are high. Historical factors, too, are important. Knipling and his coworkers at the Orlando laboratory, as noted earlier, were the first American entomologists to experiment with DDT. That compound's dramatic successes against lice and mosquitoes during World War II, plus its later triumphs, impressed Knipling and his colleagues with its tremendous power. The fact that Knipling's experience with insecticides was largely positive was of importance in his considering them as prime components for TPM-inspired experimentation.

Articulation of TPM as a coherent strategy by Knipling and his colleagues occurred in the context of successful ventures against specific insects. Insecticidal controls for lice, mosquitoes, and other species during World War II constituted the first historical root of the paradigm. Perfection of the sterile male technique against the screwworm fly constituted the second root of the strategy. Both of these sets of events were described earlier (Chapter 4), but it is now important to note an additional feature about the biological nature of these particular pest species. Each was an insect affecting man and other animals, i.e., they were vermin, the very name of which brings connotations of filth, disgust, and horror. Moreover, human infestation with these insects was associated with annoyance, the threat of serious illness, and possibly death (typhus, malaria, and myasis for lice, mosquitoes, and screwworm flies, respectively).

By definition, pests have negative characteristics, but these particular pests had especially unpleasant attributes. Their defeat was particularly important precisely because they were such horrible creatures. People value their own bodies highly, and the benefits accruing from the advances of Knipling and his colleagues were accordingly large. In fact, it may be reasonably speculated that the magnitude of suffering brought about by lice, mosquitoes, and screwworms was perceived of as so great that any hint of a technology to eradicate them would be judged with great and universal acclaim. It is not difficult to envision why Knipling began to think about eradication of screwworms even before he had perfected the sterile male technique. The justification for such thoughts can be considered intrinsic to the biological habits of the screwworm fly itself.

TPM originated largely within the USDA, but the implementation of its experiments were collaborative ventures between the USDA and state governments, state universities, private growers and their organizations, and foreign governments. The current program to suppress screwworm flies in Mexico and the southwestern U.S., for example, involves collaboration between numerous institutions in the U.S. and the Federal Republic of Mexico. A striking parallel therefore exists between the main tenet of TPM and the organizational structure from which it came and which it requires: TPM calls for ecosystem-wide efforts against a pest across its entire range irrespective of political boundaries; the USDA has responsibilities that by law range across state and international boundaries. It is difficult to imagine scientists in state agencies or universities conceptualizing the theory and implementation of insect control strategies that require such widespread collaboration between such disparate social and political entities. In an important way, therefore, TPM as a scientific construct mirrored the bureaucratic structure of the agency in which it was nurtured.

One could dismiss such a parallel between theory content and political structure as a coincidence, but the fact that it also occurred in IPM and chemical control suggests that a functional relationship existed between the structure of knowledge and the bureaucratic organization of its original home institution. The USDA was heavily involved in research under the chemical control paradigm before 1955, so it is evident that no sharp cause and effect relationship existed between strategy generation and bureaucratic structure. It is more plausible to envision a permitted/forbidden connection. The USDA's structure permitted adoption of all paradigms, while other factors determined that TPM became supreme. In contrast, the chemical industry's profit-oriented, decentralized structure permitted only research under the chemical control paradigm. Land grant universities operated as decentralized, service-oriented agencies, a structure that permitted either the chemical control paradigm or IPM. Most universities could cooperate with TPM efforts only with the support of the USDA.

Economic attributes of TPM-inspired suppression practices within the agricultural production system are difficult to assess. First, only a few cases can be identified in which the TPM-derived technology has advanced to the point of unambiguous success. Most notable are the successful eradications of screwworm flies from Curaçao and Florida, and their suppression in Texas and other areas of the Southwest. The success on Curaçao was an experiment that, because of its success, turned out to have practical benefit for livestock growers on the island. No efforts were made, however, to calculate any cost–benefit ratios. Estimates in Texas suggest that the returns were large in that savings in livestock losses and labor costs far exceeded the costs of the program.[21] Other TPM inspriations, such as the boll weevil eradication experiments, releases of pink bollworms over the San Joaquin Valley, and attacks on codling moths in the Pacific Northwest with sterile male moths, are still in an experimental stage, and it would be inappropriate and impossible to calculate any economic returns until their technical adequacy is known.

A second factor making economic evaluation of TPM difficult is that in programs to date, the government has borne a large share or all of the expenses. Benefits, if they occur, are distributed broadly among affected farmers and taxpayers in general. Collective purchasers and recipients, none of whom has a large investment or returns, make evaluation of the *distribution* of costs and benefits difficult. The NAS emphasized the importance of this point in 1975 by noting that those who benefited from releases of sterile males might be charged more of the ongoing costs of the release program.[22] Certainly until distributions of costs and benefits are better analyzed, TPM's economic attributes will remain somewhat murky. If in fact benefits to farmers from TPM-programs are in excess of their costs, TPM programs will be plums to be captured by farmers through the political process.

Large projects inspired by the TPM strategy may be political plums, but the close political cooperation needed between federal, state, private, and sometimes foreign entities is also a major weakness of technologies designed with TPM. Achieving such consensus and cooperation is far from costless in terms of time, money, and perhaps the need to compromise on issues beyond the program or experiment. When eradication, rather than mere suppression, is the goal, compliance among the different organizations involved has to be absolute, or the project is doomed to failure. Some of the political difficulties involved in launching the Pilot Boll Weevil Eradication Experiment and the Trial Boll Weevil Eradication Program were described earlier (Chapters 4 and 5) and elsewhere.[23] Technology derived from TPM manifestly does not fit the political philosophy of the U.S., which makes insect control largely a private matter. As a result, proponents of TPM will continually face a struggle in the political arena in order to conduct their experiments and implement what they consider to be proven control techniques.

Social considerations, also, militate against TPM-inspired technologies. Adoption of TPM-derived practices frequently demands cooperation, even collaboration, among farmers; yet their social organization as atomistic entrepreneurs has traditionally led them to use technical inventions as a prime weapon in economic competition with their neighbors. The fact that farmers banded together sufficiently to implement a number of TPM-derived programs demonstrated that farmers have the capacity to cooperate for these technologies, but it must not be forgotten that such efforts are in spite of, not because of, their social organization in the agricultural production system. TPM-inspired efforts are not likely to win widespread farmer approval unless other serious considerations, like insecticide resistance, leave them no alternative.

A specific instance in which social devisiveness among farmers killed the hopes of TPM entomologists occurred during efforts to begin a boll weevil eradication program in Texas in 1974. Most cotton in Texas is grown in the western parts of the state where boll weevils are potential pests but thus far have not been particularly serious in their actual damage. Economists from Texas A & M University pointed out that the high costs Texas farmers would have to pay for an eradication effort would not be commensurate with the returns they could expect from the disappearance of boll weevils from their agroecosystems. Moreover, if eradication really were effective, cotton grown in the mid-South and the Southeast would be more competitive with Texas-grown fiber.[24]

Some may have perceived the reluctance of Texas growers to support a national eradication program begun in Texas as simple-minded ludditism. More accurately, it should be seen as the rational conclusion of shrewd businessmen who had no need or desire to sponsor a technological innovation that could never help them much and might even damage their competitive position. Quite a different social organization for growing cotton would be needed to elicit the rational support of cotton growers in Texas for boll weevil eradication.

One sociopolitical feature of TPM may be seen as advantageous, in terms of its ultimate public acceptance. Specialized, expert labor, generally employed by the government, is required to implement a TPM program. If successful, the program will indirectly reduce the total amount of farm labor needed to produce a unit of food or fiber. Even if the program fails to suppress or eradicate its target, the location of the new labor in government, rather than in the farming industries, will reduce farmer reluctance to proceed with the program. IPM, as discussed below, does not enjoy this feature because IPM presumes location of new labor in the farming industries.

Philosophical considerations of current agricultural trends in the U.S. tend to favor technologies derived from TPM-based research. Historically, TPM's development followed developments in synthetic organic insecticides. Just as the chemicals were compatible with the view of farms as a machine, so too are TPM-based practices. Agroecosystems in TPM are machanistic units to be manipulated by man's will. Similarly, the sterile male technique also reinforces the image of the machine in that sterilized insect releases are the use of an engineered product, which happens to be the insect itself. In fact, it is through the sterile male technique that entomology virtually becomes one of the engineering sciences instead of a biological science. This is not to say that images of organisms as mechanistic, predictable devices do not permeate all of the modern biological sciences, but the crucial element in this technique is that man physically *remakes* the insect for his own purposes. In this way the sterile male technique stands apart, in degree if not in kind, from all other suppression techniques in entomology.

Other elements of the TPM strategy also exhibit the interventionist mode characteristic of the school. Biological control, for example, was seen by Knipling as a crucial and important suppression mechanism, but he had little faith in the ability of self-perpetuating natural enemies to render effective control. He therefore became a strong advocate of augmentative releases of natural predators and parasites of insect pests,[25] In this sense, he was a leader of more interventionist attitude toward the use of natural enemies than was characteristic of those engaged in classical biological control.

The total image projected by TPM was one of rationality and control over farm production practices. Man through his knowledge was to dominate all of nature's vagaries, including the growth and decline of insect populations. The values implicit in TPM thus precisely matched those that came to dominate capital-intensive farming. TPM-derived practices may have difficulty fitting into the agricultural production system on political and social grounds, but they are quite at home in terms of intrinsic normative judgments made by farm businessmen.

Integrated Pest Management

IPM, in contrast to TPM, developed in a partially adversarial relationship to the chemical control strategy. This is not to say that entomologists who articulated IPM did not appreciate the usefulness of insecticides. The literature of the IPM movement is replete with caveats that their suppression technologies would utilize insecticides for the foreseeable future.

Lack of a enthusiasm toward insecticides among adherents of IPM reflected theoretical and historical factors. Theoretical work by H. S. Smith, A. J. Nicholson, and others laid a foundation for the notion that biotic factors could provide a substantial and reliable suppressant effect against pest insects. This work was done in the 1930s and before, so it allowed the centrality of biological control to emerge before the advent of DDT and the other synthetic organic insecticides. Supplementing the impact of the theory was the fact that by the 1930s practical experience had already indicated that insecticides could create more problems than they solved. Curtis P. Calusen's study in 1936 of induced pest outbreaks may not have achieved long-lasting notice among all entomologists, but there is little doubt that his work was read and heeded by the California entomologists who later figured so prominently in the development of IPM.[26]

These historical roots of IPM, moreover, were based on experiences with chemicals that were considerably less than positive. Those coming to IPM from classical biological control had a tendency to view insecticides as destructive. Paul DeBach demonstrated the effectiveness of natural enemies by killing them with DDT to induce an outbreak of a pest species that was formerly controlled. He in no way condemned all uses of insecticides, but his experience demonstrated that the chemicals could destroy an otherwise highly efficient method of insect control. Similarly, every *successful* venture in biological control demonstrated that no other control method, including insecticides, could compare with biological control in terms of cost or effectiveness.

Entomologists coming to IPM from their consideration of the population dynamics of pest species and their native natural enemies, such as A. E. Michelbacher and R. F. Smith, viewed insecticides as positive tools only when used with an understanding of the ecological properties of the pest species and its natural enemies. They were, for example, more than willing to use insecticides against the alfalfa butterfly, but only when it was evident that its parasite, *Apanteles medicaginis*, was not going to exercise natural biological control. Michelbacher, Smith, and their colleagues came to see insecticides as a supplement to be used only when absolutely necessary—otherwise they would wreak havoc in an agroecosystem.

Just as TPM developed in the context of triumphs over specific pests with unique biological features, so too did IPM emerge from specific major successes. Especially important were the victories against olive scale, the alfalfa butterfly, and the spotted alfalfa aphid. The "grandfather" of all successes based on biological control, of course, was the demise of the cottony cushion scale through predation by the vedelia beetle, an event that inspires entomologists even today.

It is important to note two features about the biological habits of the insects involved in these major success stories. First, each has a significant portion of its life-cycle as an exposed, relatively immobile form. Scale insects are particularly immobile, and aphids tend to be highly sedentary except when the adult form develops wings. Larvae of alfalfa butterfly are exposed as they feed. Sedentary, exposed life forms are highly vulnerable to parasitism and predation compared to the more mobile or less exposed insects such as body lice, mosquitoes, and screwworm flies. It is simply a fact that the particular insects under study in the efforts that spawned IPM tended to have more predators and parasites that kept them under control than did the insects that were the subjects of studies leading to TPM.

A second feature of the biology of the insects upon which IPM strategies were articulated is that they were all plant pests rather than feeders upon humans or other animals. Neither deadly disease nor aesthetic horror attended the depredations of the "IPM insects." This is not to deny that both entomologists and farmers may have been frequently dismayed, frustrated, and angered by the enormous economic damage these plant pests could cause, but even ten million acres of spoiled alfalfa could not induce the emotions of one case of screwworm maggots infesting a human being.

It is plausible to speculate that the biological habits of the species involved had at least some effect on the goals toward which the various entomologists dedicated their careers. It is more difficult to question the desire to eradicate screwworm flies given the horror associated with them. In contrast, few would think it necessary to attack, for example, a population of alfalfa butterflies on an ecosystem-wide basis if simple management techniques could reliably contain the pest's damage. All people are in some ways captive of their particular experiences; the biological characteristics of various insects surely differ enough to cause different reactions in entomologists, all of which are reasonable and prudent under the circumstances.

Bureaucratic organization of the institutions in which IPM matured also was correlated with the shape of the knowledge produced. Most IPM-inspired research during the 1960s and 1970s was performed in the land grant universities with only peripheral involvement of the USDA. A common strategy and perspective unified the researchers, but they worked in decentralized laboratories and were geared primarily to the production of technology that could be used on individual farms. High attention was given to regional differences that affected the population dynamics of pest species. A decentralized research effort was, in short, geared toward the production of decentralized control technologies that could be adapted to the pecularities of each farmer in each state. Area-wide attack against a single species was not ruled out, but efforts to control the total population of a pest were not central to IPM as they were to TPM. Once again, coincidence could be invoked to explain the congruence between the structures of this paradigm and its research institutions, but similar correlations in chemical control and TPM make such a supposition seem unnecessarily weak.

IPM's ability to generate technology that fits the economic imperatives of the agricultural production has been demonstrated. Examples include cotton in Mississippi, Texas, Arkansas, and the San Joaquin Valley of California; soybeans in North Carolina and Louisiana; alfalfa and apples in Michigan, Washington, and Pennsylvania.[27] Little debate surrounds the conclusion that the probability of success for IPM research is high and, if the technology is adopted, can reduce insecticide use by 30–50% or more with monetary returns to growers equal to or exceeding those presently achieved.[28]

Distribution of benefits and costs from IPM practices has not yet been subject to serious study. Intuitively, however, it seems likely that such analyses will demonstrate at least three points. First, consumers will derive some benefits in the form of an environment less contaminated with insecticide residues. Such benefits will be nearly impossible to quantify, however. Second, some farmers will probably be disadvantaged by IPM's adoption, just as some farmers have gained while others have lost with the adoption of all previous innovations. Differential abilities to adopt new IPM-derived technology will be the cause of the discrepancies among farmers. Third, public subsidies were used to promote IPM in the 1970s and preliminary estimates suggest the marginal returns for farmer expenditures on these programs were quite large.[29] Just as TPM programs became a plum, this feature of IPM may also make IPM programs a prize to be captured through political action. These three factors suggest that the ultimate economic impact of IPM-generated expertise may be difficult to predict, but they certainly suggest that political as well as market economics will be involved in the future fate of IPM-based research and technology transfer.

Economists have noted that IPM is a substitution of expert labor for insecticides (capital) in agricultural production.[30] IPM is thus a reversal of the trends in agricultural production that have been occurring for over a century (Chapter 8). Labor for IPM programs may be employees of public agencies such as the cooperative extension services or employees of private pest consulting firms. Only the largest of farms would hire a staff entomologist.

The labor that is inserted into agricultural production in IPM functions differently than the new infusion of labor that occurs in TPM-based strategies. In IPM, the new labor must operate directly on the farmer's land year after year. Most of this labor consists of scouts and their supervisors monitoring the population trends of pests and their natural enemies. TPM, as noted above, involves the infusion of new labor skills into agriculture, but government is their likely employer and they are not generally required to work extensively on the farm.

Labor for IPM that is employed by nonfarm organizations will probably appeal to farmers, but the presence of an increased number of workers moves against the grain of economic habits created in the past century. Possibly most troublesome will be the fact that labor, regardless of how it is employed, requires management. It is also subject to disruptions, such as strikes. One of the beauties of insecticides from the farmer's viewpoint was that chemicals were inanimate objects. They required management skills, but they didn't talk back or strike. IPM places a burden on farmers to deal once again with human beings on their land, and this aspect may count against its voluntary adoption by some farmers.

IPM's underlying political framework lies somewhere between chemical control and TPM. Chemical control envisions insect problems as almost entirely the province of the private sector while TPM places enormous responsibility on the public sector to conduct insect suppression or eradication programs. IPM, in contrast, developed from a public research base but envisioned the ultimate transfer of responsibilities to the private sector. A transition period of publically subsidized scouting

TABLE II
Summary of Relationships between Entomological Expertise and Agricultural Production

Paradigm	Origins	Economic	Political	Social	Philosophical
Chemical	Decentralized, from chemical industry and many entomological laboratories.	Demonstrates high returns in many cases to farmers and the chemical manufacturers; low labor inputs by farmers and their employees; generally attractive to farmers.	Supports tradition of no government involvement as an agricultural producer; insect control a private matter; attractive to farmers.	Supports tradition of individual use of technology to gain competitive edge in farming business; attractive to farmers.	Derived from a humanistic sense of nature dominated by man's technologies; fits with capital-intensive agriculture; attractive to farmers.
TPM	Primarily from centralized USDA laboratories.	Demonstrates high returns in a few cases to farmers; low or zero labor inputs by farmers; high returns for successes and reduced labor will be attractive to farmers	Defies tradition by making government a direct participant in agricultural production; insect control partially a public matter; attractive to farmers only if	Depends upon cooperation among farmers and thus removes insect control from functioning as a competitive tool; unattractive to farmers except	Derived from a humanistic sense of nature dominated by man's technologies; fits capital-intensive agriculture; attractive to most farmers.

			without controls on their operations, or (2) it is a subsidy to their operating expenses and/or improves their profit margin.	problem is severe.	
IPM	Primarily from the land grant universities, decentralized.	Demonstrates high returns in a few cases to farmers; increased labor input by farmers or their employees and consultants; high returns will attract farmers; increased use of labor will be unattractive.	Government involved in assisting transfer of technology to private sector; insect control basically a private affair; may be attractive to farmers if it is a subsidy to their production expenses and/or improves their profit margin.	May require cooperation among farmers but in many cases serves individual farmers and can thus serve as a competitive tool; attractive to farmers to the extent it can be employed individually.	Derived from a naturalistic philosophy in which man cannot totally control nature; clashes with most assumptions of capital-intensive agriculture; not attractive to most farmers but will appeal to organic farmers and others with a strong sense of naturalism.

programs was considered necessary to launch IPM efforts, but such efforts were considered temporary, not permanent. At this point, it is unclear whether the transition mechanism as commonly envisioned will be sufficient to take IPM from the public laboratories to the private agricultural production system. IPM nevertheless has a closer match to the political traditions of American agriculture than does TPM.

Social congruence between IPM and the present agricultural production system is also intermediate compared to chemical control and TPM. Effective IPM strategies may require some cooperation between neighbors, especially to avoid the needless decimation of natural enemies on one farm that could be useful to a neighbor. Drift of insecticides or cropping practices could be the source of such problems. To the extent that IPM demands cooperation within the competitive framework of U.S. agriculture, it will be subject to the same social mismatch as TPM. The fact that most efforts in IPM have been directed toward the design of relatively decentralized techniques useful for individuals, however, makes IPM more amenable for use as a competitive force between farmers. If the strategy is cost effective regardless of a neighbor's practices, the shrewd farmers will pick it up and use it to advance their own operations.

The underlying philosophy of IPM may be at a considerable disadvantage, in terms of farmer acceptance, compared to chemical control or TPM. As discussed earlier (Chapter 7) IPM is based on a naturalistic philosophy in which man cannot attain and does not seek total control over natural forces. It envisions man as a hopefully sharp bargainer with nature but never its master. Capital-intensive farmers are not likely to be attracted by such notions. They are people who see themselves as running a machine that is beholden to their beck and call, and they have no wish to share the driver's seat with anyone so capricious as Mother Nature. The humanistic foundations of chemical control and TPM will undoubtedly lend a comparative attractiveness to those research strategies that IPM will find difficult to overcome. Development of systems analysis and computer modeling within the IPM paradigm may be the major route by which IPM-based entomologists will seek to make nature machine-like while still adhering to a philosophy that is fundamentally subservient to natural forces that are seen as unconquerable.

CONCLUDING REMARKS

This chapter argued that current insect control research and practice reflect a complex historical interaction between research strategies on the one hand and our culture's economic, political, social, and philosophical habits on the other hand. Table II summarizes the salient features of this historical legacy. Events in entomology since its inception and especially since 1945 lead me to the fundamental conclusions of this study: It is impossible to understand why insecticides became and continue to be the most widely used insect suppression practice in the U.S. without understanding the development of entomological expertise in its cultural context. Furthermore, understanding the political arena in which future intellectual battles will be fought over insecticides and alternative systems of control demands an appreciation of how that arena of knowledge came into being. Without the historical background, arguments about insect control appear superficially to be either (1) of trivial concern except to those with a direct economic interest in agricultural production, or (2) arguments over scientific fact that can be resolved easily given more research and educational efforts.

Properly understood, insect control as a science and an art should be seen to touch our deepest assumptions about the proper role of political power, our methods of organizing socioeconomic activity, and our sense of man's role in the cosmos. If resolution of the insecticide crisis is to come, it will occur primarily in the fields of values and politics and only derivatively and secondarily in science. Insects may be small and invite contempt, but efforts to deal with them evoke all of the most deeply held beliefs about what it is to be human.

REFERENCE NOTES

1. Luigi Chiarappa, Huai C. Chiang, and Ray F. Smith, Plant pests and diseases: Assessment of crop losses, *Science* 176 (1972): 769–773.
2. For a review of data from 1904 to the present, see Table 2 of David Pimentel, J. Krummel, D. Gallahan, J. Hough, A. Merrill, I. Schriner, P. Vittum, F. Koziol, E. Back, D. Yen, and S. Fiance, Benefits and costs of pesticide use in U.S. food production, *BioScience* 28 (1978): 772, 778–784 (hereafter cited as Pimentel *et al.*, Benefits and costs).
3. H. H. Cramer, *Plant Protection and World Crop Production* (Leverkusen, Federal Republic of Germany: Farbenfabriken Bayer AG, 1967), 524 pp. See also Ray F. Smith and Donald J. Calvert, "Insect pest losses and the dimensions of the world food problem," in *World Food, Pest Losses, and the Environment*, David Pimentel, ed. (Boulder, Colorado: Westview Press, 1978), pp. 17–38.
4. *Pest Control: An Assessment of Present and Alternative Technologies, Vol. 3, Cotton Pest Control* (Washington, D.C.: National Academy of Sciences, 1975), p. 59.
5. Herman W. Delvo, *Economic Impact of Discontinuing Aldrin Use in Corn Production*, ERS-557(Washington, D.C.: USDA, June 1974), 17 pp.
6. *Report on Environmental Assessment of Pesticide Programs*, State Component, Vol. 2 ([Sacramento]: Calif. Department of Food and Agriculture, 1978), pp. 4.2-11–4.2-12.

7. B. A. Croft, "Tree fruit pest management," in *Introduction to Insect Pest Management*, Robert L. Metcalf and William H. Luckmann, eds. (New York: John Wiley and Sons, 1975), pp. 473–474.
8. Martin Brown, An orange is an orange, *Environment* 17 (No. 5, 1975): 6–11. A more extensive discussion of the cosmetic damage problem and insecticide use can be found in Martin Brown, R. Garcia, C. Magowan, A. Miller, M. Mann, D. Pelzer, J. Swartz, and R. van den Bosch, *Investigation of the Effects of Food Standards on Pesticide Use*, Environmental Protection Agency Contract 68-01-2602, available from National Technical Information Service, PB 278-976, $9.00.
9. Darwin C. Hall, The profitability of integrated pest management: Case studies for cotton and citrus in the San Joaquin Valley, *Bull. Entomol. Soc. Am.* 23 (1977): 267–274.
10. EPA Completes Risk/Benefit Review of Citrus Pesticide Chlorobenzilate, Environmental Protection Agency, Press Release, July 24, 1978, 2 pp.
11. John Krummel and Judith Hough, "Pesticides and controversies: Benefits versus costs," in *Pest Control: Cultural and Environmental Aspects*, David Pimentel and John H. Perkins, eds. (Boulder, Colorado: Westview Press, 1980), pp. 169–170.
12. Review of Investigation of the Effects of Food Standards on Pesticide Use, Council for Agricultural Science and Technology, Report No. 55, Mar. 26, 1976, 44 pp.
13. Aaron G. Nelson and William G. Murray, *Agricultural Finance*, 5th ed. (Ames: Iowa State Univ. Press, 1967), pp. 3–23, 188–190. For a specific discussion of risk-bearing capacity and farmers' attitudes toward pest control, see Alexander Davidson and Richard B. Norgaard, "Economic Analysis of Pest Control," paper delivered to Conference on Plant Protection Economy, European and Mediterranean Plant Protection Organization, May 15, 1973, Brussels, 22 pp.
14. *Principles of Plant and Animal Pest Control, Vol. 3, Insect-Pest Management and Control* (Washington, D.C.: National Academy of Sciences, 1969), p. 3; *Pest Control: An Assessment of Present and Alternative Technologies, Vol. 1, Contemporary Pest Control Practices and Prospects: The Report of the Executive Committee* (Washington, D.C.: National Academy of Sciences, 1975), p. 40; *Monoculture in Agriculture: Extent, Causes, and Problems* (Washington, D.C.: USDA, n.d.), 64 pp.
15. *Pest Control: An Assessment of Present and Alternative Technologies, Vol. 2, Corn/Soybeans Pest Control* (Washington, D.C.: National Academy of Sciences, 1975), p. 77.
16. John P. Giere, Keith M. Johnson, and John H. Perkins, A closer look at no-till farming, *Environment* 6 (No. 6, 1980): 14–20, 37–41.
17. Thomas R. Dunlap, The triumph of chemical pesticides in insect control, 1890–1920, *Environ. Rev.* No. 5 (1978): 38–47 (hereafter cited as Dunlap, The triumph).
18, Pimentel *et al.*, Benefits and costs.
19. Dunlap, The triumph; idem, Farmers, scientists, and insects, *Agric. Hist.* 54 (1980): 93–107.
20. John Harvey, ed., Crops, *Farm Journal*, Dec., 1979, p. 19.
21. Charles G. Scruggs, *The Peaceful Atom and the Deadly Fly* (Austin, Texas: Jenkins Pub. Co., The Pemberton Press, 1975), p. 311.
22. *Pest Control: An Assessment of Present and Alternative Technologies, Vol. 1, Report of the Executive Committee* (Washington, D.C.: National Academy of Sciences, 1975), pp. 356–357.
23. John H. Perkins, Boll weevil eradication, *Science* 207 (1980): 1044–1050.
24. C. Robert Taylor and Ronald D. Lacewell, Boll weevil control strategies: Regional benefits and costs, *South. J. Agric. Econ.* 9 (July, 1977): 129–135.
25. E. F. Knipling, *The Basic Principles of Insect Population Suppression and Management*, U.S. Department of Agriculture, Agriculture Handbook No. 512, Sept., 1979, p. 135.

26. Curtis P. Clausen, Insect parasitism and biological control, *Ann. Entomol. Soc. Am.* 29 (1936): 201–223.
27. Carl B. Huffaker, *New Technology of Pest Control* (New York: John Wiley and Sons, 1980), pp. 94–95, 140–149, 211, 297–303.
28. *Ibid.*, p. 21.
29. Arthur Grube and Gerald Carlson, "Analysis of field scouting and insecticide use," to the American Agricultural Economics Association, mimeo, Aug. 6–10, 1978, 13 pp.
30. Darwin C. Hall, The profitability of integrated pest management: Case studies for cotton and citrus in the San Joaquin Valley, *Bull. Entomol. Soc. Am.* 23 (1977): 267–274.

Index